THE PSYCHOLOGY OF SEX, GENDER, AND JOBS

THE PSYCHOLOGY OF SEX, GENDER, AND JOBS

ISSUES AND SOLUTIONS

Edited by Louis Diamant and Jo Ann Lee

PRAEGER

Westport, Connecticut
London

Library of Congress Cataloging-in-Publication Data

The psychology of sex, gender, and jobs : issues and solutions / edited by Louis Diamant and Jo Ann Lee.
   p. cm.
 Includes bibliographical references and index.
 ISBN 0-275-96507-4 (alk. paper)
  1. Sex role—United States. 2. Sex differences—United States. 3. Sex role in the work environment—United States. 4. Sex discrimination in employment—United States. 5. Sexual harassment in the workplace—United States. I. Diamant, Louis, 1921– II. Lee, Jo Ann.

HQ 1075.5.U6 P79 2002
305.3'0973—dc21   2001021164

British Library Cataloguing in Publication Data is available.

Library of Congress Catalog Card Number: 2001021164
ISBN: 0-275-96507-4

First published in 2002

Praeger Publishers, 88 Post Road West, Westport, CT 06881
An imprint of Greenwood Publishing Group, Inc.
www.praeger.com

Printed in the United States of America

The paper used in this book complies with the
Permanent Paper Standard issued by the National
Information Standards Organization (Z39.48-1984).

10 9 8 7 6 5 4 3 2

We dedicate this book to our parents, Harry and Elizabeth Diamant and Joe and May Lee.

CONTENTS

PART III. HARASSMENT ISSUES

PART IV. SEXUAL ORIENTATION AND IDENTITY ISSUES

PART V. SOCIETAL ISSUES

PREFACE

At this writing, practically the day of the Indianapolis 500, on the television there is great fanfare over the young woman who appears the racing star—not because she is favored to win, but because she is there at all. The media hoopla tells us at least two things. The first is that a woman has arrived; the second is the novelty of that arrival. (Woman races Indy—that's news!) The event encapsulates the theme of this book, which is that a psychosocial evolution has brought about our current view of gender and sexual issues in the workplace.

We aim to inform with theory and research about the diversity existing in our society and of the potentials of all women and men. The book provides information on a range of issues, illustrating the degree to which sex and gender continue to influence judgments and decisions about others in the world of work.

Stereotypes and prejudices due to gender, nontraditional sexual behavior, and sexual orientation have led to human suffering. Barriers have been erected, preventing some individuals from achieving their fullest potentials as productive citizens in our society. We emphasize three major points:

1. Biases and ignorance have resulted in the establishment of barriers to economic well-being and employment opportunities.
2. While privately held views of gender roles and sexual orientation have been liberated, the book emphasizes the need to transfer these to the workplace to supporess discrimination.
3. There is a need for policymakers and corporate decisionmakers to be informed and involved in creating a workplace climate that openly accepts all people.

Each chapter stands alone and offers recommendations and solutions for the issue it addresses. The reader may select specific issues that are of particular concern or interest to him or her. The reader will not be at a loss if he or she skips or omits certain chapters.

The Psychology of Sex, Gender, and Jobs: Issues and Solutions is a compilation of 16 chapters, each describing how sexual behavior and gender continues to affect success in the workplace.

The introduction (Part I) deals with the clarification between "gender" and "sex," and discusses the different implications of each. It reviews the history of sexual and gender influences in the workplace in the context of psychosocial evolution.

Part II (Gender Issues) contains chapters that discuss the origins and development of gender and sexual stereotypes that form the bases for discrimination. Opinions and judgments of coworkers and employees are often influenced by perceptions of the target individual's conformity with today's traditional standards.

Part III (Harassment Issues) focuses on the sexual behavior, as distinct from the gender roles, of workers and employers. It describes harassment, its origins as a judicial issue, and the evolvement to include homosexual workers.

Part IV (Sexual Orientation and Identity Issues) deals with individuals' views of their sexual identity, orientation, and behavior, and the complex issues that are created in the workplace. One chapter deals with the search for the ideal heterosexual and the problems that notion creates in the workplace.

Part V (Societal Issues) examines issues of gender and sex that are related to customs, mores, laws, and politics. A chapter, for example, considers the transition from one working spouse (husband) to two (both husband and wife). Another chapter reviews the politics of institutions and the decisions of who may have sex with whom.

Decisionmakers in the work environment have neglected many of the issues discussed in the book. To be competitive in the global marketplace, corporate leaders must educate themselves and their employees to understand the wide range of differences that exist in the labor force. *The Psychology of Sex, Gender, and Jobs: Issues and Solutions* offers solutions to managing the workforce of today.

The comprehensive coverage in the sections and chapter topics of sex, gender, and jobs brings this book to the forefront of texts dealing with the psychological and social issues concerned with sex and gender in the workplace. For this we are indebted to the theoretical and research prowess of our contributors and to their abilities in synthesizing complex material in a highly readable fashion.

We also, almost needless to say, owe many thanks to the editors and staff of Greenwood Press for all the help, advice, and consideration they have given. We appreciate too the professional staff of Atkins Library, The University of North Carolina at Charlotte, who have been available when we needed them, especially Frada Mozenter. Special thanks are extended to Mary Olbrich, Beth Austin, and Jodi Hankins of the Psychology Department, who have been exceedingly helpful and kind, and Sasha Windholz of the College of Education. Last and perhaps most, thanks to Dr. Kim Buch who has always been there as a font of knowledge and encouragement.

Part I
Introduction

INTRODUCTION:
PAST, PRESENT, FUTURE

Louis Diamant

PROLOGUE

Lady MacBeth (on the news of Duncan's arrival): "Come, you spirits that tend on mortal thoughts! unsex me here, and fill me from the crown to the toe top full of direst cruelty. . . "

Macbeth, 1.5.38–39

Cristina Sanchez (a champion matador): "One of the main problems that I had working in the male-dominated world of Spain is machismo. . . . Some men refuse to be on the same poster and fight in the same fight with me."

New York Times Magazine, June 27, 1999, p. 17

Chamique Holdsclaw (the WNBA draft's top overall pick, when called a "female Michael Jordan"): "I'm the first Chamique Holdsclaw; Michael Jordan is a man. I'm a woman. And I think that is where the women's game has to get to, when women are recognized on their own."

Charlotte Observer, June 10, 1999, p. 2B

George H. Willliams (Oregon senator, debating women's voting rights in 1886): "When the women of this country come to be sailors and soldiers, when they come to navigate the ocean and to follow the plow; when they love to be jostled by all sorts of men in the thoroughfares of trade and business; when they love the treachery and turmoil of politics; when they love the dissoluteness of the corrupt and the smoke of the thunder and blood of battle better than they love the affection and enjoyment of home and family, then it will be time to talk about making the women voters."

Great Debates in American History cited in Tannahill, 1982

Peter Moore (president of Trinity Episcopal School for Ministry in Ambridge, Pennsylvania, responding to a declaration calling for the ordination of openly gay ministers, January 18, 2000): "God loves homosexuals, as he loves us all. But I have yet to find any support based on scripture, tradition, or reason for the idea that God approves of homosexual behavior."

Richard N. Ostling, "Religious Leaders Urge Blessing of Gay Ministers, Same Sex Unions," Associated Press, January 19, 2000

Famke Janssen (actress and former model): "If you play the pretty girl or the sidekick or whatever you call it, your career is a very short one, because the moment those looks start fading, you're over."

"Former (James) Bond Beauty Looks Past Appearances," *Charlotte Observer,* August 21, 2000, p. 2A

Humpty Dumpty (who came to mind in this author's search for authoritative definers of things such as gender orientation, discrimination, and so on): "When I use a word . . . it means just what I choose it to mean—neither more nor less."

Lewis Carroll, *Through the Looking Glass*

THE EVOLUTION OF SEX, GENDER, AND THE WORKPLACE

Sex, whether understood as an act or a biological classification, can be thought of as the dominant variable related to human survival. In infrahuman species, its story may be rather simple—and perhaps presented most simply by those who espouse male-female divisions and behaviors based on morphology and drives imbedded in instinct potential related to that biological construct. Instinct theory is a neat formula assigning preprogrammed biochemical mechanisms for what may seem to us mere mortals as most magical, mystical, and complex behaviors such as the lowly eel in a muddy Midwestern creek scooting over thousands of miles to make its way to the Sargasso Sea to reproduce and die. On the other hand, learning theories discount the notion that complex behaviors spring full blown from a rat or Rotarian, but rather rely on environmental reinforcement. This is true of the most radical sort of learning theories as well as those not basically concerned with neurology or intervening variables such as minds (Skinner, 1953) and those more at peace with mental phenomena (the cognitive behaviorists and the social learning theorists [Bandura, 1977]). From the learning theorists' point of view, environmental reinforcement (society and culture) shapes human sexual behavior. However, psychoanalytic theory, an instinct theory of sorts, claims that sexual instincts are not so much modified by the culture but, through mental activity, may actually create the culture that in turn modifies behavior. Psychoanalytic theory may say that the drives build a society to handle those very drives of instincts. However, psychoanalytic theory does not spend a lot of print on animal instincts and thus does not extrapolate or expand a theory of human behavior from animal research (Freud, 1905).

What seems more certain (and perhaps not even that certain) is that sexual behavior is likely to be a simpler matter in infrahumans than in people; sex distinction and sex behavior in animals were more likely to have reached their current states by processes of physical evolution that can be explained in Darwinian terms. Some have assumed that the systemic development of *Homo sapiens* completed about 150,000 years ago, and the development of cognitive and language ability were milestones in human evolution (Bickerton, 1990). Nobel laureate (1963) Theodosius Zombowski has asserted that with the end of physical evolution came the onset of social evolution. One might say that this should distinguish us from the beasts. This point of physical completion-conceptual nascence initiates the evolutionary aspects of general thought and behavior.

The change or evolution of "sex" to "gender" may be noticed in the gender psychology literature, where in the early editions, indexing of the "sex" is omitted or used to refer to the male-female classifier. In most current general psychology books, "sex" is presented with the modifier's identity and role, as for example in Zimbardo and Gerrig (1999). In contrast to biological sex, "gender" is a psychological phenomenon referring to learned sex-related attitudes. However, a huge (but polite) battle goes on with many a warrior attempting to clarify and deliver the definition. A most comprehensive attempt to survey the battlefield (or the landscape, or playing field, as the case may be) is given in Anselmi and Law (1998). But even the impulse to present catholicity could lend strength to the adage that sometimes "the least is the most." Space or sloth may restrict what is written here, but the notion of gender, in the expansive sense, leads as I found, not only from Anselmi and Law but by field experience, down many paths that are relevant to the workplace and scope of topics in this book. None of this will lead to an agreed upon or single accurate definition among the many people who do this sort of thing for a living. Perhaps an operational definition is a good bet when one is doing a study on gender or sex or even jobs, but, for some, even this may seem like reinventing the wheel.

When we began this book it seemed the title was clear and self-defined: sex would be what a certain president did not have with that woman, and gender would be a simple he-she matter. JoAnn Lee is an industrial organizational psychologist and I am a clinician. In a clinical framework gender is indexed only to the diagnosis of Gender Identity Disorder in the American Psychiatric Association's (1994) *Diagnostic and Statistical Manual of Mental Disorders* (DSM-IV). It is there designated as a preoccupation with getting rid of the primary and secondary sex characteristics (for example, request for hormones, surgery, or other procedures to physically alter sexual characteristics to simulate the other sex) or belief that he or she was born in the wrong body. Elsewhere this book will deal with this condition and what it means for such diagnosed individuals in the world of jobs.

Here is a complexity. Those with Gender Identity Disorder or transsexuals may be discriminated against occupationally, not because of their biological sex designation but rather for what they wish it to be. Thus sexual discrimination here will be gender discrimination in the elaborated view of gender and not in the morphological sense or sexual male-female designation. This paradigm holds true for homosexual persons where discrimination depends on knowing what they do sexually (sex behavior) rather than on a male or female designation. The military gives a striking example of the phenomenon of knowing what one does as the criterion for occupational demise or survival in its Damoclean sword policy of "Don't ask, don't tell" (about homosexuality). Homosexual service personnel, whose sexual orientation is known, fall into the discriminatory conflict because of the inferences of behaviors related to the orientation, much the same as a person with a Gender Identity Disorder finds discrimination frequently related to the behavior (acting differently from their male-female designation). In neither case is discrimination primarily related to the morphology as sexual discrimination. In the military when one tells, they know what one does. Military personnel with years of exemplary performance records have been discarded when they "came out" because of what the revelation implies about sex in the behavioral sense. How did MASH's Klinger manage it? He was a cross-dresser—possibly a fetishist transvestite but most likely heterosexual and competent—and of course that was television. Cross-dressing itself need not be labeled Transvestic Fetishism, which is a clinical disorder according to DSM-IV (1994). The diagnosis calls for the behavior being ego-dystonic (a twist in which the behavior creates the disorder, as distinguished from the disorder bringing on the behavior).

Our book title at first seemed glib and "perfect"—sex and gender fit perfectly, as identifiable and as distinct as night and day, beans and rice. Soon it became apparent that the struggle for definition was in itself intricately woven into the social and psychological occupational problems we are examining. Writers and researchers describe gender in much the same way that three blind persons are reputed to have described an elephant. The descriptions of the creature by each were very different, depending on which part of the animal they "examined."

THE DEFINING GAME

One of the things I did to gain focus in the lexical pastiche was a small and impromtu study: asking persons outside my office, in my office, in the gym, and so on, a question or two (too modest to be called interview or inventory). I have dared to use this method before (Diamant, 1975). In the current research, I asked about 25 persons, "What is meant by sex, what is meant by gender"? To summarize their response, basically "sex" meant having sex. The second meaning for "sex" was "male or female." "Gender" was virtually always defined as the distinction between male and female. One clinical psychologist said, "What?", and then quickly gave the male-female response. A respondent who is some kind of authority on language said first that it was a grammatical term, but she did it with a smile and then said male or female.

Although gender is the most commonly used indicator of male-female assignment, employment applications commonly ask for one's sex when they want that information. The application for employment with the state of North Carolina has a perforated and easily detached portion for "Equal Opportunity Information," which reads: "State Government Policy prohibits discrimination based on race, sex, color, creed, national origin, age or disability. Sex and age are bona fide occupational qualifications in a small number of state jobs . . . the information requested below will in no way affect you as an applicant. Check one: ___ male ___ female" (North Carolina, 1994).

The results of my informal investigation, whether measured by mere perusal or by nonparametric statistics, indicate with extremely high probability that when asked for a definition of "sex" without reference to anything else, the respondent will reply with "sexual behavior" or "having sex." The respondents, then giving a definition of gender, will give the male-female definition at a highly significant level when compared to anything else. We know there is more to it, but it takes another look after a pause to think about it.

For example, in this book the issues examined concerning sex as behavior and gender as male-female division do not always (if ever) fall into these neat stacks, even when they come close. If you take, for instance, sex as that most traditional form of "having sex" (heterosexual coitus), you will know only that it is a man and woman, but it is not a complete story of behavior and gender. For if that woman is an Air Force officer and that man anything else, odds are things would be a lot worse for her occupationally than if the man is an Air Force officer and that woman anything else; especially if either were married to someone other than that sex partner. Many have thought this especially so in the case of Lt. Kelly Flinn, a 1993 Air Force Academy graduate and a highly regarded pilot, who was charged with disobeying orders, lying, fraternizing, and having sex with an enlisted man. Although the Pentagon had in place, at the time of her hearing, strict penalties for adultery, enforcement was considered ordinarily weak, with cases brought to court-martial trial averaging between 11 and 22 in the 1990s. Linda Bird Franks, the author of *Ground Zero: The Gender Wars in the Military* (1997), says double standards have long been "a bone of contention and resentment in the military" and notes that the "military is coming to grips with what companies have known for a decade: banning romance, even adultery within the ranks, is a brush war that borders on the impossible to win" (p. 25). Still at the time of Franks's writing, a *USA Today*/CNN/Gallup poll revealed that 55 percent responding felt a boss should be fired for an adulterous affair and 52 percent believed that adulterers, even of equal rank, should be fired (Jones, 1997). What becomes clear is:

1. Adultery is fornication between adults, at least one of whom is married but not to the other partner.

2. That at times employers (for instance, the military) mete out punishment in that situation, which would represent employer punishment for sexual behavior between consenting adults.

3. That there can be male-female differences in the approach to punishment.

4. That the male-female distinction has nothing to do with reality and that if gender were merely another way of saying male-female as gyrating is for whirling, the next item would be unnecessary, but because it is not.

WHAT MAKES A WORKPLACE? A JOB?

The *American Heritage Dictionary* (1991) offers two definitions of a workplace: (1) A place such as an office or factory where people are employed; and (2) a workplace in general. Of the two, the latter suits the purpose of this volume best, the former being too restrictive. It was instructive to find that many dictionaries did not include the term "workplace." Scholarly papers and books frequently use the term without definition. My own edited collection *Homosexual Issues in the Workplace* (Diamant, 1993) neither indexed nor defined it in 15 chapters. It appears to be taken for granted from one's own frame of reference as an author, and often, although close to being "on the money," there are plenty of murky areas. For example, one of the more amorphous of workplaces is the home. There is the cottage industry of the home where children and adults manufacture items, perhaps for an entrepreneur or perhaps to vend on the street (which also may be a workplace). The home and a computer may represent the total workday experience for those who are self-employed as well as those whose labor is paid for by an entrepreneur. In the latter case, the physical workplace is not synonymous with "where one works," which is more truthfully "for whom one works" and who defines the job. The homemaker may consider the home his or her workplace, because current laws ordinarily entitle homemakers to a fair share of a spouse's income. In another informal survey by the author it was indicated that although a number of those in that classification do not consider themselves employed in the formal sense, they do not feel unemployed either. The *Dictionary of Occupational Titles* (U.S. Department of Labor, 1991) includes a job description for homemaker (309.354-010). It is, however, a domestic service occupation serving to a needy family provided by outside agents. For the purpose of this chapter, the workplace will, by and large, be the matrix for jobs (occupations, work, employment) done for remuneration. In an earlier perusal of sex/workplace issues (Long, 1993), even a place of incarceration (prison) was considered a workplace.

A growing number of social and behavioral scientists, however, consider spousal duties as a job, and one for which money or in-kind payment is due. Current laws in most states, in effect, make the earned income of one the income of the other. Thus, theoretically, the homemaker is remunerated for domestic labor. Of course this is not free of conceptual flaws. What if the spouse does nothing but get beauty treatments, hang out at the track, or eat chocolates in bed? Well, many folks have jobs outside the house in which the value is not obvious and others that do not seem much like work. In any event, as disputable as it may be, I choose to call the houseperson's work a job from my personal conceptual framework—especially because compensation for it seems to have some legal standing. On the other hand, there are many activities that are moneymaking occupations in which the major effort is criminal, but in this case I prefer to demur. In sum, there is a synergistic relationship between the workplace and the job in which one cannot be defined nor have an existence while leaving out the other. Operationally the workplace is where the jobs are done, described, or both, and controlled. Further, from here on "sex" and "gender" are what you say they are (and undoubtedly much more). Yet one does not have a clear picture of sex behavior without gender implications that are based on formal male-female divisions. Different expectancy of behaviors will befall a male-female designee that has little to do with biological functions, limitations, or abilities, but more to do with social, cultural, and personal beliefs. Thus criticism or kudos awarded one gender or the other on sexual conduct are related to views that are everchanging (discursive, as gender psychologists prefer to state) and to the more elaborated notion of gender.

SEX AND GENDER AT WORK: A DOUBLE ENTENDRE

A landmark court case, which may be illustrative of plasticity between sex as male-female and gender as role in a job situation, is probably *Barnes v. Costle* (1977). Until this case the federal government considered discrimination in employment on the basis of prejudice to a male-female based on that biological fact. Complaints about sexual harassment, which until then had not been considered, were, as a result of this ruling, viewed as valid and litigable under federal law.

Although the ruling in *Barnes v. Costle* (1977) deals with sexual discrimination, it does so with inclusion of harassment as a point it could not consider without taking into account gender roles and expectations. It states "but for her womanhood . . . her participation in sexual activity would never have been solicited. . . . Put another way, she becomes the target of her superiors' sexual desires because she was a woman. The circumstances adding high visibility to the role of gender in the affair."

The document's intent in using "gender" was probably a convenient means of avoiding the clumsiness of using "sex" in the male-female sense. However, the subtlety of its wording, whether or not intended, is that it supports a notion of a woman's gender role and expectancy on the part of her male employer: that women are to play a certain role that is not in the official job description.

Interestingly enough, the support for the harassment discussion lies in the claim "that no male employee was susceptible to such an approach by the appellant's supervisor." That was possible to state because there was a paucity of male complainants of sexual harassment by women and even more rarely was a complaint brought forward by men against men. The latter has a radical turn in *Oncale v. Sundowner* (1998), in which a court finds for a heterosexual man who has been sexually harassed by other men. The lawsuit was brought by Joseph Oncale who said that he was sexually pursued by his male supervisor and two other men during his four months working on a Gulf of Mexico oil rig (Epstein, 1998).

Title VII of the 1964 Civil Rights Act prohibits discrimination based on race, color, religion, sex, or national origin. In early litigation, discrimination based on sex meant picking one gender over another based on things such as tradition, convention, prejudice, or ignorance. Historically, such discrimination was largely used to block women from positions and advancements. Although these prejudicial sex proscriptions were by and large a woman's burden, men have more recently brought suits in some basic industries. Title VII more than once placed the heavy burden of justification on management for excluding one sex or another, although sex and age have been allowed as bona fide occupational qualifications. In litigation, the employers had to prove their cases. In *Diaz v. Pan American* (1971), the court said, "What we hold is that because of the nonmechanical aspects of the job, flight cabin attendants are not reasonably necessary to the normal operation of Pan Am's business. Pan Am cannot exclude all males simply because most males may not perform adequately. . . . We do not agree that in this case 'all or substantially all men have been shown to be inadequate'." In summarizing its findings the court said, "Before sex discrimination can be practiced, it must be shown that it is impractical to find the men that possess the ability that most women possess and that the abilities are necessary to the business not merely tangential."

The airline had offered the following as evidence:

1. Surveys showed that passengers preferred women to men as cabin attendants.
2. A clinical psychologist testified that women, simply because they *were* women, could provide comfort and reassurance to passengers better than men could.
3. An industrial psychologist testified that sex was the best practical screening device to use in determining whom to hire for the position.

These assertions speak to the task that lies ahead for those that deal with the legal, social, and psychological issues of job phenomena. Antidiscrimination movements were urged into place by compelling evidence with regard to gender stereotypes. Gender discrimination rulings were the vehicle on which the later sexual discrimination legislation arrived.

Once sexual harassment is a bona fide issue in sexual discrimination, it lends itself to application for same-sex harassment suits, but under a sexual behavior label not a gender expectation status. But this expansion of litigation for harassment did not immediately follow *Barnes v. Costle.* For in ensuing cases, or at least until *Oncale v. Sundowner* (1998), the courts in general, it appeared, did not know what to do with work sexual harassment involving men and men. In *Barnes v. Costle,* the "but for her womanhood" concept, which had extended sexual discrimination into the sex and harassment category, did not seem to be transferred to man-on-man harassment. It remained for the United States Supreme Court to bring the proliferation of same-sex harassment suits to closure in their conclusion statement that sexual harassment is sexual harassment if the perpetrator(s) and victim think the offensive actions or words are of a sexual nature. In the unanimous decision in *Oncale v. Sundowner,* the United States Supreme Court extended the federal prohibition on workplace sexual harassment to same-sex incidents. Chief Justice Anthony Scalia writing for the court states, "Common sense and an appropriate sensibility to social context will enable courts and juries to decide between what is legal and illegal."

Even if one eschews the psychoanalytic concept (Freud, 1930) that stresses the role of sexuality in the unconscious and in individual development, one would be hard put to deny its pervasiveness in our conscious lives. Offenses of a sexual nature apparently have a good chance of occurring, of course, if they are always in the unconscious and, as Laumann, Gagnon, Michael, and Michaels (1994) inform us, very much in the conscious minds of men (who are of the gender most likely to be cited for sexual harassment). The Laumann study of sexual behavior in the United States of 3,432 randomly selected men was the most comprehensive since its famous precursor, the Kinsey report. Laumann and colleagues found that 54 percent of men think about sex daily compared to only 9 percent of women. Those are the facts, whether the cause would be thought of as mainly biochemical or cultural indoctrination, or both. The figure given for the 54 percent of age group 18 to 59 sounds conservative if one might reckon in the unaware, the unknown, the forgotten stare, the hand movement, the touch that becomes almost denied to the toucher's conscious. Sexual issues pervade the workplace. They pervade life. So why should or would jobs be immune? A cigar is always more than just a smoke.

Workplace concerns with the broad term "sex" may be subdivided into some nearly distinct parcels: There are issues in which preferential treatment in hiring and promotion are based on the singular fact of biological morphology—an individual's genitals. It is as clear and unexamined as signs on restroom doors. It was anatomical male-female sex differences and those workplace issues that led to judicial review of the issue of discrimination by harassment. Just what constitutes "harassment" is a difficult issue in itself. Harassment as a sexually oriented behavior has numerous foci. In the strictest, isolated male-female form it might just be making life miserable for the recipient through constant verbal denigration and other obstructions to occupational success and satisfaction accomplished with a certain meanness. It is the expression of disparagement and disdain for the non-preferred gender rather than lust and seduction. Then there are the behaviors that may be described in terms such as lecherous, prurient, salacious, unsolicited, but most of all emotionally traumatic. Gutek (1985) found that 67.2 percent of 393 men were flattered by the idea of sex offered by a coworker, whereas 62.8 percent of 814 women would be insulted by a sexual invitation by a male colleague.

Certain sexual pursuits, as subsequent chapters will demonstrate, are actually ongoing affairs, which are declared to have been unwanted but were maintained (according to the complainants) under duress and related to keeping their jobs in a power relationship mastered by the employer or superior. There has recently been a spate of such revelations in the military.

Then there is the problem of sexual behavior that is unacceptable to those in charge and stressful to those engaged in romantic or erotic relationships by consensual couples whose actions are contrary to the policies of the organizations and institutions. The corporate world, which has less difficulty in dealing with adultery than does the military, still has difficulty when dealing with power relations. The military, while attempting to reduce its punitive actions regarding adulterous relationships, has far more problems in dealing with the issue of rank as exemplified by the following:

Travis Air Force Base, California. An Air Force captain who disobeyed orders to halt his love affair with an enlisted woman was dismissed from the service Sunday and ordered to serve a fifteen-day sentence. A six-member military jury decided the sentence after prosecutors argued that Capt. Joseph Belle should serve a year in prison. Belle, 35, pleaded guilty to conspiracy, disobeying a direct order, and fraternizing with Susan Redo of Huntersville, whom he married. Belle could have faced a maximum 22-year term. (*Charlotte Observer*, April 26, 1999)

Court harassment decisions were rooted in the sexual discrimination regulations of Title VII. The control of sexual conduct among consensual adults to a large degree grew out of moral conduct issues and have biblical basis in Western culture from whence also comes discrimination by the diminution of the woman's importance, according to psychoanalyst Thomas Szaz (1970). Although the enlargement of the legal view of sexual harassment was eventually to effect adjudication in cases of same-sex harassment, there has been virtually nothing done to give job protection against discrimination to those whose known sexual orientation is not heterosexual and to those whose sexual behavior and identification is different but not criminal. Nor is there federal effort, judicial or legislative, to decriminalize behavior that in some states is criminal whereas in others it is not. For instance, North Carolina criminalizes heterosexual fornication among the unmarried and all oral and anal sex regardless of one's marital status or sexual orientation. True prosecution is now seldom but to whom do such statutes give comfort?

Some of these sexual implication issues have recently drawn the attention of researchers and writers contributing to this volume. It has been noted that homosexual workers through an application of the antidiscriminating position of Title VII are protected from sexual harassment but are not afforded protection from discriminatory hiring or promotion. There are other sexual variances, not now thought of as orientation, in persons whose sexuality and gender identity leave them open to occupational problems and emotional stress unrelated to occupational competency. They often bear clinical labels such as Paraphelia and are classified in the *Diagnostic and Statistical Manual of Mental Disorders* (American Psychiatric Association, 1994). The Paraphelias comprise subclassifications that include benign cross-dressing, Tranvestic Fetishism (302.3), a cruel Sexual Sadism (302.2), and the criminally destructive Pedophilia (302.2). Read McAnulty (1995, and this volume) for elaboration. What disparate persons are sewn into this diagnostic quilt! The American Psychiatric Association (1952, 1968) once classified now pathology-free homosexuality as a disorder among Paraphelias. The history of the clinical incarceration and emancipation of homosexuality has been described elsewhere (Diamant, 1995). One would think now for reason's sake that it is time to free the cross-dresser. (Who knows, it might eventually help emotionally and occupationally.) But one should not expect a rapid new view of crossdressing. Homosexuality has not shaken the prejudice that clings from having for so long been termed a mental disorder (or a crime or a sin). As it stands currently men and women of either orientation (or bisexual) have recourse in the event of sexual harassment. Those with Paraphelias or Gender Identity Disorders are men or women in the case of harassment, but there is little protection against discrimination in employing, promoting, and firing related to their conditions.

Gay men, lesbians, and those who are considered by the American Psychiatric Association to have Paraphelias or Gender Identity Disorder are given judicial support in the cases of sexual harassment, but there is now little help in dealing with employer prejudice related to a sexual behavior propensity as long as it is not obviously a harassment situation. Thus the policy of not telling that the military adopted may protect a job at the price of closet stress or more dire consequences; for example: "Army private Calvin Glover, 18, was sentenced Thursday to life in prison with the possibility of parole for bludgeoning to death a fellow soldier who had been rumored to be gay—a case that gay rights activists said was a tragic failure of 'don't ask, don't tell' " (*Charlotte Observer,* December 10, 1999).

Certain sex issues in the workplace produce unpleasant or violently aversive reactions even though the prejudiced are at little risk of harm. One of a few studies dealing with employer perception of risk finds that employees evaluate risk on the perception of probability and magnitude. In the case of HIV/AIDS, a number of studies (Roth & Carman, 1993; Sheehan, Lennon & McDevitt, 1989) show that although many workers say they know that the risk of becoming infected is low they are still apprehensive about HIV on the job. Roth and Carman also suggest that perceptions of risk influence how legal standards are interpreted. AIDS is, it appears, continuously seen as a sexual issue regardless of how it is contracted. But even superstar basketball player Ervin "Magic" Johnson was shunned by certain other starters when he disclosed his HIV–positive status (Sorenson, 1982). Later his most antagonistic opponent relented, demonstrating the power of knowledge.

Male homosexual workers have suffered from a public germophobia almost inseparable from sexual orientation since the onset of the AIDS epidemic. This is not much more than simple homophobia, which like other phobias may be considered "a persistent irrational fear of a specific object or situation (the phobic stimulus that results in a compelling desire to avoid it). This often leads either to avoidance of the phobic stimulus or "enduring it with dread" (American Psychiatric Association, 1994, p. 770). The problems related to the homophobic reaction have been examined by Herek (1988).

Each of us is in our own sexuality closet. Sometimes we find our way out, sometimes we are let out, and sometimes there is the illusion of being out. Understanding AIDS and the reactions to it requires a deeper understanding of ourselves. One could speculate that homophobia is a reaction formation, which in psychodynamic terms, produces an opposite response to feared, unconscious fantasy. James, a waiter in my favorite deli, told me of his horror brought on by a minister customer who told one of the proprietors that he did not want to be served by a homosexual who could give him AIDS. How did James feel? "I felt rotten, how would you feel? I could have lost my job. I had just moved to a new apartment, how could I pay the rent? I am lucky that the people I work for understood."

GET THE PICTURE

I am partial to a reaction-formation concept that provides a useful explanation of oppositional shifts from morality to lechery, which has been characteristic of the workplace for centuries or at least since the industrial revolution. While the Calvinistic owner classes developed the strongest code of religiosity, sin, and purity regarding the women of their families, impulses were less fettered regarding the lower classes. Take your choice: reaction-formation, learned behavior, or (as the average Joe or Jane might say) "hypocrisy"—and as an old saying went "heaven help the poor working girl."

These sexual issues in the workplace have developed from the historical position of woman that had been attached to much biblical, biological, and social dogma as the natural and genetic order of things related to survival. It appears to be so whether these are issues of harassment of some erotic design or occupational exploitation. Industrialization increased the opportunity for wage earning as well as opportunities for exploitation and discrimination, even the discarding of women when they lost beauty and youth and thus supposedly their sexual appeal.

In lesser measure, men had to struggle to gain acceptance where women dominated. The flight attendant conflict is illustrative (*Diaz v. Pan American,* 1971). Men who could perform the flight attendant tasks as well as women suffered from discriminatory employee practices. But no one who knew the sexual mystique of these stereotypes can deny that their employer utilized that role with the largely male commercial clientele making youth and beauty and femaleness (and not competency) as the main issues that were tested for fair employment practices.

Perhaps time will see the increase of practices, situations, and conditions that promote harmonious, productive, and just relationships in matters interlinking sex and gender and jobs. This utopian view can be labeled social evolution and in that evolution the movement is basically toward personal actualization. Social evolution is to be seen as a concept apart from that of evolutionary psychology, which sees the evolvement of male and female gender role differences measurable today—a result of adaptive processes that have occurred in the sexual selection processes—understandable in Darwinian survival terms (Buss, 1994). Even Abraham Maslow's (1970) hierarchical model for individual self development (self-actualization) employs within the individual that which is operating in society: the move from biological to psychological and social mastery. A considerable segment of the corporate world has claimed faith in Maslow's psychology and a number of university schools of business include his ideas in their curricula. So would an actualized person harm or harass another? Should not harassment and actualization be mutually exclusive? Could not the postulates of the developing self apply to issues of gender, appearance, and orientation—and to people who fall in love and who relate to each other in mature sexual ways, regardless of work settings?

In this respect because of the "special needs" of the military, more rigidity has been applied to regulating relationships than in corporate life. Companies with armies of lawyers often will not interfere with an office romance unless it puts the company at risk or hurts business by damaging employee morale or credibility with the company (Jones, 1997). Jones also reports that a *USA Today*/CNN/Gallup survey revealed that 55 percent of respondents thought firing was in order when a boss has an affair with a supervisee, whereas 32 percent believed any adultery was cause for dismissal. Because many states and communities now have passed laws forbidding discrimination based on marital status, those cases in which corporations single out married people for corporate punishment for sexual adultery involving employees would not be officially allowed.

Weiss (1998) writes to the contrary (almost). In his article, "Don't Even Think about It. (The Cupid Cops Are Watching)," he investigates the problems and inequities that may occur in such relationships in the corporate world as well as the institutional sphere, especially universities. Although he cites the many dangers and penalties put in place by laws and institutional acumen, he notes the importance of context as a determinant of good or evil in workplace romance. Freud has been credited with saying, "All that matters is love and work," (Partingon, 1992), but apparently the combination in the workplace may be another (and very tricky) matter, according to Weiss (1998).

I have in this introduction attempted to bring in lines and colors that may paint the picture impressionistically—more a Jackson Pollock than a detailed blueprint. This essay is intended informationally and emotionally for what is to come in this book and perhaps in the universe of jobs. Borrowing words from Browning's Rabbi Ben Ezra, it wishes also to say "grow old along with me, the best is yet to be. . . ."

EPILOGUE

> The Rev. Vashti Murphy McKenzie (after being elected the first woman bishop in the 213-year history of the African Methodist Episcopal Church): "The stained-glass ceiling has been pierced"
> *(New York Times,* July 12, 2000, p. 1).

REFERENCES

American Heritage Dictionary (2nd college ed.). (1991). Boston: Houghton Mifflin.
American Psychiatric Association. (1952). *Diagnostic and statistical manual of mental disorders.* Washington, DC: Author.

American Psychiatric Association. (1968). *Diagnostic and statistical manual of mental disorders* (2nd ed.). Washington, DC: Author.

American Psychiatric Association. (1994). *Diagnostic and statistical manual of mental disorders* (4th ed.). Washington, DC: Author.

Anselmi, D. L., & Law, A. L. (1998). *Questions of gender: Perspectives and paradoxes.* New York: McGraw-Hill.

Bandura, A. (1977). *Social learning theory.* Englewood Cliffs, NJ: Prentice Hall.

Barnes v. Costle. 561 F2d 983 (DC Cir 1977).

Bickerton, D. (1990). *Language and species.* Chicago: University of Chicago Press.

Buss, D. M. (1995). Evolutionary psychology: A new paradigm for psychological science. *Psychological Inquiry, 6,* 1–30.

Court martial grants possibility of parole. (1999, December 10). *Charlotte Observer,* p. 1B.

Deaux, K., & Major, B. (1987). Putting gender into context: An interactive model of gender-related behavior. *Psychological Review, 94*(3), 364–389.

Diamant, L. (1975) Perceptual defense—Down but not out. *American Psychologist, 30*(9), 945.

Diamant, L. (Ed.). (1993). *Homosexual issues in the workplace.* Washington, DC: Taylor & Frances.

Diamant, L. (1995). Sexual orientation: Some historical perspective. In L. Diamant & R. McAnulty (Eds.), *The psychology of sexual orientation, behavior, and identity* (pp. 3–18). Westport, CT: Greenwood.

Diaz vs. Pan American. 422 F2d 385 388 (5th Cir 1971).

Epstein, A. (1998, March 5). Same sex harassment illegal. *Charlotte Observer.*

Franks, L. B. (1997). *Ground zero: The gender wars in the military.* New York: Simon & Schuster.

Freud, S. (1905). Three essays on the theory of sexuality. *The standard edition of the complete works of Sigmund Freud* (Vol. 7, pp. 125–245). London: Hogarth Press.

Freud, S. (1930). Civilization and its discontents. *The standard edition of the complete works of Sigmund Freud* (Vol. 21, pp. 59–74). London: Hogarth Press.

Gutek, B. A. (1985). *Sex and the workplace: The impact of sexual behavior and harassment on women, men and organizations.* San Francisco: Jossey-Bass.

Herek, G. M. (1988). Heterosexuals' attitudes toward lesbians and gay men: Correlates and gender differences. *Journal of Sex Research, 25,* 451–477.

Jones, D. (1997, June 12). Companies avoid pitfalls of punishing adultery. *USA Today,* p. 1B.

Laumann, E. O., Gagnon, J. H., Michael, R. T., & Michaels, S. (1994). *The social organization of sexuality: Sexual practices in the United States.* Chicago: University of Chicago Press.

Long, G. T. (1993). Homosexual relationships in a unique setting: The male prison. In L. Diamant (Ed.), *Homosexual issues in the workplace* (pp. 143–158). Washington, DC: Taylor & Francis.

Maslow, A. (1970). *Motivation and personality* (rev. ed.). New York: Harper & Row.

McAnulty, R. D. (1995). The paraphelias: Classification and theory. In L. Diamant & R. D. McAnulty (Eds.), *The psychology of sexual orientation, behavior, and identity.* Westport, CT: Greenwood Press.

North Carolina. (1994). P. D. 107 (Rev. 12/94).

Oncale, Joseph v. Sundowner Off Shore Services, Inc. U.S. Supreme Court 1998 No. 96-568.

Ostling, R. N. (2000, January 19). Religious leaders urge blessing of gay ministers, same sex unions. *Charlotte Observer,* p. 4A.

Partingon, A. (Ed.). (1992). *Oxford Dictionary of Quotations.* New York: Oxford University Press.

Roth, N. L., & Carman, J. (1993). Risk perception and HIV legal issues in the workplace. In L. Diamant (Ed.), *Homosexual issues in the workplace.* Washington, DC: Taylor & Francis.

Sheehan, E. P., Lennon, R., & McDevitt, T. (1989). Reaction to AIDS and other illnesses: Reported interactions in the workplace. *Journal of Psychology, 123*(6), 525–536.

Skinner, B. F. (1953). *Science and human behavior.* New York: Macmillan.

Sorenson, T. (1982). Why wouldn't Magic want to come back? *Charlotte Observer,* p. 1B.

Szasz, T. (1970). *The manufacture of madness: A comparative study of the inquisition and the mental health movement.* New York: Harper & Row.

Tannahill, R. (1982). *Sex in history.* Chelsea, MI: Scarborough House.

Travis air force base. (1999, April 27). *Charlotte Observer,* p. 1C.

United States Department of Labor. (1991). *Dictionary of occupational titles* (4th ed.). Washington, DC: Author.

Weiss, P. (1998, May 3). Don't even think about it. (The cupid cops are watching.). *New York Times Magazine,* pp. 42–47, 58–60, 68, 86.

Zimbardo, P. G., & Gerrig, R. J. (1999). *Psychology and life.* New York: Longman.

Part II
Gender Issues

2

HITTING THE CEILING: GENDERED BARRIERS TO OCCUPATIONAL ENTRY, ADVANCEMENT, AND ACHIEVEMENT

Ruth E. Fassinger

INTRODUCTION

Despite several decades of sweeping societal change, persistent and pernicious barriers to women's vocational entry, advancement, and achievement remain (Fitzgerald, Fassinger, & Betz, 1995). Moreover, recent political changes such as the dismantling of affirmative action threaten to erode what little progress has been made in creating a more equitable, hospitable workplace for women. Women continue to earn less than their male counterparts; women continue to be segregated into female-dominated jobs that offer neither status nor opportunity for advancement; women continue to enter careers that vastly underutilize their capabilities and talents; and women continue to shoulder most of the burden of managing home and family (Fitzgerald, Fassinger, & Betz, 1995). Assuming that many, if not most, women would prefer to earn fair compensation for their work, would prefer to enter a wide variety of careers that are commensurate with their abilities and motivation for achievement, and would prefer to share responsibility for family and home, their failure to do so suggests the extensive presence of factors that are inhibiting or compromising the healthy career development of women.

In fact, almost a half-century of rich scholarly literature in the vocational psychology of women has produced ample evidence of pervasive impediments to women's occupationally related choices and behaviors (Betz & Fitzgerald, 1987; Fitzgerald et al., 1995). This chapter presents an overview of the barriers to women's career development that have been documented frequently and consistently in the vocational literature. The chapter is organized into two major sections: "Problems" and "Solutions." The first section ("Problems") introduces a wide range of variables that have been implicated as inhibiting women's career development and achievement, grouped according to whether they are external/environmental barriers or internal/self barriers (cf. Betz, 1994; Betz & Fitzgerald, 1987; Fassinger, 1996). The second section ("Solutions") outlines the interventions needed to address the problems outlined in the first section, grouped according to whether they are targeted at systemic change or at particular individuals or groups. The chapter concludes with a suggested action agenda related to theory and research, intervention, and advocacy. It should be noted that it is beyond the scope of this chapter to present an exhaustive review of individual empirical studies or detailed descriptions of interventions. Rather, the focus is on presenting summaries and illustrative examples of issues identified and investigated in the vast literature on the vocational psychology of diverse women.

PROBLEMS

Barriers to women's career development negatively affect vocational behavior across a wide range of occupational processes: choice, implementation, adjustment, advancement, and achievement. In fact, many barriers (such as discrimination and stereotyping) have multiple effects on a woman's occupational behavior throughout her life. These barriers can be grouped broadly into external/environmental barriers and internal/self barriers, which are discussed in the following sections.

External/Environmental Barriers

External or contextual barriers, also termed "structural factors," are features of the environment or context—specific workplaces and organizations, the educational system, and society at large—that serve to limit access to or opportunities within those environments (Fitzgerald & Betz, 1994). Contextual barriers exist outside of the individual and can be expressed by individual persons but are rooted in societal structures such as policies, institutions, practices, ideologies, and norms. Barriers that are contextual or environmental are listed below (Betz, 1994; Betz & Fitzgerald, 1987; Fassinger, 1996), with a brief discussion of each.

Occupational Stereotyping

Pervasive beliefs about the appropriateness or suitability of particular jobs for one sex or the other, based on widely held societal and individual gender role stereotypes, serve to limit perceived occupational choices (for example, beliefs that women should not be in military combat roles or engineering preventing a woman from exploring those careers). Such stereotypes also function through employer attitudes and workplace climate to restrict actual entry into certain jobs (for instance, men being hired over equally qualified women) or opportunities to advance once in the organization (for example, women being skipped over for deserved promotions or clientele requesting male professionals). There is strong evidence that occupational stereotypes are formed early, remain evident in secondary and college years, and that the media reinforce traditional roles and expectations, exerting clear influence on the occupational perceptions and role identification of young people (Phillips & Imhoff, 1997). Research also suggests that males stereotype more and are subject to greater stereotyping than females, although negative consequences for gender role deviant behavior (such as academic or vocational success) by females is well documented in the literature (Phillips & Imhoff, 1997).

Interestingly, research suggests that purposeful exposure to models and cognitive training in the form of increased information about actual job activity can reduce gender stereotyping of occupations, but it is unclear whether such changes lead to real expansion of vocational options for women or men (Phillips & Imhoff, 1997). Moreover, there is evidence that rising numbers of women in male-dominated occupations make those careers more attractive to women but not necessarily to men (Phillips & Imhoff, 1997), suggesting relatively intractable ideologies on the part of men about women's "place" in particular career fields (also see chapter 3 in this volume).

Gender Bias in Education and the "Null Environment"

Bias against women in education (including higher education) is well documented (AAUW, 1992; Bailey, 1998; Sadker & Sadker, 1994; Touchton & Davis, 1991). Recent literature also has begun to address the unique issues facing sexual minority women (Fassinger, 1993, 1996; Harbeck, 1992; Harris, 1997; Sanlo, 1998) and women of color (Betz & Fitzgerald, 1993; Bingham & Ward, 1994) in their educational pursuits. Classroom interaction and communication patterns that exclude or marginalize, faculty behavior that ignores or belittles, faculty and peer harassment that frightens and intimidates, curriculum content and practices that alienate, extracurricular activities and organizations that exclude, testing practices that disadvantage, and the absence of women in positions of power and influence at all levels in the educational system are factors that have been cited as barriers to females' success in academic pursuits, particularly females who also are members of sexual or ethnic minority groups. Socioeconomic background also is an important, if rarely acknowledged, factor in educational achievement. One recent study (LePage-Lees, 1997) found that women from disadvantaged backgrounds who were academically successful attributed their success to the fact that they did not disclose their background to faculty, suggesting that they perceived pervasive classist attitudes in professional educators.

One educational issue that has received considerable research attention is the paucity of females in mathematics, sciences, and engineering, and the documentation of efforts to significantly increase the participation of girls and women in mathematics, the "critical filter" (Sells, 1982, cited in Betz & Fitzgerald, 1987) that regulates entry into scientific, technical, and business fields. Fassinger and O'Brien (in press) point to the intransigence of this problem by noting the example of chemistry, a field in which the "influx" of women is widely declared. In 1980, some of the top chemistry departments in the United States (Harvard, Stanford, MIT, University of Chicago, Columbia) contained either no female faculty or one woman; in 1997, after almost 20 years of very public focus on recruiting women faculty, these same departments each had one female faculty member (Brennan, 1998), suggesting that very little actual progress had been made. Similarly, Wasserman (1998) recently reported on membership in the prestigious National Academy of Sciences, noting that only 93 women are included in the membership of over 1,600, most of them concentrated in the biological sciences and very few in chemistry, physics, or engineering. Of the top 150 "Silicon Valley" companies, only 28 of the 755 senior executives are women (Corcoran, 1999), indicating that women also have not progressed very far into the management and business sectors of technical fields.

Fassinger and O'Brien (in press) point out that the blatant discrimination of the past is often replaced at present by a benign tolerance that offers no support or encouragement and leaves women even more confused and self-blaming when goals are thwarted or fail to materialize. For example, a college professor notes in passing to a female engineering student that her weak math background might bar her from the most lucrative jobs but then makes no effort to help her improve her skills. Recent work on retention of students in science, mathematics, and engineering majors (Seymour & Hewitt, 1997) supports the importance of faculty relationships for women students. Not only were female students about twice as likely as males to have chosen these majors through the active influence of someone (for instance, a teacher) important to them and arriving in college with greater expectations of having personal relationships with faculty, but female students also were more affected by faculty attitudes and behaviors (praise, criticism) than males and less able to separate their feelings about faculty from their performance in classes. An educational environment that discriminates indirectly has been termed a "null environment" (Freeman, 1979), in that it may not be particularly encouraging toward students of either sex but constitutes a form of passive discrimination against females in its failure to take into account (and therefore deliberately address) the vastly different circumstances from which male and female students come in terms of support for academic and career pursuits. The concept of the null environment represents a clarion call for proactive efforts to address educational inequities, and lack of a strong advocacy stance is viewed as adherence to a status quo that maintains women's educational disadvantage (Betz, 1989; Betz & Fitzgerald, 1987).

Occupational Discrimination

Discriminatory practices related to education and training, hiring, wages, evaluation, promotion/advancement, coworker attitudes and behaviors, and workplace climate have been widely documented in the literature on women's career development (Betz, 1994; Betz & Fitzgerald, 1987; Phillips & Imhoff, 1997; also see chapter 5 in this volume for discussion of sexual harassment). There is a great deal of research indicating that men advance faster, further, and with greater compensation than do their female peers, and differential salary patterns have remained quite consistent over time (women now earn 72 cents for every dollar earned by men, up from 63 cents 20 years ago). A recent report (Corcoran, 1999) indicated that, of the 100 best-compensated "Silicon Valley" executives, only two were women; the average compensation package (including salary, bonuses, options) for men was $1.4 million as compared to $829,922 for women, including a salary gap of $255,251 for men compared to $197,494 for women. It is important to note that documented compensation differences persist even when factors such as age, education, experience, and performance are controlled (Phillips & Imhoff, 1997), and that sexual and ethnic minority women experience the greatest disadvantage in earnings (Badgett, 1994; Bingham & Ward, 1994). Occupational status appears to be related to earning differentials, with female-dominated occupations compensated much more poorly than male-dominated occupations requiring comparable training and skill (Betz & Fitzgerald, 1987). The literature also indicates that the high levels of sex segregation in the workforce are due to discrimination, not merely to occupational "choices" made by women (Phillips & Imhoff, 1997). Gender role attitudes also have been strongly implicated in earnings differentials; for example, a "depressed-entitlement effect" has been documented, in which women in simulated work tasks pay themselves less than men for the same amount and quality of work (Jost, 1997). Similarly, marriage and parenthood are associated with higher salaries for men but lower salaries for women (Phillips & Imhoff, 1997), and evidence suggests that women often are not viewed as co-providers in dual-career families even when they earn as much or more than their husbands (Cook, 1993), again suggesting the pervasive effects of gender role ideologies on fair compensation for work.

Research also clearly documents sex differences in patterns of occupational advancement, with women consistently disadvantaged despite education, qualifications, tenure, and occupational attitudes comparable to those of men (Phillips & Imhoff, 1997). A recent study of British workers found that 55 to 62 percent of the variance in career success was attributable to sex discrimination (Melamed, 1995). Another study documented perceptions of the work environment as significantly more hostile to women than men on several dimensions, including sexist attitudes and comments, dual standards and opportunities, informal socializing, remediation policies and practices, and balancing work and personal obligations (Stokes, Riger, & Sullivan, 1995). Such perceptions have critical implications for job satisfaction and turnover; the latter study indicated that, for both men and women, the friendlier they perceived the work environment to be, the longer they planned to stay in the organization (Stokes, Riger, & Sullivan, 1995). Similarly, research on job satisfaction has demonstrated strong links to family variables and role conflict, mentoring, social support, income, and occupational rank and type, all areas in which women typically are disadvantaged relative to men (Phillips & Imhoff, 1997).

Factors associated with differential advancement opportunities for men and women that have been documented consistently in the literature include the tendency of men to promote other men, the relationship between gender and perceived job performance and evaluation resulting in poorer evaluations of women, the prevalence of sexual harassment, and the lack of resources for advancement (for example, mentors, institutional support). A recent study of faculty at 24 U.S. medical schools, for example, found that female faculty were less productive and less satisfied with their career progress than were their male counterparts, with women publishing an average of 18 journal articles to men's 29; lack of institutional support (secretarial help, grant support, and so on) as well as greater responsibility for children were implicated in this gender gap (Carr et al., 1998). Similarly, eminent female scientists in one recent study (Wasserman, 1998) cited as barriers to advancement the unfair or inaccurate assessment of women by men, lack of institutional financial support during the critical early years of their careers, lack of inclusion in "old boy" networks, lack of mentors, and persistent negative societal attitudes.

There also is evidence that the effects of discrimination may be especially high for those in nontraditional, male-dominated fields, those in low-level positions, and those who are also members of other oppressed groups, such as lesbians and women of color. For example, women do not traditionally fill firefighting jobs. A recent study of female firefighters, for example, found that they experienced more sexist events, more job stress, and lower perceived valuation by coworkers than did women in more traditional careers (Yoder & McDonald, 1998). Evidence also suggests that standing out as a male in a female-dominated field may be advantageous to men, whereas standing out as a female in a male-dominated field may not be an advantage to women (Phillips & Imhoff, 1997). This is perhaps due to the dual problems of tokenism for women—excessive demands and expectations based on being one of only a few women, as well as lack of credibility and widespread dismissal of one's efforts and accomplishments as a woman (Betz & Fitzgerald, 1987).

Another study indicated that female clerical workers, as compared to managers, experienced more work demands and less support, were more distressed and less satisfied with their jobs, and experienced greater difficulties in accessing and implementing coping strategies (Long, 1998). Klonoff and Landrine (1995) assert that "sexist discrimination is rampant in women's lives" (p. 439), especially for women of color, and other work by these authors (Landrine, Klonoff, Gibbs, Manning, & Lund, 1995) indicates that sexist discrimination contributes far more to women's psychiatric and physical symptoms (such as depressive and somatic complaints) than do more generic stressors. This is supported by other findings indicating that women's perceptions of personal and group discrimination are related to greater experiencing of depression (Klonis, Endo, Crosby, & Worell, 1997). It is thus clear that occupational discrimination exacts a high price in women's mental health and that its effects extend far beyond the workplace into other areas of women's lives.

Multiple Role Issues in the Home-Work Interface

Although ample evidence has accumulated pointing to the beneficial aspects of multiple roles (especially work roles) for women (see Crosby, 1991), there also is consensus in the literature that many women face additional challenges in their career planning and implementation due to combining work and family roles (Phillips & Imhoff, 1997; also see chapter 13 in this volume). Indeed, the presence of (heterosexual) marriage and children traditionally has been the most salient factor in women's career direction and success, and the impact of parenting on one's career trajectory continues to be experienced far more strongly by women than men (Betz & Fitzgerald, 1987; Fitzgerald & Weitzman, 1992). This is in large measure because, although women's employment patterns have shifted in recent decades to reflect greater workforce participation, higher levels of employment, and smaller families started later in life, their level of involvement in housework and childcare has not changed relative to that of men, and women continue to shoulder most of the family burden, even in dual-career couples (Cook, 1993; Fassinger & O'Brien, in press; Fitzgerald & Weitzman, 1992; Phillips & Imhoff, 1997).

Recent findings indicate that women spend over 15 hours per week on housework alone as compared to 9 hours for men (Konicus, 1999), that women spend an average of 15 hours per week more than men in both housework and childcare (Burley, 1991), and that medical school faculty mothers were found to devote 22 hours weekly to childcare whereas faculty fathers spent 14 hours caring for children (Carr et al., 1998). Moreover, there is ample evidence of continued societal endorsement of the "motherhood mandate" (Russo, 1976, cited in Fitzgerald & Betz, 1994)—the traditional expectation that women's primary fulfillment in life will be derived from bearing and caring for children. Indeed, research consistently indicates that many women exhibit strong commitment to both work and family roles (Fitzgerald & Betz, 1987, 1994; Fitzgerald & Weitzman, 1992; Spade & Reese, 1991), and this may be especially true for women of color (for example, Fassinger, 1998; Gomez & Fassinger, in press; Richie et al., 1997; Weathers, Thompson, Robert, & Rodriguez, 1994). It is also important to note that family roles for women often include caring for extended family members (aging parents) or close friends and community members, rendering multiple role issues salient for women both with and without children (Fassinger, in press). Research further suggests that women may feel more comfortable and confident about managing multiple roles if they are pursuing careers in fields traditional for women rather than nontraditional fields (Farmer, Wardrop, Anderson, & Risinger, 1995;

Phillips & Imhoff, 1997; Stickel & Bonnet, 1991); thus, women's plans to combine work and family may further contribute to pervasive sex segregation in the workplace.

Interestingly, the literature indicates that even though many women plan to combine work and family roles, they expect and want their partners/husbands to participate equitably in household and childcare responsibilities, and marital satisfaction appears to be strongly linked to perceptions of cooperation regarding domestic tasks (Phillips & Imhoff, 1997; Unger & Crawford, 1996). Related variables that influence the well-being of women juggling multiple roles are spousal views of the woman's employment, gender role attitudes of one's partner/spouse and other family members, family climate, and aspects of the work environment such as occupational rank and congruence of employment status with one's preferences (Betz & Fitzgerald, 1987; Klein, Hyde, Essex, & Clark, 1998; Phillips & Imhoff, 1997). Unfortunately, research suggests that men's expectations regarding their own participation in household labor continue to demonstrate wide discrepancies from those of women, and their actual performance of household and childcare tasks is far less than that of their female partners/spouses, even in couples who regard their relationships as egalitarian (Gilbert, 1992; Unger & Crawford, 1996). Indeed, in Wasserman's (1998) sample of eminent female scientists, many of whom were married to scientists (spouses who presumably understood the rigors of a scientific career and who were often described as "supportive"), women with children reported that they shouldered most of the responsibility for childcare.

In attempting to understand the well-documented discrepancies between men's and women's ideologies regarding work and family, some scholars point to problems in the patriarchal structure of family life that defines fathering as providing income rather than nurturing, and suggest radical changes in gender roles that will centralize connection in men's socialization (Cook, 1993; Gilbert, 1992; Silverstein, 1996). Other scholars note societal messages that subtly undermine role equality by praising women for their "superwoman" feats and men for "helping." These messages reinforce traditional gender roles in which men are seen as special if they participate at all in family life whereas women are viewed as neither needing nor deserving equality in the home (Cook, 1993; Deutsch & Saxon, 1998; Gilbert, 1992). Regardless of reasons for the impediments to more egalitarian family roles, the critical point to be made here is that it is not merely the combining of multiple roles that creates stress and compromises women's well-being, but rather the lack of concrete support in both the family and the workplace that forces women to seek individual solutions for what are pervasive environmental impediments to success in managing those roles. As one scholar summed up, "For women, it's not having a job that's bad for your health, it's having a lousy job with inadequate support for at-home responsibilities" (Baruch et al., 1983, p.180, cited in Unger & Crawford, 1996).

The structure of the workplace itself bears the blame for much of the difficulty women experience in managing multiple roles. By and large, workplaces have not provided affordable or accessible childcare, flexible working arrangements (such as job-sharing and flextime), liberal parental leave policies, and viable alternative paths to success (for instance, longer or more circuitous tenure tracks). In addition, lesbian and gay workers usually are denied even the most basic benefits for partners and children, such as medical insurance and tuition (see Fassinger, in press, for summary). Recent findings of the Families and Work Institute (1998) indicated that, of the 1,057 employers surveyed, only 9 percent offered on-site childcare, a mere 5 percent helped workers pay for childcare, and only 36 percent provided information for locating childcare. It is important to note the tangible benefits to companies offering childcare—a cost-benefit analysis by Chase Manhattan Bank of their limited policy of providing 20 days of back-up childcare in emergency situations saved the company $825,000 in reduced absenteeism in only one year, suggesting that it is fiscally sensible to provide such services. Interestingly, companies with women in top positions were six times more likely to provide childcare than were male-dominated companies (19 percent versus 3 percent), and retail trade (a field characterized predominantly by female workers in lower echelons and males in positions of authority) were the least likely to offer childcare (Boyd, Galinsky, & Swanberg, 1998). It would appear that having women in positions of power is critical in creating work environments that are supportive of workers' multiple roles and obligations.

Lack of Role Models, Mentors, and Collegial Support

The difficulty for women of negotiating male-dominated work environments is well documented, and much of this difficulty stems from lack of presence of other women as well as lack of support by men (Betz & Fitzgerald, 1987). Research on mentoring indicates that, although having mentors has positive effects on women's career advancement, there are significant barriers to obtaining mentors due to the lack of women (particularly ethnic minority women and "out" lesbians) in the upper ranks of most workplaces (Betz & Fitzgerald, 1987; Fassinger, 1996; Phillips & Imhoff, 1997). Studies indicate that individuals receive more support for advancement from same-sex workers, and also that men tend to support other men whereas women support both women and men (Phillips & Imhoff, 1997). Simple math applied to these findings suggests that men are far more likely to be in mentoring relationships than are women. This workplace reality is supported by reports from female scientists, who indicated that exclusion from information-rich "old boy" networks had constituted critical impediments to their success. This was compounded by the general lack of women in the sciences to serve as role models and supporters and to help counteract persistent negative social attitudes (Wasserman, 1998). Further support comes from studies of the career success of women of color, who consistently report difficulties in finding mentors similar to themselves, and assert the critical importance of mentoring to career achievement (for instance, Fassinger, 1998; Gomez & Fassinger, in press; Richie et al., 1997; see also Bingham & Ward, 1994).

Bias in Counseling and Testing

There is a voluminous literature in gender-related issues in counseling and psychological testing. Suffice it to say here that many of the assessment devices commonly used in career counseling have been criticized for their inaccuracy or lack of applicability to women, people of color, and sexual minority populations, and much research has explored psychometric modifications and assessment alternatives that better serve diverse populations (for example, see Betz, 1994; Fassinger, 1996; Leong, 1995). As but one example, research indicates that Holland's widely accepted hexagonal structure of interests (which underlies several interest inventories as well as the organization of many career centers, occupational resource materials, and commercial resources), although finding consistent support for adults and children across many populations and occupations, may not fit quite as well for women or for members of some racial-ethnic groups (for instance, African American males) (Fouad, Harmon, & Borgen, 1997; Rounds & Tracey, 1996; Tracey & Ward, 1998), raising questions about the applicability of assessment instruments built upon this typology. Unfortunately, not all of this important psychometric work filters down into the training of counselors and psychologists, who also may harbor their own biases regarding diversity among people, rendering the provision of counseling unhelpful at best and harmful at worst (see Fassinger, in press, for summary). Research indicates that many graduate training programs are not preparing trainees adequately in the areas of gender, sexual orientation, and race/ethnicity in counseling and therapy (see Fassinger, in press; Fassinger & Richie, 1997), which suggests that individual clients may or may not get skilled, sensitive help with their vocational concerns. Indeed, Phillips and Imhoff (1997) conclude in their recent extensive review of the literature that many existing assessment tools and interventions used in counseling continue to restrict occupational options considered by women.

In summarizing the external/environmental barriers discussed above, it should be noted that many of them overlap, creating circumstances that exponentially increase their effects. For example, consider a young woman, Sherrie, seeking advice at a university counseling or career center about whether to declare a major in chemical engineering. Research on contextual barriers strongly suggests that she may be:

1. administered an inappropriate interest inventory that fails to adequately tap her technical interests;
2. counseled by a career advisor or counselor who is steeped in stereotyped notions that females have neither the aptitude nor fortitude for the rigors of science or engineering;
3. sent to search out career information from materials and resources that reinforce occupational stereotypes (for instance, show photographs of male scientists and engineers only);

4. considering entering an engineering department in which there are no female faculty and few female students;

5. obtaining her education in an institution in which she rarely has a female professor, in which male professors and students routinely demean and harass females, in which she is ignored in her classes, and in which she will rarely if ever experience direct encouragement for pursuing a career, particularly in engineering.

If Sherrie, against all odds, decides to pursue engineering, she is likely to:

1. be or feel excluded from male-dominated clubs and organizations in engineering, as well as from informal social activities;

2. fail to receive mentoring and networking opportunities (for instance, being asked to assist a professor on a research project) that will aid her in obtaining employment;

3. continue to be undermined or ignored in her classes;

4. receive less pay than her male counterparts when she does obtain a job;

5. encounter numerous obstacles to promotion and advancement (for example, an employer who denies her a deserved promotion following a maternity leave but cites her performance as the basis of his decision);

6. experience a hostile or unwelcoming workplace climate and have little or no collegial support; and

7. find that workplace policies and norms dismiss family and home responsibilities.

If Sherrie is African American, lesbian, or disabled, her difficulties are likely to be even greater, due to the effects of a multiplicity of contextual barriers she must face (Fassinger & O'Brien, in press; Fitzgerald & Betz, 1994; also see chapters 7, 8, and 14 in this volume). It would hardly be surprising if Sherrie came to question, berate, and blame herself in these situations, thus demonstrating the link between external career barriers and those that are internal to the self, which are discussed in the following section.

Internal/Self-Barriers

Internal or self-barriers, also termed "cultural factors" (Fitzgerald & Betz, 1994), are beliefs and attitudes common to members of particular groups that serve to inhibit optimal vocational development. Often they are beliefs and attitudes that have been taught or inculcated by society (for instance, ideas about "appropriate" roles for men and women, notions of what constitutes a "normal" sexual orientation), but become translated into internalized representations of the self that are therefore self-perpetuating (Betz, 1994; Fitzgerald & Betz, 1994). Internal or self-barriers include the following, with brief explanation and discussion (Betz, 1994; Betz & Fitzgerald, 1987).

Underestimation of Capabilities

Probably the most pervasive and intractable internal barrier to a woman's career success is her own underestimation of competencies, talents, and capabilities. This self-concept construct has been operationalized and explored in many forms in the literature, perhaps most effectively as self-efficacy—that is, the expectation or belief that one can successfully perform a particular task or behavior (Betz & Fitzgerald, 1987). Originally derived from Bandura's (1977) work and first applied to women's career development by Betz and Hackett (1981, 1983; Hackett & Betz, 1981), self-efficacy is thought to affect both the types of behaviors attempted and persistence of behaviors when difficulties are encountered. The now-classic (Hackett & Betz, 1981) linkage of self-efficacy to career behavior demonstrated how the four sources of self-efficacy postulated by Bandura (1977) —performance accomplishments, vicarious learning, emotional arousal, and verbal persuasion—were compromised by female gender role socialization such that self-efficacy for many vocationally related behaviors is low for women. In particular, low or weak self-efficacy expectations were found in regard to the study and performance of mathematics, as well as for the successful completion of male-dominated majors and careers (Betz & Hackett, 1981, 1983; Hackett & Betz, 1981; Hackett, 1985).

Much scholarly attention during the past two decades has been given to the effects of self-efficacy on career development, demonstrating the debilitating effects of low self-efficacy on pursuit of and persistence in vocationally relevant tasks and particular career fields (Fitzgerald et al., 1995; Phillips & Imhoff, 1997). In addition, relationships have been demonstrated between self-efficacy and other career variables such as outcome expectations, vocational aspirations, academic success, career barriers, vocational interests, occupational congruence, and social support (Fitzgerald et al., 1995; Phillips & Imhoff, 1997). In general, the literature indicates that females continue to demonstrate lower self-efficacy and expectations for success in traditionally male interests and occupations (Betz, Harmon, & Borgen, 1996; Fitzgerald et al., 1995; Phillips & Imhoff, 1997), that self-efficacy is a stronger predictor of career choice than are past performance or achievement (Phillips & Imhoff, 1997), and that self-efficacy operates both independently and in interaction with other variables to affect vocational behaviors (Fitzgerald et al., 1995).

A small sampling of studies during the 1990s demonstrates that:

- instrumental or agentic characteristics are related to greater self-efficacy in completing career search tasks (Solberg, Good, Fischer, Brown, & Nord, 1995) and in women's choices of nontraditional careers (Fassinger, 1990; O'Brien & Fassinger, 1993);
- perceptions of academic gender bias by women are associated with lower career self-efficacy expectations (Ancis & Phillips, 1996);
- self-efficacy in combination with other career variables (for instance, ability, support, barriers) predicts persistence in engineering (Schaefers, Epperson, & Nauta, 1997);
- ethnicity is a predictor of career self-efficacy and expectations (Hackett, Betz, Casas, & Rocha-Singh, 1992; Lauver & Jones, 1991; McWhirter, Hackett, & Bandalos, 1998); and
- prevalent patterns of career self-efficacy favoring males apply in ethnic minority samples as well (Lauver & Jones, 1991; Post, Stewart, & Smith, 1991).

Interestingly, differences between males and females in self-efficacy based on Holland's interest themes (in which females demonstrate lower self-efficacy in regard to male-dominated occupations and interests) continue to characterize college samples but are less pronounced for employed adults. This suggests that women successfully engaged in an occupation are about as confident as men (Betz et al., 1996). This finding lends support to the notion that self-efficacy expectations can be altered by actual experiences of success in the workplace, and highlights the importance of intervention efforts targeted at occupational choice and entry behaviors.

Pervasive low self-efficacy expectations in females regarding mathematics (often termed "math anxiety" in the literature) have been a particularly strong focus in the vocational psychology literature because (as previously discussed) mathematics functions as a gateway into science, engineering, technical, and business careers, in which the persistent underrepresentation of women is a problem. Much controversy exists over sex differences in mathematics ability, and results of dozens of studies reveal little difference in competence or achievement when controlling for the effects of math background and preparation (Betz & Fitzgerald, 1987). However, what has been consistently documented are dramatic differences in mathematics attitudes and participation, indicating that females are less likely than males to feel confident, interested, and eager to participate in mathematics activities and coursework, placing them at enormous disadvantage in early preparation for entry into prestigious, lucrative careers (Betz & Fitzgerald, 1987). Gender socialization, attitudes of parents and educators, tools and materials for learning mathematics, classroom practices, and institutional barriers have all been cited as factors in avoidance of mathematics by girls and women, and this is an area where continued empirical attention and intervention efforts are sorely needed (Betz & Fitzgerald, 1987).

Other Attitudinal Barriers

Because gender role socialization affects a large number of personal traits, behaviors, beliefs, and attitudes, there are many vocationally relevant internal career barriers that stem from women's socialization experiences, a few of which are briefly reviewed here. Research on socialization suggests that females are likely to have been taught to be passive, emotional, nurturant, and dependent, whereas males are more likely to have learned independence, assertiveness, and self-sufficiency (see Unger & Crawford, 1996, for a summary). In addition, gender role socialization teaches females to hide their competence and intelligence (especially around males), to derive their sense of self-worth from their physical attractiveness and appeal to males, to expect to marry and bear children, to eschew competition in favor of cooperation and pleasantness, and to avoid activities and interests that are "inappropriate" for their sex (Unger & Crawford, 1996). Given these kinds of patterns, it should hardly be surprising that women might exhibit lack of decision-making skills and confidence, perceptions of insurmountable barriers and low expectations for successful outcomes, fear of the attitudes of others, guilt, and self-doubt—to name just a few of the attitudinal barriers that women face as a result of gender socialization.

As demonstrated in vocational research, there is indeed a relationship between perceptions of occupational barriers (for instance, discrimination based on sex or race) and low outcome expectations regarding careers (Hackett & Byars, 1996; Swanson, 1996). Females perceive more career barriers than males (and, therefore, have lower outcome expectations) (Luzzo, 1995). People of color perceive additional career barriers related to ethnic identity (Hackett & Byars, 1996; Luzzo, 1993; Swanson, 1996). Additional evidence suggests that females are more vocationally mature than are males (and therefore presumably more able to make appropriate career choices), but are more likely to perceive role conflicts (Luzzo, 1995), which may help to explain decisional difficulties for women. Moreover, there is evidence that women demonstrate lower career aspirations than comparably talented males (Phillips & Imhoff, 1997) and tend to attribute their successes to external factors rather than to personal effort or ability (Betz & Fitzgerald, 1987), thereby reinforcing socialized patterns of self-doubt and self-denigration.

Socialized habits of caregiving and self-denial also render women susceptible to excessive worry about the judgment of others, as well as guilt about nonparenting activities and pursuits. This can prove a difficult problem in a society fueled by media images reinforcing women's responsibility to home and hearth and warning about the loneliness and heartache of singlehood and career pursuits (one evening of viewing prime-time television should be convincing in this regard). Indeed, research indicates that work-family conflicts for women may be due in part to the simultaneous endorsement of conflicting ideologies, with more liberal attitudes held regarding work and careers and more traditional expectations toward family responsibilities (Novack & Novack, 1996). Moreover, self-doubt leaves women particularly vulnerable to internalizing negative events or aspects of the environment (discrimination, denigrating remarks about motherhood, and so on) in a cycle of self-blame that prevents effective action from being taken. An example of this phenomenon is a lesbian worker who is discriminated against in a job evaluation or by coworkers but blames herself for not being more careful in protecting her hidden identity rather than challenging the discrimination, personally or legally.

In summarizing internal or self barriers to women's career development and the way in which they interact with contextual factors discussed earlier, a return to the example of Sherrie can be instructive. Based on gender socialization patterns, it might be assumed that Sherrie has been:

1. discouraged (however subtly) from independence, assertiveness, and self-sufficiency, and encouraged to be emotional, nurturant, and passive;

2. inculcated with strong expectations that she will marry and have children someday, and that this is to be her most important adult role;

3. taught to judge her value mainly by her attractiveness to males;

4. discouraged from manifesting her intelligence and competence, especially around males;

5. discouraged from taking science, math, and technical courses in school;

6. taught that men are more appropriate for or capable of performing some activities and jobs;

7. trained to attribute her successes to factors outside herself; and

8. taught to doubt her judgment, decisions, actions, feelings, choices, needs, motivation, and capabilities.

Again, if Sherrie manages to actually pursue a career in chemical engineering, she is likely to

1. feel guilt, self-blame, and self-doubt whenever problems arise (for instance, blaming herself for losing a deserved promotion rather than being angry at her sexist employer);

2. be overwhelmed by multiple role responsibilities if she marries and has children, receiving little tangible help or support from her male partner and blaming herself for the difficulties;

3. experience excessive demands in the workplace based on being one of only a few women, and feel that she must be unfailingly responsible to others, and

4. experience general lack of self-confidence and low expectations for success in the workplace.

Moreover, if Sherrie is a lesbian, she may also be hiding her identity (and perhaps that of her partner); and if she has a mobility disability, she may be confronting the challenges of an inaccessible workplace. It is little wonder that Sherrie might often question whether having a career is worth the trouble.

SOLUTIONS

What can be done to help women like Sherrie? I have argued elsewhere (Fassinger, 1998; Fassinger & O'Brien, in press) that women's vocational problems *must* be considered problems of context. Even so-called internal or individual problems are caused by an externally driven sociocultural indoctrination and socialization process that places women at great disadvantage relative to men in educational settings, workplaces, and families. Thus, solutions to both contextual and individual problems must dismantle systemic gendered barriers that women face. Continuing to focus intervention efforts on helping individual women address their own untenable circumstances is tantamount to blaming the victim for her victimization rather than undertaking advocacy efforts aimed at pervasive societal change that would make work a more viable enterprise for women. Certainly counseling and intervention efforts targeted at particular individuals and groups can help to ameliorate problems created by existing social structures. However, it is also critical to engage in prevention and advocacy activities in order to reform education, work, and family systems that so clearly compromise women's vocational health and well-being (Fassinger, 1998; Fassinger & O'Brien, in press).

Contextual or Systemic Interventions

Many potential targets for prevention and advocacy in educational institutions, workplaces, and families have been identified that would lead to systemic change (for example, Fassinger, 1993, 1996, 1998; Fassinger & O'Brien, in press), and are summarized here briefly. In the workplace, the most important structural change needed to accommodate working parents is mandatory on-site childcare with flexible hours and acute care for temporary illnesses. Researchers can contribute to advocacy efforts by documenting the benefits to companies that accrue from instituting childcare facilities and programs. In addition, the 40- to 60-hour in-house workweek must be made more flexible, with job-sharing, flextime, liberal family leave, and work-at-home options. Again, researchers can document the benefits of such arrangements on workers and workplaces. Implementing such changes will require extensive education and lobbying efforts, in the workplace (for instance, with personnel specialists) and with policymakers, with the skills of researchers applied to synthesizing existing knowledge and engaging in program design and evaluation.

Within workplaces and educational institutions, discrimination, sexual harassment, and affirmative action must be carefully monitored and addressed. Gender-fair, gay-affirmative policies and nondiscrimination statements must be instituted in order to protect basic civil rights, for example, including gender and sexual orientation in human rights codes and offering domestic partner benefits to lesbian and gay as well as unmarried heterosexual personnel. Educational efforts designed to raise consciousness regarding diversity (gender, ethnicity, sexual orientation, disability) also should be instituted to support policy implementation and eliminate harassment or negative educational or workplace climate. Workers in the educational system, in particular (teachers, school administrators, school counselors), should be well educated in issues of diversity, and those affiliated with institutions of higher education that engage in and monitor teacher and counselor training must become involved in proactive efforts to ensure that professional training incorporates diversity. In addition, nursery school and day-care workers should receive mandatory training in gender and other diversity issues (tied to licensure or certification), in order to disrupt traditional gender socialization habits at early enough ages to have impact on children. Recent research findings support such efforts: one study, for example, demonstrated that reducing gender stereotypes in elementary school teachers produced higher aspirations among both male and female pupils (Shamai, 1994), and there is considerable evidence of the impact of teachers on female students in career aspirations as well as participation in mathematics and science (Phillips & Imhoff, 1997).

Forensic involvement is another avenue through which important social change can occur, and provides additional opportunities for scholarly involvement in advocacy roles. Particularly in the areas of sexual harassment and lesbian/gay issues, societal myths and misinformation are rampant. All personnel involved in the legal process (litigators, judges, juries) are likely to be ill informed and steeped in biases, leading to legislative and policy decisions that continue to disadvantage those already at risk. Learning how to work with the courts in providing expert testimony in these areas will go far in changing existing policy and legislative barriers faced by diverse women. Working with those involved in the training and licensing of attorneys in order to ensure the incorporation of knowledge about gender and sexual orientation also would help to build more gender-fair, gay-affirmative legislative bodies.

For those with the means for and interest in resource allocation issues, educational systems, workplaces, and communities are all viable locations for integrating educational materials and resources. For example, sex education curricula (including lesbian, gay, bisexual, and transgender issues) should be instituted in all schools, with appropriate consultants and instructors provided to help schools implement the curricula. Community and school libraries should be provided with gender-fair and gay-inclusive books, magazines, and visual media, and school curricula should be examined (and reformed where necessary) to reflect the inclusion of women, gays and lesbians, people of color, and persons with disabilities. Community and religious organizations can be provided with materials and programs to offer their constituencies in gender issues, sexual orientation, and the like. In fact, much could be incorporated into existing programs; for example, including basic education regarding the negative effects of rigid gender socialization on children in a workshop or class on pregnancy or parent training. At all levels of schooling (including higher education), resources and personnel can be provided for clubs, support groups, and centers that benefit females; for example, a career club for high school girls or a women's support center in a college or university. Again, scholars can aid such efforts through their context expertise in gender issues, as well as their skills in program design and evaluation.

A final area to target in bringing about systemic change involves family life and the role of society in continuing to reinforce traditional socialization patterns in women and men. Dramatic changes need to occur in family structures in order to make them more viable for women, and stereotypes regarding the home as primarily the woman's domain must be replaced by notions of household work (including childcare) as a shared responsibility. Because primary offenders in upholding traditional ideologies are the media, advocacy efforts are critical. Well-coordinated letter-writing campaigns can be surprisingly effective in bringing about a desired result, especially if they are very public. In addition, resources and educational materials can aid parents in teaching their children to watch visual media critically, and the Internet also may prove to be an effective vehicle for educational change efforts. Of course, individual change is the ultimate goal, and the following section focuses on interventions aimed at individuals or groups.

Individual and Group Interventions

Until sweeping social change has created a more tenable context for women workers, individually oriented interventions will be necessary in ameliorating the problems noted earlier in this chapter. Much has been written regarding vocational counseling and interventions for women (see Walsh & Osipow, 1994), although Phillips and Imhoff (1997) point out that empirical research on the process and outcome of career interventions for women has been scant. A recent study (Whiston, Sexton, & Lasoff, 1998) is promising in this regard, in that it is a comprehensive meta-analysis of career intervention studies, and its findings indicate that career interventions, especially individual counseling, are indeed effective in treating vocational problems for both women and men. In addition, the consistent documentation of particular barriers and problems (noted above) also provides guidance for the design, implementation, and evaluation of vocational interventions for women (Fassinger & O'Brien, in press).

For example, self-esteem often has been targeted as an important goal of individual counseling or small-group interventions for women. Many programs and support groups in colleges and universities focus on this theme, teaching women basic information about the harmful effects of gender socialization, as well as such strategies as cognitive reframing, assertiveness training, bibliotherapy, and other techniques to build self-esteem. Self-efficacy, particularly in regard to science and math or career pursuits in general is another commonly invoked target of intervention, with programs designed to help women conquer math anxiety by building mastery experiences and individual counseling focused around support and encouragement. Assessment of interests, abilities, values, and the like are often valuable in counseling or career advising, and (as noted previously) much progress has been made in developing gender-fair assessment devices. Institutional initiatives such as mentoring programs, student organizations (for example, an organization for women in engineering), and support groups (for example, a lunchtime discussion group for working mothers) also are ways of providing academic, career, and social support to women workers.

In general, competent, gender-fair career counseling and intervention for women must include:

1. thorough knowledge of gender issues, especially as they affect work and educational behavior;

2. knowledge and use of a wide variety of gender-fair (that is, gender-normed) assessment devices, including card sorts, fantasies, and other less formal approaches;

3. knowledge of particular groups of women as they are affected in the workplace, such as lesbians, women of color, and women with disabilities;

4. knowledge of the usefulness and limitations of various theories of vocational development for women;

5. knowledge regarding sexual harassment;

6. willingness to assume educational, preventive, and advocacy roles in helping individuals or groups; and

7. thorough self-examination on the part of the counselor to guard against sexist biases affecting counseling.

Moreover, effective intervention with women employs all of the same components of any effective counseling relationship: active listening, empathic responding, careful assessment, solid rapport, mutual goal-setting and planning, ongoing evaluation of progress and mutual feedback, providing resources, ensuring generalizability of learning, and terminating appropriately (Fassinger & O'Brien, in press).

However, Fassinger and O'Brien (in press) call for a new approach to vocational intervention with women, which builds on the competencies and skills already noted, but adds three additional critical components. The first is a deliberate focus on raising consciousness and providing a sociopolitical analysis of the contextual factors involved in an individual's problems and decisions, so that self-blame is minimized and personal empowerment is maximized within that context. This includes analysis of the counseling relationship itself as a potential purveyor of societal ideologies and demands, and requires a deliberate minimizing of power differences between the counselor and client to convey deep respect to the client and confidence in her own power to solve her problems.

The second element in this approach is a conscious and consistent destruction of the false dichotomy between work life and home or personal life. Fassinger and O'Brien (in press) point out that the "one overarching truth" (p. 15) found in the literature on the vocational psychology of women, is that, for many if not most women career and personal concerns are inextricably linked, and that the arbitrary dichotomizing of the two domains (a legacy from turn-of-the-century sociopolitical shifts that relegated women to the home and men to the workplace) prevents women (and men) from effectively being able to integrate their work and home lives without feeling guilty and being judged negatively. Such a dichotomizing forces them to feel that they must choose between the two and perpetuates problems of multiple role overload by disengaging men from household and childcare tasks and by preventing women from seeking environmental solutions (for instance, mandatory on-site childcare), rather than personal solutions (for example, time management) to their problems. In addition, it is particularly destructive to lesbians, in that it reinforces what already may be a rigid separation of work and home in order to protect a stigmatized identity. In counseling and interventions, this approach would require education and consciousness raising, as well as encouragement of women (and men) working together to bring about local change. Research supports such an approach, in that there is evidence that deliberate planning for multiple roles is associated with lower role conflict and more effective problem solving (Phillips & Imhoff, 1997).

The third element of the intervention approach advocated by Fassinger and O'Brien (in press) is the recognition that most women's lives will include significant interactions with men—in families, schools, workplaces, and communities. Therefore, men *must* be targeted for interventions that involve extensive education and consciousness raising. Fassinger and O'Brien note that "it is not enough to attempt to empower women to challenge patriarchal structures and the nonegalitarian attitudes of individual men, because such an approach still places the burden for social and political change squarely on the shoulders of individual women" (in press, p. 17). Men, who control power structures through patriarchy, must themselves be involved in personal and social change, or women's lives cannot improve. In counseling and intervention, this implies teaching men basic information about gender socialization and helping them to develop relationships with women built on respect, sharing, and interdependence. This kind of information can be incorporated into community parenting classes, high school and college career classes and workshops, educational programming for college fraternities and athletic teams, as well as in individual counseling and advising at all levels.

CONCLUSIONS

By way of summary, it should be clear that "women's issues" in the workplace are composed of gendered barriers created and maintained by society, that must be attacked vigorously by both women and men in building more equitable work and family environments. This requires a proactive approach—involving commitment to prevention and advocacy roles aimed at pervasive social change—rather than merely continuing attempts to ameliorate existing problems.

Because most psychologists, counselors, and other mental health professionals have been trained in fairly traditional, intrapsychic approaches targeting individual problems, assuming advocacy and preventive roles will require radical changes in the professional training and certification of mental health professionals (Fassinger, 1998, in press; Fassinger & O'Brien, in press). For example, training programs must include coursework and practica in policy, forensics, program evaluation, and consultation. Gender issues must be infused into the curricula through required as well as optional courses, and research will need to be taught as not only a scientific enterprise but also as a political act that has critical policy and advocacy implications. Counseling practica must integrate "vocational" and "emotional/personal" counseling foci in order to bridge the dichotomy between work and home or personal life.

In addition to formal curriculum transformation efforts, the climate of training programs must be examined for the promotion of subtle biases (for instance, senior white male faculty wielding all the power) or unfair advantage given to some students or faculty over others (for example, awards or teaching assistantships consistently given to males). Perhaps the most serious impediment to program reform is that existing faculty (who are unlikely to have been trained themselves in prevention and advocacy) will require continuing education and in-service activities to build their own competencies in these areas. Moreover, supervisors in internships and externships from outside the training program will need monitoring in order to ensure training that is gender-fair and sensitive to the needs of diverse women, both supervisees and clients (see Fassinger, in press; Fassinger & Richie, 1997; Fassinger & O'Brien, in press, for more detailed discussion and suggestions regarding training). Finally, training programs must attend to more deliberate integration of the professional and personal lives of both students and faculty, so that dichotomous work-home ideologies are not being unwittingly reinforced by the invisibility of personal interests and commitments outside the program. Conscious efforts to incorporate the myriad complexities of gender into training programs can contribute to more proactive participation of mental health professionals in creating workplaces that are sane, fair, and supportive for women.

REFERENCES

A.A.U.W. (1992). *How schools shortchange girls.* New York: Marlowe & Company.

Ancis, J. R., & Phillips, S. D. (1996). Academic gender bias and women's behavioral agency self-efficacy. *Journal of Counseling and Development, 75,* 138–144.

Badgett, M. V. L. (1994, May-June). Equal pay for equal families. *Academe,* 26–30.

Bailey, S. M. (1998). The current status of gender equity research in American schools. In D. L. Anselmi & A. L. Law (Eds.), *Questions of gender: Perspectives & paradoxes* (pp. 461–472). Boston: McGraw-Hill.

Bandura, A. (1977). Self-efficacy: Toward a unifying theory of behavioral change. *Psychological Review, 84,* 191–214.

Betz, N. E. (1989). Implications of the null environment hypothesis for women's career development and for counseling psychology. *Counseling Psychologist, 17,* 136–144.

Betz, N. E. (1994). Basic issues and concepts in career counseling for women. In W. B. Walsh & S. H. Osipow (Eds.), *Career counseling for women* (pp. 1–42). Hillsdale, NJ: Erlbaum.

Betz, N. E., & Fitzgerald, L. F. (1987). *The career psychology of women.* New York: Academic Press.

Betz, N. E., & Fitzgerald, L. F. (1993). Individuality and diversity: Theory and research in counseling psychology. *Annual Review of Psychology, 44,* 343–381.

Betz, N. E., & Hackett, G. (1981). The relationship of career-related self-efficacy expectations to perceived career options in college women and men. *Journal of Counseling Psychology, 28,* 399–410.

Betz, N. E., & Hackett, G. (1983). The relationship of mathematics self-efficacy expectations to the selection of science-based college majors. *Journal of Vocational Behavior, 23,* 329–345.

Betz, N. E., Harmon, L. W., & Borgen, F. H. (1996). The relationships of self-efficacy for the Holland themes to gender, occupational group membership, and vocational interests. *Journal of Counseling Psychology, 43,* 90–98.

Bingham, R. P., & Ward, C. M. (1994). Career counseling with ethnic minority women. In W. B. Walsh & S. H. Osipow (Eds.), *Career counseling for women* (pp. 165–196). Hillsdale, NJ: Erlbaum.

Brennan, M. B. (1998). Reshaping affirmative action. *Chemical & Engineering News, 76,* 17–31.

Bond, J. T., Galinsky, E., & Swanberg, J. (1998). *The 1997 national study of the changing workforce.* New York: Families and Work Institute.

Burley, K. A. (1991). Family-work spillover in dual-career couples: A comparison of two time perspectives. *Psychological Reports, 68,* 471–480.

Carr, P. L., Ash, A. S. Friedman, R. H., Scaramucci, A., Barnett, R. C., Szalacha, L., Palepu, A., Moskowitz, M. A. (1998). Relation of family responsibilities and gender to the productivity and career satisfaction of medical faculty. *Annals of Internal Medicine, 129,* 532–538.

Cook, E. P. (1993). The gendered context of life: Implications for women's and men's career-life plans. *Career Development Quarterly, 41,* 227–237.

Corcoran, E. (1999). Women in technology compare experiences, challenges at meeting. *Washington Post,* January 23, 1999.

Crosby, F. J. (1991). *Juggling.* New York: Free Press.

Deutsch, F. M., & Saxon, S. E. (1998). The double standard of praise and criticism for mothers and fathers. *Psychology of Women Quarterly, 22,* 665–683.

Farmer, H. S., Wardrop, J. L., Anderson, M. Z., & Risinger, R. (1995). Women's career choices: Focus on science, math, and technological careers. *Journal of Counseling Psychology, 42,* 155–170.

Fassinger, R. E. (1990). Causal models of career choice in two samples of college women. *Journal of Vocational Behavior, 36,* 225–248.

Fassinger, R. E. (1993). And gladly teach: Lesbian and gay issues in education. In L. Diamant (Ed.), *Homosexual issues in the workplace* (pp. 119–142). Washington, DC: Taylor & Francis.

Fassinger, R. E. (1996). Notes from the margins: Integrating lesbian experience into the vocational psychology of women. *Journal of Vocational Behavior, 48,* 160–175.

Fassinger, R. E. (1998, August). *Gender as a contextual factor in career services delivery: A modest proposal.* Paper presented at the annual meeting of the American Psychological Association, San Francisco, CA.

Fassinger, R. E. (1998, September). *Still I rise: Career journeys of prominent U.S. women.* Paper presented at the 50th Anniversary Symposium of the Student Personnel Assistant Program, Department of Higher Education and Student Affairs, Ohio Sate University, Columbus, OH.

Fassinger, R. E. (In press). Gender and sexuality in human development: Implications for prevention and advocacy in counseling psychology. In S. D. Brown & R. W. Lent (Eds.), *Handbook of counseling psychology* (3rd ed.). New York: Wiley.

Fassinger, R. E., & O'Brien, K. M. (In press). Career counseling with college women: A scientist-practitioner-advocate model of intervention. In D. A. Luzzo (Ed.), *Career development of college students: Translating theory and research into practice.* Washington, DC: American Psychological Association.

Fassinger, R. E., & Richie, B. S. (1997). Sex matters: Gender and sexual orientation in training for multicultural counseling competency. In D. Pope-Davis & H. Coleman (Eds.), *Multicultural counseling competencies: Assessment, education and training, and supervision* (pp. 83–110). Thousand Oaks, CA: Sage.

Fitzgerald, L. F., & Betz, N. E. (1994). Career development in cultural context: The role of gender, race, class, and sexual orientation. In M. L. Savickas & R. W. Lent (Eds.), *Convergence in theories of career choice and development,* pp. 103–118. Palo Alto, CA: Consulting Psychologists Press.

Fitzgerald, L. F., Fassinger, R. E., & Betz, N. E. (1995). Theoretical advances in the study of women's career development. In W. B. Walsh & S. H. Osipow (Eds.), *Handbook of vocational psychology* (2nd ed., pp. 67–109). Hillsdale, NJ: Erlbaum.

Fitzgerald, L. F. & Weitzman, L. M. (1992). Women's career development: Theory and practice from a feminist perspective. In Z. Leibowitz & D. Lea (Eds.), *Adult career development* (2nd ed., pp. 124–160). Alexandria, VA: National Career Development Association.

Fouad, N. A., Harmon, L. W., & Borgen, F. H. (1997). Structure of interests in employed male and female members of U.S. racial-ethnic minority and nonminority groups. *Journal of Counseling Psychology, 44,* 339–345.

Freeman, J. (1979). How to discriminate against women without really trying. In J. Freeman (ed.), *Women: A feminist perspective* (2nd ed., pp. 194–208). Palo Alto, CA: Mayfield.

Gilbert, L. A. (1992). Gender and counseling psychology: Current knowledge and directions for research and social action. In S. D. Brown & R. W. Lent (Eds.), *Handbook of counseling psychology* (2nd ed., pp. 383–418). New York: Wiley.

Gomez, M. J., & Fassinger, R. E. (in press). Career paths of notable Latinas: A qualitative study. College Park, MD: University of Maryland.

Hackett, G. (1985). The role of mathematics self-efficacy in the choice of math-related majors of college women and men: A path analysis. *Journal of Counseling Psychology, 32,* 47–56.

Hackett, G., & Betz, N. E. (1981). A self-efficacy approach to the career development of women. *Journal of Vocational Behavior, 18,* 326–339.

Hackett, G., Betz, N. E., Casas, J. M., & Rocha-Singh, I. A. (1992). Gender, ethnicity, and social cognitive factors predicting the academic achievement of students in engineering. *Journal of Counseling Psychology, 39,* 527–538.

Hackett, G., & Byars, A. M. (1996). Social cognitive theory and the career development of African-American women. *Career Development Quarterly, 44,* 322–340.

Harbeck, K. M. (Ed.). (1992). Coming out of the classroom closet: Gay and lesbian students, teachers and curricula. New York: Harrington Park Press.

Harris, M. B. (Ed.). (1997). *School experiences of gay and lesbian youth: The invisible minority.* New York: Harrington Park Press.

Jost, J. T. (1997). An experimental replication of the depressed-entitlement effect among women. *Psychology of Women Quarterly, 21,* 387–393.

Klein, M. H., Hyde, J. S., Essex, M. J., & Clark, R. (1998). Maternity leave, role quality, work involvement, and mental health one year after delivery. *Psychology of Women Quarterly, 22,* 239–266.

Klonis, S., Endo, J., Crosby, F., & Worell, J. (1977). Feminism as life raft. *Psychology of Women Quarterly, 21,* 333–345.

Klonoff, E. A., & Landrine, H. (1995). The schedule of sexist events: A measure of lifetime and recent sexist discrimination in women's lives. *Psychology of Women Quarterly, 19,* 439–472.

Konicus, J. (1999, January 23). Down and dirty: Leaving housework in the dust. *Washington Post,* p. C-4.

Landrine, H., Klonoff, E. A., Gibbs, J., Manning, V., & Lund, M. (1995). Physical and psychiatric correlates of gender discrimination: An application of the schedule of sexist events. *Psychology of Women Quarterly, 19,* 473–492.

Lauver, P. J., & Jones, R. M. (1991). Factors associated with perceived career options in American Indian, White, and Hispanic rural high school students. *Journal of Counseling Psychology, 38,* 159–166.

LePage-Lees, P. (1997). Struggling with a nontraditional past: Academically successful women from disadvantaged backgrounds discuss their relationship with "disadvantage." *Psychology of Women Quarterly, 21*, 356–385.

Leong, F. T. L. (Ed.). (1995). *Career development and vocational behavior of racial and ethnic minorities.* Mahwah, NJ: Erlbaum.

Long, B. C. (1998). Coping with workplace stress: A multiple-group comparison of female managers and clerical workers. *Journal of Counseling Psychology, 45*, 65–78.

Luzzo, D. A. (1993). Ethnic differences in college students' career maturity and perceptions of barriers to career development. *Journal of Counseling Psychology, 37*, 382–388.

Luzzo, D. A. (1995). Gender differences in college students' career maturity and perceived barriers in career development. *Journal of Counseling and Development, 73*, 319–322.

McWhirter, E. H., Hackett, G., & Bandalos, D. L. (1998). A causal model of the educational plans and career expectations of Mexican American high school girls. *Journal of Counseling Psychology, 45*, 166–181.

Melamed, T. (1995). Barriers to women's career success: Human capital, career choices, structural determinants, or simply sex discrimination. *Applied Psychology, 44*, 295–314.

Novack, L. L., & Novack, D. R. (1996). Being female in the eighties and nineties: Conflicts between new opportunities and traditional expectations among white, middle class, heterosexual college women. *Sex Roles, 35*, 57–77.

Phillips, S. D., & Imhoff, A. R. (1997). Women and career development: A decade of research. *Annual Review of Psychology, 48*, 31–59.

O'Brien, K. M., & Fassinger, R. E. (1993). A causal model of the career orientation and career choice of adolescent women. *Journal of Counseling Psychology, 40*, 456–469.

Post, P., Stewart, M. A., & Smith, P. L. (1991). Self-efficacy, interest, and consideration of math/science and non–math/science occupations among college freshmen. *Journal of Vocational Behavior, 38*, 179–186.

Richie, B. S., Fassinger, R. E., Linn, S. G., Johnson, J., Prosser, J., & Robinson, S. (1997). Persistence, connection, and passion: A qualitative study of the career development of highly achieving African American-black and white women. *Journal of Counseling Psychology, 44*, 133–148.

Rounds, J., & Tracey, T. J. (1996). Cross-cultural structural equivalence of RIASEC models and measures. *Journal of Counseling Psychology, 43*, 310–329.

Sadker, M., & Sadker, D. (1994). *Failing at fairness: How our schools cheat girls.* New York: Simon & Schuster.

Sanlo, R. L. (Ed.). (1998). *Working with lesbian, gay, bisexual, and transgender college students: A handbook for faculty and administrators.* Westport, CT: Greenwood Press.

Schaefers, K. G., Epperson, D. L., & Nauta, M. M. (1997). Women's career development: Can theoretically derived variables predict persistence in engineering majors? *Journal of Counseling Psychology, 44*, 173–183.

Shamai, S. (1994). Possibilities and limitations of a gender stereotypes intervention program. *Adolescence, 29*, 665–680.

Silverstein, L. B. (1996). Fathering is a feminist issue. *Psychology of Women Quarterly, 20*, 3–37.

Solberg, V. S., Good, G. E., Fischer, A. R., Brown, S.D., & Nord, D. (1995). Career decision-making and career search activities: Relative effects of career-search self-efficacy and human agency. *Journal of Counseling Psychology, 42,* 448–455.

Spade, J. Z., & Reese, C. A. (1991). We've come a long way, maybe: College students' plans for work and family. *Sex Roles, 24,* 309–321.

Stickel, S. A., & Bonnet, R. M. (1991). Gender diferences in career self-efficacy: Combining a career with home and family. *Journal of College Student Development, 32,* 297–301.

Stokes, J., Riger, S., & Sullivan, M. (1995). Measuring perceptions of the working environment for women in corporate settings. *Psychology of Women Quarterly, 19,* 533–549.

Swanson, J. L. (1996, August). *How do women perceive career barriers? Theoretical and measurement issues.* Paper presented at the annual meeting of the American Psychological Association, Toronto, CA.

Touchton, J. G., & Davis, L. (1991). Fact book on women in higher education. New York: American Council on Higher Education and Macmillan.

Tracey, T. J., & Ward, C. C. (1998). The structure of children's interests and competence perceptions. *Journal of Counseling Psychology, 45,* 290–303.

Unger, R., & Crawford, M. (1996). *Women and gender: A feminist psychology* (2nd ed.). New York: McGraw-Hill.

Walsh, W. B., & Osipow, S. H. (Eds.). (1994). Career counseling for women. Hillsdale, NJ: Erlbaum.

Wasserman, E. R. (1998). Women in the National Academy: Their lives as scientists and as women. *Magazine of the Association of Women in Science, 27,* 6–10.

Weathers, P. L., Thompson, C. E., Robert, S. & Rodriguez, J. (1994). Black college women's career values: A preliminary investigation. *Journal of Multicultural Counseling and Development, 22,* 96–105.

Whiston, S. C., Sexton, T. L., & Lasoff, D. L. (1998). Career-intervention outcome: A replication and extension of Oliver and Spokane (1988). *Journal of Counseling Psychology, 45,* 150–165.

Yoder, J. D., & McDonald, T. W. (1998). Measuring sexist discrimination in the workplace: Support for the validity of the schedule of sexist events. *Psychology of Women Quarterly, 22,* 487–491.

3

MEN AND WOMEN
IN CROSS-GENDER CAREERS

Susan R. Furr

Betty did not start out to be a trailblazer when she became the first woman hired in the repair and installation unit of her local telephone company. She had always enjoyed working with her hands and welcomed the opportunity to enter a higher paying job. Although she loved the work, she missed the social connections with other women. No longer could she swap recipes or feel comfortable discussing children. To fit in, she learned to talk about sports and cars. She never felt harassed, but she also never felt included. She initially developed a sisterly role that eventually evolved to being "mom" as younger men entered the unit. She often brought in their favorite foods, and they developed a protective stance, making sure she never walked to the parking lot alone. None of these accommodations were ever vocalized. Upon retirement, she reflected that she felt she had earned respect but believed no one ever understood the emotional sacrifice she made to be a good "team player."

Betty's situation illustrates one of the many difficulties experienced by both men and women who enter careers dominated by the other gender. The issue involves a complex combination of identifying intrapersonal factors that support the interest in a career, interpersonal factors that impact whether one is encouraged to pursue and sustain a career, and systemic factors that influence the culture, values, and norms of the organization. Although the organization is only responsible for the impact of the systemic factors, managers may find it beneficial to understand the process of career development that leads to the choice of a nontraditional career.

Making a decision to enter a career in which one would be a gender minority is a complicated choice. In order to make any type of career decision, a person must evaluate his or her own skills, interests, and values and then match these characteristics with a career opportunity that will allow their expression. When the career is atypical for that person's gender, an added layer of frustration is encountered. First, a high probability exists that the person has no exposure to role models who can demonstrate that this option is feasible and desirable. Another added obstacle is lack of support to pursue the career from both family and community. As will be discussed later in this chapter, social systems are highly resistant to change and are geared toward maintaining current norms. So when an individual, whether a student in a local high school or a displaced homemaker, expresses an interest in a nontraditional career, this interest is likely to be met with responses ranging from disbelief to ridicule. Consequently, a person who pursues an occupation in which he or she will be a gender minority must be highly motivated, whether by a strong interest in the actual activities of the job or the benefits and monetary rewards of the work.

In this chapter, the dynamics of pursuing a nontraditional job will be described along with an exploration of the consequences of being a gender minority. Although males and females share some similarities when entering cross-gender careers, the overall impact on the individual is different; therefore, females entering occupations traditionally dominated by males will be discussed separately from the experience of males entering occupations traditionally dominated by females. Reasons that organizations are having difficulty adjusting to nontraditional employees will be examined through the framework of systems theory. In addition, change and transition in the workplace will be explored in terms of what the workplace can do to become more inclusive of the workforce of the twenty-first century.

GENDER SEGREGATION IN THE WORKPLACE

Work is no longer strictly gender-typed, yet these stereotypes remain and continue to influence who is welcomed into what types of occupations (Reskin & Hartmann, 1986). Even with the immense strides made by women and men in employment, women are still viewed as too emotional or illogical for management positions and men seen as not nurturing enough to teach young children or care for the elderly.

Some stereotypes have contributed directly to job segregation. One gender is identified as possessing a trait that is seen as directly relevant to a job. It is then assumed that the other gender is deficient in this area. For example, women's superior dexterity has been cited as the reason for most clerical workers being female (Kessler-Harris, 1982). However, prior to 1920, the vast majority of secretaries were male, and clerical work was seen as part of the male managerial role (Cassell, 1991). Women's lesser physical strength and their alleged intolerance of harsh working conditions have been cited as reasons for not hiring women in construction (Reskin & Hartmann, 1986), and female peers believed that males could not make accurate judgments with regard to disciplining and supervising children (Robinson, 1981). Rather than evaluating the individual's suitability for a position, these stereotypes lead to half of the population being excluded from consideration for certain jobs.

However, in spite of these barriers, women and men have continued to pursue career interests in nontraditional fields, thus changing the face of many occupations. In order for organizations to thrive in today's economic marketplace, it will become necessary for employers and managers to recruit and retain the best-qualified workers regardless of gender (Rizzo & Mendez, 1990). By understanding the workplace experiences of the nontraditional worker, success of both the worker and the organization will be enhanced.

WOMEN IN A "MAN'S WORLD"

Although there have always been a few exceptional women to enter traditionally male occupations, it has only been since the 1970s that large numbers of women have sought to enter both professional and blue-collar positions previously dominated by men. Prior to 1970, three major occupational categories (operatives, farm managers, and managers) actually became more male-dominated whereas clerical work became more female-dominated (Reskin & Hartmann, 1986). The occupations that moved to greater gender integration were professional and sales positions along with domestic services, crafts, and labor. Since 1970, there has been a substantial increase in the number of women managers (Rytina & Bianchi, 1984), physicians (Cartwright, 1987), and lawyers (American Bar Association, 1986). Although some increase in participation of blue-collar positions has occurred, these fields still tend to be dominated by males (U.S. Bureau of Labor Statistics, 1997). Therefore, women entering professional positions traditionally dominated by men will be discussed separately from women entering blue-collar positions traditionally dominated by men.

Women in the Professions

Even with the increasing numbers of women medical students, it will be at least the year 2010 before females comprise 25 percent of practicing physicians in the United States (Cartwright, 1987). Gender differences become apparent from a female's first contact with the medical profession. During medical school interviews, women were asked more frequently about their plans for marriage and children whereas men were asked more often about their reasons for pursuing medicine and the selection of a specialty (Marquat, 1990). Research shows that women were more likely than men to have been physically harassed during training and that the harassers were of a higher professional status (Komaromy, Bindman, Haber, & Sande, 1993). Female medical students also were more likely to experience inappropriate sexual behavior from patients than were male medical students (71 percent versus 29 percent) and frequently encountered this behavior more than once (Schulte & Kay, 1994). Consequently, not only do women physicians encounter inappropriate behavior from within the profession, this behavior is also present in the general work environment. When faculty were questioned about abuse, two thirds of the respondents agreed that the students' complaints were valid. The faculty who disagreed were primarily male and believed that female students were too sensitive (Kane, 1995).

Men and women physicians display different strengths in their training. In taking medical history, female physicians talked 40 percent more than male physicians and the patients of female physicians talked 58 percent more. Female physicians engaged in more positive talk, partnership building, question asking, and information giving (Roter, Lipkin, & Korsgaard, 1991). Male physicians reported more concern about areas of patient charts and documentation, malpractice litigation, physician oversupply, peer review, and interaction with patients, and they tended to be more satisfied with their medical career. Female physicians placed greater value on the psychosocial aspects of medicine than did male physicians (Hojat, Gonnella, & Xu, 1995).

Although selection of specialty is generally thought to be a free choice, women physicians continue to be overrepresented in the fields of internal medicine, pediatrics, obstetrics/gynecology, family practice, and psychiatry (Cartwright, 1987). Women physicians are more likely to work in clinics serving the indigent, to complete primary care training, and to pursue generalist careers (Bickel & Ruffin, 1995). The reasons for this imbalance are not straightforward but may arise from a mix of limited opportunities and different personal motivation. Women have reported lack of opportunity to gain surgical experience and are rarely represented in fields such as sports medicine or research and administration (Riska & Wegar, 1993). In addition to lack of opportunity, women may choose less prestigious and lower paying specialties in order to fulfill other values. Women physicians give more weight to factors such as patient contact, the family, and working fewer hours (Berquist et al., 1985). In fact, women physicians report that the primary source of stress in medicine came from the conflict between career and personal lives, with sexual harassment being the second greatest source (Firth-Cozens, 1987). The perception that women physicians with children are less committed to their careers has been used to limit their access to positions of authority and the current structure of the work favors those without childcare responsibilities (Lorber, 1993).

Women in the field of law report similar patterns of response from male attorneys. Sexist behavior is encountered frequently in that women lawyers are more likely than men to report hearing sexist jokes and remarks, to be referred to by first name, to be asked about professional status, and to receive compliments about appearance rather than achievement (MacCorquodale & Jensen, 1993). Less discrimination was found in recruitment and hiring than on the job, and those women with strong career aspirations actually encountered more sexual harassment than those women with lower career aspirations (Rosenberg, Peristadt, & Phillips, 1993).

Although few differences were found between men and women lawyers in terms of dominance in patterns of speech interaction, both men and women clients demonstrated greater deference to men lawyers (Bogoch, 1997). Once again, the gender discrimination extends to the larger work environment. Women also reported that they hear judges address attorneys differently according to gender and that male attorneys were given more attention and credibility (MacCorquodale & Jensen, 1993). Male attorneys have been seen as being more successful in the development of social capital (social relationships that form a resource the individual can draw upon in his or her professional life). Even when controlling for differences in measures of social capital favorable to a firm's monetary goals, a preference was given to men in partnership decisions (Kay & Hagan, 1998).

Other professions also create additional barriers for the entry of women. In the field of management, the use of stereotypes has been formalized into acceptable organizational behavior. When identifying the characteristics of a good manager, the model that emerges is a masculine one in which the successful manager is aggressive, competitive, firm, and just (Rizzo & Mendez, 1990). Yet research has shown that men and women managers were found to use similar approaches to supervision when access to power resources was held constant (Instone, Major, & Bunker, 1983). Power rather than management style may account for supervision differences.

Women in science generally occupy lower level positions relative to their male counterparts despite having comparable levels of expertise, and the representation of women scientists steadily declines as one moves higher up on the career ladder (Pattatucci, 1998). Male and female engineers with virtually identical qualifications and work attitudes were found to have dissimilar occupational status (Robinson & McIlwee, 1991). Even though the majority of women in science choose to either postpone childbearing until their careers are established and a substantial minority choose not to have children, the career disparity remains. Although male engineers generally report that women are completely accepted and treated the same as men, researchers have found significant differences in terms of job assignments, travel, and promotions (Kirkham & Thompson, 1988). The more strongly the culture of an engineering office is identified with the male gender, the more difficulty a woman engineer will encounter with occupational status and mobility.

Women in Law Enforcement and Military

Although both policework and the military may be considered professional level occupations, these areas differ from the white-collar positions mentioned previously. These positions are particularly associated with traditional male gender characteristics, and when women enter these fields, they create a threat to the established culture associated with the occupation (Leger, 1997). Women present challenges to job definition in that if the job has been based on masculine characteristics such as physical strength, the ability of women to perform the same tasks threatens the definition of masculinity when women can do the "men's work" (Hertz, 1996). For example, men in the military who serve in the role of "protector" have difficulty accepting those whom they are supposed to protect (women) as equals.

Because use of force is sometimes necessary in policework, the role of physical strength seems to be a legitimate concern. However, it has been shown that in situations where force is required, women may perform as well as men by using alternative techniques such as karate (McDowell, 1992). Characteristics such as the ability to think clearly and quickly have been shown to be more important than physical strength in measuring police effectiveness (Sherman, 1973). During potentially explosive situations, female officers are more likely to use their communication skills to negotiate an appropriate outcome (McDowell, 1992). Although in other professions women stated that they were accepted after proving they could do the job, women police officers reported that they had to prove themselves repeatedly (Brown, 1994).

Because of the necessity of shiftwork in these positions, additional stressors may occur. Although women who participated in shiftwork did have more off-the-job work stress due to domestic duties, they did not display more severe psychosocial or health impairments (Beermann & Nachreiner, 1995). A fear that working night shifts together may lead to inappropriate behavior between men and women was cited as a problem for wives of men in the military (Hertz, 1996). Not only do changes in the gender composition of the workforce affect the gender majority employed in those positions, there is also an impact on their broader social networks. These social networks may serve to reinforce the idea that such changes are negative and should not be accepted, thus increasing the difficulty of the nontraditional worker being accepted into the organization.

Women in Blue-Collar Occupations

Perhaps the arena that has been most resistant to acceptance of women has been blue-collar employment. Blue-collar females are more likely to experience harassment from coworkers and animosity from supervisors than are female white-collar workers (Palmer & Lee, 1990). Less than 9 percent of the employees in skilled crafts, repair, and precision production are women (Mansfield et al., 1991). Studies of women working in traditionally male jobs show that women face many problems: sexual harassment, discrimination, hostility and sabotage, withholding of training opportunities, and supervisory indifference (Shostak, 1985). Significantly more harassment and sex discrimination were experienced by tradeswomen than women working in other male-dominated areas such as transit. Tradeswomen reported more isolation, loneliness, noise, and general undesirability of the job (Mansfield et al., 1991). Because skills in the trades are usually obtained during apprenticeships or on the job, tradeswomen are more dependent on the assistance and support of their coworkers for success on the job. If this support is withheld, chances of success are further diminished.

The primary reasons given by women for pursuing skilled trades are better pay, fringe benefits, security, training, and future promotional opportunities (Palmer & Lee, 1990). Even though women in these traditional blue-collar positions reported greater satisfaction with salary than women in secretarial positions and had positive feelings of accomplishment and independence, female workers also reported dissatisfaction with perceived opportunities for advancement (Mansfield et al., 1991).

It has been proposed that as men gain more experience with women in nontraditional jobs, male attitudes will become more positive. Palmer and Lee (1990) found support for this idea among supervisors who had previous work experience with women, but they did not find more positive attitudes among coworkers who had previous work experience with women. Perhaps supervisors still retain a degree of power in the workplace and have developed an identity separate from the work being done by these nontraditional women. Therefore they feel less threatened by the change in job definition.

Dynamics of Entering a Traditionally Male-Dominated Career

Regardless of the level of position sought by women in these traditionally male careers, several dynamics emerge that interfere with the level of success that can be obtained. One of the primary theories in this area has been proposed by Kanter (1977) and will be explored in relationship to women in nontraditional careers. First, Kanter defines the difference between tokens and dominants. Tokens are those members of the minority population who are not treated as individuals but typically treated as symbols or representatives of their category. Kanter proposes that there are three dynamics associated with group composition: visibility, polarization, and stereotyping.

Because of their limited numbers, tokens are highly visible in the organization. They often capture more than their share of the attention, which can increase performance pressure. This pressure can result in either overachievement or underachievement. An added pressure is the fact that tokens are seen as representing the entire category of women so that every mistake or failure is attributed not to the individual but to the entire gender. Often characteristics not related to achievement on the job, such as physical appearance, get undue attention.

Polarization refers to the process of creating a division between the dominants and the tokens by emphasizing the differences between the two groups. The dominant's culture becomes exaggerated, and the tokens are expected to show their loyalty by accepting the culture of the dominant group. For example, women may be subjected to sexual innuendoes, swearing, and "dirty" jokes and are expected to accept these as conditions of the job. Polarization may include being isolated from social interaction such as not being included in informal discussions or lunchtime activities. Also included in polarization is the process of heightened differentiation where the dominants highlight the differences between themselves and the tokens. For example, women in construction are often reminded of their lesser physical strength.

Finally, women face being stereotyped into traditional female behavior by the dominant male group. Male coworkers expect the females to fit into a limited set of feminine roles (such as Betty's "Mom" role in the opening vignette), which may be contradictory to the expectations of the job. If the female refuses to fit into one of the roles, she may be seen as too aggressive or tough, traits that would be rewarded in male employees. Such a situation creates a double bind in which the female is either too feminine for the job or too masculine to be an acceptable female.

Another way of conceptualizing the issues faced by women in nontraditional occupations is by examining three levels of interaction: dynamics between individuals, dynamics involving group identity, and organizational dynamics (Kirkham & Thompson, 1988). Often, organizations believe they are responsible only for what happens on the system or organizational level. Managers who recognize and address both the interpersonal and group dynamics can facilitate the integration of women into the organization.

When examining dynamics between individuals, personal prejudice emerges as the primary problem. Men in situations where few women are employed may be unsure how to relate appropriately to women on the job. Women in these situations frequently report that they do not feel that they are treated as full-fledged professionals. Male coworkers may refer to them as "girls" or joke that they should be home having babies. Often, men make statements about women not being as smart as men or see women coworkers as someone to flirt with. If women try to address these interpersonal issues, they may be accused of being too sensitive.

If the male group identity in an organization is strong, women may experience a collective impact from the behavior of the group. Individuals within the group probably are unaware of this impact, and, when confronted, would respond that they did not intend to discriminate. For example, if men in a workgroup play basketball together during lunch, they may share information related to work in an informal manner. Even though this is a social activity, it has an impact on the work setting and results in the women employees not having access to the same information as men employees.

Women also report that men change the direction of conversation when a woman enters the room. Conversations often become lighter, and politics are not discussed resulting in women feeling like they are not taken seriously (Kirkham & Thompson, 1988). Again, women face a dilemma about whether to confront these problems. On one hand, they do not want to be perceived as troublemakers by addressing sexist comments and exclusionary behavior. Yet if these issues are not addressed, women continue to be at a disadvantage in the work environment. The biggest asset in this situation is when a female employee has a male "ally" who can voice similar opinions and help coworkers recognize their tendency to stereotype (Rizzo & Mendez, 1990).

Because most high level managers in traditionally male-dominated occupations are male, most senior executives are unaware of how company policies and practices affect women. Because managers may have little experience supervising female employees, they may rely on assumptions on how to respond to issues. In their desire to protect female employees, managers may limit a woman's travel or late evening hours. But in placing these limitations, managers inadvertently send the message that women are less capable than their male coworkers. Without equivalent field experiences, women may find access to future job assignments limited. Consequently, organizational policies and their impact on women must be examined if women are to be fully included in the organization.

Two major issues that emerge across all three levels of interaction are job assignment and feedback. Job assignment can be influenced by personal bias of an individual supervisor, by managers as a group who withhold challenging jobs for fear women may leave or lack long-term commitment, and by informal organizational policies that limit travel (Kirkham & Thompson, 1988; Wentling, 1995). On the issue of feedback, an individual male manager may be reluctant to give critical feedback to female employees because he believes that she would not be willing to change. Although males often get feedback through their informal network groups, women generally are excluded from this source of information and often do not receive critical information about performance until it is too late to make corrections. Because women are less likely to receive this ongoing coaching and mentoring, a corporate policy of formal feedback may be inadequate to meet their needs for information that will foster continual improvement (Stuart, 1992; Wentling, 1995). Quarterly evaluations may fulfill the company requirement but may be insufficient for those employees isolated from other sources of feedback. On the surface, the policy concerning feedback appears fair because all employees receive feedback with the same frequency. But when there are informal sources of feedback available to one group of employees and denied to another group, the issue of equity becomes more complex and needs to be examined on the organizational level.

MEN DOING "WOMEN'S WORK"

Because many more fields are male-dominated than female-dominated, females have faced more constraints in the job market and have made a greater effort to cross the gender barriers (Jacobs, 1993). In general, jobs in male-dominated fields offer better pay and benefits, authority, and independence than jobs in female-dominated fields. For women, the switch to a male-dominated field may offer many enticing benefits, which offset the stressors of sexual harassment and discrimination. Consequently, one is more likely to find women employed in male-dominated fields than men employed in female-dominated fields.

Not only do males find that female-dominated jobs offer fewer monetary and social rewards, they also discover that they may pay a "prestige penalty" in that their masculine image may be challenged (Jacobs, 1993). Men may develop a vested interest in maintaining their masculine ideal as a source of power and self-respect, which would make it even more difficult for them to enter female-dominated fields (Acker, 1990). In spite of these adverse situations, there are still many instances of men who choose to enter traditionally female positions. At times, these men encounter dynamics similar to those faced by women entering traditionally male fields. Yet, they often choose different behavioral responses based on maintaining identification with their higher status as males.

Men in Female-dominated Occupations

Nursing, elementary education, and secretarial work are three female-domi-nated occupations that have small contingents of male employees. Men in nursing report that they do encounter some of the situations described by Kanter (1977). Increased visibility accompanied by performance pressure has been reported by male nurses (Heikes, 1991). But whereas females respond to this pressure by over-achieving or underachieving, male nurses responded only by overachieving. In general, male tokens appear to benefit from the increased visibility of entering a female-dominate occupation (Floge & Merrill, 1986).

The issue of polarization appears to have two components—social isolation and heightened differentiation between dominants and tokens. When discussing social isolation, male nurses described being excluded from informal social gatherings and conversations, which is similar to the female token experience. However, on the issue of heightened differentiation, tokens appear to be the ones to define themselves differently from the dominants. Male nurses will often emphasize their specialty (for instance, psychiatric nurse or nurse anesthetist) and highlight their interest in science and the technical aspects of nursing as opposed to the nurturing aspects as a way of distancing themselves from the dominants (Heikes, 1991). This pattern contradicts what Kanter proposed when discussing women as tokens in a male-dominated occupation. The dynamic of assimilation also affected male nurses but in the opposite way in which it affects female tokens. Male nurses often are mistaken for physicians, which reflects status elevation unlike the status level-ing that occurs when female attorneys are mistaken for clerical workers. Although this status elevation may initially seem positive, male nurses view it as negative because it implies they are working in positions inappropriate for a man.

In the field of education, females comprise 70 percent of all teachers and 88 percent of all elementary teachers (Allan, 1993). However, men still hold the ma-jority of principalships and upper administrative positions. When interviewed, men in elementary schools reported that they perceived that they received prefer-ential treatment in the hiring process. The reason for this preference was expressed as a need for male role models for the students. But this hiring preference at times was accompanied by conflicts with the female staff who questioned the male's qualifications for the position. Male elementary teachers believed they were watched more carefully (high visibility) to see how they would respond to the nur-turing aspects of the position. In order to form trust and cooperation with the fe-male teachers, male teachers may have to relinquish traditionally male interests in order to fit into the informal social network (polarization). Men report that women would share things among themselves that they would not share with men (Robin-son, 1981).

But these male elementary teachers also engaged in heightened differentiation by emphasizing their differences from female teachers by activities such as coaching sports. A paradox is created if the male teachers emphasize their masculinity too much because it contradicts their image as an emotionally sensitive teacher. In addition, males reported they refrained from demonstrating caring qualities because they did not want to invite suspicions of abuse. Behavior that was considered natural from women was often off-limits to men (Allan, 1993).

Men in childhood education also face stereotyping in terms of job behavior. Often they are welcomed into a school because they are expected to be strong disciplinarians. They may be viewed as handymen and asked to do heavy lifting and repair work. Although some men do not mind these expectations, others view them as a form of discrimination that highlights their minority status (Robinson, 1981). From this perspective, the three situations described by Kanter (1977)—visibility, polarization, and stereotyping—appear to be present for men in childhood education.

Until the early 1900s, secretarial work was a male-dominated occupation and was considered an apprenticeship for management. As organizations became more complex, an extensive middle management evolved, which led to secretaries having specialized technical skills unrelated to management (Pringle, 1993). In today's world, men reject the label of "male secretary," so it becomes difficult to even identify men who perform the functions of a secretary. These positions often are classified as "administrative" or "managerial assistants," because a male secretary may be thought to have some problem with his masculinity (stereotyping). Once a male secretary is hired, he appears to receive favorable treatment in that he is treated as a "junior" manager (polarization/heightened differentiation). He generally receives more explanation of processes, makes speedier progress through the system, and is paid more (Pringle, 1983). Although men can type, they often decline to do so, which may be another way for them to increase the differentiation from female secretaries. Male bosses support this differentiation, perhaps due to their own discomfort of placing another male in a subservient position.

Role Entrapment

Men in female-dominated occupations may be placed in four different roles that serve to stereotype men (Heikes, 1991). Often men who choose to enter a traditionally female organization are seen as "ladderclimbers." Because men are expected to be aggressive in pursuing their careers, this expectation carries over into cross-gender occupations. Women in these occupations may view men as a threat to their own aspirations to move into higher positions. A second role in which men may be placed is that of "troublemaker." In some organizations dominated by females, a preference was given to those who were docile and who did not question policy (Allan, 1993). Because men typically have exhibited more autonomy, they are more willing to assert opposing professional opinions. This behavior may not be rewarded by those expecting a more complaisant employee.

The role of "he-man" is commonly encountered in that men are expected to use their "superior" physical strength. Although this behavior may establish masculinity, males often resent this expectation. It is interesting that females value the unique capabilities men bring to the job whereas males in traditional occupations do not find value in the unique qualities females bring to the job. For example, female business owners in traditionally male fields have been found to communicate more effectively with employees (Smith, Smits, & Hoy, 1992), yet these skills are not often identified as an important trait for managers.

Although males in female-dominated occupations do not attempt to fight the first three stereotypical roles, the role of "homosexual" elicits strong reactions due to the stigmatizing nature of the label. This label is more likely applied to males in traditionally female occupations by those outside of the occupation. It is assumed that any man who deviates from traditional expectations must be less than fully masculine. Fear of this label keeps some males from pursuing nontraditional career interests, leaving the field to those who are either confident about or unconcerned with their gender identity.

It appears that the status difference, which exists, between males and females in the larger society influences the expectations of males and females who enter nontraditional occupations. Token status may be of some benefit to males who enter female-dominated occupations, but males also face stereotypes, which may result in those occupations being less desirable. Traits such as assertiveness, ambition, and physical strength that assist men in other careers may create stress when exhibited in work settings with different expectations. Because men frequently use work to establish their masculine identity, men in female-dominated occupations may see their masculine identity (part of which is higher income for self and family) constantly challenged and find it difficult to remain in the occupation without some redefinition of position.

WHY CHANGE IS DIFFICULT

In order to understand why change can be difficult, it is essential to understand systems (Cusins, 1994; Deming, 1993). A system is a complex organization of interdependent parts in which change in one part affects the other parts. Systems are resistant to change; in fact one of the primary characteristics of a system is the mechanism of homeostasis. Homeostasis is the process by which a system tries to maintain its current internal state by adjusting its processes. To maintain this equilibrium, a system may employ a number of approaches. The first method a system may try is to get the deviant element to conform to commonly accepted norms. If the deviant element can adjust to the expected behavior, then the system reestablishes its balance. When a person of a different gender enters a traditional workplace, that person is expected to do the job in the same way as the majority of the employees. Little consideration is given to alternative ways of behaving that might be just as effective. The system prefers to assimilate the new element into the usual method of performance rather than accommodate any differences.

If the new element is not able to be assimilated, then an effort will be made to expel that element in order for the homeostasis to be maintained. By all of the forces of the system joining together, pressure can be asserted on the deviant element to leave the system. For example, coworkers can create very harsh working conditions for new employees by limiting information, withholding instruction, and excluding the person from social interaction. If these conditions are unpleasant enough, the new employee may decide that the personal costs are too great to remain and "fight the system."

Systems do have the ability to accommodate change when that change is seen as necessary for the survival of the system. Adjustments will be made to retain those elements seen as valuable to the maintenance of the system. Women may be helped in systems that need increased numbers of employees to accomplish the work. When employees from traditional male groups are not available, women may be seen as a benefit to the system. But if women are viewed as invading the system, they may not be welcomed into the workgroup. In a system traditionally dominated by men that is seen as highly desirable employment for men, women may not be accommodated by the system. For example, a woman employee may be criticized if she cannot handle the heavy lifting but an experienced male employee with a health problem may be provided with assistance through the informal social network so that he can continue working. The system has to value the change if that change is to be accommodated.

The workplace system is challenged when its gender composition changes. Because the minority gender is usually in a token status, the majority gender will resist the changes they believe will result from this invasion of the minority. The more that gender identity is associated with the job, the more the system will resist the change. There is some belief that if a large enough proportion (critical mass) of the workforce changes, the system will be forced to accommodate the new employees. Although the idea of critical mass has been seen as a means of getting the system to change, this process may not occur. Some evidence indicates that even when the number of women reaches a critical mass, the male employees still resist their inclusion (Ott, 1989). Even increased numbers does not mean that those in the minority will form a cohesive group with common goals (Pattatucci, 1998). In their efforts to demonstrate that they belong with the majority, those in the minority may try to prove that they are the exception and not identify with others in the minority (Leger, 1997). In essence, the demands of the system override the cohesion of those in the minority.

CHANGE VERSUS TRANSITION

In the majority of situations where a job has been dominated by one gender, a dramatic legal or social change has been the impetus for opening the job to the other gender. For example, in 1972 the U.S. Congress amended Title VII of the 1964 Civil Rights Act that prohibited discrimination by both public and private employers. This legislation provided the legal foundation for women to pursue previously denied positions. Because these job opportunities were initiated by forces outside of the occupation, change was thrust upon the organization but in many cases was not accepted by the organization. Just because a change occurs, or is mandated, does not mean that it will be embraced by those affected by the change. What happens in an organization when a change is implemented but not fully accepted by the system? One interesting conceptualization of this problem is based on the understanding of the differences between change and transition as proposed by William Bridges (1991). Change is when there is a shift in the external situation and results in the work not being accomplished in exactly the same way as before. But just because the situation has changed, it does not mean the change will work. The people who actually carry out the work must also change or they will try to maintain the status quo. Consequently, an organization must examine the process of transition—moving the people in the organization from the old situation to the new one.

Transition is the process by which employees are given the opportunity to deal with their internal reactions to change. Any type of change creates a sense of loss, which is accompanied by feelings of grief. If these feelings are not addressed, the employees will express them through resisting the change. The old way of doing things must be allowed to end before a new beginning can occur. People resist change for many reasons. First, they may not understand why the change is occurring. For many workers, if a situation has been working well, there is no reason to change it. Another reason for resistance is their lack of knowledge about how change will affect the work setting. An employee initially may be more interested in how the change impacts him or her on a personal level than how the change might affect the organization. This focus on self may be accompanied by resentment over what has been lost. Resentment may be directed toward the organization and management for forcing the change upon the workers. Workers who do not see themselves benefiting from the change will experience the most resentment.

Uncertainty creates anxiety and stress for any workforce, and increased stress can affect productivity and safety. Because gender changes in the work setting often have been propelled by outside legal forces, those currently in the job may wonder about the effect on promotions and advancement. Someone who has waited for an opening on a different shift or as a supervisor may fear that the new hires will be given priority for these opportunities. When there is a lack of knowledge about how the changes will affect the individual workers, there is a tendency for them to "fill in the blanks" with their own interpretations of what the change means to them on an individual level. Speculation tends to lead to the "worst case scenario," which in turn further fuels the anxiety over the unknown.

MANAGING TRANSITION

As a manager, one needs to first ask who may lose something because of the change. Those affected may include members of the workgroup, those who interact with the workgroup, and those who supervise the workgroup. Once those who are affected are identified, then it is important to determine what might be lost. Although managers often tend to think in terms of material losses (wages, raises, promotions), one needs to consider psychological losses as well. When someone of another gender enters the workforce, the identity associated with the job changes. If the employees define the work as "a real man's job," the presence of women will challenge that definition. Concurrent with the loss of definition may be a sense that prestige and status have been lowered. The social relationships also will be affected in that the informal ways of interacting and communicating may no longer be acceptable. For example, in an organization that has been tradition- ally female, building the informal communication network through communicat- ing about personal information is quite common. A male employee may be less in- clined to reveal this personal information and consequently not be seen as a "team player."

To help employees move to a point of letting go of the past, labeled as the "end- ing phase," it is important to address what the loss means to those affected. First, employees need to know in advance that a change is going to happen. Unfortu- nately for many employees, the first awareness that a gender minority is entering their work sphere occurs the day the person shows up for work. Many managers do not want to "make a big deal" out of this type of change fearing that they will create an even bigger problem if they draw attention to it. But in most cases, infor- mation is power so letting employees know a change is about to occur gives time to address the emotional reactions to change.

Addressing employee's fears about what will be lost and what will be different is one way to soften the impact of the change. This approach means that employ- ees are allowed to voice any concerns they have and that the concerns will be ac- knowledged by management. Acknowledging concern does not mean that the de- cision is going to be reversed but just that managers understand that life on the job will be different in the immediate future. Such a discussion also allows unreason- able fears and expectations to be disputed. For example, if employees mistakenly believe that the seniority system will be abolished in order to promote the gender minority group, this concern can be alleviated immediately by providing accurate information to the concerned employees.

Supervisors and managers need to be made aware that this transition period in- volves grieving the loss of the past and that employees may go through periods of anger, sadness, and even depression. Sometimes, employees may try to bargain for a return to the old ways. It is extremely important that the supervisor or man- ager not give "mixed messages" that suggest that if this person(s) does not work out, the employees will return to the old work atmosphere. Employees must get a clear message that the gender integration of the job is not an experiment but a per- manent redefinition of the job.

Once a degree of closure has been obtained from the ending phase, the organi- zation moves into what Bridges (1991) terms the "neutral zone." This phase may be seen as the psychological resting place in which the intense emotions triggered by the change have decreased, but a full commitment to the new structure has not yet been made. The change has actually taken place, but the system has not ac- commodated and embraced the change. When there is a major social change such as a gender redefinition of the workplace, it may take several years for this accommodation to take place. As a manager or supervisor, the most important role one can take is that of communicator. The neutral zone can be a confusing and discouraging time, and employees need to know that the system is concerned about their well-being. They also need to know how the change fits into the long-range plans of the organization.

Supervisors and managers need to remain open to hearing about how the change is impacting the work setting and recognize the difficulty of making the accommodations. For example, males were unsure how to accommodate women firefighters because they must share living quarters and showering facilities (Floren, 1997). Sensitive supervisors acknowledge these difficulties while helping those affected move to solutions to the problems. As much as possible, those affected by the change (both the gender majority and minority) need to be included and involved in the discovery of solutions. Individuals often make a greater commitment to the change process if they have had a voice in determining how to solve the problem. Change can provide the impetus for innovation, and managers need to find ways to both encourage and support creative solutions to problems resulting from the change. Perhaps the introduction of a gender minority into the workplace would be a good time to reexamine the everyday practices on the job and make needed improvements for all employees.

As employees move through the neutral zone, they will move to a point of a new beginning in which the changes are being accepted. In this phase, employees benefit from receiving coaching on behaviors appropriate to the new setting and from having input into the new practices expected on the job. Employees may need to review their career opportunities in order to minimize the perceived losses based on the inclusion of the gender minority. Most importantly, employees need opportunities to form a new group identity that includes the gender minority. Finding ways to celebrate workteam success as opposed to individual achievements can reinforce the importance of all members of the team.

SUPPORTING THE GENDER MINORITY

Increased involvement of the total work setting in the change process is essential to creating an environment that supports the success of the gender minority. However, the needs of the individuals who cross gender lines must be addressed. If the gender minority is to find a place in a nontraditional career, a number of steps can be taken to enhance this process.

Whenever possible, career counseling should be offered to those individuals who are interested in pursuing a career where he or she will be a minority. This counseling should examine the most satisfying and stressful elements in the occupation. If the new employee has an understanding of the formal and informal values and attitudes held by the workgroup, he or she will be better equipped to respond to behavior that seems inappropriate and will be less inclined to self-blame when rejecting behavior is encountered. Along with this understanding, the employee needs to be aware of how to communicate about inappropriate behavior when it occurs. Inappropriate behavior should not be excused just because the established employees want to maintain the status quo.

Careful screening of applicants related to the ability to complete job tasks in a reasonable way would help ensure that the nontraditional employee can be successful on the job. A male without skills in operating office equipment or a female who is unfamiliar with construction practices may be unprepared for nontraditional employment unless job training will be provided. Just hiring a person to meet legal expectations of being an equal opportunity employer will not change the workplace. But it is also essential that job requirements unrelated to job performance be reconsidered. Irrelevant height or weight requirements, which have been used to exclude groups of people from jobs, have been ruled illegal (Leger, 1997).

On-the-job workshops are needed for supervisors and coworkers as a way to address stereotypical attitudes toward the gender minority. Until individuals are able to recognize the prejudices they bring into the workplace, behavior change will not occur. In addition to increasing awareness, clear concise guidelines concerning appropriate versus inappropriate behavior must be communicated to all employees and then enforced in a consistent manner. Although some employees will change behavior because it is the right thing to do, others only respond when faced with consequences for negative behavior. Regulations without enforceable consequences are ineffective.

First-line supervisors are in a position of power where they can influence the work situation. These are the individuals in the organization who can create a climate of acceptance or rejection. If it is obvious to employees that the supervisor does not welcome the gender minority, employees will believe they have the right (and perhaps even the expectation) to act inappropriately toward the nontraditional worker. Consequently, it may be beneficial to involve these supervisors in setting the standards for the employees to be hired so that the supervisors know the employees meet the qualifications.

First-line supervisors may be charged with implementing policies that they may oppose personally. Therefore it is critical to involve these supervisors in training and reward them for efforts to assist gender minority employees. Because it is the responsibility of these supervisors to ensure an equitable distribution of challenging assignments, give adequate feedback, and provide access to important job information, they can facilitate the success of the nontraditional worker.

First-line supervisors may need to become allies for the gender minority when awkward situations are encountered. When the gender minority speaks up about an uncomfortable situation, he or she is assumed to be too sensitive. But when a member of the gender majority voices the same concern, there is a higher probability that concern will be heard by the other employees. The first-line supervisors and their managers can assist the gender minority by becoming aware of disruptive or prejudicial behavior that impacts work behavior and then addressing this behavior without putting the gender minority "on display." For example, if a male manager observes sexually explicit material in the work area, he may want to state that he disapproves of that material being present at work rather than stating that the female employee may not appreciate seeing the material.

Those in positions of management need to examine their own personal biases and implement behavior changes. Learning not to generalize about people as a group but to consider each individual for his or her own capabilities is a skill that can be developed. Whenever a supervisor or manager encounters a statement such as "men just are not sensitive to patient needs" or "women can't handle the dirty work," the person in a position of power needs to challenge that statement and see if a specific situation has occurred that needs to be addressed or if the statement is just a stereotype being used to exclude those in a minority position. Because stereotypes tend not to be accurate, they need to be dismissed.

One trait of a successful manager is the ability to utilize the different talents available in the workforce to solve different work problems. If a manager is able to identify abilities possessed by those who are gender minorities, not only will he or she improve the overall performance of the workgroup but also will provide recognition for the contributions of the nontraditional employee. When the scientific interest of a male nurse or the communication skills of a female police officer are used to obtain a successful outcome to a work problem, the entire workgroup benefits. Focusing on the varying contributions that lead to team success can enhance the worth of the individual team members.

If the organization expects the gender minority to progress successfully beyond entry-level positions, the organization needs to ensure that the employee receives continued training in both work skills and leadership. Training in administration, politics, financial management, and resource management often are learned through delegation of projects. Gender minority employees need equal consideration when these assignments are distributed. But because the gender minority employee is often excluded from informal networks, he or she may not immediately come to mind when assignments need to be made.

On an organizational level, policies should be examined to find those that might be discriminatory, such as travel requirements, leave policies, and benefits. One controversial area is developing flexible work schedules to accommodate employees who have significant family responsibilities. From a traditional viewpoint, employees should be willing to accept the established work schedule when entering a job. Yet many organizations are losing valuable resources when extensive overtime or shiftwork interferes with family needs. Both blue-collar and white-collar positions are in a state of transition as employees are seeking alternatives that allow for interruptions in the career path or periods of part-time employment.

One additional issue that needs consideration is the involvement of unions in the changing workplace. In the past, a higher proportion of "failures" of women in traditionally male occupations involved unionized employees (Reskin, 1986). Union cooperation is another way to integrate women into blue-collar jobs that have been dominated by men. By utilizing the power of the union to recruit, train, and support nontraditional employees, greater access to skilled jobs can be provided, and the union will benefit from an additional source of membership.

CONCLUSIONS

The workplace of the future will be highly dependent on finding the best-qualified employees regardless of gender. Although both males and females are affected by traditional gender roles, the phenomenon of gender segregation has had greater consequences for females who have been excluded from many higher paid positions. Because men in traditionally male positions have a tendency to define their masculinity through the job, they have offered greater resistance to women entering their occupations than vice versa.

Women who enter occupations traditionally dominated by males face more obstacles than males who enter female-dominated occupations. For males, the increased visibility appears to be a benefit whereas it is a detriment to females. When a female errs on the job, that error is generalized to all females. However, both males and females face exclusion from informal social networks and therefore are not part of the necessary communication networks.

Many organizations focus on helping the gender minority "fit" into the existing work environment, but true change will only occur when the system is restructured to accommodate the needs of both genders. Because systems are resistant to change, it is the responsibility of management to provide training, supervision, and support for those in the system who can most influence the acceptance and accommodation of the new employees. As mentioned in the opening example, nontraditional employees can perform the work successfully. Yet it has been the responsibility of these employees to make all of the adjustments to the work environment rather than the environment adjusting to the needs of the new employees. If organizations are to thrive, learning to value the unique contributions of each employee is essential for proving a viable and stable workplace.

REFERENCES

Acker, J. (1990). Hierarchies, jobs, bodies: A theory of gendered organizations. *Gender and Society, 4,* 139–158.

Allan, J. (1993). Male elementary teachers: Experiences and perspectives. In C. L. Williams (Ed.), *Doing women's work* (pp. 113–127). Newbury Park, CA: Sage.

American Bar Association. (1983). *A review of legal education in the United States—Fall 1977 through Fall 1983: Law schools and bar admission requirements.* Chicago: Author.

Beermann, S., & Nachreiner, F. (1995). Working shifts—Different effects for men and women? *Work and Stress, 9,* 289–297.

Berquist, S. R., Duchac, B. W., Schalin, V. A., Zastrow, J. F., Barr, V. L., & Borowiecki, T. (1985). Perceptions of freshman medical students of gender differences in medical specialty choice. *Journal of Medical Education, 60,* 379–383.

Bickel, J., & Ruffin, A. (1995). Gender-associated differences in matriculating and graduating medical students. *Academic Medicine, 70,* 551–559.

Bogoch, B. (1997). Gendered lawyering: Difference and dominance in lawyer-client interaction. *Law and Society Review, 31,* 677–712.

Bridges, W. (1991). *Managing transitions: Making the most of change.* Reading, MA: Addison Wesley Longman.

Brown, M. C. (1994, September). The plight of female police. A survey of NW patrolmen. *The Police Chief,* 50–53.

Cartwright, L. K. (1987). Occupational stress in women physicians. In R. Payne & J. Firth-Cozens (Eds.), *Stress in health professionals* (pp. 71–87). Chichester, UK: Wiley.

Cassell, C. (1991). A woman's place is at the word processor: Technology and change in the office. In J. Firth-Cozens & M. West, *Women at work: Psychological and organizational perspectives* (pp. 172–184). Philadelphia: Open University Press.

Cusins, P. (1994). Understanding quality through systems thinking. *TQM Magazine, 6,* 19–27.

Deming, W. E. (1993). *The new economics for industry, government, education.* Cambridge, MA: MIT Center for Advanced Engineering.

Firth-Cozens, J. (1987). The stress of medical training. In R. Payne & J. Firth-Cozens (Eds.), *Stress in health professionals* (pp. 3–22).. Chichester, UK: Wiley.

Floge, L., & Merrill, D. (1986). Tokenism reconsidered: Male nurses and female physicians in a hospital setting. *Social Forces, 64,* 925–947.

Floren, T. M. (1997). Firefighter. In M. Martin (Ed.), *Hard-hatted women: Life on the job* (pp. 156–170). Seattle, WA: Seal Press.

Heikes, E. J. (1991). When men are the minority: The case of men in nursing. *Sociological Quarterly, 32,* 389–401.

Hertz, R. (1996). Guarding against women? Responses of military men and their wives to gender integration. *Journal of Contemporary Ethnography, 25,* 251–284.

Hojat, M., Gonnella, J., & Xu, G. (1995). Gender comparisons of young physicians' perceptions of their medical education, professional life, and practice: A follow-up study of Jefferson College graduates. *Academic Medicine, 70,* 305–312.

Instone, D., Major, B., & Bunker, B. (1983). Gender, self-confidence, and social influence strategies: An organizational simulation. *Journal of Personality and Social Psychology, 44,* 322–333.

Jacobs, J. A. (1993). Men in female-dominated careers: Trends and turnover. In C. L. Williams (Ed.), *Doing women's work* (pp. 49–63). Newbury Park, CA: Sage.

Kane, F. J. (1995). Faculty views of medical student abuse. *Academic Medicine, 70,* 563–564.

Kanter, R. (1977). Some effects of proportions on group life: Skewed sex ratios and responses to token women. *American Journal of Sociology, 82,* 965–990.

Kay, F., & Hagan, J. (1998). Raising the bar: The gender stratification of law-firm capital? *American Sociological Review, 63,* 728–743.

Kessler-Harris, A. (1982). *Out to work.* New York: Oxford University Press.

Kirkham, K., & Thompson, P. (1988). Managing a diverse work force: Women in engineering. In R. Katz (Ed.), *Managing Professionals in Innovative Organizations* (pp. 564–575). Cambridge, MA: Ballinger Publishing Company.

Komaromy, M., Bindman, A., Haber, R., & Sande, M. (1993). Sexual harassment in medical training. *New England Journal of Medicine, 328,* 322–326.

Leger, K. (1997). Public perceptions of female police officers on patrol. *American Journal of Criminal Justice, 21,* 231–249.

Lorber, J. (1993). Why women physicians will never be true equals in the American medical profession. In E. Riska & K. Wager (Eds.), *Gender, work, and medicine: Women and the medical division of labour* (pp. 62–76). London: Sage.

MacCorquodale, P., & Jensen, G. (1993). Women in the law: Partners or tokens? *Gender and Society, 7,* 582–593.

Mansfield, P., Koch, P., Henderson, J., Vicary, J., Cohn, M., & Young, E. (1991). The job climate for women in traditionally male blue-collar occupations. *Sex Roles, 25,* 63–79.

Marquat, J. A. (1990). The influence of applicants' gender on medical school interviews. *Academic Medicine, 65,* 410–411.

McDowell, J. (1992, February 17). Are women better cops? *Time,* 70–72.

Ott, R. M. (1989). Effect of the male-female ratio on work: Policewomen and male nurses. *Psychology of Women Quarterly, 13,* 41–57.

Palmer, H. T., & Lee, J. A. (1990). Female workers' acceptance in traditionally male-dominated blue-collar jobs. *Sex Roles, 22,* 607–626.

Pattatucci, A. (1998). Trespassers on private property. In A. Pattatucci (Ed.), *Women in science: Meeting career challenges* (pp. 1–14). Thousand Oaks, CA: Sage.

Pringle, R. (1993). Male secretaries. In C. L. Williams (Ed.), *Doing women's work* (pp. 128–151). Newbury Park, CA: Sage.

Reskin, B. F., & Hartmann, H. I. (1986). *Women's work, men's work: Sex segregation on the job.* Washington, DC: National Academy Press.

Riska, E., & Wegar, K. (1993). Women physicians: A new force in medicine? In E. Riska & K. Wegar (Eds.), *Gender, work, and medicine: Women and the medical division of labour* (pp. 77–93). London: Sage.

Rizzo, A., & Mendez, C. (1990). *The integration of women in management: A guide for human resources and management development specialists.* New York: Quorum Books.

Robinson, B. E. (1981, March). Contemporary man in childhood education. *Educational Forum,* 307–311.

Robinson, J., & McIlwee, J. (1991). Men, women, and the culture of engineering. *Sociological Quarterly, 32,* 403–421.

Rosenberg, J., Peristadt, H., & Phillips, W. (1993). Now that we are here? Discrimination, disparagement, and harassment at work and the experience of women lawyers. *Gender and Society, 7,* 415–433.

Roter, D., Lipkin, M., Korsgaard, A. (1991). Sex differences in patients' and physicians' communication during primary care medical visits. *Medical Care, 29,* 1083–1093.

Rytina, N. F., & Bianchi, S. M. (1984). Occupational reclassification and changes in distribution by gender. *Monthly Labor Review, 107,* 11–17.

Schulte, H. M., & Kay, J. (1994). Medical students' perceptions of patient-initiated sexual behavior. *Academic Medicine, 69,* 842–846.

Sherman, L. (1973). A psychological view of women in policing. *Journal of Police Science and Administration, 1,* 383–394.

Shostak, A. (1985). Blue-collar worker alienation. In C. Cooper & M. Smith (Eds.), *Job stress and blue-collar work* (pp. 7–18). Chichester, UK: Wiley.

Smith, P. L., Smits, S. J., & Hoy, F. (1992). Female business owners in industries traditionally dominated by males. *Sex Roles, 26,* 485–496.

Stuart, P. (1992). What does the glass ceiling cost you? *Personnel Journal, 71,* 70–80.
U.S. Bureau of Labor Statistics. (1997, January). *Employment and earnings.* Washington, DC: U.S. Government Printing Office.
Wentling, R. M. (1995). Breaking down barriers to women's success. *HRMagazine, 40,* 79–82.

4

AGE AND BEAUTY: STEREOTYPES AS FACTORS IN WOMEN'S CAREERS

Rosemary Booth

Women have always worked. They have always made meaningful contributions to the economy. In preindustrial times, women's work was ordinarily centered in the home. With the changes wrought by the industrial revolution, women ventured out of the house to work but in limited numbers and in limited occupations. Most women worked in gendered occupations such as education, nursing, household domestic, clerical, textiles, and garment work. It wasn't until World War II that women took positions that previously had been considered men's work, that is, work not suitable for women. Women helped the war effort by filling in for the absent men wherever they were needed, including working in factories, flying airplanes, and driving trucks. But this was a temporary situation resulting from difficult times and one not expected to continue. At war's end, women were expected to turn these jobs over to the returning servicemen and once again return to their homes; or if they had to work, seek positions more appropriate for females, for instance, as nurses, teachers, and secretaries. Most women did just that, but others enjoyed their new-found independence and challenges. What they had started as a temporary wartime measure now appealed to them on a full-time basis. They wanted to pursue careers. However, their efforts met with resistance; and for the most part, women were unsuccessful in obtaining positions outside the traditional women's occupations. During the 1940s and 1950s, the expectation was that women worked because they needed to, not because they wanted to.

WOMEN'S LABOR FORCE PARTICIPATION

It wasn't until the feminist movement in the early 1960s that women began to join the workforce in record numbers and pursue careers. After World War II, 31.8 percent of women worked. By 1984, that number had increased to 53.4 percent and of these, two thirds of women ages 23 to 54 were employed (Wolf, 1991). Recent labor statistics indicate that these numbers continue to rise. The percentage of the workforce between the ages of 36 and 54 is expected to increase to 48 percent by 2005 with the number of women between the ages of 35 and 44 projected to be 17.1 million (Gordon & Whelan, 1998). Prior to the women's movement, women had jobs, not careers. Careers, as defined by Stroh, Brett, and Reilly (1992), are patterns of work-related experiences, and successful careers are characterized by ever-increasing salaries, levels, promotions, responsibilities, recognition, respect, and freedom (Larwood & Gutek, 1987; Powell & Mainiero, 1992).

Currently women comprise nearly one half of the U.S. labor force, and more than one half of the students obtaining bachelor and master's degrees, 40 percent of those receiving law degrees and one third of MBA degree recipients are women (Catalyst, 1996). Yet 75 percent of American women continue to work in traditional "women's jobs," jobs that are ill paid and emphasize physical attractiveness (Wolf, 1991). In 1972, women held 17 percent of managerial positions; by 1995, 42.7 percent. Yet they are clustered in entry-level or mid-level managerial positions; women hold less than 5 percent of executive positions (Ragins, Townsend, & Mattis, 1998). In 1990 *Fortune* magazine reported that women comprised .05 percent (19 of 4,012) of the highest paid officers and directors of the 1,000 largest U.S. industrial and service companies (Fierman, 1990). Similarly, in 1993, Catalyst (1993), a research and advisory organization to advance women in business, reported women held only 5.9 percent of the total directorships of *Fortune* 500 industrial firms.

GLASS CEILING: BARRIER TO ADVANCEMENT

Much has been written about the "glass ceiling," that invisible barrier to advancement that seems to be pervasive in corporate America. Over 92 percent of women executives recognize its existence but disagree with the CEOs of the *Fortune* 1000 about its cause. In a recent study, CEOs attribute women's lack of success to a general lack of management or line experience or of not having been in the pipeline long enough. On the other hand, female executives attribute their lack of success to corporate culture (Ragins et al., 1998). In an earlier study, CEOs of some of the same companies seemed to agree with the female executives. The CEOs acknowledged that stereotypes continue to negatively affect women's career mobility (Fierman, 1990). There seems to be more to the glass ceiling than just lack of time and experience. Men who completed graduate school 20 years ago are poised for promotion to senior management, but the women who graduated with them are not (Fierman, 1990). Similarly, recent reports indicate that women graduating from top schools are paid less than their male counterparts

("The Best," 1990). Earlier studies indicated that although females with MBAs were initially paid as much as men, within 10 years their salaries fell behind that of their male counterparts by nearly 20 percent (Devanna, 1987; Wallace, 1989). Researchers have explored these phenomena by considering issues such as sexual harassment, sex role stereotyping, childcare issues, and women's traits and characteristics, including age and attractiveness. Admittedly, discrimination based on age and appearance also applies to men; however, it appears to have a more adverse effect on women's careers than on men's.

JOB VERSUS CAREER

The change in focus of women from having jobs to having careers has major implications for women's participation in the workforce. In the period between the end of World War II and the beginning of the women's movement, the positions women held as nurses, teachers, or secretaries were seen as either a source of a supplemental income to their husbands or a temporary measure until women married and had children. This was the era of suburban growth, which glorified the role of the housewife and homemaker. It was expected that women would focus primarily on their responsibilities as homemakers. Thus, the work they did outside the home was a job; the job was an end in itself, not a position that would lead to a series of ever-increasing work experiences and responsibilities. The women did not expect to advance in their work and it wasn't expected they would remain for long periods of time (Gutek & Larwood, 1987).

Careers, on the other hand, as stated previously, are a series of work-related experiences and jobs over a period of time (Stroh et al., 1992). Careers represent a progression up a hierarchy or of increasing responsibility or of freedom to select the manner in which to complete one's assigned tasks. A career can include a number of jobs in one organization or a series of related positions in a number of organizations. At least that is the model most men follow for their careers. Women's careers, however, differ from men's, primarily because of four issues: (1) Women select jobs that limit their advancement opportunities; (2) women accommodate their careers to their spouses; (3) women accept primary responsibility for their children; (4) women face constraints based on stereotypes and discrimination in their career advancement (Gutek & Larwood, 1987).

CAREER SELECTION

As soon as the young, female college graduate looks for her first position and the start of her career, she begins to encounter obstacles. Women, more so than young men, are guided toward careers in human resource management, public relations and communications, or other similar administrative positions. Research has shown that experience in line management positions, those with profit and loss responsibility, is critical for career advancement. Whereas young men are encouraged to seek out such careers, women immediately put themselves at a disadvantage by accepting assignments in areas such as human resource management and communication. These are relatively dead-end jobs with little opportunity for advancement. One explanation for women being guided to these positions is that women may be viewed as softer, gentler, and more sympathetic and thus fit better into these areas. Another explanation may be the employer's perception that women lack commitment to their job or career.

Frequently, women don't recognize they will have a career. Through the socialization process, women come to expect they will marry and have the primary responsibility for the home. Thus, unlike young men who are socialized to find a job, build a career, and work until retirement, women's focus is more complex. Rexroat and Shehan (1984) found that women's long-range work plans significantly impacted their work role behavior and influenced their employment decisions. Women who expected to combine the responsibilities of a home and a family with their career and remain in the workforce did so regardless of changes in their marital and parenting status. In addition, these women coordinated their work and family roles to ensure extensive and continuous employment. On the other hand, many women make poor decisions when evaluating job assignments and their relation to their career progression. They fail to recognize the relationship of each position to the successive work-related experiences that comprise a career. Thus, when they decide they want a career, either through personal choice or environmental factors, they find they are at a disadvantage. They have held a series of unrelated positions, rather than adhering to a consistent pattern of career-enhancing assignments. Women who originally did not expect to be employed over extended periods of time were less committed to long-term employment. With this in mind, they were frequently less focused on selecting the best opportunity or most challenging assignment in the early stages of their career (White, 2000).

Oftentimes the stereotypical belief that women will marry and have a family in the very first stages of their careers may result in discrimination based on age. Employers, either consciously or unconsciously, look at a woman in her early or middle twenties just starting out on a career and hesitate to employ her because they fear she will leave to marry, have a family, or follow her spouse (Devanna, 1987). Recent research shows marked differences between early career experiences of men and women. A 1995 report by the Federal Glass Ceiling Commission found that women lack management training, opportunities for career development, access to critical developmental assignments and networks of communication, and rotation to line or revenue-producing positions. Although in recent years women have made substantial progress in obtaining similar developmental experiences similar to men, Ohlett, Ruderman, and McCauley (1994) found that differences continue. They express concern that these differences may be a result of subtle discrimination, which is difficult to identify.

CAREER AND FAMILY

Women have trouble relinquishing the roles of housewife and mother (Hochschild & Machung, 1989). They continue to assume principal responsibility for home, family, and social life in addition to career responsibilities (Hartmann,

1987; Morrison & Von Glinow, 1990). Data show that many women with success-ful careers choose to remain single or childless (Schneer, & Reitman, 1995), but such a decision is difficult to share readily with a prospective employer. And, even if an applicant did share the information, it is doubtful she would be believed. From the employer's viewpoint, the risk of hiring a young woman is great. It re-quires a large commitment of time, money and training on the part of an employer to establish someone in a career. This is a serious investment in an individual for an employer concerned about a woman's commitment to her career and organiza-tion. Thus, women of childbearing age frequently experience subtle age discrimi-nation. Their employers do not offer them the training and career-enhancing as-signments so vital for their advancement. In addition, women frequently find it difficult to identify a mentor, also necessary for career advancement, either be-cause male potential mentors doubt a woman's commitment to her career or the fear of accusations of sexual harassment or perceptions of favoritism. Women can only hope that the recent emphasis on the benefits of diversity and the tight labor market will encourage employers to select well-qualified candidates, whether male and female, and work to retain them.

CAREER INTERRUPTIONS

Women's childbearing affects their careers. The early years in one's career are critical for gaining experience, developing a reputation as a high achiever, secur-ing mentoring relationships, and completing challenging assignments. It is during this period that women must address the issue of having children. Some choose to take extended leaves from their careers to raise children. Others decide either to remain childless or postpone having children until they establish their careers. For those who postpone having children, when they do take a maternity leave, they limit their time away from the office (White, 2000). Once they have children, they work to balance their work and family priorities. Oftentimes, their employer's cor-porate culture or structure is not supportive of their needs. Because the traditional career model continues to adhere to the male model, women frequently find their employers are not family-friendly. Thus, although willing to remain in the work-force, women are forced to temporarily abandon their careers to focus on their family responsibilities. These career interruptions negatively impact their future income and career advancement. When they choose to return to work, they find they are out of the mainstream of activities and lacking in current technical exper-tise. Recent innovations in employment structure, such as telecommuting and job sharing, however, are beginning to help young women juggle career and family commitments. In the current tight labor markets, employers are more receptive to finding ways to keep good workers. Telecommuting, using technology to work from home, or unique work arrangements such as job sharing or part-time work enable a woman to maintain her position while caring for her family. Although not as advantageous as full-time job commitment, these innovations allow the women to remain current and visible in their fields until they can resume their careers full-time. On the other hand, some women resolve the conflict between family and ca-

reer commitments by becoming entrepreneurs. They opt out of the restrictive corporate environment and create a firm more conducive to their multiple roles.

APPEARANCE AND CAREER POTENTIAL

Considerable research indicates that the applicant's appearance affects the hiring process for both men and women. Numerous studies have shown that attractive people are selected and promoted more often than less attractive individuals.
Heilman and Stopeck (1985) determined that attractiveness induced a halo effect
in the work setting in relation to hiring decisions and assessments of employee potential. However, being attractive can be a double-edged sword. Research demonstrates that attractiveness is a help or hindrance depending on the sex of the applicant and the nature of the job sought. Spencer and Taylor (1988) found that
physical attractiveness is a liability for women if it exaggerates the perception of
gender-related attributes. They noted that the more attractive a woman is perceived to be, the less suitable she will be judged for occupying a job that is
thought to require "male characteristics." This also holds true for the potential for
advancement. Thus, attractiveness puts female candidates for managerial positions
at a disadvantage because existing research equates good managers with "male
characteristics" (Heilman, Block, Martell, & Simon, 1989). It appears women
need to be unattractive and to demonstrate masculine characteristics to succeed in
management careers.

Recent highly publicized cases, however, appear to contradict the premise that
one must be unattractive to advance. Ann Hopkins was denied a partnership at
Price Waterhouse because she was "too masculine." Although technically qualified, she was criticized for being aggressive, harsh, and impatient, characteristics
frequently cited as male traits. She was advised to walk, talk, and dress more
femininely, and to wear jewelry and makeup (Fierman, 1990). Hopkins was
caught in a double bind. If she chose to adopt a more feminine style, it was very
likely that she would be considered less technically competent. Yet, when she
demonstrated "masculine traits," she was evaluated harshly for lacking femininity.
Hopkins subsequently sued and won a sex discrimination case against Price
Waterhouse.

Christine Craft, a former Kansas City anchorwoman, was fired for being too old
and too unattractive (Wenske, 1983). According to Craft, appearance on air is
more important for women than it is for men. In her lawsuit, she noted that of all
the anchor people over 40, 97 percent were male and the remaining 3 percent were
women who didn't look their age. Craft sued for sex discrimination. After years in
litigation and conflicting judgments, the Supreme Court ruled against Craft.

The well-known TV correspondent Leslie Stahl, in a 1999 interview on the television show *20/20,* reminisced about the early days of women as network reporters. She noted that the first women reporters, of which she was one, were all
young, attractive, and blond. She observed how appearance was important for

women in those days but apparently not for men referencing, in particular, for Walter Cronkite's appearance. Wolf (1991) contends that most male television reporters would be unemployed if a single standard was applied to both men and women. Stahl observed that while appearance is still a factor for both men and women, women are recognized for their technical competence now as well.

In an occupation less visible than television reporting, Moss (1984) reported a waitress whom she thought particularly competent but was fired because the customers didn't like her. The restaurant manager explained to Moss that the men who come into the restaurant "want to see a pretty face" (p. 68). Similarly, National Airlines fired a stewardess for being four pounds over their weight limit and Xerox Corporation withdrew a job offer to a woman because of her weight. A fifty-four-year-old woman was fired without warning because her boss wanted to look at someone younger to lift his spirits (Wolf, 1991). These examples add credence to Bell's (1989) contention that discrimination because of factors of physical attractiveness usually arises solely because the woman is seen as a sex object before she is seen as a productive worker.

Since 1971, frequent court cases have recognized that employers have a right to set appearance standards for employment. Although such standards have never been defined, and the informal rules of the appropriateness of appearance keep shifting, these standards have frequently been used against women. A female police officer was fired for "looking like a lady," and a supervisor lost her job for "dressing like a woman." In another case, a woman who was young, beautiful, and carefully dressed lost a sexual harassment suit when the court ruled that her beauty and dress could be interpreted as provoking the harassment (Wolf, 1991).

APPEARANCE AND JOB TYPE

Attractiveness as a help or hindrance for career development depends on the sex of the applicant and the nature of the job sought. Heilman and Sawuwatari (1979) found that the job type influenced the impact of women's attractiveness on her evaluation. Attractiveness was beneficial for female employees only when the job type was clerical. When the job type was managerial, attractiveness was a deterrent to favorable performance evaluation. In a later study, Spencer and Taylor (1988) found that attractive women in managerial positions were rated more favorably than unattractive women, but the attractive women were perceived to have performed well because of good luck or supervisory favoritism. Jackson (1983) reported similar findings. She found an interaction between gender and perceived attractiveness in sex-typed occupations, supporting the assumption that gender traits mediate the influence of attractiveness in occupation advancement decisions. Thus, behaving in a manner that does not conform to stereotypical views should ultimately be a potent antidote to a feminine appearance. Conversely, women who chose to pursue traditionally male careers are negatively affected by factors that emphasize their femininity (Heilman & Stopeck, 1985). Wolf (1991) contends that beauty "is determined by politics and in the modern age in the west, it is the last best relief system that keeps male dominance intact" (p.12). Although research indicated attractiveness is not an asset for a woman's career advancement, it does appear to have a positive effect on her salary progression. Frieze, Olson, and Russell (1991) found that for more attractive women with MBAs, appearance did not affect their starting salaries, but their appearance had a positive effect on their salaries as their careers progressed over time. It appears that attractiveness affects men and women differently.

CAREER TRANSITION

A career model that might be evolving for women includes early career entry; brief interruption for family responsibilities, and subsequent return to the labor force until retirement (White, 2000). However, at 40 women are perceived as old. Stereotypes about midlife and older women as unattractive, passive, or incompetent are still pervasive in the American work force (National Partnership for Women and Families, 1999). Women past 45 rarely are offered an interview or even an application form for skilled jobs. For unskilled jobs, which pay the minimum wage, age discrimination is less evident. Because few women qualify for pensions (and when they do, their payments are significantly less than what men receive), it is in these jobs where many middle-aged women work until they are eligible for social security at 62 or even beyond to supplement their small social security payments (Maupin, 1984). Most women can't save for retirement because of their meager wages, yet their retirement needs are frequently greater than that of men because women live longer and thus are dependent on their retirement funds longer. Despite the fact the average woman lives 40 years after her last child enters school and 25 years after her last child marries (Bell, 1989), current statistics show that women's income peaks around age 40. Yet, because of their career interruptions and their lower wages, women usually work longer than men.

PERCEPTIONS OF OLDER WORKERS

Age discrimination against older workers is well documented. One half of all jobs are closed to people over 55, one quarter to those over 45 (Bell, 1989). A number of reasons are given for employers' reluctance to hire older workers. Some employers perceive older workers as lacking the energy and commitment of younger workers, some think older workers are less willing to work long hours, and others believe older workers do not like working for someone considerably younger than themselves (Steen, 1998).

Many common myths surround the older worker. There is the perception that older employees' ability to perform declines with age. There is also the misconception that older workers are not interested in retraining and learning new skills. Quite the contrary might be true. Older workers are enthusiastic about learning new skills if they believe the skills will be in their self-interest. Some people believe that older workers should retire to make way for younger workers. Others believe that older workers won't be willing to leave the job, therefore mandatory retirement is necessary, even though it is illegal now. There is also the perception that older workers have a higher absentee rate than younger. This is not true. An analysis of attendance records of older employed persons by Paul and Townsend (1993) determined their attendance records equaled that of younger workers. What employers are finding now is that older workers are a valued and necessary component in their workforce. It is anticipated that retention of older workers will be a major focus of employers as the baby boomers reach retirement age. Many economic forecasts predict a shortage of skilled labor within the next 20 years and employers will be looking to the older worker to fill the void. It is unknown whether this will prove advantageous for the older female worker or if employers will continue to be influenced by stereotypical perceptions of older women.

Currently, though, it is well documented that both men and women experience age discrimination. However, women are more likely than men to believe that their advancing age is a serious impairment. One explanation for this can be attributed to the negative stereotypes in the media of middle-aged women. Research has demonstrated that the age group rated most severely was women over 40 (Bell, 1989). Wolf (1991) contends that it is a male model that portrays aging in women as "unbeautiful." It is her position that women become more powerful as they age, and men fear these powerful women. Thus, men have created the myth that aging is unattractive and older women lack status and importance. It is too early to tell how the first cohort of women who sought careers rather than jobs will be treated as it approaches retirement age. Because the women's movement began in the early 1960s, it is only now that career women are reaching retirement age. Time will tell if they will be treated any differently from women in previous decades.

RETIREMENT

There is considerable documentation that financial concerns cause women to work longer than men. Interrupted work cycles and low wages result in women needing to supplement their incomes as long as possible. Statistics indicate the gap between men's and women's wages is lessening, but women still earn less than men. One can only hope that as women achieve career success, they will also be able to make adequate financial provisions for their retirement.

On a social level, women adapt to retirement better than men. Frequently, men find retirement difficult because they lose the status and prestige that came with their career identity. They don't know what to do with their time. Women, on the other hand, are closer to their families; thus they are sheltered from the isolation one experiences when one retires (Bell, 1989). It can also be projected that women have less prestige and status to lose when they retire because very few have achieved the career success of their male counterparts. Thus, the balance women have maintained between their family and career responsibilities during their careers helps them achieve happiness and contentment in retirement.

SUMMARY

Women are attaining more career success, but they are still far from achieving equity with men in career progression. Stereotypes continue to have an adverse impact on working women. Being attractive can be a double bind for them. Although it is well known that attractiveness might help women obtain a position early in their careers, it can work against them as they progress. People attribute women's success to their appearance rather than to their skills. This is particularly true if the women's career is in an area not recognized as "women's work."

Women are also aware that their age works against them. They are either too young or too old. When they first enter the labor force, employers worry about their family responsibilities and how they will interfere with the woman's career responsibilities. Employers hesitate to invest in training and developing young women. As women reach middle age, the time when they should be achieving career success, women encounter age discrimination.

Since the feminist revolution, women have made significant strides in pursuing careers. However, there is still a long way to go. With women approaching 50 percent of the labor force, employers must focus on adapting career models to women's needs and eliminating stereotypical attitudes towards career women. It is in the best interest of employers to recognize the value of women employees.

REFERENCES

Bell, I. P. (1989). The double standard: Age. In J. Freeman (Ed.), *Women: A feminist perspective* (4th ed., pp. 236–244). Mountain View, CA: Mayfield.

The best companies for women. (1990, August 6). *Business Week,* 49–55.

Catalyst. (1993). *Women on corporate boards: The challenge of change.* New York: Author.

Catalyst. (1996). *Women in corporate leadership: Progress and prospects.* New York: Author.

Devanna, M. A. (1987). Women in management: progress and promise. *Human Resource Management, 26,* 469–481.

Federal Glass Ceiling Commission (1995). *Good for business: Making full use of the nation's human capital.* Washington, DC: Government Printing Office.

Fierman, J. (1990, July 30). Why women still aren't getting to the top. *Fortune,* pp. 40–42, 46, 50, 54, 62.

Frieze, I. H., Olson, J. E., & Russell, J. (1991) Attractiveness and income for men and women in management. *Journal of Applied Social Psychology,* 1039–1057.

Gordon, J. R., & Whelan, K. S. (1998). Successful professional women in midlife: How organizations can more effectively understand and respond to the challenges. *The Academy of Management Executive, 12,* 8–27.

Gutek, B. A., & Larwood, L. (1987). Women's careers are important and different. In B. Gutek & L. Larwood (Eds.), *Women's career development* (pp. 7–14). Newbury Park, CA: Sage.

Hartmann, H. E. (1987). The family as the focus of gender, class, and political struggle: The example of housework. In S. Harding (Ed.), *Feminism and methodology.* Bloomington, IN: Indiana University Press.

Heilman, M. E., Block, C. S., Martell, R. F., & Simon, M. C. (1989). Has anything changed? Current characterizations of men, women and managers. *Journal of Applied Psychology, 74,* 935–942.

Heilman, M. E., & Saruwatari, L. R. (1979). When beauty is beastly: The effects of appearance and sex on evaluations of job applicants for managerial and nonmanagerial jobs. *Organizational Behavior and Human Performance, 23,* 360–372.

Heilman, M. E., & Stopeck, M. H. (1985). Being attractive, advantage or disadvantage? Performance based evaluations and recommended personnel actions as a function of appearance, sex, and job type. *Organizational Behavior and Human Decision Processes, 35,* 202–215.

Hochschild, J. S., & Machung, A. (1989). *The second shift.* New York: Viking.

Jackson, L. A. (1983). Gender, physical attractiveness, and sex role in occupational treatment discrimination. The influence of trait and role assumptions. *Journal of Applied Social Psychology, 13,* 443–458.

Larwood, L., & Gutek, B. (1987). Working towards a theory of career development. In B. Gutek and L. Larwood (Eds.), *Women's career development* (pp. 170–184). Newbury Park, CA: Sage.

Maupin, J. (1984). Older working women. In A. M. Jagger & P. S. Rothenberg (Eds.), *Feminist frameworks: Alternative theoretical accounts of the relation between women and men* (2nd ed., pp. 45–47). New York: McGraw-Hill.

Morrison, A. M., & Von Glinow, M. A. (1990). Women and minorities in management. *American Psychologist, 45,* 200–208.

Moss, Z. (1984). It hurts to be alone and obsolete: The aging woman. In A. M. Jagger & P. S. Rothenberg (Eds.), *Feminist frameworks: Alternative theoretical accounts of the relation between women and men* (2nd ed., pp. 66–69). New York: McGraw-Hill.

National Partnership for Women and Families (1999). Sex and age discrimination. [Online.] Available: www.nationalpartnership.org//workandfamily/workplacedoublediscrimin/sa_discrim.htm. January 17, 1999.

Ohlett, P. J., Ruderman, M. N., & McCauley, C. D. (1994). Gender differences in managers' developmental job experiences. *Academy of Management Journal, 37*(1), 46–47.

Paul, R. J., & Townsend, J. B. (1993). Managing the older worker—Don't just rinse away the gray. *Academy of Management Executive, 7,* 67–74.

Powell, G. N., & Mainiero, L. A. (1992). Cross-currents in the river of time: Conceptualizing the complexities of women's careers. *Journal of Management, 28,* 225–237.

Ragins, B. R., Townsend, B., & Mattis, M. (1998). Gender gap in the executive suite: CEOs and female executives report on breaking the glass ceiling. *The Academy of Management Executive, 12,* 28–42.

Rexroat, C., & Shehan, C. (1984). Expected versus actual work roles of women. *American Sociological Review, 49,* 349–357.

Schneer, J. A., & Reitman, F. (1995). The impact of gender as managerial careers unfold. *Journal of Vocational Behavior, 47,* 290–315.

Spencer, B.A., & Taylor, G. S. (1988). Effects of facial attractiveness and gender on causal attributions of managerial performance. *Sex Roles, 19,* 273–285.

Stahl, L. (1999, January 6). *20/20.* Personal observation.

Steen, M. (1998, July 20). Age-old dilemma. *InfoWorld, 29,* 1–4.

Stroh, L.K., Brett, J. M., & Reilly, A. H. (1992). All the right stuff: A comparison of female and male managers' career progression. *Journal of Applied Psychology, 77,* 251–260.

Wallace, P. A. (1989). *MBAs on the fast track.* New York: Harper & Row.

Wenske, P. (1983, August 15). The TV anchor case: A firing for appearance sake? *The National Law Journal,* p. 6.

White, B. (2000). Lessons from the careers of successful women. In M. J. Davidson & R. J. Burke (Eds.), *Women in management current research issues* (Vol. II, pp. 164–176). London: Sage.

Wolf, N. (1991). *The beauty myth: How images of beauty are used against women.* New York: Anchor Books.

Part III
Harassment Issues

5

WOMEN EXPOSED: SEXUAL HARASSMENT AND FEMALE VULNERABILITY

Sue Norton

AN OVERVIEW OF SEXUAL HARASSMENT

Sexual harassment is recognized as a form of sexual discrimination under Title VII of the Civil Rights Act (CRA) of 1964. Title VII prohibits employment discrimination based on an individual's race, color, religion, sex, or national origin. According to Title VII, it is an unlawful employment practice for an employer to fail or refuse to hire or to discharge any individual or otherwise discriminate with respect to compensation, terms, conditions, or privileges of employment because of race, sex, religion, color, or national origin. Title VII does not refer to sexual harassment per se, but to discrimination based on gender.

Interestingly, as some experts (Colson, 1996; Snaden, 1996) have noted, the drafters of the Civil Rights Act of 1964 did not originally intend to include gender as a protected class within the statute. In fact, Representative Howard Smith, a Southern legislator and ardent segregationalist, in a last-minute attempt to thwart the passage of the Civil Rights Act, inserted the word "gender" into the proposed legislation with the hope that this would demonstrate the absurdity of the bill and thus prevent its ratification. There had been no prior hearings or debate on the insertion of gender.

The statute did pass, thereby including women as a class of protected individuals. Because of the last-minute nature of the inclusion, there was no discussion or debate on the gender issue or its possible ramifications, nor is there substantive legislative history vis-à-vis gender. Given this lack of legislative history, gender discrimination in employment—with its complicated subdivisions of pregnancy discrimination and maternity leave, fetal protection, sexual harassment, and appearance requirements—has been a difficult issue for courts, regulatory agencies such as the Equal Employment Opportunity Commission (EEOC), and individuals and businesses.

The lack of legislative history is especially telling in the sexual harassment arena. It would seem reasonable to continue this overview by simply saying "sexual harassment as a particular form of gender discrimination is defined as . . . ." In reality, defining harassment has been difficult and is a problem with which policymakers, courts, and researchers have long struggled. Skaine (1996) notes that defining sexual harassment is both simple and complex. It is simple because harassment is unwelcome sexual behavior. It is complex because harassment can involve behaviors that in other contexts—for instance, outside the workplace—are considered positive and reaffirming. In fact, Childers (1993) notes that it is accurate to say that *some* sexual harassment is actionable under Title VII. A basic problem that has plagued the courts is that there is no consensus on what types of behaviors constitute sexual harassment.

Several often-cited definitions of sexual harassment are noticeably different in their wording and implications. Crosthwaite and Priest (1996), for example, mention a definition of sexual harassment as "unsolicited nonreciprocal male behavior that asserts a woman's sex role over her function as a worker" (p. 67). This definition implies that only males commit harassment, and only females can be the victims of harassment. MacKinon (1979) defines it as "the unwanted imposition of sexual requirements in the context of a relationship of differential power." She further clarifies this by mentioning more specific examples: "situations of persistent verbal suggestion, unwanted physical contact, straightforward proposition, and coerced intercourse . . . including insult, pressure, or intimidation having gender as its basis or referent" (p. 4).

In 1980, the EEOC (Bureau of National Affairs, 1981) established guidelines that define sexual harassment more broadly: "Sexual harassment is unwelcome sexual conduct when such conduct has the purpose or effect of unreasonably interfering with an individual's work performance or creating an intimidating, hostile, or offensive work environment" (p. 45). Although the EEOC guidelines do not have the effect of law, courts have often explicitly relied on them in the adjudication of sexual harassment decisions. As Childers (1993) notes, the guidelines seem to suggest that some incidents of unwelcome sexual conduct may not "unreasonably" interfere with work performance and may not create a hostile working environment. This begs another question: Is there such a thing as "reasonable" interference with work performance? According to these guidelines, therefore, only some forms of unwelcome conduct are actionable as sexual harassment.

TWO CATEGORIES OF SEXUAL HARASSMENT

A helpful prelude to exploring factors that may contribute to women's vulnerability to harassment is to provide more substance vis-à-vis definitions and examples of sexual harassment. This is critical, because vulnerability may be at least partially a function of the type of sexual harassment alleged to be occurring. Sexual harassment complaints generally fall into one of two broad categories: quid pro quo and hostile environment. Each of these will be discussed in more detail.

Quid Pro Quo Harassment

Typically, quid pro quo, the original cause of action for sexual harassment under Title VII, refers to a situation in which an employee is forced, directly or indirectly, to choose between giving in to a supervisor's sexual demands or forfeiting an economic benefit, such as a pay increase, a promotion, or continued employment. The landmark quid pro quo case, according to many legal experts (Grose, 1995) is *Barnes v. Costle* (1977).

In this case, Ms. Barnes, the complainant, was hired as an administrative assistant at the Environmental Protection Agency (EPA) at the GS-5 level. During a preemployment interview, she alleged, the director of the EPA promised that she would be promoted to grade GS-7 within 90 days. Shortly after she actually began working for the EPA, she claimed, the director initiated requests for sexual favors. He repeatedly asked her to join him for social activities after office hours; she repeatedly refused to do so. He repeatedly made remarks to her that were sexual in nature. He repeatedly suggested to her that if she had an affair with him, her employment status would be enhanced. Ms. Barnes continually resisted his "overtures," and responded to his contention that "many executives have affairs with their personnel" (p. 988) by stating that she preferred their relationship to remain strictly professional. The director then began a campaign to belittle her and to strip her of her job duties, eventually culminating in the decision to abolish her job in retaliation for her refusal to grant him sexual favors.

Ms. Barnes initially sought informal and then internal resolution of the matter but was unsuccessful. She then filed a lawsuit. The district court originally dismissed her complaint, concluding that such practices as demanding after-hours sex are not the type of discrimination that should be proscribed by Title VII. The allegations were deemed to be an "inharmonious personal relationship," that regardless of how reprehensible the conduct is, does not constitute an arbitrary barrier to continued employment.

After the district court ruling, Ms. Barnes sought a review from the U.S. Court of Appeals. The court of appeals heard Ms. Barnes's appeal, and concluded that Title VII must be construed liberally to achieve its objective. When Title VII was enacted, Congress recognized that it would be pointless to try and enumerate specific proscribed practices. Rather, the court of appeals concluded, each case must be judged according to the underlying principles of Title VII. Thus even though the behavior she complained of was not specifically mentioned in Title VII, the behavior could certainly be considered a gender-based barrier to employment. Consequently, Ms. Barnes won.

Hostile Environment Harassment

As MacKinon's (1979) definition suggests, the cause of action of sexual harassment has evolved to incorporate the concept of a hostile work environment—an atmosphere so sexually charged that the employee/victim may be uncomfortable, embarrassed, or even unable to work effectively. A hostile environment may be created in a variety of ways, including sexist or sexually oriented comments, jokes, or questions by colleagues or supervisors, physical touching, sexually oriented posters or cartoons in the work area, leering, or the proverbial "elevator eyes," to name but a few.

The original hostile environment sexual harassment case is *Meritor Savings Bank v. Vinson* (1986). In this case, the federal Supreme Court recognized that a hostile environment exists when sexual conduct has "the purpose or effect of unreasonably interfering with an individual's work performance or creating an intimidating, hostile, or offensive work environment" (p. 71). The plaintiff, Ms. Mechelle Vinson, was employed by the defendant bank for roughly 4 years until she was discharged for excessive use of sick leave. She sued her supervisor, Sidney Taylor, and the bank under Title VII, alleging that she had been the victim of sexual harassment by Taylor. Taylor had hired Vinson in 1974 as a teller trainee. During her first year on the job, Taylor invited her out to dinner and suggested that they have sexual relations. She initially refused his advances, but out of fear of losing her job, she agreed. Thereafter, Taylor made repeated demands for sexual favors, forcing Vinson to engage in sexual relations during and after business hours. Vinson estimated that she had intercourse with Taylor 40 to 50 times between 1975 and 1977. Taylor also fondled her in front of other employees, followed her into the women's restroom when she went there alone, exposed himself to her, and even forcibly raped her on several occasions.

Allegedly because of her fear of Taylor, Vinson never reported the problem to any of Taylor's superiors, and never used the bank's complaint procedure. The bank and Taylor denied all allegations of sexual misbehavior on his part. The bank also claimed that it could not be held responsible even if there was sexual activity, because it did not know of any sexual misconduct by Taylor.

Vinson spent several years moving through progressively higher levels of the court system. Lower courts concluded that although the situation was unfortunate, it reflected the behavior of consenting adults. Eventually, the case reached the federal Supreme Court. This court was not convinced that "consent" had occurred. Given that Taylor was and had always been Ms. Vinson's superior, with power over such work-related outcomes as raises, promotions, demotions, and so on, the Court established what has come to be known as the Meritor rule. This rule says that whenever there is a built-in power differential (for instance, a boss and a subordinate), the boss generally cannot use "consent" as a defense, given that "consent" may be due to fear of saying no.

The Court also developed a two-part definition of what constitutes a hostile environment under Title VII: The complainant must show that the sexual conduct was (a) sufficiently severe or pervasive so as to alter the conditions of the victim's employment and create an abusive working environment, and (b) unwelcome—that is, the complainant did not desire the sex-related conduct to take place.

According to Koen (1989), in *Vinson,* the Supreme Court resolved some issues in sexual harassment, but left many others unanswered. How severe and pervasive must the harassment be? How should offensiveness be determined or measured? How should a court determine whether or not conduct is unwelcome?

Some cases of sexual harassment, particularly those involving quid pro quo, are fairly obvious. If, for example, a supervisor says, "You must sleep with me or I will fire you," there is little ambiguity about whether or not harassment is occurring. However, it might be useful to know what factors could make a woman more vulnerable to quid pro quo harassment, and what characteristics predispose a perpetrator to engage in such behavior.

Identifying hostile environment sexual harassment, on the other hand, is often considerably more difficult. Since *Vinson,* according to Brown and Germanis (1994), lower courts have struggled to articulate some general rules about when alleged conduct is unwelcome. Such general rules would be helpful, because they would help clarify expectations about appropriate workplace behaviors and perhaps even provide general definitions or standards about what appropriate really means.

FACTORS CONTRIBUTING TO FEMALE VULNERABILITY

Legally, sexual harassment is not limited to the harassment of women by men but can encompass harassment of men by women and even same-sex harassment. Despite the popular assumption that "it's perfectly legal to sexually harass a man," both males and females are protected, by federal law, from illegal sexual harassment, and both males and females have been accused of—and found guilty of—committing harassment.

This legality notwithstanding, it is true that the vast majority of complaints about harassment come from females alleging harassment from males. In fact, according to statistics kept by the EEOC, roughly 90 percent of all harassment complaints filed between 1980 and 1990 involved females alleging harassment from males (Mathis & Jackson, 1997). Likewise, Skaine (1996) notes that some 42 percent of female respondents in surveys done by the U.S. Merit Systems Protection Board (in both 1980 and in 1988) reported that they had been harassed, whereas only 15 percent of men reported being harassed. Fitzgerald (1993) cites a disturbing government estimate that roughly 12,000 female federal workers were the victims of rape or attempted rape by supervisors or coworkers in a mere 2-year period. The parallel between sexual assault and sexual harassment is appropriate. Most experts recognize that the majority of sexual assaults—in fact, as many as one out of every seven—are not reported. Similarly, many instances of sexual harassment may also go unreported, possibly because those who are most vulnerable to harassment are also vulnerable economically. Thus although Fitzgerald (1993) insightfully notes that true epidemiological studies do not exist, large-scale surveys of working women suggest that approximately one out of two women will be harassed at some point during their academic or working lives or both.

Based on such statistics, it seems obvious that females are more vulnerable to sexual harassment in the workplace than are males. The next step, then, is to determine why—to identify factors/problems/unresolved legal issues that might affect women's vulnerability. To discuss possible contributing factors in a straightforward, consistent way, the following framework will be used:

- Problem: first, the problem(s) will be identified; this may involve unresolved legal issues, ethical dilemmas, organizational factors, individual factors, and so on.
- Solution: second, potential and actual solutions will be presented
- Conclusion: finally, the effectiveness (or potential effectiveness) of solutions will be discussed.

Three different sets of factors will be discussed, although it is recognized that there may be some overlap, and factors that may affect women's vulnerability do not necessarily fall with absolute precision into one and only one area. Many women, therefore, may be vulnerable for a number of different reasons.

The first factor that will be examined concerns an as-yet unresolved legal issue. In essence, this centers on gender differences in definitions of harassment. Do men and women really define harassment differently? In other words, is behavior that the "average" man would consider acceptable or appropriate viewed similarly by the average woman? To the extent that definitions or standards are very different, such differences could certainly contribute to women's increased vulnerability, particularly in a male-dominated work environment. This factor may be especially significant in the context of legal standards of reasonableness. If men and women do indeed have very different standards of what constitutes a "reasonable" environment or "reasonable" behavior, a "one-size-fits-all" legal standard of "reasonable" may be unrealistic and ineffective in helping create and maintain a comfortable work environment for all employees, male and female.

A second and complex set of potential factors affecting vulnerability is related to the first: perception and the influence of stereotypes on those perceptions. To what extent are perceptions of what is appropriate versus inappropriate in the workplace affected by external social mores, gender-related stereotypes, and so on? The discussion of the possible role of perception will focus on both individual perceptions and legal rulings. At the level of individual employees, to what extent do individuals, both males and females, base their expectations about workplace behavior on their experiences in the larger society? At the level of the legal system, to what extent should external social mores be considered in determining whether a hostile environment exists? Should the fact that a certain behavior is acceptable or condoned in society mean that same behavior should be acceptable in the workplace? If men and women have different expectations about appropriate cross-gender interactions in general, these differences in background and socialization may affect their experiences with harassment, both in the probability of experiencing harassment and in willingness to report harassment.

A third section will review the individual or micro factors—such as age, marital status, job level or physical appearance—that might affect women's vulnerability

to harassment. For example, are married or single women more vulnerable? Are
new employees more vulnerable? Finally, some general conclusions about the issue of harassment and directions for future research will be provided.

DO MEN AND WOMEN DEFINE HARASSMENT DIFFERENTLY?
THE REASONABLE PERSON/REASONABLE WOMAN/REASONABLE
VICTIM DEBATE

*Problem: Men and women may have very different standards of what consti-
tutes reasonable, thus making general legal standards difficult to establish.*

The issue of whether men and women differ in their definitions of sexual harassment—particularly hostile environment sexual harassment—has generated
much debate among researchers and lawmakers. Pollack (1990), for example,
notes that often behavior that women find offensive is accepted as "normal" or appropriate by men. Therefore, men may not believe a woman's versions of events,
or may question why a woman is or claims to be offended. Further, even when
women's reports of harassment are believed, men are often unconvinced that
women suffer any real harm from the behavior. For example, a man may say,
"Well, okay, I made a pass at her in the copy room, but what's the big deal?" Likewise, Childers (1993) argues that men and women often have very different perceptions of what is appropriate sexual conduct in the workplace (and in general)
and, therefore, different standards of what conduct is offensive or harassing.

Gutek (1995) notes that since social scientists started conducting systematic research on sexual harassment, it has become a truism that harassment has a large
subjective component. Also, she notes, it is generally assumed that women are
more likely than men to label similar or identical experiences sexual harassment,
suggesting that women have a broader definition of what constitutes harassment
than men do.

*Solution: Recognize the limitations of the reasonable person standard and ex-
plore other, more flexible ways of determining reasonableness.*

One effect of this assumption of different definitions is that it has been difficult
to clearly define reasonableness—that is, what is reasonable or unreasonable in
defining hostile environment. Differences in terminology may initially seem very
subtle. Some legal scholars have argued in favor of a "reasonable person" standard, whereas others advocate "reasonable woman" or even "reasonable victim."
The concern is that "reasonable person" may implicitly mean "reasonable man,"
and if men and women do indeed have different standards of reasonableness, this
may perpetuate an environment designed around male norms and thus leave
women more vulnerable to hostile environment sexual harassment.

A classic illustration of the inherent weakness of the reasonable person standard is provided by the case *Rabidue v. Osceola Refining* (1993). Although this
case is discussed in more detail below, certain elements are relevant in this discussion. In this case, the female plaintiff (and other female employees) were repeat-

edly referred to by a male coworker in highly pejorative terms, with "whore" and "fat ass" among the least offensive. The coworker also said of the plaintiff, "All that bitch needs is a good lay." He and other male employees insisted on displaying pornographic pictures of women in common areas. In one such picture—displayed for eight years—a naked, prone woman with a golf ball on her chest was lying beneath a fully clothed man who was yelling "Fore!" Using the reasonable person standard, the Sixth Circuit Court concluded that the obscenities, comments, and pictures, though "annoying" (p. 622), were not so terrible as to have seriously affected the plaintiff or other female employees. In fact, the court focused more on the plaintiff's supposedly "argumentative and uncooperative nature" (p. 615), apparently completely disregarding the possibility that her demeanor at work may have been a product of—or at least exacerbated by—the uncomfortable work environment.

The contention of some experts is that a reasonable woman standard would recognize the probability of different male-female standards and thus do more to protect women from harassment. In *Barbetta v. Chemlawn Services Corporation* (1987), for example, the plaintiff provided evidence of the posting of sexually oriented posters and calendars, use of vulgar comments by employees and supervisors, and unwanted physical contact of a sexual nature. The court stated that this conduct provided a basis for a hostile environment claim, because it could seriously affect the psychological well-being of a reasonable woman and interfere with her ability to perform her job. The fact that male employees had not complained about the sexually oriented material was irrelevant: If a reasonable woman would find the material offensive, that and that alone should provide a basis for a sexual harassment claim.

Likewise, in *Ellison v. Brady* (1993), the court applied the reasonable woman standard to protect a woman complaining of long-term harassment from a colleague. The plaintiff was in a difficult situation because of the actions of a male coworker. He repeatedly asked Ms. Ellison out on dates, which she turned down. He wrote a number of very detailed notes about his intense feelings for her. She was sufficiently frightened by his actions that she complained to her supervisor. After exhausting her administrative remedies, she decided to file a formal complaint. The district court determined that her allegations did not constitute a hostile environment, concluding that the behavior in question was "isolated and generally trivial" (p. 877)—a puzzling conclusion, given that the conduct had lasted for many months. On appeal, the Ninth Circuit Court adopted the reasonable woman standard, saying specifically that a reasonable woman could consider the conduct sufficiently severe and pervasive to constitute an actionable hostile environment claim, even if the conduct would not bother a reasonable man.

Although the use of a reasonable woman standard has some appeal, and possibly some advantages over the reasonable person standard, there are still several potential problems. The most basic problem is that a reasonable woman is difficult to define. Childers (1993), for example, notes that over the years, much criticism has been directed at the women's movement for being predominantly white and upper middle class, and possibly ignoring the circumstances and experiences of women of color and poor women. Thus "reasonable woman" may be implicitly synonymous with "reasonable upper middle class white woman," and may produce a skewed understanding of what women as a group identify as offensive sexual conduct. This is particularly significant in light of the demographics of the population of female victims (see below). Thus neither reasonable person nor reasonable woman are adequate standards for protecting the most typical victims of sexual harassment.

An even more serious problem is that the reasonable woman standard may sometimes be applied in a way that is disastrous for a female plaintiff. In the *Rabidue* case, for example, the district court that initially heard the case did apply a reasonable woman standard and concluded that an "average female employee" would find the conduct Ms. Rabidue complained of to be "trivial" or "merely annoying." The difficulty lies in attempting to determine what "typical" (p. 622) female employee means—of particular concern when the majority of judges are male.

An alternative to reasonable person and reasonable woman is reasonable victim. In essence, this standard would evaluate the offensiveness of the conduct from the point of view of the victim in that specific set of circumstances. This would allow for recognition of potential social and power differences between men and women and would also eliminate the possibility of general stereotyping of women as all the same. Childers (1993) notes that reasonable victim will eliminate the tendency to cling to a standard that may implicitly favor a male perspective. It will also eliminate the difficulty in attempting to define the "typical" or "average" woman.

Conclusion: A reasonable victim standard may provide a viable frame of reference for determining whether a hostile environment exists, because it would focus consideration on a specific victim or victims in a specific set of circumstances.

STEREOTYPES AND THE PERCEPTION OF SEXUAL HARASSMENT

Problem: Stereotypes—many of which are held by both men and women—may contribute to women's vulnerability by reinforcing patterns of power and sexism.

As noted above, sexual harassment—particularly hostile environment sexual harassment—has a large subjective component. It is often the perception of behavior or work environment that is problematic. Thus external social mores and stereotypes may play a significant role in determining standards of appropriate versus inappropriate behavior. A number of gender-related stereotypes may dramatically affect how "acceptable" behavior is defined. If what is "acceptable" (or in some cases actually expected or condoned) in society in general is also then implicitly or overtly considered acceptable in organizational settings, this may greatly increase women's vulnerability. Pechman (1993) notes that a problem in defining hostile environment is the extent to which consideration should be given to the prevalent mores in society. While an exhaustive discussion of gender-related stereotypes is beyond the scope of this chapter, several stereotypes may be of particular importance in the context of sexual harassment.

Gender and Power

Childers (1993) argues that sexual harassment is less about sex than it is about power, and that two dimensions of power—one related to job status and one related to gender—must be considered in evaluating a sexual harassment allegation. Grauerholz (1994) contends that individuals or groups in power (most often men) come to perceive power differently than those not in power (usually women). The white middle class, she argues, socializes women to be cooperative and associative; it socializes men to be competitive and domineering. Males are socialized to dominate both females and other males through verbal and nonverbal behaviors. Thus if both men and women are accustomed to the idea that it is appropriate for men to dominate and women to be submissive, women as a group are much more likely to be the targets of men's aggression. Although no one would argue that women are raised to believe that quid pro quo harassment is perfectly acceptable or "just part of the natural order of things," this power and gender stereotype could increase the likelihood of quid pro quo harassment occurring. Depending on the male's attitude, he might feel that he is expected to be aggressive toward a woman; he may even feel that it is his "right" to be aggressive and exercise his power. And depending on a variety of other individual factors (see below), the woman might find it difficult to deflect or protest his aggression. Paetzold and Shaw (1994) contend that we must not forget that sexual harassment in organizations represents the power and control that patriarchy has given men over women. Little systematic research addressing the issue of socioeconomic differences exists. For example, it is unclear whether these socialization trends are universal or vary across socioeconomic level.

Even at lower levels of harassment, women may feel offended or threatened by aggressive behaviors such as leering, unwelcome touching, dirty jokes, and so on. But if she has been socialized to be submissive and accommodating, she may feel that it is inappropriate for her to protest. In other words, she may feel that "boys will be boys." Indeed, Gruber and Smith (1995) note that women generally give fairly nonassertive responses to harassment when the harassment is not severe.

Gender and Sexual Responsibility

Another stereotype mentioned by many experts is that women are often assumed to be the guardians of proper sexual behavior. The cliche is that a man is entitled to "sow his wild oats." Even if such behavior (which implies promiscuity and a lack of sexual responsibility) is not overtly condoned, it tends to be regarded with a "boys will be boys" mentality, or a wink and a nod. Men may be stereotyped as being naturally more promiscuous, more sexually aggressive, and so on, whereas women are regarded as being the responsible party. A man who makes suggestive comments, talks about his sex life, or actively pursues the opposite sex is perceived much differently from a woman who behaves the same way.

We have only to listen to such expressions as "she asked for it" to see how this stereotype may operate in general. In fact, even in the context of sexual assault, such myths as "why was she dressed like that?" or "why did she go to a bar in the first place?" help underscore the sad fact that it is the woman who is somehow assumed to be responsible for the behavior of the man. The assumption seems to be that he can't control his behavior, so it's her job to do so.

In the context of harassment, this stereotype may be harmful in several related ways. First, it may make it difficult for a woman to complain, fearing that it is *her* credibility that will be questioned. For example, she may be concerned about what a complaint about sexual harassment says about her, along the lines of "What was she doing that he came on to her? Nice girls don't get harassed." Jensen and Gutek (1982) found that some women do blame themselves for the harassment, and are thus less likely to report it. In fact, Bravo and Cassedy (1994) mention a common myth about sexual harassment: "Women who make it clear that the behavior is unwelcome don't get harassed" (p. 28). The implication is that either the woman did something to invite the harassment, or she failed to make it clear that the harassment was unwelcome. After all, if it really bothered her, she'd say so, wouldn't she? If he keeps it up, it must be her fault for not doing something about it.

Second, such stereotypes will unfortunately affect efforts at education and long-term prevention. If we continue to focus mostly on what the woman must have done, or—the focus of this chapter notwithstanding—how women might make themselves less vulnerable, we will fail to focus on the real source of the harassment: the male's behavior. Again, this is analogous to sexual assault: Although it is worthwhile to provide advice to females on how they can reduce their odds of being assaulted, ultimately, we need to recognize that women are not assaulted because of how they dress or where they go or how they identify themselves on the mailbox in their apartment building.

The Objectification of Women

Portraying women as sex objects—or even (at a lower level) judging a woman's value largely by her physical attractiveness—may affect women's vulnerability to harassment in the work place. Numerous experts (Davis, 1990; Henderson-King & Henderson-King, 1997) in a variety of fields have discussed the objectification of women. In advertising, for example, attractive (often scantily clad) women have long been used to sell a variety of products, from beer to cars. The implication, of course, is that a "babe" goes along with the product.

Even in magazines directed at women, advertising and article content is often largely devoted to ways in which women can take steps to improve their appearance. Overall, both women and men may be socialized to believe that a woman's value is determined primarily by her appearance, so the more attractive she is, the better. The net result may be that there is an assumption that it is acceptable—perhaps even de riguer—to look, study, evaluate, comment, and judge women's appearance. It may be assumed, in other words, that it is perfectly acceptable to discuss women in terms of their physical attractiveness and sex appeal, or to display pictures or images of women who meet the criteria. Perhaps this means making remarks about the breasts of a female coworker. Perhaps it means displaying pictures of buxom women in bikinis as an ideal of femininity. Bravo and Cassedy (1994) mention myths about sexual harassment that may reinforce this stereotype, such as "you can't blame a guy for looking" or "women send mixed signals" (p. 31). The end result may be a no-win situation for many women. If a woman is not sufficiently attractive or sexy or alluring, she may be devalued for failing to meet the ideal of femininity. If she is attractive, however, her attractiveness is taken as license to look, comment, or perhaps even touch.

In the context of professional relationships, the objectification of women may work to devalue a woman's professional achievements. If she is still ultimately judged on how she looks, she is less likely to enjoy the kind of power that comes primarily from professional accomplishments. This, in fact, may be conflated with men's and women's different perceptions of what is reasonable. Childers (1993) provides an example of this conflict. If a man tells a female coworker that she always looks very nice when she comes to work, and that he'd love to take her out to dinner sometime, is this harassment? In his opinion, he may feel that he's simply being friendly and pursuing a potential date. In her opinion, she may think that she can't be taken seriously as a colleague if he's focusing on her appearance and asking her out.

In the often-cited case, *Rabidue v. Osceola Refining Company* (1986), also mentioned earlier, the Sixth Circuit Court of Appeals found that the conduct complained of by the female plaintiff was not sufficiently pervasive or severe so as to constitute illegal harassment. The plaintiff's supervisor made obscene comments to her and was in general vulgar and crude. Other male employees displayed nude and scantily clad pictures of women in their work areas, including the picture of a naked, prone women with a golf ball between her breasts. The court stated that the obscenities, although annoying, were not so startling as to have seriously affected any female employee. The majority of the court focused on Ms. Rabidue's supposedly "irascible" and "opinionated" personality and her alleged inability to work with others. The court did not consider the possibility that these traits were caused by, or at least exacerbated by, the environment in the workplace.

Most significantly with respect to the issue of the objectification of women, the pictures posted on office walls, according to the court, had minimal effect on the work environment when considered in the context of a society that condones, publicly features, and commercially exploits erotic material. In essence, the court ruled that because erotic material is prevalent and widely accepted in society in general, why should it be censored in the workplace? This is a puzzling conclusion, given that it is precisely because of the existence of such social problems as racism and sexism that fair employment laws such as Title VII were deemed necessary. If sexism in the workplace is allowed because society as a whole is sexist, it is unclear how fair employment laws are supposed to apply to protect employment rights.

Conclusion: Sexual harassment may often be something of a vicious cycle, where the sexism and stereotyping that compromise the economic advancement of women are echoed in the workplace in such a way so as to perpetuate those problematic stereotypes.

How to combat these perceptions and stereotypes? It is difficult to imagine how any individual woman could change deeply engrained stereotypes that affect her. Certainly, encouraging women to be assertive about their professional roles and to separate professional roles from stereotypical feminine roles may result in tiny or local advances. However, the larger issue is the society that encourages male dominance/female compliance, a double standard, and the objectification of women. Perhaps a viable starting point is to focus on education as a means of gradually changing perceptions and stereotypes. Sexual harassment education has been used on some college campuses to combat the problem in educational settings. Rather than concentrate mostly on how women can make themselves less vulnerable, such education addresses *male* roles and responsibilities. Similar educational efforts in the workplace directed at reducing sexual harassment might be beneficial in the long run.

Solution: Explore ways to educate both males and females to recognize and, ideally, avoid or reduce, the stereotypes that contribute to women's vulnerability to harassment.

INDIVIDUAL FACTORS

Problem: A variety of individual factors may make women more vulnerable to harassment and also make them less likely to complain.

As noted above, it is often difficult—and in fact, it may be unrealistic—to assume that the factors contributing to women's vulnerability are independent. In addition to unresolved or ambiguous legal standards and the influence of stereotyping and perception, women may also be more vulnerable to harassment depending on a variety of individual characteristics and circumstances. A number of individual factors have been studied in attempts to identify which women might be most vulnerable to sexual harassment. It should be noted, however, that interpretation of the significance of these factors can be difficult, as the factors that render a woman more vulnerable to harassment may also make her less likely to formally complain. In addition, the stereotypes mentioned above may exert considerable influence, particularly if a woman feels that her credibility and professionalism will be questioned.

The first Merit Systems Protection Board (MSPB) study indicated that of those female victims reporting sexual harassment, 50 percent were trainees, 67 percent were between the ages of 16 and 19, and 47 percent earned a low income (Skaine, 1996). Skaine (1996) notes that many subsequent studies have compared results with those of the MSPB.

Level in Organization

According to Skaine (1996), one potentially important individual factor concerns level in the organization. Given the significance of power in situations of sexual harassment, it is reasonable to expect that those women (and potentially those men) in lower level positions are naturally more vulnerable.

Some researchers have expressed organizational level as a function of income—for instance, higher income level = higher status. In the MSPB study, of women who reported that they had experienced sexual harassment of some type, women earning $121 per week or more experienced mostly verbal harassment, whereas those earning $92 per week or less experienced mostly physical harassment. Although it is unclear what might explain this finding, a possible explanation is that those in lower level positions are simply easier prey. There are more people above them, so the likelihood of someone misusing power, even in a very overt way, increases. Also, given their lack of economic power, they may be less likely to complain, although this would best be addressed by anonymous surveys.

A number of other researchers addressed the victim's salary rate. Robinson-Beeman (1980), for example, found that higher incidence rates of sexual harassment were associated with women at higher income levels, whereas the Merit Systems Protection Board (1981) found little variation among salary grades. Terpstra and Cook (1985) argue that rather than reflecting the relative incidence rate, complainant salary distribution can more likely be explained by financial status: People with a reasonable income may be more likely to file a formal complaint because they have the financial means to do so. Indeed, level in organization is quite often conflated with factors such as education and income, thereby making summary conclusions difficult. Some experts (Gutek, 1995; Terpstra & Cook, 1985) have found that educated women are more likely to report that they would be insulted if propositioned at work. To the extent that education equals higher organizational status, it would be reasonable to speculate that better educated women are harassed less frequently, simply because they are usually in higher level positions. Also, well-educated women may have a better understanding of their legal rights and more confidence in finding another job and thus may be less reluctant to complain.

Other researchers have found contradictory results. Some have focused their attention more specifically on occupation. Professionals (for instance, scientists, engineers, lawyers, and teachers) may be less likely to file formal charges, perhaps due to a strong professional network and concerns over reputation and quality of future references. As noted above, there are often negative opinions of the victim's behavior, and fears of what might travel through a professional grapevine may dissuade some professional women from filing. Still another consideration in this context is the source of the harassment. Although well-educated women may be less likely to be harassed by superiors, harassment can also come from peers. Skaine (1996), for example, notes that males might be inclined to harass well-educated female peers if they perceive that such women constitute a significant threat to their job status. Fitzgerald (1993) notes that prevalence rates of sexual harassment are highest, in fact, in workplaces where women have traditionally been underrepresented. Here again, women often face something of a no-win situation: Because traditionally male-dominated occupations tend to carry higher pay and better status, women might seek education and training to gain entry to such occupations. If they are perceived as an economic threat by men in those occupations, however, their work environment and long-term work experience might be significantly compromised by various forms of sexual harassment.

Another consideration vis-à-vis organizational level is tenure. It is reasonable to speculate that there may be an inverse relationship between tenure and vulnerability to harassment. A new employee does not "know the ropes," and is typically eager to please and reluctant to make waves (Dusky, 1996). Because women are much more likely to change jobs during their work lives than are men, women are, de facto, more vulnerable to harassment based on lack of job tenure.

The last consideration that will be mentioned in this context is employee performance. Many organizations attempt to systematically measure or assess job performance to make decisions about employment-related outcomes such as raises, promotions, demotions, and so on. The effect of performance on vulnerability to harassment could go both ways. On one hand, an employee whose performance is judged to be poor may feel less secure, less confident about finding another job, less comfortable saying "no," less likely to be credible. Therefore, women whose job performance is less than stellar may be more vulnerable to harassment. On the other hand, women whose performance is exemplary, particularly those in male-dominated occupations, may be perceived as a significant threat, thus making them more vulnerable to certain kinds of harassment.

Although the philosophy of systematic performance appraisal is commendable, the reality may be much different. In settings in which there is little or no effort made to identify objective, appropriate criteria and measure employees against those criteria, there may be little consistency or objectivity. When an annual performance review, for example, includes "measurement" of such vague constructs as "attitude," the results may unfortunately be biased and inaccurate. Imagine, for example, the reaction of a supervisor whose subordinate has formally complained about his sexist behavior. Thus even with additional research in this area, it may be difficult to make meaningful generalizations. Unless there is confidence that an appraisal system is straightforward, consistent, and objective, it is unclear how to best tease out a possible relationship between job performance and vulnerability.

Age

Most studies suggest that younger women are more vulnerable to harassment than are older women. The MSPB survey, for example, indicated that 67 percent of the victims were between the ages of 16 and 19. Maypole and Skaine (1982) report that some 92 percent of the female victims in their study were in their twenties or thirties (Skaine, 1996). Some researchers (Fitzgerald & Ormerod, 1993) point out that caution must be used in interpreting this statistic. Victims of sexual harassment have been mythologized as sexy or "hot," for instance, a randy older boss pursuing a sexy, alluring young female employee. The reality is that age is often—and obviously—strongly related to factors such as experience and tenure. A young woman almost always has less work experience, less tenure at an employer, and thus less power.

Marital Status

Another individual factor that has been studied is marital status. Most studies indicate that single women experience harassment more often than do married women. In the MSPB report, for example, 53 percent of single women reported being harassed, compared to 37 percent of married women (Skaine, 1996). It is quite possible that some male coworkers and supervisors believe it is socially acceptable to pursue relationships with single females at work; thus when harassment takes the form of repeatedly asking someone out on a date or even frequently complimenting someone on their appearance, it may be a function of a male attempting to pursue a romantic relationship with a seemingly available woman. In addition, a single woman may fear complaining, as she may not have the support of another paycheck, thus making her economic situation somewhat more precarious. However, some studies have found very different results vis-à-vis marital status. Maypole and Skaine (1983), for example, found that 92 percent of the females reporting harassment were married. Marital status, in fact, may be something of a red herring in harassment situations. Vulnerability may be more a function of factors such as organizational power.

Race/Ethnicity

Although woefully little systematic data is available, some researchers argue that Hispanic women and African American women are more likely to be victims of harassment. Gutek (1985), for example, in an anonymous survey that went beyond reported harassment, found that roughly one third of 824 harassment victims studied were non-White, a percentage indicating considerable overrepresentation of minorities in the class of victims. It is tempting to argue that this may because they are stereotyped as more promiscuous or "easy" or "hot," but a far more practical explanation (Fitzgerald & Omrerod, 1993) is economic need. Because minorities in general and minority females in particular may be concentrated toward the lower end of the economic ladder, by definition they have less power in their respective organizations. And they may feel less confident about finding another job or about being taken seriously if they complain.

Conclusion: A variety of individual factors may affect a woman's vulnerability to harassment and also her willingness to formally complain about harassment. Research results on many of these factors are often either contradictory or nonexistent.

As noted above, many individual characteristics may make a woman more vulnerable to harassment, particularly in light of the unresolved legal issues and a number of sexist stereotypes. Unfortunately, such factors may also make a woman less likely to formally complain about harassment, thus many studies admittedly underestimate the true prevalence of harassment. An appropriate research agenda will thus involve large-scale studies with diverse respondent populations to ask about both reported and unreported harassment experiences. An appropriate organizational agenda might emphasize being cognizant of the relationship between organizational power (or lack thereof) and vulnerability to harassment. Concerted efforts to then focus on education and prevention, as well as aggressively dealing with formal complaints of harassment, may reduce the frequency of such harassment over the long run.

Solution: Collect more systematic data on frequency of harassment and develop organizational policies that focus on prevention and support toward women who might be most vulnerable.

CONCLUSION

Sexual harassment is a complex set of behaviors and experiences that may have compounding effects on both individuals and businesses. Although it seems to be a relatively new phenomenon, based on applicable legislation and case law, it is, in reality, an age-old problem. Fitzgerald (1993), for example, notes that sexual harassment has been a fixture of working life since women first offered their labor for sale in the marketplace. The harassment of working women and their resistance to such harassment in America is documented in historical research accounts as early as colonial times. It is troubling that some two centuries later, roughly half of all women are victims of harassment at some point in their working lives.

Something as seemingly simple as defining harassment is difficult, as the plethora of definitions mentioned above illustrates. Even the EEOC's definition may be inadequate or confusing when superimposed against real-life behavior and experiences. Sexual harassment is further complicated by the fact that contextual factors such as workplace demographics are significant. Indeed, the panoply of factors reviewed above may often interact to affect both vulnerability to harassment and likelihood of reporting harassment.

Some summary statements on harassment might include the following. First, it is essential to understand that harassment is pervasive and may affect the employment experiences of virtually all working women at some point in their work lives. Even though victims do not have to demonstrate serious psychological injury (Colson, 1996; Gehring, 1994), there may still be significant and costly adverse consequences for organizations as well as individual victims that are far beyond the obvious cost of a lawsuit. Increased turnover, decreased morale, or a deterioration in trust and in the quality of intercollegial relations may represent huge costs. Indeed, additional research on both short- and long-term individual and organizational consequences is necessary.

Second, it is reasonable to advocate legal standards that attempt to recognize the complexity of sexual harassment. The reasonable victim standard, for example, attempts to take context into account rather than applying a "one-size-fits-all" definition to all actions and all circumstances. Given the often-subjective nature of many alleged instances of sexual harassment, a legal framework that can recognize the uniqueness of different victims in different circumstances would be helpful.

Third, it may be beneficial to focus more effort on prevention. Although women can take steps to reduce their vulnerability, women—indeed, any victims—ultimately are harassed not because of what they do or how they dress but because of the socialization of the harasser. If the workplace or society implicitly condones behavior that is demeaning and even offensive to women, that must be recognized and corrected. Given that women still have not achieved economic equality (Norton, 1994), identifying and removing obstacles to women's continued economic progress, including sexual harassment, is essential. The goal, ultimately, is a workplace that is comfortable and free from harassment for all employees.

REFERENCES

Barbetta v. Chemlawn (1987). 669 FSupp 569.

Barnes v. Costle (1977). 561 F2d 983.

Bravo, E., & Cassedy, E. (1994). Yes, the 9 to 5 guide to combating sexual harassment. In K. Fintersbusch & G. McKenna (Eds.), *Taking Sides* (pp. 24–27). Guilford, CT: Dushkin Publishing Co.

Brown, B. B., & Germanis, I. L. (1994). Hostile environment sexual harassment: Has *Harris* really changed things? *Employee Relations Law Journal, 19*(4), 567–578.

Bureau of National Affairs (1981). *Labor relations reporter: EEOC guidelines on sexual harassment* [Vol. 107(23)]. Washington, DC: Author.

Childers, J. (1993). Is there a place for a reasonable woman in the law? A discussion of recent developments in hostile environment sexual harassment. *Duke Law Journal, 42,* 854–904.

Colson, K. A. (1996). *Harris v. Forklift Systems, Inc.*: The Supreme Court moves one step closer to establishing a workable definition for hostile work environment sexual harassment claims. *New England Law Review, 30,* 441–474.

Crosthwaite, J., & Priest, G. (1996). The definition of sexual harassment. *Australasian Journal of Philosophy, 74*(1), 66–82.

Davis, S. (1990). Men as success objects and women as sex objects: A study of personal advertisements. *Sex Roles, 23*(1–2), 43–50.

Dusky, L. (1996). *Still unequal.* New York: Crown Publishers, Inc.

Ellison v. Brady (1991). 54 FEP Cases 1346.

Fitzgerald, L. F. (1993). Sexual harassment: Violence against women in the workplace. *American Psychologist, 48*(10), 1070–1076.

Fitzgerald, L. F. & Ormerod, A. J. (1993). Breaking silence: the sexual harassment of women in academia and the workplace. In F. L. Denmark & M. A. Paludi (Eds.), *Psychology of women: A handbook of issues & theories* (pp. 181–298). Westport, CT: Greenwood Press.

Gehring, T. J. (1994). Hostile environment sexual harassment after *Harris*: Abolishing the requirement of psychological injury. *Thurgood Marshall Law Review, 19,* 450–474.

Grauerholz, E. (1994). Gender socialization and communication: The inscription of sexual harassment in social life. In S. C. Bingham (Ed.), *Conceptualizing sexual harassment as a discursive practice* (pp. 68–99). Westport, CT: Praeger.

Grose, C. (1995). Same-sex harassment: Subverting the heterosexist paradigm of Title VII. *Yale Journal of Law and Feminism, 7,* 375–398.

Gruber, J. E., & Smith, M. D. (1995). Women's responses to sexual harassment: A multivariate analysis. *Basic and Applied Social Psychology, 17*(4), 543–562.

Gutek, B. A. (1995). How subjective is sexual harassment? An examination of rater effects. *Basic and Applied Social Psychology, 17*(4), 446–467.

Henderson-King, E., & Henderson-King, D. (1997). Media effects on women's body esteem: Social and individual factors. *Journal of Applied Social Psychology, 27*(5), 399–417.

Jensen & Gutek, B. A. (1982). Attributions & assignment for responsibility in sexual harassment. *Journal of Social Issues, 38*(4), 121–136.

Koen, C. M. (1989). Sexual harassment: Criteria for defining hostile environment. *Employee Responsibilities and Rights Journal, 2*(4), 289–301.

Maypole, D. E., & Skaine, R. (1983). Sexual harassment in the workplace. *Social Work, 28*(5), 385–390.

MacKinon, C. A. (1979). *Sexual harassment of working women: A case of sex discrimination.* New Haven, CT: Yale University Press.

Mathis, & Jackson (1997). *Human resource management* (8th ed.). Minneapolis, MN: West Publishing.

Meritor Savings Bank v. Vinson (1986). 477 U.S. 57.

Norton, S. M. (1994). Pregnancy, the family, and work: An historical review and update of legal regulations and organizational policies and practices in the United States. *Gender, Work, & Organization, 1*(4), 217–226.

Paetzold, R. L., & Shaw, B. (1994). A postmodern feminist view of "reasonableness" in hostile environment sexual harassment. *Journal of Business Ethics, 13,* 681–691.

Pechman, L. (1993). Emerging issues in hostile work environment sexual harassment. *New York State Bar Journal, 65*(3), 38–41, 59.

Pollack, W. (1990, Spring). Sexual harassment: Women's experiences versus legal definitions. *Harvard Women's Law Journal,* 35–85.

Rabidue v. Osceola Refining Company. (1986). 805 F2d 611.

Robinson-Beeman, R. (1980). *Sexual harassment in the workplace.* Master's thesis, Sangamon State University, Illinois.

Skaine, R. (1996). *Power and gender: Issues in sexual dominance and harassment.* Jefferson, NC: McFarland & Co.

Snaden, S. L. (1996). Baring it all at the workplace: Who bears the responsibility? *Connecticut Law Review, 28,* 1225–1258.

Terpstra, D. E., & Cook. S. E. (1985). Complainant characteristics and reported behaviors and consequences associated with formal sexual harassment charges. *Personnel Psychology, 38*(3), 559–574.

6

HETEROSEXUAL MEN AS TARGETS: THE SHADOW SIDE OF SEXUAL HARASSMENT

Ronald B. Simono

As with many writers, Tang and McCollum (1996) saw the EEOC's definition of sexual harassment as reflecting situations that would arise when females were the sole objects of behavior that could include "verbal abuse, sexist remarks regarding a woman's body, ogling, etc." with the assumption being that sexual harassment is something that is perpetrated only by men upon women. In citing the EEOC definition, Tang and McCollum underlined that it included,

Unwelcome sexual advances, requests for sexual favors, and other verbal or physical conduct of a sexual nature constitutes sexual harassment when (1) submission to such conduct is made either explicitly or implicitly a term or condition of an individual's employment, (2) submission to or rejection of such conduct by an individual is used as a basis for employment decisions affecting such individual, or (3) such conduct has the purpose of unreasonably interfering with an individual's work performance or creating an intimidating, hostile, or offensive work environment. (p. 54)

The purpose of this chapter is to look at sexual harassment of men in the workplace. The focus here will be heterosexual men because the topic of the harassment of gay men or men who are perceived to be gay is the subject of another chapter in this text.

LANDMARK CASES AND PUBLIC PERCEPTIONS OF SEXUAL HARASSMENT OF MEN

The problem of sexual harassment of men in the workplace was arguably first brought to the attention of the general public through Michael Crichton's (1994) book, *Disclosure,* and the film by the same title starring Michael Douglas and

Demi Moore in 1995 as well as by broad media coverage of Joseph Oncale's suit against Sundowner Offshore Services. *Disclosure* involved a man, portrayed by Michael Douglas, being harassed by his female superior, portrayed by Demi Moore. The Oncale case involved a man being harassed by his male supervisors. In 1986 the Supreme Court of the United States had ruled unwanted sexual overtures on the job illegal but seemed to have avoided attempts to set the legal boundaries for sexual harassment.

Articles in the *Wall Street Journal,* the *Christian Science Monitor, US News and World Report, Jet,* and *Time* (see references) covered the Joseph Oncale story from the moment his case was filed to a lower court ruling that threw out his case and finally onto the U.S. Supreme Court. Labor legal experts differed on whether Title VII of the Civil Rights Act applied to same-sex harassment situations. However, in the spring of 1997, the Justice Department urged the Supreme Court to hear this case and the stage was set for a precedent-setting decision. Three separate same-sex sexual harassment suits had been refused a hearing by the Court one year earlier. The Court settled the question of this application of Title VII on March 4, 1998, when they ruled unanimously that same-sex harassment in the workplace was a violation of federal civil rights law. Justice Antonin Scalia asserted, "We see no justification in the statutory language or our precedents for a categorical rule of excluding same-sex harassment claims from the coverage of Title VII" (Supreme Court backs, p. 128). Although this outcome was welcomed by gay rights advocates, the issue of the sexual orientation of Mr. Oncale or the defendants was not addressed (Bull, 1997).

Joseph Oncale, an oil rig worker for Sundowner Offshore Services, accused his male supervisors in 1994 of behavior that clearly would be prohibited by Title VII of the Civil Rights Act if such behavior were to occur between individuals of opposite gender. He was a heterosexual father of two, and the alleged perpetrators were heterosexual. While working on an offshore oil rig he charged these male supervisors with physical assault of a sexual nature as well as intimidating threats; the assaults and the threats were alleged to have occurred in 1991. Out of fear, he eventually quit his job and filed suit after his reports to company officials went unheeded. When the Supreme Court was hearing his case, sexual harassment claims by men totaled about 11 percent of all such cases filed at the EEOC with most of these being same-sex harassment (Marquand, 1997). Two years earlier, Merrick (1995) reported a survey done in Britain during the week that the movie *Disclosure* opened. Seven percent of a sample of 400 men and women reported knowledge of male employees being harassed by female coworkers. This was in contrast to a survey (Townsend & Luthar, 1995) reported by the U.S. Merit Systems Protection Board, which put the percent of men reported being sexually harassed as high as 15 percent compared to 40 percent for women.

How does one distinguish boorish and crude behavior from something that would meet definitions for sexual harassment? Writing in *Time,* John Cloud (1998) observed that in the Oncale case Justice Scalia had noted that the Supreme

Court was not establishing a "general civility code" (p. 55), and David Savage (1998) wrote in the *ABA Journal* that nothing in this ruling forbids "horseplay" among men.

This issue concerning harassment of men was raised a decade earlier in 1982 in the United States District Court, Western District of Wisconsin. In that case, David Huebschen, supervisor in the Bureau of Social Security and Disability Insurance for the State of Wisconsin, alleged that his immediate supervisor, a female, demoted him because he refused to continue a sexual relationship with her in the fall of 1979, a liaison that had been started with mutual consent. The court decided in favor of the plaintiff. In the 1990s, there were other charges of sexual harassment of men but none received the attention that the Joseph Oncale situation did. For example, at Jenny Craig, Inc. (Carton, 1994), male employees complained of sexual harassment that took the form of "lewd comments" and inappropriate behavior from female employees. One year later, David Papa, an employee of Domino's Pizza charged his supervisor, a female, with firing him after he had rebuked her sexual advances, a dismissal that came after she had previously nominated him for "manager of the year." He reported that when he talked to prospective employers about his complaints of sexual harassment at Domino's against a female supervisor, he was met with disbelief as if such a situation could not have happened to a man. This was the first time that a case where a female perpetrating sexual harassment of a man resulted in a federal judge deciding in favor of the plaintiff, a decision which resulted in a $237,000 award for Mr. Papa (The chain must pay, 1995). Two years later a male stockbroker in Stamford, Connecticut, claimed that he was pressured to have sex with his female supervisor and he filed a complaint with the Connecticut Commission on Human Rights and Opportunities. He alleged that the company vice president had told him to have sex with his supervisor "for the company." The stockbroker did, but when he decided not to continue the relationship he feared he would lose his job although the company denied these allegations after an internal investigation found "no grounds" for the complaint (Broker says, 1997). The world of finance continued to be challenged when in the late 1990s (Davis, 1998) Eric Kurschus, a man in his early thirties making $117,000 a year as a sales assistant, consented to a sexual encounter with the wife of his boss at Paine-Webber. This notion of mutual consent was similar to aspects of the relationship present in the Huebschen case mentioned above. The Paine-Webber case became quite acrimonious when charges and countercharges were leveled, and Kurschus was arrested and charged with forcing his supervisor's wife to have oral sex. After he lost his job, he sued his boss and his boss's wife for malicious prosecution and he sued Paine-Webber alleging sexual harassment stating that his boss's wife's aggressive pursuit of him led to the problems in the first place. Finally on May 19, 1999, the seriousness of same-sex harassment was underscored when an El Paso, Texas, jury awarded $7.3 million to a shoe salesman who said that he had been sexually harassed by his male boss (Same sex verdict, 1999).

MEN AND SEXUAL HARASSMENT: PROBLEMS OF PERCEPTION AND DEFINITION

When talking about men as the objects of sexual harassment, Gutek writing in 1985 said, "Sexual harassment is not a problem for them" (p. 158). She acknowledged that her research found that men reported behaviors directed toward them that would indicate interest in sexual involvement from women but that the men were not likely to experience this as harassment or to report the kinds of negative effect upon their work or career advancement that was reported by females. Certainly, Gutek's work in the middle 1980s helped to establish the notion that sexual harassment presents fewer problems for men even though there is evidence of situations that have occurred with male employees. Gutek (1985) presented survey data that showed that when men were the objects of sexual harassment, they were likely to be slightly older than the average male worker; when married, less likely to report experiences of sexual harassment than unmarried men did; education, occupation and income were not related in her study to sexual harassment when reported by men. Specific behaviors directed at men such as being sexually touched or required to date or have sex with a woman at work were often seen by the men as having positive outcomes for them or to have taken place in the context of a mutually rewarding relationship. This was never the case from the standpoint of women in this study who were objects of such behavior.

Other influential writers have viewed sexual harassment as primarily a women's issue. When looking at higher education, Paludi (1990) presented the issue of sexual harassment on college and university campuses as a problem perpetrated by male professors with status and power used to coerce, subtly or otherwise, undergraduate and graduate female students. Although it seems valid to assume that this would be the situation in most cases of sexual harassment on college and university campuses, one is left to wonder whether or not men on any campus would find it as difficult to level a complaint as would his counterpart in business and industry. There would seem to be less stigma in an academic environment to a man complaining that he was the victim of sexual harassment than in corporate/industrial America, which arguably is less open or sympathetic to such a claim from men.

Fitzgerald, Swan, and Magley (1997) raised a good question as to whether something that may be offensive to men when coming from other men in a male-dominated workplace is really the same as harassment. These authors did a very good job of pointing out the methodological problems in researching the extent to which men in the workforce are sexually harassed and that using the same questionnaires to survey men and women assumes that sexually explicit or implicit behavior has no meaning or impact separate from gender. Some men may be put off by or find tasteless, stories, jokes, and pranks perpetrated by other men in the workplace but probably for the most part they would not see such behaviors as harassment specifically directed at them. Therefore, the point is well taken that questionnaires that assume identical responses from both genders to such actions would be problematic. However, others (Pryor & Whalen, 1997) have taken a different slant and have looked at the extent to which the person being mistakenly labeled as homosexual might be associated with harassment from other men. They reported that male-to-male sexual harassment is much more common than thought, apart from whether one is labeled gay or not, and often takes the form of inappropriate inquires, comments, and humor.

When looking at sexual harassment research, Vaux (1993) explored assumptions that characterized men as the perpetrators of violent behavior toward women and questioned the validity of seeing most men as potential perpetrators and most women as potential victims. Vaux acknowledged that such sweeping generalizations, prevalent since the 1980s, have undermined writing and research in the area of sexual harassment. Another particular slant seemed present in Colker's (1995) very thought-provoking article, which suggested that sexual harassment complaints on the part of white heterosexual men are at times given more validity in our system and that more is required of women in terms of successfully pleading their cases. She broadened her discussion of sexual harassment doctrine to include other kinds of gender-based discrimination and asserted that more was asked of women, racial minorities, and gay and lesbian people in demonstrating harm than was asked of white heterosexual men. She underscored a good point that sexual advances are intended to demean and objectify the victim and that whether the reason for the attraction is heterosexuality or homosexuality should not make any difference. Certainly when men are harassed by other men there will always be official and unofficial inquiries as to whether the person lodging the complaint is heterosexual or homosexual as if a determination one way or the other would validate or invalidate a man's claim. This assumption that any male who has been harassed by other males is homosexual was called into question by the Oncale case cited earlier.

RESEARCH STUDIES ON SEXUAL HARASSMENT OF MEN

In the late 1980s, Vaux (1993) was part of a research project at a midwestern university that looked at sexual harassment and utilized the Sexual Experiences Questionnaire. Although when this survey was done, men and women were included, the participation of men was seen as a "political safeguard" (p. 119). The level of harassment reported by females was similar to those in other studies at that time, but surprise was registered by the rates of harassment reported by men, which were considerably higher than expected, often similar to the rates of females. The types of sexual harassment reported twice as often by women than men were sexual seduction and sexual imposition, both being reported by graduate students. The author speculated that men might be excluded from theoretical discussions of sexual harassment as well as empirical studies because there is a sense that men are not exposed to significant harassment, which leads to their potential as victims being dismissed. This has been reflected by other observers who see sexual harassment as oxymoronic when applied to stereotypic males who experience such things as unwanted sexual advances from females.

When men in the Vaux study talked about the kinds of things that they experienced as harassment, they usually included telling suggestive stories, crude sexual remarks, being treated differently due to one's gender, and gender stereotyping. Vaux noted that, "The experiences most frequently reported by women and men were similar for all forms of harassment. To simply assert that a particular experience is offensive to women but not to men, that an item captures harassment in the case of women but not men, is to express dogma" (p. 122). Vaux did acknowledge that we often find in some men's reflections of sexual harassment experiences a bit of self-satisfaction when women direct their attention to them. Problematic with this survey that Vaux did was the possibility that this high number of men reporting harassment was more indicative of isolated and scattered events rather than any harassment of a chronic nature.

Similar to the specific incidents reported earlier, Vaux discussed the different shapes that harassment might take, including direct physical harm such as assault, psychological harm, abuse of power, and sexism. Individual cases cited earlier in this chapter included those that had to do with psychological harm as well as an abuse of power and, in the Oncale case, physical assault.

Berdahl, Magley, and Waldo (1996) cited Michael Crichton's book (1994), *Disclosure* as illustrating that as women come into more power in corporations and other organizations, the number of men who present with complaints of sexual harassment will increase significantly. In reviewing work in the area of the sexual harassment of men, these authors concluded that specific behaviors that often are part of sexual harassment have very different precipitating events, meanings, and consequences for males and females from both a personal and organizational perspective. As was true in some of the individual cases cited earlier in this chapter, these authors mentioned that the men involved often reported that the sexual relationship was initially consensual. They also reinforced the notion that most studies done in this area have shown that it is difficult to find men acknowledging negative results in their lives as a result of sexual harassment from women. In the cases cited earlier in this chapter, men experienced some loss of control in their personal life as well as their work life and a sense of security associated with both was lost. Although the authors acknowledged that both men and women could sexually harass a male subordinate, more weight and importance in wrongdoing seemed to be attached to men in power harassing female subordinates because of the "sociohistorical context" present in the situation of a male supervisor and a female subordinate. This kind of thinking would almost make it impossible to develop a "sociohistorical context" that would say that men could be sexually harassed by a female superior. Because each event is invalidated due to a lack of historical context, how do these events accumulate ever to the extent that they could be considered history? Sounds very much like a Catch-22. It seems unlikely that the individual male victims in these situations fearing loss of job, and so on, are impressed by this abstraction of a "sociohistorical context" or the reality of their own physical superiority. These authors think that sexual harassment perpetrated upon men is less threatening for these men than it is for women because of the smaller amount of social and physical power that is present when a male is harassed by a female and therefore, would be less likely to result in significant psychosocial stress.

Berdahl et al. (1996) point out that there are different types of gender harassment. Some men may be turned off by "lewd jokes, sexual comments, and 'beefcake photos'" (p. 532) but do not experience the tension and anxiety that women experience when similar stimuli are presented. In one of two studies that these authors presented, they expected to find that men were going to be less emotionally threatened by harassment from women and, therefore, would be likely to report less anxiety. This would seem to be the case also because it would make sense that when men are the objects of unwanted sexual advances from women, it is socially desirable not to record that this is a problem for them. These authors used the Sexual Experiences Questionnaire and used revisions of the instrument applicable to men. They found that both men and women indicated that sexual coercion would be the most anxiety-provoking form of harassment and that men reported that unwanted sexual attention from women including instructors and professors was nonthreatening. The subjects were 138 male and female students from a midwestern university. The second study looked at 1,156 employees of a West Coast public utility; the authors used the Sexual Experiences Questionnaire with the revision for men. Men in this study reported that they would be least bothered by gender harassment, slightly more bothered by unwanted sexual attention, and most troubled by sexual coercion. For these men the most frequent comment was that the respondent had not been sexually harassed. When present, the type of sexual harassment these men mentioned most was unwanted sexual attention. Gender harassment was the next most common, which included sexually explicit language and conversation, negative stereotyping of men, and harassment for deviating from stereotypic male gender roles. Miller (1997) reinforced the extent to which stereotypic thinking about men would lend itself to harassment of men who did not go along with prevalent gender norms and how a lack of stereotypic masculine behaviors would result in being labeled as homosexual or called names by both men and women peers. Gender harassment includes behaviors that are aimed at men or women who do not adhere to stereotypic roles as men or women. Sexual harassment refers to behaviors that result in a person being the object of unwanted behavior aimed toward sexual gratification.

Berdahl et al. (1996) found that about half of the men, in contrast to women, found the sexual harassment to be a positive experience and about half found it to be negative. These authors also found that a large majority of the men indicated that they would confront anyone who harassed them or report the behavior whereas women were more likely to be passive. They also found that in both studies of the college students as well as the public utility workers that sexual coercion would be the most offensive thing with which to cope. Although earlier in this chapter it was pointed out that there were individual men who find sexual harassment of this kind to be offensive, there is strong support in these studies to show that very often men are experiencing these harassing behaviors as positive either because they find some of the crude behavior and jokes entertaining or because the attempts by females to sexually coerce them are somehow seen as satisfying to their egos or maybe even validating of their masculinity. The authors concluded that "actual rates of sexual harassment [are] much lower for men than for women and . . . men [experience] what women have identified as sexual harassment as less stressful and threatening than women do" (p. 544). This does not negate the fact that some individual men will suffer greatly from sexual harassment. When there are negative consequences, it is more likely to be when men are harassing other men because of all the other issues that become involved. These include invalidation of stereotypic male characteristics, the assumption of homosexuality, and so on. Although for the male victim of a female sexual coercion/harassment, such behaviors can be stressful and threatening, these incidents are probably going to be less frequent than in male-on-male sexual harassment.

Other writers have reinforced the idea that men and women have different perceptions of sexual harassment including the fact that women have a broader view of what behaviors constitute sexual harassment and tend to view these behaviors as carrying more negative consequences than do men (Pryor, Geidd, & Williams, 1995). Pryor et al. make a good point that the frequency of reported incidents of sexual harassment will be correlated with the attitudes that an organization has about sexual harassment. Although their focus was on women, when men are victims, social (that is, organizational) norms are most likely to affect a man's inclination to report or even experience behavior as harassment when it is directed toward him. Pryor et al. discussed the presence of soft porn photos and other displays as part of the negative atmosphere to which women are subject in some corporations. On the other hand, there is anecdotal evidence that in some work settings female employees have "beef-cake" pictures up that might arouse the same kinds of tensions in men. This phenomenon was part of the problem at Jenny Craig, Inc. In some studies (Pryor et al., 1995) men who were likely to sexually harass women viewed themselves as hypermasculine and connected ideas about social dominance and sexuality in ways that may also fit those cases mentioned earlier in which women harassed men. The issue of power was obvious because these women were supervisors or supervisor's spouses. It is ironic that there is the potential that those men who experience harassment from women as positive view themselves as experiencing something that validates their masculinity. This may be why it is difficult to know what kind of behavior is harassing for men and what is not because some men see behavior with sexual content as positive and reaffirming of their masculinity if perpetrated by females.

There is some work (Struckman-Johnson & Struckman-Johnson, 1997) that has shown that the "attractiveness" of the perpetrator might influence a man's perception. These authors looked at 142 college men from a small midwestern university and had them view a series of vignettes. In earlier work, the Struckman-Johnsons had found that 43 percent of the college men in their sample had reported at least one incident of "pressured or forced sexual contact" with a woman since the age of 16. We have seen that men seem to have a range of reactions to sexual coercion from women including both negative and positive and that generally they were less negative than women were to such coercion. These authors were interested in the extent to which they could predict that men would react favorably to a woman's coercive sexual advance if it were perceived to be a desirable sexual opportunity. These authors had found earlier that men were more likely to have positive reactions regardless of behavior if a very attractive woman was involved even if low or moderate force was part of the behavior. This phenomena that they called a "beauty bias" certainly would complicate this issue. With these 142 men, the Struckman-Johnsons looked at the status of having a girlfriend or not having a girlfriend and also the status of whether the female perpetrator was very attractive. They found that whether or not the male had a girlfriend did not affect outcome, but the attractiveness rating did. Men who were instructed to assume the status of having a girlfriend had a slightly negative to neutral reaction to the advance from a woman but men who were told to assume that they had no romantic partner had a slightly positive response. These authors showed how a person's commitment to another person might affect whether they would experience coercive sexual advance as harassment. They also looked at the extent to which the attractiveness of the perpetrator would influence whether something was seen as harassing. Both of these phenomena influenced men's responses to hypothetical coercive sexual advance. They also found that men who would be considered to have more conservative sexual standards were in general not receptive to an advance from a woman and served in the author's terms as a "gate-keeper." Interestingly enough, among young college people this is a role that we assume has been given to females, whereas in this study it indicated that there are some young men who adopt that role. As we might expect, the study also showed that there are a group of young men who are less conservative in terms of their sexual standards and, therefore, had a positive response to the advances from women. Finally, it was interesting to note that in this sample, 66 percent of the men indicated that they would not consent to have sex with the woman presented in the vignette. In an earlier study these authors found that 71 percent of the men said that they would reject the moderately forceful advance from a woman whom they had known for only a few hours. Of course these studies have been looking primarily at vignettes, and it would remain to be seen what would happen *in vivo*.

Ivy and Hamlet (1996) also looked at a college population when studying sexual harassment that occurred between peers (that is, relationships not based on any kind of overt power or status differential) and the extent to which these could be equally troubling or even more troubling than harassment where power relationships were involved. As others have, these authors found gender differences regarding the severity of harassing behaviors, with women perceiving certain behaviors as harassing and as more severe than men. They cited earlier work with peer sexual harassment among a group of social workers where they found that 36 percent of the females had seen themselves as having been the victims of sexual harassment as compared to 14 percent of their male peers. In the study with the college population, Ivy and Hamlet looked at the student's own experience with sexual harassment by a peer, the extent to which a student knew that other students had been victims of peer sexual harassment, and, finally, the student's opinion as to whether peer harassment was a problem on this university campus in the southwest. They had students do the surveys because they felt that peers would be more open with other students than they would with faculty types. Of the 824 undergraduate students surveyed, 384 (47 percent) indicated that they had been the victims of peer sexual harassment. Of the female subjects, 281 reported that they had been such a victim whereas 103 males indicated that they had been a victim of peer sexual harassment. Women's responses ranged from one isolated incident to over 200 times over the course of their career at the school, whereas male subjects indicated a frequency of 1 to 50 times. For the female respondents who were victims, 99 percent of the harassers were men. A similar percentage of women were perpetrators when men were harassed. The six most frequently reported settings in which peer sexual harassment occurred for both female and male targets were primarily at a party or social activity, at work, or at the residence be it dorm, apartment, or their home. Also included were behaviors that occurred in the classroom and, more so for men than for women, at clubs or bars. For men, nonverbal sexual harassment occurred with less frequency than verbal whereas female targets mentioned harassment by peers that included a wide range of verbal and nonverbal behaviors. The authors conclude,

Although male targets' accounts of classmate harassment was significantly fewer in number than females', the episodes were nonetheless revealing. Predominant verbal harassment involved comments about physical appearance and body parts; comments of a sexual nature, such as descriptions of desired sexual activity with the target; asking questions about assignments as segues to asking more intimate questions; repeatedly being asked out or telephoned by female classmates; and offers of sexual favors in exchange for help on assignments or exams. One repeated comment emergent from male, but not female targets, involved female classmates talking in sexual ways about their own body parts, which made male respondents uncomfortable (p. 157).

In terms of the most frequent nonverbal forms of harassment, the responses from female and male targets were similar.

Ivy and Hamlet (1996) did a second study in order to look at the lack of agreement between men and women as to what constitutes harassment. This time there were 163 students completing the questionnaire with 60 percent of them female and 40 percent of them male. Two particular items produced significant gender differences. Behavior that was an implied or overt sexual threat produced significantly different responses. Female subjects gave significantly more severity to overt sexual threats than did male participants. Another behavior (attempted or actual kissing) produced significantly different responses with females seeing this as more significant. This study was convincing that peers could harass peers and both males and females could be perpetrators and victims. It also confirmed what had been seen in other studies in different settings. More women than men tend to be targets of all forms of sexual harassment, and there are more negative consequences for women than for men. The fact that 68 percent of the women had been harassed by male peers as compared to only 25 percent of the men should send a message in terms of how we look at institutional environments whether education or business. The fact that women are more likely to be objects of harassment does not lessen the impact that it has on the 25 percent of the men but shows a much bigger problem with women as victims. It also showed that women are more likely to be the objects of ongoing behavior that includes unwanted sexual advances as well as verbal harassment whereas men experience as harassing more isolated and singular events such as a variety of verbalizations from women. This survey showed that women were the objects of more nonverbal communication by which their privacy was invaded either physically or by clear sexual reactions to their physical appearance. These authors reflected how in a university environment male students may respond better to clear-cut behavioral definitions of what harassment is because they are not able apparently to pick up on the subtle nuances that women are.

Wolf et al. (1991) studied 87 senior medical students who were issued a Mistreatment Questionnaire developed by the American Medical Association's Office of Education Research. Sexual harassment was included among the items of mistreatment. Fifty-two percent of the respondents reported mistreatment that they would consider to be sexual harassment with reports of sexual harassment being vastly different for men and women. The difficulty with this study was that it lumped sexual harassment or discrimination together. When one parcels out what would meet the definition for sexual harassment, 61.5 percent of the women were reporting "sexual slurs" as the most common type of sexual harassment whereas 11.5 percent of the men were reporting "sexual slurs." Sexual harassment was perpetrated most often by residents or interns or both. Women perceived significantly higher levels of sexual harassment than did men. For men, 69 percent or higher reported no harassment.

Katz, Hannon, and Whitten (1996) emphasized that in order to be seen as sexual harassment, behavior must be received by the victim as "repetitive, unwelcome, and inherently coercive" (p. 35). Their study included 197 college undergraduates at a west-coast private university. These participants were asked to respond to a 60-item questionnaire that included a number of interactions between a male and a female in one of three situations as follows: (1) The workplace, involving a married supervisor and an unmarried subordinate; (2) a college campus, involving an unmarried professor and one of his or her unmarried students; and (3) two college students, who dated before and meet at a party. The results showed that the gender of the observer of the incident was as important as was the gender of the harasser. Males and females had very similar views about sexual harassment when the behavior was initiated by a man and directed at a woman. However, when the harassment was initiated by a woman and directed at a man, men rated the interactions as less harassing than women did. Regardless of the situation, men rated harassment by a woman less negatively than women did. This seems congruent with some of the other findings in which harassment of men by women, even though meeting EEOC definitions, is seen by some men as positive or certainly less negative and to some extent something that has a positive or satisfying outcome.

When looking at graduate students, Cairns and Hatt (1995) found that 2.4 percent of the men and 9.3 percent of the women had reported having experienced some kind of sexual harassment with men reporting sexual harassment as generally involving female peers as the perpetrators and occurring primarily in a social context. The author cited a university policy on sexual harassment that included "unwanted sexual solicitation or advances," behavior that was "coercive or unwelcome" and also any kind of "physical or verbal conduct" that would be sexually offensive and finally the "display of offensive material" (p. 170). A total of 985 surveys were completed at this institution. The initial question in the sexual harassment section of the survey asked these participants to report whether or not they believe that sexual harassment was a problem at the university. Sixteen percent stated that it was a problem there and women (20 percent) were more often than men (11 percent) to believe that sexual harassment was a problem on campus. A second question asked whether or not the respondents had been sexually harassed during their graduate program. To this response, 45 women and 11 men indicated that they had been sexually harassed. For these 11 men, the behavior that was harassing was primarily physical, in the form of unwanted touching, or verbal, in the form joking, vulgar comments, and sexist remarks. In this sample male graduate students were most likely to experience harassment from female staff and peers, and the most frequent locations for harassment incidents were the classrooms and laboratories, elevators or hallways, the department lounge, student offices, and professor's offices, or off-campus social events. As in other settings, these authors felt that students that experienced harassment would probably be without peer support if they wished to lodge a complaint. This is particularly the case for men because other men may see such complaints as reflecting negatively on their masculinity not to see harassment by a female as ego-boosting. Once again, as in other studies, more females than males are harassed significantly but also underscored was the extent to which the sexual harassment of male students is probably given far less attention than warranted.

Struckman-Johnson (1988) speculated as to why there was an underreporting of the sexual victimization of men by women, part of which was attributed to the "societal myth that men cannot be sexually exploited by women" (p. 234). Her work in this field has indicated that there is little to be found about the frequency of men being sexually coerced by women with whom they are involved in a social or dating relationship. She looked at a sample of 623 students at a large midwestern university and found that of the 355 women in the sample, 22 percent of them had reported that they had been forced to engage in sexual intercourse on a date at least once during their lifetime, whereas 43 (16 percent) of the 268 men had reported at least one forced sex episode in their lifetime. While at the university, the frequency was less with 13 percent of the women and 9 percent of the men having experienced a forced sex episode. Unlike women, most of the men in this study reported that they were coerced into sex by psychological "tactics" with several men describing verbal pressure from their partners. These forced sex escapades affected men and women differently. Most of the females immediate and long-term reactions were negative, with the most common being a chronic insecurity and uneasiness around men. Most of the men felt neutral about the episode when it happened and the remainder were divided between feeling positive or negative with very few men experiencing any long-term effects on their lives. Although a significant number of men and women on a college campus had been coerced into sexual intercourse, it seems to once again have had longer term negative problems for women than for men and also to have been perceived at the time that it happened as more negative by women than by men. Again, we may be seeing the power differential between men and women plus the fact that for men this may be something they would be reluctant to report even if it was negative or something that is satisfying to a variety of ego needs. On college campuses and maybe other settings "both men and women engage in a continuum of sexually exploitive behaviors ranging from verbal pressure to use of physical restraint and force" (p. 240).

Populations other than college students have been studied. Rubin and Hampton (1997) looked at members of the American Psychological Association, who were in retrospect evaluating their graduate school experience in terms of sexual harassment. Questionnaires were mailed to 750 members of the APA and 240 (32 percent) were returned completed. One question asked whether a student had offered sexual favors for some reward, and more men than women reported that this behavior was more likely to occur. Female respondents reported being more uncomfortable than male respondents when the instructor initiated a personal relationship and when the instructor made an attempt to stroke, caress, or touch them. When they looked back at their graduate school years, more females than males reported experiencing at least one unsolicited sexual advance by an instructor. The question was posed as to why there was a lack of discomfort for many of the men in terms of sexual harassment. It was postulated by these authors that men were less attuned to these kinds of behaviors in a social or work setting and that men are rarely the recipients of sexually harassing behaviors from those who are superior to them in an administrative structure.

Waldo, Berdahl, and Fitzgerald (1998) were concerned about the fictional portrayal promoted in the film and book *Disclosure* and the suggestion of how more frequently than is reported men are sexually harassed. These writers did not seem to give much credit to the public's ability to distinguish fact from fiction. Most are either in a work or education setting and probably can determine with some objectivity that women are more likely to be the victims of harassment and that this couple portrayed by Michael Douglas and Demi Moore were more works of fiction than fact. The authors underscored as others have that men and women are going to attach different meanings to the same behavior in work and school situations for many reasons including individual personality differences, organizational structure, and societal norms. As pointed out in Berdahl et al. (1996), Waldo et al. advised that any kind of research instruments used to look at sexual harassment cannot be those simply developed with women in mind and then applied to a male population. They also reinforced the notion that men not only identify things seen in research with women such as unwanted sexual attention and sexual coercion as harassment but also hostility evoked in other men when not living out the traditional heterosexual male role. Waldo et al. highlighted a study done by the United States Merit Systems Protection Board done in 1981 that reported that almost 25 percent of the male targets of sexual harassment identified men as perpetrators compared to 72 percent who reported women as perpetrators. A similar study done by the same group in 1995 reported that 21 percent of the male targets identified men as perpetrators compared to 65 percent who reported women as perpetrators. When there were cases of female-to-male sexual harassment, it most often contained unwanted sexual attention or sexual coercion.

In the study that Waldo et al. (1998) conducted, they looked at the relative frequency and types of men's experiences of potentially sexually harassing behaviors, the gender of the perpetrators, and whether this harassment met psychological definitions for the experience of harassment among three samples. The first came from a large public utility company in the northwest totaling 378 men. The second were male faculty and staff numbering 209 at a large midwestern university, and the third, a sample of 420 men from a western agribusiness operation. In all three samples just under half of the men indicated they had experienced at least one of the potentially sexually harassing behaviors identified at least once. When it came to gender harassment, more men reported experiencing lewd and offensive comments than sexual coercion and unwanted sexual attention. In each sample, men reported that male peers were more likely than women to target them for sexual harassment. Across all types of harassment, 52.7 percent of the men from the public utilities sample identified men or mostly men as the perpetrators, compared to 30.1 percent who identified women or mostly women as the perpetrators and the 17.2 percent who identified both men and women. From the faculty and staff sample, 50.2 percent of men reported that men or mostly men were the perpetrators, 31.7 percent reported that women or mostly women were the perpetrators, and 19.1 percent identified both men and women for the reported incidents. In the agribusiness corporation sample, 39.8 percent of the men reported that men harassed them, compared to 31.9 percent who identified women as perpetrators and 28.3 percent who described both male and female perpetrators.

Men in the public utility sample were significantly more likely to report obscene comments and adverse reactions should they go against the stereotypic male gender role. Unwanted sexual attention and sexual coercion came equally from men and women, and negative remarks about men were more common from women. In the faculty and staff sample, responses were similar except that no men reported sexual coercion. In the agribusiness corporation sample, again, responses were similar to the other two samples with the exception that men in this group were more likely to report experiences of unwanted sexual attention from women and were not more likely to experience enforcement of the male gender role from other men. Most of these men (70.4 percent) in the agribusiness group reported that coworkers had been the perpetrators.

IMPLICATIONS OF THE RESEARCH RESULTS

These three studies by Waldo et al. with such contrasting populations strongly support the notion that male-to-male sexual harassment is more prevalent than one would assume from published research as well as from popular sources such as newspapers, news magazines, and fictional media. This is particularly true when we take a broad definition of sexual harassment and include more than just unwanted sexual attention and negative remarks about men. It also should be noted that in all three of these settings administrators, supervisors, managers, and so on, were predominately men, indicating that the position of power might have as much to say about the sexual harassment of men as it does for women at least in terms of the kind of atmosphere that is established in any organization. In all these samples, the most significant problem for men seemed to be focused around the enforcement of stereotypic male roles. Men in these settings who strayed from these roles probably suffered significant consequences and faced chronic problem situations.

Implications from Waldo et al. suggest that we need to look beyond the low frequency female-to-male sexual harassment to the kind of environments that might be more likely to promote sexual harassment of men. There certainly would be some environments where reporting would not occur because of the tone set by the organization. A man who would report such behaviors would reinforce the notion that got him in trouble with his peers in the first place. To be in a work situation where a man is not meeting some unwritten code of male behavior can be very threatening and intimidating and certainly affect the overall quality of his life.

We need a reminder that although the focus here has been on typical settings, exaggerated forms of this kind of behavior exist in other places. Struckman-Johnson et al. (1996) surveyed 1,800 men and women in a midwestern state prison system. Although removed from sexual harassment per se we can look at the extent to which research has looked at the abuse of men. Of 516 male respondents 20 percent had been pressured or forced at least once to have sexual contact against their will while incarcerated. These authors pointed out that many individuals regardless of environments are challenged by the notion of a heterosexual man being forced to participate in sexual acts against his will. This is a bias that probably not only operates in prison situations but cuts across school, business, and industries, therefore, inhibiting men from reporting such behavior. There was also some hint that in such violent situations men can feel even more of a stigma than women in being raped and reporting a rape because again this is so contrary to the general view of masculinity. The authors noted that men who have been sexually victimized in prison are afraid of being found out if they seek help or identify perpetrators and, therefore, things go unreported. For less dramatic reasons there are probably similar inhibitions for men in all environments in terms of reporting sexual harassment in the form of sexual coercion.

SUMMARY

Twenty years after a court case dealing with the sexual harassment of men, such behavior continues to be seen by definition as something that men do to women almost exclusively. Some writers on this subject find it difficult to include men as possible targets of harassment, a bias well addressed by Vaux (1993). For some scholars in this field, the inclusion of men as potential victims seems to stretch their closed ideological framework. We have seen that this way of thinking does not minimize the negative effects that harassment can have on individual men. The ramifications of this go far beyond the kind of public attention given to fictional accounts we saw in *Disclosure*. When men are the objects of sexual harassment, it can take the form of male-to-male harassment or female-to-male harassment. It can be inferred from studies in this area that we have two mutually exclusive groups of men who are targets of harassment: men who are harassed by other men with the accompanying questions about masculinity and sexual orientation and men who are targeted by women who demonstrate sexually coercive behavior.

Whether men are harassed by other men or by women, the potential is present for significant harm. There is enough evidence in the literature to show it can happen, does happen, and should be addressed by the same level of seriousness given to all forms of harassment regardless of target. In general, men report fewer immediate consequences as well as less long-lasting harm from sexual harassment than do women, but this seems to depend on the specific behaviors perpetrated and whether males or females were doing the targeting. Chronic intimidation by other men with threats to physical safety and doubts about one's masculinity would affect a man in ways similar to worse-case scenarios for women. There is no doubt that some men are flattered when behavior that is clearly within the definition of sexual harassment is directed at them. This is seldom if ever the case when women are targeted. Men who are targets face different challenges in confronting situations in which they are harassed. If women "hit" on them and this is experienced as offensive, their wish to address the problem is undermined by the incredulity of the whole matter. On the other hand, if a man is the perpetrator, then embedded in the situation are questions about one's masculinity and sexual orientation. Except in the Jenny Craig, Inc. case cited earlier, there did not seem to be a pervasive atmosphere of harassment when men were the objects of this behavior from females as we see in some organizational settings when women are targeted by men. Men who are the targets of sexual harassment seem to have been caught up in singular and isolated events, which nevertheless could still have significant consequences on their lives.

REFERENCES

Berdahl, J. L., Magley, V. J., & Waldo, C. R. (1996). The sexual harassment of men? Exploring the concept with theory and data. *Psychology of Women Quarterly, 20,* 527–547.

Broker says his boss sexually harassed him. (1997, April 22). *New York Times,* p. B7.

Bull, C. (1997, November 25). Same-sex harassment. *The Advocate,* p. 30.

Cairns, K. V., & Hatt, D. G. (1995). Discrimination and sexual harassment in a graduate student sample. *Canadian Journal of Human Sexuality, 4*(3), 169–176.

Carton, B. (1994, November 29). Muscled out? At Jenny Craig, men are the ones who claim sex discrimination—Workers say female bosses make lewd comments and denied promotions—Biceps as new office tokens. *Wall Street Journal,* p. A1.

Cloud, J. (1998, March 16). Harassed or hazed? *Time,* 151, 155.

Colker, R., (1995). Whores, fags, dumb-assed women, surly blacks, and competent heterosexual white men: The sexual and racial morality anti-discrimination doctrine. *Yale Journal of Law and Feminism, 7*(2), 195–225.

Crichton, M. (1994). *Disclosure: A novel.* New York: Knopf.

Davis, A. (1998, November 23). Socializing of a staffer and boss's wife spells woe at brokerage firm. *Wall Street Journal,* p. A1.

Felsenthal, E. (1997, May 27). Justice Department urges court to hear harassment case. *Wall Street Journal,* p. B3.

Felsenthal, E. (1997, June 10). High court to rule on whether law bars same-sex harassment. *Wall Street Journal,* p. B20.

Fitzgerald, L. F., Swan, S., & Magley, V. J. (1997). But was it really sexual harassment? Legal, behavioral, and psychological definitions of the work place victimization of women. In W. O'Donohue (Ed.), *Sexual harassment: Theory, research, and treatment* (pp. 5–28). Boston: Allyn & Bacon.

Gutek, B. A. (1985). *Sex and the workplace.* San Francisco: Josey-Bass.

Hetter, K., & Jest, T. (1998, March 16). Harassment's sharper edges. *U.S. News and World Report, 124,* 28.

Huebschen v. Department of Health and Social Services, et al. (1982). Civil Action No. 81-C-1004, United States District Court, Western District of Wisconsin.

Ivy, D. K., & Hamlet, S. (1996). College students and sexual dynamics: Two studies of peer sexual harassment. *Communication Education, 45,* 149–166.

Katz, R. C., Hannon, R., & Whitten, L. (1996). Effects of gender and situation on the perception of sexual harassment. *Sex Roles, 34*(1/2), 35–43.

Marquand, R. (1997, December 4). Is same-sex harassment illegal? *Christian Science Monitor, 20*(7), 1.

Merrick, N. (1995, March 9). Survey discloses harassment of men at work. *People Management,* p. 10.

Miller, L. L. (1997). Not just weapons of the weak: Gender harassment as a form of protest by Army men. *Social Psychology Quarterly, 60*(1), 32–51.

Paludi, M. A. (Ed.). (1990). *Sexual harassment on college campuses: Abusing the ivory power.* Albany: State University of New York Press.

Pryor, J. B., Giedd, J. L., & Williams, K. B. (1995). A social psychological model for predicting sexual harassment. *Journal of Social Issues, 51*(1), 69–84.

Pryor, J. B., & Whalen, N. J. (1997). A typology of sexual harassment: Characteristics of harassers and the social circumstances under which sexual harassment occurs. In W. O'Donohue (Ed.), *Sexual harassment: Theory, research, and treatment* (pp. 129–151). Boston: Allyn & Bacon.

Rubin, L. J., & Hampton, B. R. (1997). Sexual harassment of students by professional psychology educators: A national survey. *Sex Roles, 37*(9/10), 753–771.

Same-sex verdict. (1999, June 14). *National Law Journal,* p. B18.

Savage, D. (1998). Signs of disagreement. *ABA Journal, 84,* 50.

Struckman-Johnson, C. (1988). Forced sex on dates: It happens to men, too. *Journal of Sex Research, 24,* 234–241.

Struckman-Johnson, C., & Struckman-Johnson, D. (1997). Men's reactions to hypothetical forceful sexual advances from women: The role of sexual standards, relationship availability, and the beauty bias. *Sex Roles, 37*(5/6), 319–333.

Struckman-Johnson, C., Struckman-Johnson, D., Rucker, L., Bomby, K., & Donaldson, S. (1996). Sexual coercion reported by men and women in prison. *Journal of Sex Research, 33*(1), 67–76.

Supreme Court backs same-sex harassment suit. (1998, March 5). *Facts on File, 58,* 128–129.

Supreme Court rules same-sex harassment on the job is illegal. (1998, March 23). *Jet, 93,* 39.

Tang, T. L., & McCollum, S. L. (1996). Sexual harassment in the workplace. *Public Personnel Management, 25*(1), 53–58.

The chain must pay male sex-harassment victim. (1995, November 24). *New York Times,* p. A28.

Townsend, A. M., & Luthar, H. K. (1995, May). How do the men feel?. *H. R. Magazine,* pp. 92–96.

Vaux, A. (1993). Paradigmatic assumptions in sexual harassment research: Being guided without being misled. *Journal of Vocational Behavior, 42,* 116–135.

Waldo, C. R., Berdahl, J. L., & Fitzgerald, L. F. (1998). Are men sexually harassed? If so, by whom? *Law and Human Behavior, 22*(1), 59–79.

Wolf, T. M., Randall, H. M., Von Almen, K, & Tynes, L. L. (1991). Perceived mistreatment and attitude change by graduating medical students: A retrospective study. *Medical Education, 25,* 182–190.

7

THE UNPROTECTED:
THE SEXUAL HARASSMENT
OF LESBIANS AND GAYS

M. Karen Hambright and James D. Decker

The genesis of sexual harassment as a legal issue began with the enactment of Title VII of the Civil Rights Act of 1964 and the creation of workplace guidelines by the Equal Employment Opportunity Commission (EEOC, 1980). Yet the development of sexual harassment as a psychological, organizational, and civil rights issue has continued into the present millennium because interpretation and enforcement of policy is contingent on the evolving legal definition.

According to *The New Shorter Oxford English Dictionary,* the verb "harass" is a pejorative derivation of the French "harer," which means to "set a dog on." In modern usage the verb means "to trouble by repeated attacks," and "to subject to constant molesting or persecution" (Brown, 1993, p. 1188). In legal terminology, sexual harassment is a form of federally prohibited employment discrimination and is actionable in either of two forms: quid pro quo, or creation of a hostile environment (cf. specific definitions below). Psychologists and other social scientists define and classify sexual harassment dichotomously as well, that is, according to whether the harassing behavior is an expression of sexual attraction or an expression of hostility toward the target individual (Pryor & Whalen, 1997). In all cases the target individual is subjected to unwelcome behavior on the part of the harasser. However, the development of specific behavioral definitions of prohibited conduct and the enforcement of sexual harassment policy are formidable tasks given the individual variation in what is considered suitably offensive behavior and the troubling variety of meanings for the terms "sex" and "sexual."

As social scientists, we want to understand and ultimately prevent such unwelcome and discriminatory behavior in the workplace and elsewhere. Yet sexual harassment is neither singular nor monolithic in form (O'Donohue, 1997); it is not a problem limited to the stereotypical chauvinistic male employer or supervisor and his attractive young female employees, nor is it limited to heterosexuals. Instead, there are numerous possible types arising from the combinations of gender, sexual orientation, behavior, and motivation that complicate interpretation, litigation, and scientific investigation. Still, court records and social science research clearly indicate that sexual harassment (regardless of current actionability) is a pervasive and mounting problem for lesbian women and gay men in the U.S. workplace (Herek, 1984; Pryor & Whalen, 1997; Schneider, 1982).

Table 7.1 illustrates the complexity arising from the interaction of gender, sexual orientation, and behavioral role of individuals involved. As shown in the table, there are 16 possible types of sexual harassment resulting from the combination of these three variables. Note that the legal prototype and most prevalent form (Greenlaw & Kohl, 1981) is referred to here as "traditional sexual harassment" and is represented by the cell in row 4, column 3. The types in which lesbians and gay men are targets of sexual harassment are represented by the eight cells in the two columns on the left half of the table. Although suspected causal motivation for these types of harassment includes homophobia (that is, unfavorable attitudes and affects toward homosexual individuals; Schreier, 1995), sexism, and sexual attraction, the main focus here is on sexual harassment of lesbian and gay targets that is thought to be motivated by homophobia. We also address sexually harassing behavior that is motivated by sexual attraction toward a lesbian or gay target. However, we do not closely examine sexual harassment of heterosexual individuals who are suspected or believed to be homosexual, or other types involving heterosexual targets, for such analysis is beyond the scope of this chapter.

Sexual harassment may be manifested in numerous forms, thus it is unlikely to be singular in causation, development, or function. Following a brief history of the development of sexual harassment law, we examine the people, contexts, behavior patterns, development, suspected causation, and consequences of sexual harassment of lesbians and gays. We conclude with a call for application of research findings and strategies necessary for reduction and elimination of these forms of discrimination, and for the extension of legal protection to homosexual individuals in the workplace.

THE LEGAL GENESIS OF SEXUAL HARASSMENT

The U.S. government enacted Title VII of the Civil Rights Act in 1964. Title VII declares it unlawful "for an employer . . . to discriminate against any individual with respect to his compensation, terms, conditions, or privileges of employment because of an individual's sex" (Civil Rights Act, 1964). The inclusion of the term "sex" to the proposed legislation is an interesting and important ingredient in the development of sexual harassment law.

At the midnight hour, "sex" was added to the original Civil Rights Bill in an attempt to defeat the legislation. Representative Howard Smith of Virginia, a principal opponent of the bill, added the amendment, which was calculated to muster

Table 7.1
Psychological Typology of Sexual Harassment: Variants Based on Sexual Orientation, Gender, and Behavior Role

		Target (Receives)			
		Homosexual		*Heterosexual*	
		Female	*Male*	*Female*	*Male*
Homosexual	*Female*	Homosexual Female/ Homosexual Female	Homosexual Female/ Homosexual Male	Homosexual Female/ Heterosexual Female	Homosexual Female/ Heterosexual Male
Harasser (Does)	*Male*	Homosexual Male/ Homosexual Female	Homosexual Male/ Homosexual Male	Homosexual Male/ Heterosexual Female	Homosexual Male/ Heterosexual Male
Heterosexual	*Female*	Heterosexual Female/ Homosexual Female	Heterosexual Female/ Homosexual Male	Heterosexual Female/ Heterosexual Female	Heterosexual Female/ Heterosexual Male
	Male	Heterosexual Male/ Homosexual Female	Heterosexual Male/ Homosexual Male	Heterosexual Male/ Heterosexual Female	Heterosexual Male/ Heterosexual Male

    Sexual Harassment of Lesbian or Gay Targets

    Traditional Sexual Harassment

opposition to the bill's passage. The plan backfired and the amendment containing "sex" was passed as part of the Civil Rights Act of 1964 (Goodman-Delahunty, 1998). Because the amendment was part of a tactical maneuver to defeat the Civil Rights Act, virtually no legislative debate was held in Congress concerning the proper interpretation or application of the term "sex." In essence, this left the courts in the middle of a legal quagmire without any legislative guidance on how to define or apply the concept of "sex" in Title VII issues (Locke, 1996).

Title VII of the 1964 Civil Rights Act does not specifically mention the concept of sexual harassment, but it does make it unlawful for employers with 15 or more employees to discriminate against any applicants or employee "because of . . . sex." Federal law in this area is, therefore, largely a court-constructed creation, evolving over nearly three decades. Court decisions and guidelines of the Equal Employment Opportunity Commission have been the driving force in this area (Brookins, 1998; George, 1998).

The early courts took a narrow, traditional approach to the word "sex," interpreting it to apply in situations where females were denied employment because male employers did not believe that women could or should be engaged in work outside the home. These early cases were straightforward and based on an established set of factors borrowed from cases involving race. The legal test that evolved was known as a "but for" analysis, meaning that a court would inquire as to whether the employer would have denied employment but for the plaintiff's sex (Locke, 1996).

In a series of court cases, including *Barnes v. Costle* (1977), and *Bundy v. Jackson* (1981), the District of Columbia Circuit Court of Appeals along with other federal courts continued to expand the definition of "sex" under Title VII to include a test for sexual harassment claims (Locke, 1996). In 1986, the United States Supreme Court determined in *Meritor Savings Bank v. Vinson* that sexual harassment equaled sex discrimination under Title VII. Mechelle Vinson, an employer of Meritor Savings Bank, had engaged in sexual relations with her supervisor 40 to 50 times over the tenure of her employment. Vinson stated that she agreed to these relations out of fear of losing her job. After an analysis of the elements required for a quid pro quo sexual harassment claim, the U.S. Supreme Court held that Vinson had, in fact, established a claim under Title VII (Brookins, 1998; George, 1998).

As noted above, there are two basic actionable types of sexual harassment. The first is referred to as quid pro quo sexual harassment. This occurs when submission to "unwelcome" sexual advances, propositions, or other conduct of a sexual nature is made an express or implied condition of employment, or where it is used as the basis of employment decisions affecting job status or tangible employment benefits. As the name suggests, this form of harassment involves actual or potential economic loss such as termination, transfer, or achievement of performance ratings as a consequence of the employee's refusal to exchange sexual favors demanded by a supervisor or employer for employment benefits (Storrow, 1998; Thomas, 1998).

The second actionable form consists of unwelcome sexual conduct, which is of such severity as to alter a condition of employment by creating an "intimidating, hostile, or offensive working environment." The essence of a "hostile environment" claim is a "pattern or practice" of offensive behavior by the employer, a supervisor, coworkers, or nonemployees so severe or pervasive as to interfere with the employee's job performance or create an abusive work environment. (Thomas, 1998, p. 4)

In *Harris v. Forklift Systems, Inc.* (1993), the U.S. Supreme Court ruled that hostile environment sexual harassment need not "seriously affect psychological well-being" of the victim in order to violate Title VII (Thomas, 1998, p. 5).

Harris also addressed the standard of reasonableness to be applied in judging sexual harassment claims. Justice O'Connor presented a two-part analysis, both components of which must be met for a violation to be found. "First, the conduct in question must create an objectively hostile work environment—an environment that a reasonable person would find hostile and abusive. Second, the victim must subjectively perceive the environment to be abusive" (Thomas, 1998, p. 6).

During the 1990s, courts also grappled with the issue of same-sex harassment—when both harasser and target are of the same gender—and have often reached widely differing conclusions (Brookins, 1998; George, 1998; Locke, 1996). Fifth Circuit courts simply ruled that same-sex harassment was not covered by Title VII (for example, *Garcia v. Elf Atochem North America,* 1994). In *Oncale v. Sundowner Offshore Services, Inc.* (1998), the U.S. Supreme Court overruled the Fifth Circuit decisions, and unanimously held that workplace harassment is actionable as sex discrimination under Title VII where the harasser and the target are of the same sex (George, 1998). Although this Court decision appears to have cleared the confusion surrounding the sex of harassers and targets, many new and uncharted issues have sprung from this expansion of sexual harassment, particularly those regarding the actual or suspected sexual orientation of the individuals involved.

The *Oncale* case began in the summer of 1991, when Joseph Oncale took a job with Sundowner Offshore Services, Inc. to work on an oil rig off the coast of Louisiana. Oncale quit his job only four months later, stating that he was a victim of ongoing sexual harassment from three of his male coworkers. Oncale alleged that on several occasions he was forcibly subjected to sexually humiliating actions against him by certain male coworkers in the presence of the rest of the crew; specifically, two coworkers had physically assaulted him in a sexual manner and sodomized him with a bar of soap, coworkers repeatedly used anti-gay slurs about him, and one had threatened him with rape (George, 1998; Storrow, 1998).

In May of 1994, Oncale filed suit in the District Court for the Eastern District of Louisiana claiming that he had been discriminated against in his employment because of his sex, in violation of a provision of Title VII of the Civil Rights Act of 1964. However, precedent was against Oncale on this issue. The U.S. Court of Appeals for the Fifth Circuit, which had jurisdiction over Oncale's district court, had held in *Giddens v. Shell Oil Co.* (1993) and again in *Garcia v. Elf Atochem North America* (1994) that sexual harassment of a man by another man is never actionable under Title VII. Because of these rulings, U.S. District Judge G. Thomas Porteous, Jr. ruled against Oncale and granted Sundowner's request for summary judgment, dismissing the case before going to trial. On appeal to the Fifth Circuit, the ruling of the lower court was affirmed. Oncale filed a *writ of certiorari* with the U.S. Supreme Court on October 9, 1996, which was granted on June 9, 1997 (Thomas, 1998).

Oncale and his legal counsel argued that his case deserved a hearing on its merits, that a man is just as capable of sexual harassment against another man as he is of discriminating against a woman because of her sex, and that the language of Title VII is gender-neutral and thus does not summarily dismiss same-sex harassment suits. The attorneys contended that the key to determining whether workplace behavior constituted sexual harassment should be the same in same-sex cases as in opposite sex cases: If the behavior and advances are "unwelcome" and "unreasonable," then they are unlawful (Thomas, 1998).

Sundowner's legal position argued that Title VII's purpose had been to remedy past discrimination against women, and that to interpret the law to include same-sex harassment would unduly broaden the law into a statute that would, in effect, ban all sexual expression in the workplace. Sundowner's lawyers pointed out that Congress's recent attempts to pass legislation banning same-sex discrimination were evidence that Title VII, as written, did not address this issue. It was also argued that because harassment may have sexual overtones, it does not mean that the harassment occurred "because of" the victim's sex (Thomas, 1998).

On March 4, 1998, the United States Supreme Court in a unanimous decision, ruled in favor of Oncale and stated that federal workplace rules under Title VII bar sexual harassment between members of the same sex. Justice Antonin Scalia, who wrote the *Oncale* opinion, stated that the Court was ending "the bewildering variety of stances" taken by federal courts in the past few years (*Oncale v. Sundowner Offshore Services, Inc.,* 1998; Thomas, 1998).

Justice Scalia wrote that although finding "male-on-male sexual harassment in the workplace was assuredly not the principal evil Congress was concerned with when it enacted Title VII," he and the Court concluded that "statutory prohibitions often go beyond the principal evil to cover reasonably comparable evils" like those alleged by Oncale. The Court further ruled that "harassing conduct need not be motivated by sexual desire to support an inference of discrimination on the basis of sex" (*Oncale v. Sundowner,* 1998, p. 4).

In rejecting Sundowner's contention that liability for same-sex harassment would transform Title VII into a "general civility code for the American workplace," Justice Scalia wrote, "the prohibition of harassment on the basis of sex requires neither asexuality nor androgyny in the workplace: It forbids only behavior so objectively offensive as to alter the "condition" of the victim's employment. Conduct that is not severe or pervasive enough to create an objectively hostile and abusive work environment—an environment that a reasonable person would find hostile or abusive—is beyond Title VII's purview" (Oncale v. Sundowner, 1998, p. 4).

The *Oncale* decision in many ways created more confusion in the law than it has cleared up. Some contend that the *Oncale* decision will expose more lesbians and gay people to harassment suits, whereas others argue that the ruling now means that homosexual people are protected by Title VII against workplace discrimination. In truth, the reality seems to be somewhere in the middle. The *Oncale* decision demonstrated an awareness within the highest levels of our legal system that same-sex harassment exists, and that it most often is not about sexual attraction but about subordination (*Oncale v. Sundowner Offshore Services, Inc.,* 1998; Thomas, 1998).

Oncale reversed a number of Fourth and Eleventh Circuit Court decisions such as *Fredette v. BVP Management Assoc.,* 1997; *Hopkins, v. Baltimore Gas & Elec. Co.,* 1996; *Mayo v. Kiwest Corp.,* 1996; *McWilliams v. Fairfax Co. Bd. of Supervisors,* 1996 and; *Wrightson v. Pizza Hut of America, Inc.,* 1996. These cases held that federal civil rights law only covered same-sex sexual harassment when it could be proven that the harasser had sexual feelings or desires for the victim. This requirement had the practical effect of singling out lesbians, gay men, and bisexuals as the only class of people *against* whom Title VII same-sex sexual harassment claims could be brought successfully. Under that interpretation, homosexuals could not bring federal claims against heterosexual same-sex harassers. Lesbians and gays could never be victims, only the perpetrators of same-sex sexual harassment (George, 1998; *Oncale v. Sundowner Offshore Services, Inc.,* 1998; Thomas, 1998).

The *Oncale* ruling eliminated the discrimination against homosexuals in sexual harassment suits by making clear that neither the gender nor the sexual orientation of the harasser or target is relevant. The crucial issue, as the Court stated, is whether the harassing conduct itself was "so objectively offensive" as to "create an environment that a reasonable person would find hostile or abusive" and therefore equivalent to discrimination because of sex (Thomas, 1998, p. 6).

As our society moves beyond *Oncale,* the larger question in this area seems to be: Will homosexual people be able to utilize the ruling in *Oncale* to fight same- or opposite-sex sexual harassment originating in homophobic sentiment? This legal decision did not address numerous underlying social issues in America, for instance, it is still perfectly legal under federal law to discriminate against someone in the workplace on the basis of sexual orientation. Although states such as Massachussetts, Minnesota, and Wisconsin have passed laws that prohibit discrimination on the basis of sexual orientation, in the vast majority of American states, employers are free to refuse to hire people because of their sexual orientation and can fire them for the same reason. At present, federal civil rights law does not preclude people from using antihomosexual epithets in the workplace or from withholding a pay increase or promotion merely because an employee is homosexual. As the legal system fleshes out the myriad issues surrounding sexual harassment, it remains to be seen whether *Oncale v. Sundowner Offshore Services, Inc.* (1998) will become one of the important milestones on the path to civil rights for lesbians, and gay men, or merely an anomaly within the American legal system.

PSYCHOLOGICAL ASPECTS OF THE SEXUAL HARASSMENT OF LESBIANS AND GAYS

Sexuality is a multifaceted, yet fundamental component of human development, identity, societal roles, and social relationships. Moreover, it is a basis for the moral and legal treatment of all individuals in human societies. Unfortunately, in the United States, prejudice, discrimination, oppression, and neglect based on sexual orientation are not only prevalent but normative (Forstein, 1988). Sexual harassment of lesbians and gay men is a widespread and invidious characteristic of the American workplace (Ames, 1996; Goodman-Delahunty, 1998; Long, 1996; Pryor & Whalen, 1997). The persistent irritation, torment, or occurrence of unwelcome sexual advances in the workplace compound the psychological, socio-economic, and physical hardships endured by lesbian women and gay men in a so-ciety that has been described as both heterosexist and homophobic in attitudes and behavior (D'Augelli & Rose, 1990; Forstein, 1988; Griffin, 1998). Therefore, we consider sexual harassment a major civil rights, occupational, and psychological issue involving people with homosexual orientation.

Target Population

As targets of the inappropriate behavior or negative attitudes or both, lesbians and gays form a distinct nonethnic, multicultural group (Elliot, 1993). Yet the "ho-mosexual lifestyle" or culture of these individuals is itself a stereotype, and in re-ality, there is no uniform or homogeneous culture of homosexual individuals. In-stead, contrary to popular stereotypes, the homosexual population is a mosaic of numerous and highly diverse people and a profusion of lifestyles. Indeed, not all people who are homosexual are young, middle-class Whites, and moreover, there is little professional or individual recognition of the differences between and among lesbians and gays (Ames, 1996; Long, 1996). However, in this chapter we consider lesbian and gay people together, as a single, but heterogeneous popula-tion, largely because of the paucity of sexual harassment research that differenti-ates between lesbians and gay men. Yet we realize the limitations of such an overly simplistic analysis, and in no way intend to diminish the importance or relevance of bisexual, transexual, or otherwise nonheterosexual individuals, and the coarseness of our analysis reflects that of existing social science literature. Further, we are grateful for and have relied heavily on the literature review of Pryor and Whalen (1997). We followed their approach of examining Person vari-ables (individual and idiosyncratic) and Situation variables (historical, sociocul-tural, professional, legal, political, educational, and organizational context), in-cluding the interaction between them in regard to the development and prevention of sexually harassing behavior (Pryor & Whalen, 1997).

Behavior Patterns

All forms of sexual harassment typically occur repeatedly, and involve one per-son's will imposed upon another. Yet the same behavior patterns may be used to express both sexual attraction and hostility. In the case of hostile sexual harass-ment, any sexual nature of the behavior is considered secondary to the hostility felt and expressed toward an outgroup individual (Pryor & Whalen, 1997). The most commonly reported behavior patterns used by sexual harassers of lesbians and gays include the following: sending love letters or hate mail; flirtation and unwelcome sexual advances or propositions; sexual "horseplay" in the form of touching, pinching, tickling, grabbing, or stripping the target; indecent exposure; sexual assault; attempted rape; sexual banter or epithets; sexual jokes; display or distribution of sexual or pornographic materials; taunts using perjoratives; offensive gestures or jokes about one's appearance; and ingroup favoritism limiting access to resources (O'Donohue, 1997).

However, patterns of harassing behavior in same-sex (that is, intragender) harassment, differ from those of opposite-sex (that is, intergender) harassment (Foote & Goodman-Delahunty, 1999). Their review of the research indicates that male same-sex harassment is predominantly expressed in crude and offensive behavior (for example, obscene stories, jokes, gestures, homosexual perjoratives and epithets, and degrading remarks concerning the target's masculinity) and rarely in terms of unwanted sexual attention or coercion. In contrast, women who are targets of same-sex harassment report far more unwanted sexual attention and coercion than crude and offensive verbal and gestural behavior. In other words, females report more quid pro quo same-sex harassment, and males report more hostile environment same-sex harassment (Foote & Goodman-Delahunty, 1999).

Person Variables

Sexual harassment generally involves a power differential between coworkers (O'Donohue, 1997). Target individuals may be subordinate to the harasser in organizational, educational, or socioeconomic rank, or in priority of access to limited resources. Gender and other personality factors may also contribute to any perceived inequality of coworkers. Herek (1989) reported that females, in general, are more likely to be targets of sexual harassment than men, which appears to imply that lesbians are targeted more frequently than gay men. Consistent with this characterization, an early survey of lesbians and heterosexual women (Schneider, 1982) found that proportionately more lesbians than heterosexual women reported being targets of sexually harassing behavior at least once. However, lesbian and gay targets may be subordinated arbitrarily by virtue of their outgroup status as homosexuals. Further the gender difference in frequency of occurrence may be a function of males being less likely to report sexual harassment due to fear of being perceived as weak, subordinate, or effeminate (Foote & Goodman-Delahunty, 1999).

Whether acting out of sexual attraction or hostility, sexual harassers are most likely male, even when the target is male (Herek, 1989; Pryor & Whalen, 1997). In other words, the number of males reporting same-sex harassment is significantly greater than that of females, and therefore, contrary to the findings above, gay men may be the targets of sexual harassment significantly more often than lesbians (Foote & Goodman-Delahunty, 1999). This interpretation is consistent with research indicating that males are more biased against homosexual individuals than are females, and in contrast to the greater frequency of female targets of sexual harassment in general, males are more biased against males who may be homosexual than against females who are or may be lesbian (Seltzer, 1992). Indeed, many males are sexually aroused by images of female-female sexual behavior in erotica (Forstein, 1988).

In addition, the social location, educational level, age, academic performance, use of principled moral reasoning, and level of exposure are personal characteristics that are inversely related with negative attitudes toward homosexuals (Pryor & Whalen, 1997; Van de Ven, 1994). Positive correlates of homophobia include male gender, the endorsement of traditional sex-role stereotypes, low self-esteem, political conservatism, religious fundamentalism, and living in the southern United States (Britton, 1990, D'Augelli & Rose, 1990; Herek & Capitano, 1996; Holtzen & Agresti, 1990; Kurdek, 1988; Pryor & Whalen, 1997; Seltzer, 1992). The psychiatric characterization of individuals holding negative attitudes and affects toward homosexual individuals is that of someone who is insecure and uncomfortable with sexual and emotional relationships (Forstein, 1988).

On the assumption that certain individuals have proclivities for certain behaviors, Pryor (1987) developed the Likelihood to Sexually Harass (LSH) test, a test instrument designed to identify males most likely to use power for sexual gain. Three studies using this instrument found that men who have high LSH scores sometimes behave in a sexually harassing way. However, these investigations did not indicate that sexual harassment is solely the product of an individual's gender or deviant personality, but that it is also a function of certain social situations (Pryor & Whalen, 1997).

Situation Variables

Situational correlates of sexual harassment include the job gender context, that is, workplace gender ratio (Fitzgerald et al., 1997). For just as males are more likely than females to harass, traditionally male-dominated occupations and workplaces where males outnumber females seem to foster sexual harassment in general, and in particular, that of suspected or actual lesbians and gays (Pryor & Whalen, 1997). In a survey of 192 lesbians and 121 heterosexual females, Schneider (1982) found that sexual harassment of lesbians was more than four times more common in workplaces with ≥80 percent male employees, than in workplaces with ≥80 percent female employees. In traditionally "blue collar" occupations (for instance, military, law enforcement, and construction), females (in general) are likely targets of both hostile and sexual attraction-based harassment, and males are likely targets of hostile sexual harassment. In traditionally "pink collar" occupations (for instance, clerical, nursing, and education), females are likely to be targets of unwelcome advances motivated by sexual attraction, and males are likely targets of hostile homophobic harassment. In other words, women in blue-collar occupations are often stereotyped as the "iron woman" lesbian, and in pink-collar occupations, stereotyped as the "temptress." Likewise, males in pink-collar occupations are often stereotyped as effeminate homosexuals (Foote & Goodman-Delahunty, 1999; Goodman-Delahunty, 1998).

Workplaces associated with sexual harassment were further characterized by Pryor and Whalen (1997), who reported that environments in which there is real or perceived competition or differential access to resources among employees, hostile sexual harassment is more likely. Other aspects of the organizational or workplace climate appear to foster sexual harassment and homophobia, particularly those that promote a sense of an all-male club. Sexually harassing behavior appears to become normative (that is, everyone else does it, so it must be okay) in workplaces in which such behavior by some occurs openly. Sexually harassing behavior is also associated with highly sexualized environments, that is, where nonharassing and consensual sexual relationships and behavior are common. Miscommunication (particularly that involving socially naive or unskilled individuals) may readily lead to sexual harassment in workplaces with nonprofessional atmospheres such as those in which males and females are dressed in some provocative way (Pryor & Whalen, 1997).

Consequences

Both immediate and long-term consequences of sexual harassment experienced by lesbian and gay targets include observable events as well as subjective phenomena. The objective results include: decreased work productivity, denial of resources or opportunities, economic loss, injury, illness, pregnancy, economic entrapment in an abusive workplace environment, and voluntary or involuntary job loss. The cognitive and affective consequences experienced by all targets, especially lesbians and gays, include: feelings of irritation, intimidation, persecution, and invalidation; increased anxiety, depression, anger, misery and hopelessness; and decreased motivation, job satisfaction, and self-esteem (Fitzgerald et al., 1997). Foote and Goodman-Delahunty (1999) report that for same-sex harassment, both males and females experience shame and humiliation in response to their harasser's behavior.

Causation and Development

With the exception of gender, the Person characteristics associated with harassing behavior or anti-homosexual attitudes, or both listed above, develop as a function of individual experience. Individual differences in learned skills and attitudes may predispose some to engage in sexually harassing behavior. For example, socially naive individuals lacking the skills necessary to interpret interpersonal cues and anticipate responses, could easily misinterpret a coworker's speech or behavior and respond with inept overtures and awkward sexual advances. Consistent with the prevalence of males as harassers, Pryor and Whalen (1997) report that numerous investigations have found a gender bias in social perception, that is, that males have a greater tendency to misinterpret social behavior such as eye contact or physical proximity, and perceive it as conveying sexual intent or proceptivity of the targeted individual. In other words, males are likely to fail to perceive a "no" in response to their sexual advances to mean just that. This could account for sex-

ual harassment that is motivated initially by sexual attraction toward both heterosexual females and lesbians. However, the inability to distinguish friendliness
from seductiveness is also positively correlated with failure to distinguish assertiveness from hostility (Pryor & Whalen, 1997), and this may contribute to hostile
harassment of women in general and to the persistence of the manly lesbian
stereotype as well (Pryor & Whalen, 1997).

Psychologists and other social scientists agree that the experiential deficits such
as the lack of appropriate role models, opportunities for learning interpersonal
skills, and moreover, exposure to homosexual individuals, contribute to the development of negative attitudes and sexually harassing behavior (Pryor & Whalen,
1997). Such negative attitudes are described elsewhere in the literature as misogynistic, sexist, heterosexist, and expressions of homoprejudice and homo-
anathema (Britton, 1990; Bhugra, 1987; Forstein, 1988; Pryor & Whalen, 1997).

For example, Herek and Capitano (1996) found that there is a reciprocal relationship between contact with and attitudes regarding homosexual individuals.
Social skills and attitudes are learned during socialization and throughout life. Social Identity Theory (Tajfel & Turner, 1986) explains that the basis for forming attitudes about others is the categorization of people into ingroups and outgroups
(that is, "we" and "they"). Individuals assigned to outgroups are disfavored, rewarded less, perceived as having fewer positive attributes, and are generally devalued (Tajfel & Turner, 1986). The likelihood of an individual being perceived as
belonging to one's own ingroup seems to be a function of contact and familiarity.
Thus lesbians and gay males may become targets of hostile sexual harassment due
to their categorization as outgroup members by heterosexual individuals who are
inexperienced and unfamiliar with homosexual individuals.

Ingroup-outgroup categorization begins in childhood and is learned in the
home, the church or temple, and in school (Pohan & Bailey, 1997; Tajfel &
Turner, 1987). These attitudes can be based on arbitrary or slight differences
among individuals. Gender and sexual orientation are Person factors with which
individuals in American society readily learn to categorize others (Pryor &
Whalen, 1997). In 1993, the American Association of University Women Educational Foundation conducted a survey of 1,632 U.S. school children ages 8 to 11
regarding their responses to various hypothetical situations involving 14 types of
harassment (cited in Pohan & Bailey, 1997; Pryor & Whalen, 1997). The type receiving the strongest negative responses was that of being called or labeled lesbian
or gay: 87 percent of females reported that they would be "very upset" were this to
happen, as did 85 percent of the males surveyed. Even actual physical abuse did
not provoke this extreme response among males. Further, 23 percent of males and
10 percent of females surveyed reported that they had personally been harassed
and accused of being homosexual (cited in Pohan & Bailey, 1997; Pryor &
Whalen, 1997). Pohan and Bailey (1997) reported personal narratives of adolescents describing how they had been called "faggot" and "queer" and were spit
upon, pushed, and ridiculed by their schoolmates. Obviously, many American

adolescents are exposed to and develop homophobic attitudes. The lack of recognition by educators and parents of the severity and ramifications of these forms of learned intolerance and actual discrimination increases the turmoil of childhood and adolescence (Pohan & Bailey, 1997).

Though socialization is key to the development of negative attitudes associated with sexual harassment, the interactions of specific workplace (that is, Situation variables) and individual characteristics (that is, Person variables) are proximate factors suspected in the causation of sexual harassment in general, and of lesbians and gays in particular. Yet causation of sexual harassment has also been investigated at a higher level of analysis. The influence of historical, societal, and institutional paradigms are examined as ultimate causal factors of sexual harassment. According to Kitzinger (1996) and Livingston (1996), sexism and heterosexism are societal paradigms and are essentially systems of oppression that have been in place for nearly 4,000 years. Sexism is a misogynistic belief system. It is a form of gender bias that values males over females and supports male rule. Heterosexism is a related system of beliefs and institutions that supports heterosexuality as the norm and treats any other sexual orientation as either nonexistent or abnormal (Livingston, 1996). Long (1996) described heterosexism as a form of multicultural bias that is essentially an ethnocentric lens through which many cultures, including our own, view the world. Herek (1990) described a general "heterosexist" ideology in American society, which disowns, denigrates and stigmatizes any nonheterosexual form of behavior, identity, relationship, or community. Indeed, Pharr (1998) stated that heterosexism creates the climate for homophobia and its systematic display in societal institutions (for instance, workplaces, religious institutions, and schools).

A number of investigators suggest that psychological theory has contributed substantially to the antihomosexual attitudes in Western societies (Britton, 1990; Livingston, 1996; Lugg, 1998). For example in Freudian theory, homosexuality is an immature and undeveloped form of adult sexuality (Britton, 1990). Psychiatry, psychology, as well as other social sciences have been accused of promoting heterosexism in their presumptions that (1) heterosexuality is "normal" and "healthy," and other sexualities are deviant and pathological; (2) that theory and data apply or generalize from heterosexuals to nonheterosexuals; and (3) that the heterosexual lifestyle provides normative standards by which to compare other sexualities (Long, 1996).

Forstein (1988) and Long (1996) hold the professions of psychiatry and psychology primarily responsible for many of the problems endured by lesbians and gays, because of the initial classification of homosexual orientation among the psychiatric disorders described in the original *Diagnostic and Statistical Manual* (DSM; American Psychiatric Association, 1952). The idea that antihomosexual attitudes and behavior are inappropriate and problematic only developed following the removal of homosexual orientation, and later that of egodystonic homosexual orientation, as a psychiatric diagnoses in the *DSM-III-R* (APA, 1987). Unfortunately, antihomosexual attitudes have only slightly diminished among the general population and within these professions (Forstein, 1988), and only recently has the mental health profession begun attempts to prevent heterosexist discrimination (Rothbulm & Bond, 1996).

However, the conceptualization of homosexuality as an illness, deviance, or perversion has a long and rich history that predates all of the social sciences and has contributed the development of a mythology of homosexuality (Bhugra, 1987; Britton, 1990; Lugg, 1998). Myths developing from this conceptualization are widely accepted today in American society, and include such ideas as: homosexual individuals recruit others into their "lifestyle" (read sexuality), prey upon children, and that they are the primary reason for the AIDS epidemic. According to Lugg (1998), the myth of harm to children is a time-worn but deliberately constructed spectacle of fear. For example, gypsies were said to steal children, Jews to eat them, witches to sacrifice them, and now, homosexuals seduce and recruit them. Britton (1990) and Lugg (1998) attribute more responsibility for this mythology and prejudice to Western Christian theology in which homosexuality is sin, than to the mental health professions and social sciences. In particular, Lugg accuses the "Religious Right," a major conservative political force in the United States, of the strategic creation and use of homophobia to influence social policy and individual behavior. For example, in order to engender political support and purposefully promote intolerance, the Religious Right often proclaims as "the Gospel truth" that homosexuals recruit and molest children, despite the unequivocal evidence to the contrary, and it portrays homosexuality as an abomination that threatens Western civilization, Christian salvation, and the theologically supported heterosexist status quo (Lugg, 1998).

Thus, it should come as no surprise that antihomosexual campaigns have flourished coincident with the AIDS epidemic of the late twentieth century, as they did in medieval and earlier times of epidemics of bubonic plague, and later in the eighteenth century when syphilis was a major epidemic. The Church and the medical professions in their attempts to cope with rampant disease and death, strongly influenced public treatment and opinion of individuals who were, or were suspected of being, homosexual (Bhugra, 1987). Professional and religious bias toward homosexual individuals has now carried over into the public education system. According to Lugg (1998), the Religious Right has subjected the U.S. public education system to blistering attacks regarding its possible moral influence on children by depicting public schools as promoting homosexuality through sexuality education, and in system-wide attempts to teach and promote tolerance and the appreciation of diversity (Lugg, 1998). These attacks have misrepresented educational curricula as promoting disease, abortion, promiscuous sexual behavior, and especially, homosexual behavior. However, many social scientists and civil rights advocates feel that if education in the United States is to be criticized, it should be for failing to create an awareness of and sensitivity to homosexual people, as well as the many issues surrounding sexual orientation. Forstein (1998) criticized postsecondary, and particularly graduate programs, for failing to utilize more recent and scientifically sophisticated literature in the training of professionals that would help to debunk and dispel the myths and stereotypes of lesbians and gays that are ubiquitous in American society today.

Griffin (1998) believes that heterosexism (which includes homophobia) is a pervasive social disease that is widely accepted due to the promotion by the popular media, wherein heterosexuality is given more validity, location, and voice. The consequence is that homosexual individuals live in silence, unrecognized, and thus must fight for the notion that they exist and that they deserve the same civil rights as heterosexuals (Griffin, 1998). It has only been since the 1990s that mention of homosexuality was acceptable on broadcast television and in other popular media. However, the controversy that ensued over the highly popular, but later cancelled, American television series *Ellen,* in which the main character "comes out" as a lesbian, exemplifies the tenacious heterosexism of sponsors and consumers of popular media, and their outcry at any deviation from the longstanding tendency to portray lesbians and gays negatively, if at all (Pryor & Whalen, 1997). Some readers may also recall the ludicrous extremes to which the antihomosexual politics of the Religious Right reached in the recent and highly publicized, openly homophobic attack of a character from a public television show for toddlers entitled *Teletubbies.* The character named "Tinkie Winkie" attracted the wrath of Reverend Jerry Falwell, who has denied stating that Tinkie Winkie's purple pelage, delta shaped antenna, and magic bag symbolized and promoted the "homosexual lifestyle" (Falwell sees gay, 1999).

The legal profession has not escaped accusations of responsibility for current heterosexist and homophobic societal views, and it has been blamed for its significant contribution to the neglect, intolerance, and persecution of homosexual individuals. Herek (1990; Portwood, 1995) argued that the profession of law has not protected homosexual citizens the way it would protect any other victimized group of people. Goodman-Delahunty (1998) described U.S. legal doctrine as replete with policies reflecting heterosexist beliefs about gender, and that there have been few exceptions to the systematic biases in the courts in favor of males over females. Further, the legal proscription of sexual behavior has historically been and continues to be quite heterosexist in ideology and rationale. Homosexual behavior is widely criminalized, and as indicated in the title of this chapter, civil rights disproportionately lean toward heterosexuals (Goodman-Delahunty, 1998).

Although some investigators assume historical and societal factors are more responsible for the present treatment of lesbians and gays than are individual attitudes and behavior, social scientists are striving to end the oppression by attempting to change the latter, and to ultimately create a more egalitarian paradigm. Their research has provided a number of suggestions for changing individual behavior and attitudes, and for effecting broad societal and institutional change in the treatment of homosexual individuals as well.

Research Applications and Potential Solutions

Modification of individual behavior and attitudes requires learning. Elimination of the myths surrounding homosexuality that flow from unrestrained ignorance is essential; therefore, we must educate people (Griffin, 1998). However, individuals attempting to do so should first examine their own language, knowledge or lack thereof, prejudice, stereotyping, and insensitivity (Kitzinger, 1996; Long, 1996). For example, by initially assuming as most people do, that a coworker is hetero-sexual unless told otherwise, one dismisses and invalidates anyone who is not. Systematic attempts to increase exposure and familiarity include developing per-sonal and professional relationships with lesbians and gays, and by gaining knowledge about the history of the gay rights movement, and especially about the personal suffering and societal consequences of antihomosexual attitudes and ac-tions (Long, 1996). Numerous studies have found that increasing exposure to ho-mosexual individuals is associated with more positive attitudes and tolerance (Ames, 1996; Bruce et al., 1990; D'Augelli & Rose, 1990; Holtzen & Agresti, 1990).

For individuals who are lesbian or gay, the most promising strategy for promot-ing change and ending the stigma associated with homosexual orientation is "coming out," for personal disclosure also appears to increase positive attitudes toward homosexuals as a group (Herek & Capitano, 1996).

Pryor and Whalen (1998) made a number of suggestions to improve workplace treatment of lesbians and gays. Negative attitudes may be modified by exercises designed to break down some of the ingroup-outgroup barriers, for instance, exer-cises such as those reported successful in race relations literature. Workplace training in interpersonal social skills would benefit the skilled, as well as unskilled and socially naive individuals, by decreasing the risk of miscommunication. More specific to sexual harassment, organizations need to establish and circulate policy, grievance procedures, and to provide support programs for all targets of sexual harassment (Greenlaw & Kohl, 1981). Again education is key, and organizations should provide accurate and current information to their employees regarding the treatment of others, especially that of lesbians and gay men, and other minority groups (Pryor & Whalen, 1997).

Education about heterosexism, homophobia, and sexual harassment should not be limited to the workplace, however (Sandler & Shoop, 1997). Instead, Rothblum and Bond (1996) recommended that this information be part of the general cur-riculum in social science, developmental psychology, the psychology of diversity, social work, aging, obstetrics, public health, and family practice programs. The importance of practitioner education and expertise should be emphasized in the training of professionals to protect individuals from both physical and mental health risks; to practice sensitivity in the assessment, intervention and recognition of the issues facing lesbians and gays, but also to serve as models for affirming these individuals and others in our communities. As such, practitioners need to be self-conscious about how their language reflects or undermines their own goals regarding heterosexism and treatment of lesbians and gay men (Kitzinger, 1996; Rothblum & Bond, 1996).

Although the consequences of sexual harassment in general, and of hostile expressions of homophobia toward lesbian and gay targets in particular, are basically the same—subordination and oppression—investigators should not assume common causes on the basis of common outcomes. More narrowly focused research is needed to determine causality for all forms of sexually harassing behavior. Furthermore, because the homosexual population is diverse, its diversity should be reflected not only in training and intervention, but in the research on which policy should be based as well (Rothblum & Bond, 1996). Ames (1996) specifically called for research that differentiates lesbians and gays and that focuses on issues and interventions specific to these two distinct groups of people. Goodman-Delahunty (1998) suggested that the test instruments used in much research regarding sexual harassment were developed to measure traditional sexual harassment involving heterosexuals, and therefore, test instruments need to be developed for nonheterosexual individuals. She suggested further that we need to identify differences in the legal, economic, and organizational power of males and females, and how specific situations and social structures treat men and women differently. Documenting how our society is gendered and unequal in its expectations or opportunities will lead to more research on, and application of, mechanisms for change (Goodman-Delahunty, 1998).

Others have called for more investigation of the effectiveness of current and developing workplace educational interventions (Pryor & Whalen, 1997). Accordingly, in an attempt to improve the quality of research, the American Psychological Association has formed a task force to provide guidelines for those wishing to engage in nonheterosexist research, and to decrease the stereotyping and stigmatization of females and nonheterosexual individuals. Further, they suggest that individual researchers should not selfishly place their professional reputation over the need for analysis of controversial and socially significant issues such as these (Rothblum & Bond, 1996).

Because of the historical reinforcement of the stigmatization of homosexual people by its initial psychiatric classification and subsequent declassification of homosexuality as a mental disorder, some feel that psychology and psychiatry are the professions most obligated to improve the current situation (Forstein, 1988; Simoni, 1996). However, others such as Kitzinger (1996), believe that these professions are not as objective and scientific as they seem, and that they are inappropriate disciplines to challenge or prevent antihomosexual attitudes and sexual harassment of lesbians and gay men, given the original conceptualization that lingers in the professions today. Kitzinger pointed out that the modern oppression of lesbians and gays is more subtle and invidious than the previous diagnostic categorization. Psychology and psychiatry no longer prohibit same-sex sexual behavior, instead they shape and construct lesbian and gay identities, and politics, in their own image and own languages, that is, the experience of homosexuals has been "psychologized." For example, in current undergraduate texts, heterosexuality is depicted as the norm and homosexuality is presented under headings of dysfunction and deviancy, rather than both being integrated into a general discussion of sexual orientation. Kitzinger further accuses psychology and psychiatry of portraying lesbians and gays as victims, while forgetting that it is the heterosexist oppressors (that is, harassers) whose attitudes, behavior, and effects on society are the real problems, and not the actual or suspected homosexual individuals who are targeted (Kitzinger, 1996).

Schreier (1995) called for a fundamental paradigm shift in education, the mental health professions, and in the workplace, from the promotion of tolerance (which is no more than acknowledgment) to the promotion of nurturance (which views females and nonheterosexual individuals as invaluable and an indispensable part of our culture; Schreier, 1995). However, Pharr (1998) stated that change in individual behavior is most often preceded by change in public ideas. In other words, many people need some sort of public reinforcement to help turn appropriate attitudes into appropriate actions. So how do we as psychologists and social scientists go about changing public policy? Livingston (1996) believes that change does not occur because it is right, but because those involved in effecting change have a vision, a systematic plan for dealing with tactics of the oppressors, that they organize and assemble, for large coalitions are not ignored.

CONCLUSION

Therefore, we call for accountability across professions and academic disciplines. We believe strongly that more rigorous systematic investigation of the heterosexist ideology, oppression and harassment of lesbians and gay men in our society, will allow for improved education of professionals, as well as others, in the workplace, schools, and popular media. Furthermore, change in legal and organizational policy may be effective methods for dealing with the patently oppressive treatment that lesbians and gays endure in the United States today. Indeed, in order to significantly diminish employment discrimination against lesbians and gays, the inclusion of sexual orientation among the enumerated bases in Title VII may ultimately be necessary. Hence, we advocate the combined application of research-based methods for change in order to effect increased legal protection, sensitivity to, and improved treatment of lesbians and gay men in the workplace and in American society at large.

REFERENCES

American Psychiatric Association: Committee on nomenclature and statistics. (1952). *Mental disorders: Diagnostic and statistical manual* (DSM). Washington, DC: Author.

American Psychiatric Association. (1987). *Diagnostic and statistical manual of mental disorders* (3rd ed., rev.) (DSM-III-R). Washington, DC: Author.

American Psychiatric Association. (1994). *Diagnostic and statistical manual* (4th ed.) (DSM-IV). Washington, DC: Author.

Ames, L. J. (1996). Homophobia, homo-ignorance, homo-hate, heterosexism, and AIDS. In E. D. Rothblum & L. A. Bond (Eds.), *Preventing heterosexism and homphobia* (pp. 239–252). London: Sage.

Barnes v. Costle (1977). 561 F2d 983, 990 n55 (D.C. Cir.).

Bhugra, D. (1987). Homophobia: A review of the literature. *Sexual & Marital Therapy, 2*(2), 169–177.

Britton, D. M. (1990). Homophobia and homosociality: An analysis of boundary maintenance. *Sociological Quarterly, 31*(3), 423–439.

Brookins, R. (1998). A rose by any other name . . . The gender basis of same-sex sexual harassment. *Drake Law Review, 46,* 441–538.

Brown, L. (1993). *The new shorter Oxford English dictionary on historical principles.* Oxford: Clarendon Press.

Bruce, K. E., Shrum, J. C., Trefethen, C., & Slovik, L. F. (1990). Students' attitudes about AIDS, homosexuality, and condoms. *AIDS Education and Prevention, 2,* 220–234.

Bundy v. Jackson. (1981). 641 F2d 934 (D.C. Cir.).

Civil Rights Act of 1964. (1994). Title VII, 42 U.S.C.A.,_sections_2000e to 2000e-17.

D'Augelli, A. R., & Rose, M. L. (1990). Homophobia in a university community: Attitudes and experiences of heterosexual freshmen. *Journal of College Student Development, 31,* 484–491.

Elliott, J. E. (1993). Career development with lesbian and gay clients. *Career Development Quarterly, 41,* 210–226.

Equal Employment Opportunity Commission. (1980). *Final guidelines on sexual harassment in the workplace* (45 Fed. Reg. 74676). Washington, DC: U.S. Government Printing Office.

Falwell sees gay in Teletubby. (1999, February 11). *New York Times,* p. A2.

Fitzgerald, L. F., Drasgow, F., Hulin, C. L., Gelfand, M. J., & Magley, V. J. (1997). Antecedents and consequences of sexual harassment in organizations: A test of an integrated model. *Journal of Applied Psychology, 82*(4), 578–589.

Foote, W. E., & Goodman-Delahunty, J. G. (1999). Same-sex harassment: Implications of the *Oncale* decision for forensic evaluation of plaintiffs. *Behavioral Sciences and the Law, 17,* 123–139.

Forstein, M. (1988). Homophobia: An overview. *Psychiatric Annals, 18*(1), 33–36.

Fredette v. BVP Management Assoc. (1997). 112 F3d 1503 (11th Cir.).

Garcia v. Elf Atochem North America (1994). 28 F3d 446 (5th Cir.).

George, M. C. (1998). Because of sex: Same-sex harassment claims under Title VII of the Civil Rights Act of 1964. *Law & Psychology Review, 22,* 251–269.

Giddens v. Shell Oil Co. (1993). 12 F3d 208 (5th Cir.).

Goodman-Delahunty, J. (1998). Approaches to gender and the law: Research and applications. *Law and Human Behavior, 22*(1), 129–143.

Greenlaw, P. S., & Kohl, J. P. (1981). Sexual harassment: Homosexuality, bisexuality and blackmail. *Personnel Administrator, 26*(6), 59–62.

Griffin, G. (1998). Understanding heterosexism: The subtle continuum of homophobia. *Women & Language, 21*(1), 33–39.

Harris v. Forklift Systems, Inc. (1993). 510 U.S. 17.

Herek, G. M. (1984). Beyond "homophobia": A social perspective on attitudes toward lesbians and gay men. *Journal of Homosexuality, 10,* 1–21.

Herek, G. M. (1989). Hate crimes against lesbians and gay men: Issues for research and policy. *American Psychologist, 44,* 948–955.

Herek, G. M. (1990). The context of anti-gay violence: Notes on cultural and psychological heterosexism. *Journal of Interpersonal Violence, 5,* 316–333.

Herek, G. M., & Capitano, J. P. (1996). "Some of my best friends": Intergroup contact, concealable stigma, and heterosexuals' attitudes toward gay men and lesbians. *Personality & Social Psychology Bulletin, 22*(4), 412–424.

Holtzen, D. W., & Agresti, A. A. (1990). Parental responses to gay and lesbian children: Differences in homophobia, self-esteem and sex-role stereotyping. *Journal of Social and Clinical Psychology, 9*(3), 390–399.

Hopkins, v. Baltimore Gas & Elec. Co. (1996). 77 F3d 745 (4th Cir.).

Kitzinger, C. (1996). Speaking of oppression: Psychology, politics and the language of power. In E. D. Rothblum & L. A. Bond (Eds.), *Preventing heterosexism and homophobia* (pp. 3–19). London: Sage.

Kurdek, L. A. (1988). Correlates of negative attitudes toward homosexuals in heterosexual college students. *Sex Roles, 18*(11–12), 727–738.

Livingston, J. A. (1996). Individual action and political strategies: Creating a future free of heterosexism. In E. D. Rothblum & L. A. Bond (Eds.), *Preventing heterosexism and homophobia* (pp. 253–265). London: Sage.

Locke, S. S. (1996). The equal opportunity harasser as a paradigm for recognizing sexual harassment of homosexuals under Title VII. *Rutgers Law Journal, 27*(2), 338–415.

Long, J. K. (1996). Working with lesbians, gays, and bisexuals: Addressing heterosexism in supervision. *Family Processes, 35*(3), 377–388.

Lugg, C. A. (1998). The religious right and public education: The paranoid politics of homophobia. *Educational Policy, 12*(3), 267–283.

Mayo v. Kiwest Corp. (1996). 94 F3d 641 (4th Cir.).

McWilliams v. Fairfax Co. Bd. of Supervisors. (1996). 72 F3d 1191 (4th Cir.).

Meritor Savings Bank v. Vinson (1986). 477 U.S. 57.

O'Donohue, W. (1997). *Sexual harassment: Theory, research, and treatment.* Boston: Allyn & Bacon.

Oncale v. Sundowner Offshore Services, Inc. (1998). 523 U.S. 75.

Pharr, S. (1998). *Homophobia: A weapon of sexism.* Little Rock, AK: Chardon Press.

Pohan, C. A., & Bailey, N. J. (1997, Fall). Opening the closet: Multiculturalism that is fully inclusive. *Multicultural Education,* 12–15.

Portwood, S. G. (1995). Employment discrimination in the public sector based on sexual orientation: Conflicts between research evidence and the law. *Law & Psychology Review, 19,* 113–152.

Pryor, J. B. (1987). Sexual harassment proclivities in men. *Sex Roles, 17,* 269–290.

Pryor, J. B., & Whalen, N. J. (1997). A typology of sexual harassment: Characteristics of harassers and the social circumstances under which sexual harassment occurs. In W. O'Donohue (Ed.), *Sexual harassment: Theory, research, and treatment* (pp. 129–151). Boston: Allyn & Bacon.

Rothblum, E. D. & Bond, L. A. (Eds.). (1996). *Preventing heterosexism and homophobia.* London: Sage.

Sandler, B. R., & Shoop R. J. (1997). What is sexual harassment? In B. R. Sandler & R. J. Shoop (Eds.), *Sexual harassment on campus: A guide for administrators, faculty and students* (pp. 1–21). Boston: Allyn & Bacon.

Schneider, B. A. (1982). Consciousness about sexual harassment among heterosexual and lesbian women workers. *Journal of Social Issues, 38,* 75–97.

Simoni, J. M. (1996). Confronting heterosexism in the teaching of psychology. *Teaching of Psychology, 23*(4), 220–226.

Seltzer, R. (1992). The social location of those holding antihomosexual attitudes. *Sex Roles, 26*(9–10), 391–398.

Schreier, B. A. (1995). Moving beyond tolerance: A new paradigm for programming about homophobia/biphobia and heterosexism. *Journal of College Student Development, 36*(1), 19–26.

Storrow, R. F. (1998, February). Same-sex sexual harassment claims after Oncale: Defining the boundaries of actionable conduct. *American University Law Review,* 677–745.

Tajfel, H., & Turner, J. C. (1986). The social identity theory of integrating conflict. In W. G. Austin & S. Worchel (Eds.), *The social psychology of intergroup relations* (pp. 33–47). Pacific Grove, CA: Brooks/Cole.

Thomas, G. (Ed.). (1998). Same-sex harassment: Civil rights law and workplace discrimination (special issue). *Supreme Court Debates, 1*(1).

Van de Ven, P. (1994). Comparisons among homophobic reactions of undergraduates, high school students, and young offenders. *The Journal of Sex Research, 31*(2), 117–124.

Wrightson v. Pizza Hut of America, Inc. (1996). 99 F3d 138 (4th Cir.).

Part IV
Sexual Orientation and Identity Issues

8

DISCRIMINATION AGAINST GAYS, LESBIANS, AND THE HIGHLY ANDROGYNOUS

Vern L. Bullough

Throughout much of Western history homosexuals have been looked upon by society with considerable disfavor. They have been feared, loathed, tolerated, treated with compassion, regarded as sick or mentally ill or sinners, but not generally accepted by most of society. When the American states began legislating on the topic, they changed the sinner into a law breaker. When the medical community treated the subject, they regarded it as a form of pathology. As Eric Marcus (1992) said, "The Churches say we're sinners. Psychiatrists say we're sick. Capitalists say we're subversive. Communists say we're immoral" (p. 249). Usually it was only the most androgynous who were identified as homosexuals, so much so that for a time there was belief that homosexuality represented a third sex. Quite clearly, those identified as homosexuals, sometime erroneously, have generally been stigmatized in some way or another. It was only in the last part of the twentieth century that official attitudes began to change.

These past attitudes have to be emphasized because although official attitudes have begun to change, the public mind still holds considerable misunderstanding and apprehension about homosexuality, lesbianism, and any kind of gender dysphoric person. Changes in attitudes have not taken place in a vacuum but rather have been in part a result of better understanding of same-sex behavior by numerous investigators, and in part by the willingness of homosexuals, lesbians, and gender dysphoric people to come out in the open, to organize, and to campaign for changes in the law, and in the process win over more and more segments of the general public to agree with them. As a historian, looking back at the changes of the past half century, changes seem radical, much more radical than could have been predicted or even hoped for by the gay community in 1950.

Among the studies contributing to the change were the Kinsey reports, which demonstrated that far more people had same-sex experiences to the point of orgasm than people traditionally believed (Kinsey, Pomeroy, & Martin, 1948; Kinsey, Pomeroy, Martin, & Gebhard, 1953). Other studies soon followed demonstrating that the stereotypes held by society were often wrong. Evelyn Hooker (1957), for example, found that the standard projective technique tests used by psychologists could not distinguish a homosexual male from a heterosexual one, despite widespread belief that they could. It is a measure of the psychologists' belief in the efficacy of their own tests (something that I do not have) that they accepted the results rather than saying their tests were not particularly accurate. The belief in new "scientific" studies had powerful influence on society. Not only did much of the public accept the results but more importantly so did the gays, lesbians, and gender dysphoric individuals themselves. This is not the place to examine or even list these studies, including some of my own, but the result was a new understanding of same-sex activities, symbolized by the changes made by the American Psychological Association and the American Psychiatric Association in the 1970s, removing it from the category of pathological behavior.

It is not enough simply to have data challenging traditional attitudes; there also has to be effective means of communicating these findings to the public and even more importantly the organization of groups agitating for change. The last half of the twentieth century saw radical changes in the role and status of Blacks, women, ethnic minorities, the physically and mentally impaired, and previously stigmatized sexual minorities. Homosexuals in the United States, encouraged by the publicity given to Kinsey's data on the widespread extent of same-sex relationships, began organizing in the post-World War II period in many of the larger American cities. The center of much of the initial activity was in Los Angeles, where the Mattachine Society first appeared and the first homosexual magazine, *ONE,* was published. Although the Mattachine started as a secret society, *ONE* was open and above board, as was the reorganized Mattachine and other groups. This meant that some individuals had to come out of the closet and more and more did so. Many of the early victories were on issues such as the right to send a magazine about homosexuality through the mail or the appearance of the word *homosexual* in a telephone directory. Gays and lesbians soon found they were not alone, and organizations such as the American Friends Service Committee and the American Civil Liberties Union campaigned to change the laws about homosexuality. Once the barriers began to fall, they did so with an ever-quickening pace. Symbolic of the change was the Stonewall demonstrations in New York City in 1969, which suddenly made homosexuality and gender dysphoric behavior a subject of attention in the nation's press, which previously had ignored such activities. It also marked the movement of the center of homosexual activities from Los Angeles and San Francisco to New York City. More and more individuals came out in the open, proclaiming themselves gay or lesbians, and what had been an underground political movement became a public one.

Coming out was essential to effective political survival. Sometimes it seems change takes place so rapidly. The more research that is done emphasizing same-sex activities as part and parcel of the human spectrum, the more people come out, and the pace of change escalates. Coming out initially was confined to people who acted as spokespersons for the movement, a sort of selfless step taken on behalf of others. Gradually, however coming out came to mean something more. Gay liberationists began to argue that coming out was not only a profoundly political act, but one that offers enormous personal benefits to an individual.

The open avowal of one's sexual identity, whether at work, at school, at home, or before television cameras, symbolized the shedding of the self-hatred that gay men and women internalized, and consequently it promised an immediate improvement in one's life. To come out of the "closet" quintessentially expressed the fusion of the personal and the political that the radicalization of the late 1960s exalted. (D'Emilio, 1983).

Coming out is a necessity in identifying discrimination against those engaged in same-sex activities because one who is closeted had difficulty benefiting from any antidiscrimination laws. Does a person who is homosexual but who has not admitted it to any of his colleagues and who is denied a promotion or a raise have any evidence that such action was based on his or her sexual activity during non-business hours? It well might have been, because he or she might not be as closeted as he or she thought, but it would be much more difficult to document than discrimination against a woman or a racial minority or a physically disabled individual or even an elder person, the other categories upon which antidiscrimination legislation has so far been based. Although there are many androgynous people who might seem to many to be homosexual or lesbian, androgynous people are not necessarily homosexual or lesbian, and homosexuals and lesbians are not necessarily androgynous. It is only when a person is public about his or her same-sex preference, that there is any chance of proving discrimination.

From the 1960s on, there has been a growing body of law and legislation outlawing discrimination, first against Blacks, then against women, then against the physically handicapped, and finally against homosexuals, lesbians, and gender nonconformists. The results have been impressive. Most importantly, the results have not been confined to the United States, but are worldwide, reflecting a radical change in attitudes toward same-sex behavior.

Fourteen countries, as of this writing, have national laws that protect gays, lesbians, and bisexuals from discrimination: Canada, Denmark, Finland, France, Iceland, Ireland, Israel, the Netherlands, New Zealand, Norway, Slovenia, South Africa, Spain, and Sweden. Twelve states, as of this writing, have extended legal protection to sexual minorities, whereas 35 have removed sodomy from the criminal code. On the national level, the United States Supreme Court has ruled that an amendment of the Colorado state constitution passed by a referendum banning antidiscrimination laws based on sexual orientation violated the equal protection clause of the U.S. Constitution and was, therefore, unlawful. This ruling has to be regarded as a landmark victory for equal rights, and should provide an important precedent for future U.S. antidiscrimination cases. In Australia, as of this writing, the Australian parliament is considering national legislation to prohibit discrimination based on sexual orientation, and several states have already enacted such legislation including New South Wales, South Australia, Northern Territory, and Capital Territory.

Various programs and agencies of the United Nations have also taken steps to encourage member states to make discrimination against same-sex relationships illegal. The International Labor Office of the United Nations, after conducting a survey examining issues of discrimination in employment based on sexual orientation, recommended the inclusion of sexual orientation in a new protocol to extend the protective applications of its 1958 Convention. The *Home Development Report* (Levine & Watson, 1999) issued by the Development Program included a "Human Freedom Index," an index ranking 88 countries by 40 indicators of democracy, including the personal rights of consenting adults to have same-sex relationships. The High Commission for Refugees (Levine & Watson, 1999) has stated that "homosexuals may be eligible for refugee status on the basis of persecution because of their membership of a particular social group" (p. 20). It holds that when a government is unwilling or unable to protect their gay and lesbian citizens, they should be recognized as refugees.

Various conferences held by the United Nations have also taken stands on the discrimination of those engaged in same-sex activity including the Fourth World Conference on Women, the Economic Council of Europe's Regional Platform for Action, the International Conference on Population and Development's Plan of Action, and Habitat II Summit's Global Plan of Action. Regional human rights organizations such as the Council of Europe have established a right to privacy while the European Court of Human Rights has ruled that those states that are signatories to the European Convention cannot criminalize same-sex relations because such laws violate personal rights to privacy. The European parliament has adopted a resolution calling on all member states to end unequal treatment of gays, lesbians, and bisexuals, and to initiate steps to reduce violence against such groups.

Several Non Government Organizations (NGOs) such as Amnesty International, the International Human Rights Law Group, the Human Rights Watch, the International Planned Parenthood Federation, and the International Humanist and Ethical Union, have included protection from discrimination on sexual orientation in their programs (Levine and Watson, 1999).[1]

These accomplishments are impressive, but discrimination still exists, and unfortunately it is sometimes tragic. This was illustrated in the United States was the by case of Matthew Shepard who in October 1998 was tied to a fence post, brutally beaten, and left to die by two men, simply because he was homosexual. Such incidents only remind us that although homosexuals have come a long way in achieving their rights, there is still a long way to go.

Most of the U.S. gay rights groups in the 1970s concentrated on convincing elected officials to protect homosexual citizens from discrimination by adding sexual orientation or similar phrases to existing antidiscrimination law, which often included provisions forbidding discrimination based on race, color, creed, sex, and religion. Age is also in the process of being added. Gays and lesbians also focused on combating police harassment, overturning state sodomy laws, providing a variety of services to local gay communities, and increasing visibility in the media. This was not always easy and for every two steps forward, there is often a backward step as well.

In 1977, for example, the pop singer and spokeswomen for the Florida orange juice industry, Anita Bryant, joined Jerry Falwell, the founder of the Moral Majority and a popular television evangelist, and other religious fundamentalists to campaign with sympathetic district attorneys, police, and the press, against giving rights to gays. They succeeded in having gay rights legislation repealed in Miami, Florida; this encouraged them to mount a nationwide crusade that led to repeal of gay rights legislation in St. Paul, Minnesota; Wichita, Kansas; and Eugene, Oregon. Though Bryant has since retired from the battle, the network she mobilized still remains active. The quick success of her network was neutralized as the gay movement and its allies gave battle on the west coast. Voters in California defeated the statewide antigay Briggs initiative that would have permitted local school districts to dismiss or deny employment to homosexual teachers, and in Seattle, voters overwhelmingly turned back an effort to repeal the city's gay rights protection. Some of the religious leaders in the antigay crusade became victims of their own initial success. Billy James Hargis, who built an empire in Tulsa around his Crusade for Christian Morality, was accused of having sex with several male students. Hargis admitted some of the charges but justified his actions by citing the friendship between David and Jonathan in the Bible. One result of the defeats suffered from the Anita Bryant crusade, as well as the admitted sex activity of Hargis, was a period of renewed militancy for the gay and lesbian movement marked by the 1979 national march on Washington by 75,000 to 100,000 gay rights supporters.

Giving renewed strength to the gay and lesbian campaign for equal rights was the outbreak of the AIDS epidemic in the 1980s, which had resulted in the death of over 23,000 individuals by the end of 1986. Many, many more were diagnosed as having the HIV virus including individuals such as the basketball star Magic Johnson. Having the virus did not necessarily mean a person was a homosexual, but some of the more militant in the gay community used it as a justification for "outing." Randy Shilts, for example, said,

By definition, the homosexual in the closet [has] surrendered his integrity. This makes closeted people very useful to the establishment: once empowered, such people are guaranteed to support the most subtle nuances of anti-gay prejudice. A closeted homosexual has the keenest understanding of these nuances, having chosen to live under the subjugation of prejudice . . . [and] is far less likely to demand fair or just treatment for his kind, because to do so would call attention to himself. (Quoted in Johansson & Percy, 1994, p. 226)

Many gays were outed publicly by Michelangelo Signorile and *OUTWEEK* in the early 1990s, but after the closing of that publication such outings have been less frequent.

Increasingly gays and lesbians have committed themselves to the gay movement and to going public, although many remain reluctant to do so. Stephen Sondheim, who only allowed his homosexuality to be made public in 1999 (Secrets, 1999), said he previously stayed closeted because he felt it was in his best interest to do so. He now felt the time was ripe to do so. Sondheim has never had an openly gay character in his work although in 1995 in a authorized revision of *Company,* he introduced homosexuality into the story by having a man make an incomplete pass at Bobby, the central character in the story. In that same year, however, he objected to a Seattle production of *Company,* which without asking permission made Bobby bisexual and changed the sexual orientation of two of the couples in his circle of friends. Ellen DeGeneres, who had gone public with her lesbianism a year earlier, however had her popular TV series canceled. Whether it was her openly gay lifestyle or whether it was for other reasons remains unclear, which only emphasizes the difficulty of determining whether or not discrimination exists. Ellen was certainly allowed the freedom to have her character develop as a lesbian, but supposedly after high initial interest, audience viewing dropped, and it was this that allegedly caused the cancellation. In a sense, the DeGeneres case emphasizes that even when a person is willing to state publicly their sexual persuasion, it is still difficult to label her show's cancellation as due to discrimination. The proof that it was not will probably be her ability to be sought by producers and directors for important roles. Discrimination without being open is even more difficult to prove, as the Tom Hanks character in the 1993 movie, *Philadelphia,* illustrated.

Few cases of real discrimination reach public attention because discrimination in the workplace is both open and subtle and can take many forms. In spite of President Clinton's "Don't Ask Don't Tell" policy for gays in the armed forces, discrimination remains enshrined in the military, in business, and in all-American institutions such as the Boy Scouts. Discrimination most often takes the form of a hostile atmosphere, but it also exists in corporate benefit policies, and company perquisites that do not apply to gay partners. As Friskopp and Silverstein (1995) reported in their study of the gay and lesbians graduates of the Harvard Business School,

Discrimination can be pervasive throughout an organization or limited to a particular department. It may be rampant among upper management or manifest in a few isolated lower individuals. It may be directed against those "queers," or it may be targeted against a specific individual who is known or suspected of being gay. (p. 70)

The first kind of reaction is what might be called impersonal because it is not directed against any individual. It is a lack of nondiscrimination policies in the institutions, as well as tolerance of certain kinds of hostile behavior, that permits, if not encourages, a hostile environment to develop. But even in organizations with nondiscrimination policies, discrimination against individuals can and does exist. Often, however, it is the fear of the unknown that is worse than the actual discrimination. One 1993–1994 survey (Friskopp & Silverstein, 1995) found that it was closeted gay people rather than the openly gay or lesbian who were most likely to report that they suspected they were discriminated against because they did not fit in. Many who believed they had been passed over for promotion or were fired for being gay admitted that they saw the discrimination as ambiguous because they did not know if anyone actually knew they were gay. Interestingly those who felt threatened by discriminatory circumstances and who chose to fight back usually achieved highly positive results for their career.

Outing is not always voluntary. In the survey of the Harvard Business School graduates, those who were involuntarily outed as gays were more likely to be outed by a fellow gay or lesbian than by their heterosexual colleagues. In some cases, a disgruntled ex-partner did the outing; in others gay activists who saw outing as a means of getting publicity for the gay community, did the outing, whereas others were simply outed inadvertently; that is, they had come out in one forum and found the information carried over to their workplace, which they had not intended. Most, however, who were outed, whether maliciously or inadvertently, suffered career damage (Friskopp & Silverstein, 1995). The question is whether they would have suffered such damage if they had outed themselves in conditions more favorable to presenting their side.

Discrimination varies according to the type of company one works for. Those employed in companies associated with the defense industry, that serve children, or that are connected with conservative or fundamentalist religious groups face special challenges. Almost all the gay or lesbian individuals working in such areas are almost completely closeted, and most have "horror stories" of fellow gays who had been treated badly by their companies. This might well be changing in some defense and military support businesses because of a change in the process of security clearance, which favors those gays and lesbians who are open about their sexual orientation in their security interviews over those who try to hide it. Stereotypes about companies that discriminate are not always accurate. The Disney company, a major family-oriented business, has large number of gay and lesbian employees, and most of them are open about it. Disney even gives insurance rights to the partners of their employees.

Large manufacturers and consumer products firms as well as construction, real estate, transportation, and utilities companies, rank second only to the defense industry or firms with close connection to fundamentalist religious groups as not being particularly sophisticated about gay issues. Many of these corporate cultures favor sameness and the situation of gays in them is the same as that of Jews or Blacks or women. Most management-level employees working in these industries remain cautious about their gay identity. Probably people who appear to be too androgynous simply do not make it. This not so true of the factory or mill worker employed by these companies. This is because unions often protect their minority employees. (Johansson & Percy, 1994). For example, one case in which I was involved dealt with a factory worker undergoing male-to-female surgical reassignment. The man had worked on the line long enough to acquire considerable seniority before deciding for gender reassignment. The employer, a major auto manufacturer, was very helpful, although they were reluctant to leave the person in the same job. They transferred her (she was already beginning to undergo hormone treatment) to another job. The other employees had some fun at the expense of their ex-coworker, including the sign put up by the replacement on the line stating that "the last person who held the job had lost his balls." My advisee found this interesting and could laugh about it herself. The one difficulty she had was determining which bathroom to use. Neither the men nor the women wanted her in their bathroom and so the company arranged for a separate bathroom to be used, which was not too far away from where she worked.

Somewhat less likely to discriminate against gays and lesbians are the banking and institutional investment companies, at least on the management level, perhaps because several key employees in these industries had been outed. In the *Fortune* 50 service companies, telecommunications, and allied services, individuals were more likely to be outed than in other organizations (Bullough & Bullough, 1995; Johansson & Percy, 1994).

Discrimination tends to vary by geographic location (Johansson & Percy, 1984). Most gay professionals who work in small towns or cities in the south or midwest remain heavily closeted, and very much concerned with being exposed. There are less closeted and more open gays in the larger cities. Being hired, promoted, or fired is a subjective process, and if an employee is out and has reliable witnesses to the hostile working environment that he or she is in, it is easier to claim discrimination.

What seems likely is that unless government abandons attempts to prevent discrimination, which seems unlikely to me, increasingly more jobs will be covered by nondiscrimination legislation. Already the sexual harassment legislation has been applied to gay and lesbian victims in states without fair employment practice acts. This is bound to be extended. To ultimately be successful, however, there needs to be enough feeling of security for individuals to admit they are gay or lesbian, or transgendered or gender dysphoric. There still are large numbers of individuals who either see no problem in keeping silent about their sex preferences or who are so fearful of what will happen that they dare not identify as gay or lesbian, that discrimination is still difficult to prove. Blacks, women, and the physically disabled have set the path. Gays and lesbians still have a political struggle to equal these other stigmatized groups, but to be protected, they have to be out in the open, and many gays and lesbians might find this too great a danger to contemplate.

NOTE

1. For more detail see the *Fact Sheet* issued by International Gay and Lesbian Human Rights Commission (IGLHRC), 1360 Mission St., San Francisco, CA 94103. See also D. Sanders, "Getting Lesbian and Gay Issues on the International Human Rights Agenda," *Human Rights Quarterly, 18* (1996), 67–106; "Promoting Lesbian and Gay Rights through International Human Rights Law" (New York Center for Constitutional Rights, 1996); J. D. Wilets, "International Human Rights Law and Sexual Orientation," *Hastings International and Comparative Law Review, 18,* 1(1996), 1–120; J. D. Wilets, "Using International Law to Vindicate the Civil Rights of Gays and Lesbians in United States Courts," *Columbia Humana Rights Law Review, 27,* 1(1995, Fall), 33–56; L. R. Helfer and A. M. Miller, "Sexual Orientation and Human Rights: Toward a United States and Transnational Jurisprudence," *Harvard Human Rights Journal, 9*(1996), 103.

REFERENCES

Bullough, V. L., & Bullough, B. (1995). Sexual attitudes: Myths and realities. Buffalo: Prometheus Books.

D'Emilio, J. (1983). *Sexual politics, sexual communities: The meaning of a homosexual identity in the United States, 1940–1970.* Chicago: University of Chicago Press.

Friskopp, A., & Silverstein, S. (1995). *Straight jobs: Gay lives.* New York: Scribners.

Hooker, E. (1957). The adjustment of the male overt homosexual. *Journal of Projective Techniques, 21,* 18–31.

Johansson, W., & Percy, W. A (1994). *Outing: Supporting the conspiracy of silence.* New York: Haworth Press.

Kinsey, A., Pomeroy, W., & Martin, C. (1948). *Sexual behavior in the human male.* Philadelphia: W. B. Saunders.

Kinsey, A., Pomeroy, W., Martin, C., & Gebhard, P., (1953) *Sexual behavior in the human female.* Philadelphia: W. B. Saunders.

Levine, A., & Watson, S. C. (1999). Fact sheet worldwide antidiscrmination laws and policies based on sexual orientation. *Siecus Report, 28*(2, December and January), 19–20.

Marcus, E. (1992). *Making history: The struggle for gay and lesbian rights.* New York: Harper.

Secrets, M. (1999). *Steven Sondheim: A life.* New York: Knopf.

9

THE SEARCH FOR THE IDEAL
HETEROSEXUAL ROLE PLAYER

Michelle J. McCormick

This chapter addresses three major questions: (1) What is the nature of hetero-sexuality as a normative ideal in society? (2) What impact has heterosexuality had as a normative ideal in the workplace? (3) Is there evidence of any change regarding this ideal? Answering the first question is important because of the intersection between sexuality and gender in society's views. Heterosexuality defines the ideal sexual orientations for men and women, whereas social definitions of masculinity and femininity define the ideal expression of heterosexual behavior.

The second question is important because normative expectations shape and constrain individual options in everyday life. Prevailing expectations with regard to heterosexuality have different implications for women and men, hence different social consequences for compliance and deviance. As a result, these views encourage behavior that tends to uphold a patriarchal pattern of gender relations in important areas of society such as the workplace, in spite of attempts to change the pattern of gender relations through legal or other macrostructural means.

The importance of the third question is that it raises the possibility of changes in the impact of sexuality on gender definitions and gender relations, with corresponding changes for women and men in the workplace and beyond. If the treatment of heterosexuality as the norm maintains the pattern of male dominance, then any change in the norms regarding sexuality can challenge this pattern. It thus can be argued that current views regarding gender and sexuality appear to be in a state of flux, which may lead to the emergence of a new "ideal."

THE HETEROSEXUAL IDEAL

The search for the ideal heterosexual role player begins with a look at how this role has been defined. Heterosexuality has a long history as a normative tradition for most societies, including our own. It does not operate on its own, however.

Instead, its role in defining ideal sexual behavior has been intimately bound up with prevailing views of gender (Schwartz & Rutter, 1998). Therefore, the heterosexual ideal needs to be examined within that context. The basic relationship has been one of mutual influence, with heterosexuality defining the normative masculine-feminine sexual orientations, whereas behaviors traditionally associated with gender definitions have defined normative heterosexual behavior.

The view of heterosexuality as the "normal" sexual orientation has been long and widely held in our society (Rosenbluth, 1997) and is generally viewed as a moral imperative (Connell, 1987; Rich, 1980). The acceptance of this view has been so strong that it is often taken for granted as a tacit assumption, even in social scientific discourses on gender and sexuality (Rich, 1980). Justified by religion and enforced by law, the assumption that heterosexuality is the exclusive pattern for normal sexual expression has been so ingrained in western thought that the term *heterosexual* was not developed and used explicitly until 1868 (Foucault, 1978; Katz, 1995). Even then, its meaning as a normal sexual orientation did not become the prevailing definition until around 1901; prior to that, the general meaning was as "an *abnormal or perverted* sexual appetite toward the opposite sex" (Penelope, 1993, p. 262; emphasis added).

Heterosexuality represents a strongly sanctioned behavioral mandate, its normative force greatly enhanced by its inclusion in the expectations defining the traditional gender roles. The association between heterosexuality as the ideal sexual expression and the traditional definitions of gender appears quite strong in prevailing views. For instance, people who engage in stereotypically masculine or feminine behaviors are generally perceived as heterosexual if their sex is gender-consonant, but as homosexual if it is not (Deaux & Lewis, 1984). Similarly, people whose facial features are perceived as cross-gender—a man with a "feminine" face or a woman with "masculine" features—tend to be perceived as homosexual (Dunkle & Francis (1990).

Men generally hold less tolerance for homosexuality than do women (D'Augelli & Rose, 1990; Herek, 1988; Kurdek, 1988), suggesting a greater association with homophobia for traditional masculine attitudes than for traditional views of femininity. For both sexes, however, traditional gender definitions and rejection of homosexuality appear to be highly related (Herek, 1988; Kite & Deaux, 1986; Whitley, 1987). It is not surprising, therefore, that the prevailing view among both women and men in U.S. society appears to be that heterosexuality is the only natural form of sexual expression (Kane & Schippers, 1996). The heterosexual mandate, or "compulsory heterosexuality," appears to be a central aspect of gender in modern society (Connell, 1987; Rich, 1980).

Just as heterosexuality impacts gender by defining the ideal sexual orientation, gender impacts heterosexuality by defining the gender-appropriate behaviors for its expression. Traditional gender expectations are strongly reflected in prevailing views of how women and men should express their sexuality. The main theme in gender-based behavioral expectations has been the manifestation and reinforcement of patriarchy, or male dominance (Doyle, 1983; Rich, 1980), and the traditional norms for heterosexual behavior share this theme.

Byers (1996) offers a useful conceptualization of prevailing views regarding heterosexual behavior that demonstrates the relationship of these views with the traditional gender roles. She presents a delineation of the major characteristics of what she calls the "traditional sexual script," or TSS, representing the most common set of expected behaviors for sexual interaction in the United States. That these behaviors presuppose heterosexuality is made explicit by her research (1996, p. 9). She lists and discusses six characteristics, which may be synopsized as follows (Byers, 1996, pp. 9–10):

1. Men are "oversexed" and women are "undersexed."

2. Women's worthiness and status are viewed to be reduced by sexual experience but men's worthiness and status are seen as enhanced.

3. Men are the active initiators, women the passive recipients of attention in sexual situations.

4. Women are expected to control sexual access, placing limits on the level of sexual activity in which they engage with their male partner.

5. A woman's value and status are considered to be enhanced by being in a romantic relationship. She is thus expected to behave in a way that maintains the man's romantic interest in her, even while she is restricting sexual access.

6. Women are expected to be emotional, sensitive, and nurturing; men are expected to be unemotional, relatively insensitive, and self-focused.

Traditional gender expectations are clearly reflected in these characteristics. For instance, the traditional views of masculinity and femininity define them as bipolar sets. Thus the expected traits and behaviors that comprise them are seen as mutually exclusive, so that masculine traits contain no "feminine'" elements and vice versa (Deaux & Kite, 1987). This expectation is even stronger for the masculine role than for its counterpart (Pleck, 1981, 1995). The traditional sexual script follows this pattern as well. There is no allowance for behavioral overlap in how men and women might appropriately express their sexuality. Instead, "being masculine" requires "not being feminine" and vice versa.

For example, Levant (1997) points out that "avoiding all things feminine" (p. 13) is one of the normative expectations for traditional masculinity, which is reflected in sexual norms for men that encourage the avoidance of such "feminine" traits as sexual passivity or emphasis on emotional intimacy over physical pleasure. He points out the connection with traditional gender norms, in which men are socialized to develop characteristics such as competitiveness and emotional stoicism. On one hand, these characteristics are beneficial for men because they support a patriarchal framework for society; but on the other hand, they discourage closeness and emotional involvement in sexual relationships, according to Levant (1997, pp. 13–14).

Traditional masculinity and femininity are not just mutually exclusive in their conceptualization, they are also represented as polar opposites. Thus a second way the defining characteristics of the traditional sexual script reflect traditional gender expectations is by following a pattern of complementarity. The genders are perceived as complementary in the traditional view, so that the association of a trait or behavior with one gender is matched by an expectation for its opposite with the other gender (Deaux & Lewis, 1984; Foushee, Helmreich, & Spence, 1979). For example, according to traditional definitions of masculinity, strength, leadership, rationality, and dominance are typical male traits. Their opposites—weakness, being a follower, irrationality, and submissiveness—are ascribed to females in the traditional views of femininity. Interestingly, these traits (and others) and their complementary distribution are remarkably uniform in the prevailing notions of masculinity-femininity found among Americans, as well as among members of other Western and non-Western societies (Williams & Bennet, 1975; Williams & Best, 1982).

This complementary pattern of traits also appears in the traditional expectations for heterosexual behavior. For instance, each characteristic in Byers's (1996) formulation of the traditional sexual script involves a complementary pair of traits for men and women, defining their respective heterosexual expression in behavioral opposites. Men are oversexed, thus women are seen as undersexed; men's value is enhanced by sexual experience whereas women's value is reduced; men actively pursue sexual activity, whereas women passively receive sexual advances; and so forth. From this perspective, women's sexuality is defined as fundamentally different from men's in a way that supports the patriarchal views of male dominance and control (Weinberg, Swensson, & Hammersmith, 1983), just as is found in the traditional gender definitions.

A third pattern found in the traditional sexual script reflecting the traditional gender definitions is the devaluing of women. The complementary pairs of traits or behaviors constituting the traditional gender definitions typically involve one term that is positively valued in society and another that has a lesser or even negative social value. The general pattern of assignment for these paired traits or behaviors is for the positively valued one to be associated with masculinity and the negatively valued one to be part of the definition of femininity (Broverman et al., 1972; Rosenkrantz, 1968).

Byers's (1996) delineation of the traditional sexual script shows a similar pattern. For instance, sexual experience is seen to enhance men's social worth, but to decrease that of women. Men are cast as the leaders, a positively valued role, as the initiators of sexual activity, whereas women are the passive recipients of the man's active advances. In this manner, the traditional sexual script both follows and reinforces the general pattern of male dominance and superiority traditionally defined for the genders.

THE HETEROSEXUALIZED WORKPLACE

Heterosexuality as a normative ideal, reinforced by and reinforcing the traditional gender definitions, has had a profound influence on the framework of society. Feminists argue that gender imbues every component of society, shaping the components to conform to the expectations defining these roles through the process of engendering. Schwartz and Rutter (1998) describe this process as one in which "social processes have determined what is appropriately masculine and feminine and that gender has therefore become integral to the definition of the phenomenon" (p. 3). For example, they point out that the inclusion of gender assumptions is so much a part of the institution of marriage that same-sex marriage appears innately impossible to most people (1998).

Nowhere is the engendering of society more clearly exemplified than in the workplace. Although earlier works (Acker & Van Houten, 1974; Feldberg & Glenn, 1979; Ferguson, 1984; MacKinnon, 1979; Moss Kanter, 1977) delved into the issue of gender as a force shaping work relations and organizational structure, Acker (1990) presents the first systematic proposal for a theory of gendered organizations. She starts by pointing out that the organizational structure of the workplace is far from gender-neutral, as is often assumed, but instead is founded upon an underpinning of assumptions about gender. However, she goes on to say, the engendered nature of work and the workplace is often hidden, with masculine assumptions regarding gender and sexuality being taken as the sex-neutral representation of the abstracted Universal Worker. Thus, "images of men's bodies and masculinity pervade organizational processes, marginalizing women and contributing to the maintenance of gender segregation in organizations" (1990, p. 139).

As demonstrated earlier, gender and sexuality are enmeshed in a close, two-way interaction. Schwartz and Rutter even go so far as to say that gender is the most important dimension of sexuality (1998). Thus an important conclusion reached by conceptualizing a *gendered* workplace is that it is also *sexualized*, so that sexuality is "part of the processes of control in work organizations" (Acker, 1990, p. 140). However, given the strength of the heterosexual mandate, it is perhaps more appropriate to say that the modern workplace is *heterosexualized*. Just as the behavioral prescriptions and proscriptions of traditional masculinity and femininity have infused the workplace, structuring male-female work relations and occupational circumstances, so have the prescriptions and proscriptions of the traditional sexual script so aptly described by Byers (1996).

This may be a fairly new development linked to the emergence of the modern bureaucratic work organization. Based on her review of earlier works (Burrell, 1984; Foucault, 1979; Hearn & Parkin, 1983; Morgan, 1986) dealing with sexuality in work organizations, Acker (1990) concludes that the historical development of large organizations as originally all-male institutions allowed them to suppress heterosexuality as an organizational concern. The suppression of sexuality in the workplace was seen as necessary because of its potential to disrupt the orderly execution of business. Excluding women from work organizations was an easy means of controlling the occurrence of at least one form of sexual activity, heterosexual relations.

The focus was on the suppression of heterosexuality in particular, however, not sexuality in general. Acker cites Burrell (1984) in this regard, noting that homosexuality was not affected by excluding women from organizations. Indeed, she points out, promoting heterosexuality would be a major way to control homosexuality if that were the concern. Thus the prohibition of heterosexuality was part of the process of separating the home and the workplace rather than an attempt to banish sexuality altogether.

And yet, Acker (1990) notes that the attempt to control heterosexual influences by excluding women did not create a workplace unaffected by heterosexual norms. Instead, male heterosexuality—in the form of dominance enactment, minimal concern with emotional involvement, and low involvement in reproduction and childcare—permeated the modern bureaucratic organization even when male exclusivity was maintained. The normative expectations representing traditional masculine sexuality became part of the conceptualization of the ideal worker, even though sex (and sexuality) was not explicitly acknowledged.

One key result was that female sexuality became defined as a disruptive influence: "Women's bodies—female sexuality, their ability to procreate and their pregnancy, breast-feeding, and child care, menstruation, and mythic 'emotionality'—are suspect, stigmatized, and used as grounds for control and exclusion" (Acker, 1990, p. 152). Thus the norms regarding heterosexuality served as an ideology supporting male dominance, a dogmatic justification for patriarchy that set the stage for maintaining women's traditionally subordinate position in the modern workplace even before their entry into the workforce.

The stigmatization of women's sexuality has profound consequences for their general position in the workforce relative to men. For instance, Acker (1990) demonstrates the connection between gender segregation and widespread beliefs regarding the "disruptiveness" of women's sexuality, noting that these beliefs have often been used to justify the relegation of women in the workforce to low-status, low-income occupations. This situation is well exemplified by attempts to use arguments regarding women's reproductive function to limit their workforce participation.

The so-called "protective" laws, which commonly placed restrictions on where, how long, or time of day women may work, were typically justified on the grounds that women needed protection, shorter hours, or day-only employment so as not to interfere with their roles as mothers. The first serious challenge to this type of paternalistic policy, *Muller v. Oregon* in 1908, resulted in the Supreme Court upholding a law excluding women from jobs that required lifting more than 30 pounds or working at night on the grounds it was correct to protect women in this fashion due to their reduced muscle strength and childrearing function (Baer, 1991, p. 23). Similarly, In the 1948 case *Goesart v. Cleary,* the Supreme Court upheld Michigan's right to forbid most women from working as bartenders because of the need to work at night and "to protect women from unruly drinkers" (Baer, 1991, p. 28).

With the passage of the Civil Rights Act of 1964, such blatant discrimination was no longer legal. Nonetheless, women continue to be discriminated against regarding one aspect of their childrearing function—pregnancy. Mandatory maternity leaves are currently illegal for most occupations, with the notable exception of airline attendants, since the Supreme Court overturned such a policy in their decision regarding *Cleveland Board of Education v. La Fleur* (Baer, 1991, p. 106). However, challenges regarding restrictions placed on women's entry or performance in jobs that may pose a threat to a developing fetus have been unsuccessful (hence the continuing policy of mandatory maternity leave for female flight attendants; Baer, 1991, p. 105). For instance, *International Union, UAW v. Johnson Controls* challenged the policy of a battery manufacturer to exclude women from positions that involved exposure to lead. The justification offered by the company was that lead had been shown to be potentially harmful to fetal development.

Another relevant influence of heterosexual dogma is the sexualization of women in the workforce as part of their employment (MacKinnon, 1979), which Acker (1990) notes often involves jobs that serve men. In this manner, occupations defined as female-appropriate are imbued with the behavioral expectations associated with traditional feminine heterosexuality, becoming "feminine heterosexualized" occupations.

The position of secretary provides a good example of a "feminine heterosexualized" occupation. The view that secretarial work is "women's work" is so pervasive that it is commonly asserted that male secretaries are very rare. But as Pringle (1997) notes, this is more a manner of semantics than reality. She points out that, although there are many men who perform work that is secretarial in nature, they typically are given a title other than "secretary," such as "administrative assistant." According to Pringle, this has occurred as a result of the changeover of secretarial work from a male-dominated to a female-dominated occupation, with a concomitant devaluation of its social status and income potential.

Hence "secretary" now denotes a feminized, low-status position whose occupants are often defined in sexualized terms. Pringle (1997), for instance, discusses the common images of secretaries as either "office wives" or as what she calls "dolly birds," "with large breasts, long legs, and short skirts" (p. 360). These are both sexualized images, albeit with different implications. The ingrained sexual content of the occupational definition of "secretary" is made even more explicit by the common assumption that male secretaries are gay. Pringle points out, "This is both a conventional way of interpreting a male sexuality that is perceived as lacking power and a statement about the place of sexuality in people's perceptions of the boss/secretary relation" (p. 360). It is not surprising, then, those men performing secretarial work might choose to avoid questioning of their sexuality by eschewing the title.

The conceptualization of certain occupations that imbues them with either masculine or feminine sexuality is so pervasive in the workplace that it has even appeared as justification for sex discrimination in legal cases. In the landmark 1971 Supreme Court hearing of the case *Diaz v. Pam American World Airways,* the airlines argued that its refusal to hire men as flight attendants was justified because this was a "feminine" occupation that required empathetic and nurturing skills natural to women (Mackinnon, 1979). Women were thus best suited to meeting the needs and preferences of their customers (Baer, 1991).

This argument was rejected by the Supreme Court and marked the end of airline stewardship as a female-only occupation. However, the 1976 Supreme Court case of *Laffey v. Northwest Airlines* demonstrates that the occupation continued to hold its sexualized image for women. The airline had been brought to trial on charges of sex discrimination because of company policies that required female flight attendants, but not male attendants, to wear contact lenses if they required vision correction and to be subject to weight checks and maximum height restrictions (Baer, 1991, p. 84). The only basis for this policy would be the maintenance of a "sexy" image for the women. This policy was also overturned, but the "Fly Me" image of flight attendants remains a part of popular culture.

Women also encounter special problems that demonstrate the heterosexualized nature of the workplace when employed in traditionally male-dominated occupations. The use of markers of traditional femininity such as makeup proclaims a woman as heterosexual (Dellinger & Williams, 1997). Women in professional sports, for example, often go to great lengths to demonstrate their heterosexuality and publicly affirm their femininity (Kolnes, 1995). Thus frequent comparisons to Michael Jordan led women's basketball player Chamique Holdsclaw to exclaim, "I'm the first Chamique Holdsclaw. Michael Jordan is a man; I'm a woman. And I think that is where the women's game has to get to, when women are recognized on their own" (Mehrtens, 1999, p. 1B).

The basic dilemma for women in professional sports is that athleticism is equated with both masculinity and heterosexuality in prevailing social views, which may be normalizing for men but presents a paradox for women (Messner, 1996, p. 225). Thus, to be a professional athlete automatically calls a woman's femininity and sexuality into question. This dilemma, representing a struggle for acceptance as a woman along with acceptance as an athlete, pressures female athletes to consciously and continually assert their femininity in gender-appropriate displays of dress, hair styling, and makeup while not playing their sport, in order to counteract the stigmatizing association with masculinity gained while on the playing field (Kolnes, 1995).

The traditional view of femininity presents a pattern of traits and behavior that has commonly been seen as inappropriate for "masculine" occupations (MacKinnon, 1979). Yet a woman may be penalized if she does not successfully counteract the masculinizing implications of holding such an occupation, even though her performance is exceptional. The case *Price Waterhouse v. Hopkins*, brought before the Supreme Court in 1988, involved a situation in which a woman was denied promotion for not being "feminine" enough (Goldstein, 1994). Even though she had an outstanding work record, her superiors refused to elevate her position in the company on the grounds that she was aggressive, sometimes used foul language, and behaved in an "unladylike" manner. In other words, she had behaved like a man and was being punished for this gender incongruity. The plaintiff argued that this constituted sex discrimination through gender stereotyping; the Supreme Court agreed (Goldstein, 1994).

Thus societal norms regarding heterosexuality have a pervasive influence on the workplace, constraining the behavior of both sexes. However, because norms regarding masculine sexuality are generally consonant with workplace expectations, it is women who are most likely to be put to the disadvantage in the heterosexualized workplace.

IS THE IDEAL CHANGING?

The power of tradition is tremendously strong—nonmaterial cultural components, such as the values and norms regarding sexual behavior, are the slowest and hardest cultural aspects to change (Ogburn, 1964). Nonetheless, there is indication that heterosexuality's power as a normative ideal is waning, and that the traditional sexual script may be giving way to new, more egalitarian behavioral norms for heterosexual relations.

The traditional views regarding the norm of heterosexual identity and heterosexual behavior have long held sway, supported by religious and secular ideologies. Until very recently, even the social sciences were virtually unanimous in their support. To give an example, Garner (1990) points out that starting with the work of Sigmund Freud, psychoanalysis defined the "normal" woman as heterosexual, adding that "Its aim—though unspoken, unacknowledged, and perhaps unknown—was to socialize women to suit the ends of patriarchy as we know it in the Western world" (p. 164). Chodorow (1989) further explicates the psychoanalytic assumption that heterosexuality is the norm, noting that according to the Freudian view, the psychosocial means through which any sexual orientation other than heterosexuality is acquired is through a sexually repressive upbringing, which leads to "sexual perversions" (p. 67).

The most recent exposition of the view that traditional assumptions regarding heterosexuality are "natural" is found in sociobiology. Sociobiological arguments generally assume that social behaviors have their roots in a genetic heritage that results from the biological processes of natural selection (Buss, 1994, 1998; Wilson, 1978, 1980). From this bioevolutionary perspective, for example, woman's role as primary child caretaker is explained as part of a necessary sexual division of labor tied to species survival and now built into human sexuality (Chodorow,

1978). Noteworthy is that it is assumed that the primary and overriding function of human sexuality is reproduction, whereas any possible benefit associated with sexual pleasure is ignored as irrelevant (Wilson, 1978). This is not surprising when it is considered that as late as 1966, when Masters and Johnson published their seminal work on human sexual response, it was generally believed that orgasm in females was either a myth or an aberration (Lancaster, 1979).

Following this focus on the reproductive function of sexuality, sociobiological theory argues that the traditional pattern of heterosexual behavior is grounded in the notion of "minimal parental investment" (Baldwin & Baldwin, 1997). The difference between the sexes is seen to be grounded in differences in the level of commitment to childcare necessary to ensure offspring to pass on one's genes (Baldwin & Baldwin, 1997). Women have the higher level of commitment, according to this view, because they hold responsibility for gestation, lactation, and primary childcare until the child reaches adulthood. Men, on the other hand, have no further need to be involved in childcare once they have accomplished the impregnation of the female. Thus natural selection has worked to produce differences in heterosexual expression for the sexes that are biologically determined.

According to sociobiology, then, the differences in the amount of time and energy needed to ensure the production of offspring and the subsequent passage of one's genes to future generations has led to biologically bolstered differences in the sexual behavior of women and men. Due to their need to invest more time in their offspring, women develop less desire for indiscriminate mating and a greater degree of discrimination in mating. Men, on the other hand, enhance their genetic success by mating with as many females as possible; a more discerning male reduces his potential contribution to the future gene pool. Because these differences are argued to be inherent and therefore immutable, this theory represents an ideological argument that upholds the traditional sexual script, lending the force of science to the voice of tradition in maintaining the heterosexual ideal.

However, even in the face of such strong support, there is evidence that prevailing views regarding the normative nature of heterosexuality are changing. Although belief that heterosexuality is the natural order still prevails among the majority of women and men (Kane & Schippers, 1996), social attitudes have become more tolerant toward same-sex relationships than they were prior to the 1960s (Schwartz & Rutter, 1998). According to nationwide studies, over three quarters of adults in the United States believed that homosexuality was morally wrong in the 1970s, but this proportion has dropped to just over half in more recent surveys (National Opinion Research Center [NORC], 1996). Even more suggestive of increasing tolerance for sex orientations other than heterosexuality is that in these same recent surveys, the majority of respondents indicated they thought gays deserve equal opportunities in the workplace. Thus the heterosexual normative ideal may still be quite strong, but it does appear to have lost some of its force.

The traditional sexual script for heterosexual relations also appears to have lost ground in recent times. For women, the change in the traditional script appears to involve a move toward more freedom and control, with recognition of the female capacity for sexual pleasure. In a study of U.S. sex manuals from 1950 to 1980, Weinberg et al. (1983) clearly demonstrate this trend. They found that the traditional sexual script, or what they label the "different-and-unequal model," dominated the sex and marriage manuals of the 1950s and continued to be predominant into the early 1970s. At this time, they found the manuals switching to a new model that they termed "humanistic sexuality." Weinberg et al. (1983, p. 317) describe this model as one that de-institutionalizes sexuality by taking it out of the marital context and treating it as a basic human quality. The sexual act is not depersonalized, however, because it is assumed to involve a loving relationship, being viewed as an act between caring partners in which sexual pleasure for both is pursued in an atmosphere of exploration, experimentation, and fun.

One important difference between the humanistic sexuality model and the traditional sexual script is that equality between sexual partners is emphasized. Weinberg et al. (1983) note that in these manuals women are portrayed as active and enthusiastic participants on an equal basis with their partners, while the enactment of traditional sex roles is often explicitly denounced.

The researchers note the emergence of yet another sexual model for women in manuals published from 1975 to 1980, which they call the "sexual autonomy" model. This model is noteworthy in that it grants even more freedom for women by portraying women's sexuality as separate from men's (p. 319). The portrayal of women in this model is as "independent agents, self-sufficient and in control of their own sexuality. . . . Men are cast out of the role of sexual leader and expert, and women are told to take responsibility for their own sexual satisfaction" (p. 318). According to Weinberg et al., this model in conjunction with the model of humanistic sexuality has proved to be very popular with the manuals' readers. The researchers note important implications: First of all, there is the gaining of respectability for women who exhibit sexual competence, something denied by the traditional sexual script. Second, they note that the position of women relative to men in heterosexual relationships is strengthened. Finally, the models grant women control of their own sexuality in ways denied to them by the traditional sexual script.

Changes in the behavioral norms regarding women's sexual expression cannot occur in a social vacuum, however, but necessitate changes in men's sexual prescriptions and proscriptions as well. This need is especially meaningful in light of the oft-noted association between the traditional sexual script and male aggression and violence toward women (Brownmiller, 1975; Byers, 1996; Clark & Lewis, 1977). Recent work regarding the social psychology of men has attempted to address the issue of changing the traditional male sexual role (Brooks, 1997; Levant, 1995, 1996, 1997; Pleck, 1981, 1995).

The general approach taken is that the traditional expectations regarding the male gender role in general and male sexuality in particular have pathological consequences, not just for women or society, but for men themselves. Pleck (1981, 1995) delineates harmful effects for men in developing a model for male gender socialization, or the "gender-role strain paradigm." He points to three general ways in which traditional expectations regarding masculinity have created difficulties for men (1995, p. 12). First, he argues, many men suffer from "gender-role discrepancy," an incongruity between what is expected from them according to the traditional gender role and what they can actually achieve. This leads to negative psychological consequences such as low self-esteem. The second problem is that socialization into masculinity is in itself stressful and problematic with possible long-term negative effects, a problem Pleck (1995) calls "gender-role trauma." Finally, there is the problem of "gender-role dysfunction," in that the successful fulfillment of many of the traditional expectations for masculinity can have inherently negative side effects for either the men themselves or for other people. He points, for example, to the low level of family participation defined as acceptable by traditional masculine views.

Building upon Pleck's gender-role strain paradigm, Levant (1995, 1996) explores the dysfunctional aspects of traditional views on male sexuality. His main criticism is that these views promote "nonrelational sex," which he defines as "the tendency to experience sex as lust without any requirements for relational intimacy, or even for more than a minimal connection with the object of one's desires" (Levant, 1995, p. 10). Brooks (1997) refers to the problems associated with the traditional sexual script for men as "the centerfold syndrome," which he defines as "a set of psychosexual attitudes and behaviors that is characteristic of most heterosexual men (some more than others) as well as reflective of the many ways in which normative male sexuality is problematic" (p. 28).

However, these dysfunctional consequences may be encouraging a change in attitude among many men. For example, a survey of 120 male undergraduates found a majority of respondents rejecting the traditional male sexual script, at least in principle. For instance, most respondents disagreed with the statement that "Men should always take the initiative when it comes to sex" while agreeing with the statement that "A man should love his sex partner" (Levant et al., 1992). And in her research, Byers (1996) found that although common, the traditional sexual script was not normatively typical in all its aspects, at least when applied to dating behavior. Her findings led her to conclude that, though behaviors such as coercion and taking the initiative in sex were more common for men than for women, there was considerable overlap in women's and men's sexual behavior. She further concluded that the prevailing perceptions regarding what constitutes ideal sexual behavior for women and men are converging. Thus it is suggested that changes in the traditional sexual script may be occurring that involve a merging of the gender-linked expectations, eliminating the traditional pattern of male dominance and blending the scripts into one equally shared pattern.

CONCLUSIONS AND IMPLICATIONS

The answers offered to the questions raised at the beginning of this chapter be-speak both the power of tradition and the possibility of change. To start with, the exploration of heterosexuality's nature as a normative ideal in society illustrates the intimate and interactive relationship between sexual norms and social defini-tions of gender. The impact of heterosexuality on gender traditionally has been that heterosexuality stands as the normative imperative for male and female sexual orientations, operating as the sole standard of acceptability against which all other sexual orientations are judged and defined as normal or deviant. The heterosexual mandate in turn has been affected by gender expectations, in that the social norms for appropriate expression of heterosexual behavior follow the patterns of mean-ing found in the more general traditional views of gender. As with the traditional perceptions of masculinity and femininity, the traditional sexual script defines fe-male and male sexual roles as bipolar, complementary opposites. Furthermore, ex-pected traits and behaviors are assigned such that those valued by society are asso-ciated with men, whereas those that are less valued are ascribed to women. Thus, the traditional sexual script operates to support patriarchy and male advantage, just as do traditional views of femininity and masculinity.

Exploring the second question brought forth the notion of a heterosexualized workplace, with occupations and work settings defined and designed to reflect tra-ditional norms regarding heterosexuality. The attempt to control heterosexual in-volvement as an impediment to work efficiency has encouraged the exclusion of women from occupations and settings, usually resulting in lower status and lower paying jobs for the female side of the workforce. This has been exacerbated by the normative role of male heterosexuality in the workplace, serving as part of the standardized definition of the ideal worker. Thus, although the constraints raised by the permeation of sexual norms in the social construction of the workplace may create problems for both women and men, it is women who have been put to the greatest disadvantage.

Even though the weight of tradition stands well behind the norms of compul-sory heterosexuality and sexual behaviors promoting male dominance, the search for an answer to the third question suggests that current attempts to change these norms do exist. Heterosexuality may be losing its force as a behavioral mandate, allowing other sexual orientations to gain more social tolerance. And work regard-ing changes in the traditional sexual script raises the possibility that heterosexual behavioral norms are moving toward a merged script for both sexes rather than a divergent pattern, with men and women sharing egalitarian sexual roles that em-phasize equal control, initiative, and pleasure.

What might these changes portend for the heterosexualized workplace? There appears to be no reason to think that the influence of prevailing sexual norms on the workplace will disappear. However, if prevailing views are indeed growing more tolerant of alternative sexual orientations, then the heterosexual nature of the influence may decrease. The workplace would remain *sexualized*, but not *het-*

*eros*exualized. Coupled with the possible trend toward greater equality between women and men in sexual matters, the sexualized nature of the workplace may lose its constraining force on women's position in the workforce.

REFERENCES

Acker, J. (1990, June). Hierarchies, jobs, bodies: A theory of gendered organizations. *Gender & Society, 4*(2), 139–158.

Acker, J., & Van Houten, D. (1974). Differential recruitment and control: The sex structuring of organizations. *Administrative Science Quarterly, 19,* 152–163.

Baer, J. A. (1991). *Women in American law: The struggle toward equality from the New Deal to the present.* New York: Holmes & Meier.

Baldwin, J. D., & Baldwin, J. I. (1997, April). Gender differences in sexual interest. *Archives of Sexual Behavior, 26*(2), 181–210.

Brooks, G. R. (1997). The centerfold syndrome. In R. F. Levant & G. R. Brooks (Eds.), *Men and sex: New Psychological perspectives* (pp. 28–57). New York: Wiley.

Broverman, I. K., Vogel, S. R., Broverman, D. M., Clarkson, F. E., & Rosenkrantz, P. S. (1972). Sex-role stereotypes: A current appraisal. *Journal of Social Issues, 28*(2), 59–78.

Brownmiller, S. (1975). Against our will: Men, women, and rape. New York: Simon & Shuster.

Burrell, G. (1984). Sex and organizational analysis. *Organizational Studies, 5,* 97–118.

Buss, D. M. (1994). *The evolution of desire: Strategies of human mating.* New York: Basic Books.

Buss, D. M. (1998, February). Sexual strategies theory: Historical origins and current status. *Journal of Sex Research, 35*(1), 19-31.

Byers, E. S. (1996). How well does the traditional sexual script explain sexual coercion? Review of a program of research. *Journal of Psychology & Human Sexuality, 8*(1/2), 7–25.

Chodorow, N. (1978) *The reproduction of mothering: Psychoanalysis and the sociology of gender.* Berkeley: University of California Press.

Chodorow, N. (1989). *Feminism and psychoanalytic theory.* New Haven, CT: Yale University Press.

Clark, L., & Lewis, D. (1977). *Rape: The price of coercive sexuality.* Toronto: The Woman's Press.

Connell, R. W. (1987). *Gender and power: Society, the person and sexual politics.* Stanford, CA: Stanford University Press.

D'Augelli, A. R., & Rose, M. L. (1990) Homophobia in a university community: Attitudes and experience of heterosexual freshmen. *Journal of College Student Development, 31,* 484–491.

Dellinger, K., & Williams, C. L. (1997, April). Makeup at work: Negotiating appearance rules in the workplace. *Gender & Society, 11*(2), 151–177.

Deaux, K., & Kite, M. E. (1987). Thinking about gender. In B. B. Hess & M. M. Ferree (Eds.), *Analyzing gender* (pp. 92–117). Newbury Park, CA: Sage.

Deaux, K., & Lewis, L. L. (1984). Structure of gender stereotypes: Interrelationships among components and gender label. *Journal of Personality and Social Psychology, 46*(5), 991–1004.

Doyle, J. A. (1983). *The male experience.* Dubuque, IA: Wm. C. Brown.

Dunkle, J. H., & Francis, P. L. (1990). The role of facial masculinity/femininity in the attribution of homosexuality. *Sex Roles, 23*(3/4), 157–167.

Feldberg, R., & Glenn, E. N. (1979). Male and female: Job versus gender models in the sociology of work. *Social Problems, 26,* 524–538.

Ferguson, K. E. (1984). *The feminist case against bureaucracy.* Philadelphia: Temple University Press.

Foucault, M. (1978) *The history of sexuality. Vol. I: An introduction* (R. Hurley, Trans.). New York: Pantheon Books. (Original work published 1976)

Foushee, H. C., Helmreich, R. L., & Spence, J. T. (1979). Implicit theories of masculinity and femininity: Dualistic or bipolar? *Psychology of Women Quarterly, 3,* 259–269.

Garner, S. N. (1990). Feminism, psychoanalysis, and the heterosexual imperative. In R. Feldstein & J. Roof (Eds.), *Feminism and psychoanalysis* (pp. 164–181). Ithaca, NY: Cornell University Press.

Goldstein, L. F. (1994). *Contemporary cases in women's rights.* Madison, WI: University of Wisconsin Press.

Hearn, J., & Parkin, P. W. (1983). Gender and organizations: A selective review and critique of a neglected area. *Organizational Studies, 4,* 219–242.

Herek, G. M. (1988). Heterosexuals' attitudes toward lesbians and gay men: Correlates and gender differences. *Journal of Sex Research, 25,* 451–477.

Kane, E. W., & Schippers, M. (1996, October). Men's and women's beliefs about gender and sexuality. *Gender & Society, 10*(5), 650–665.

Katz, J. N. (1995). *The invention of heterosexuality.* New York: Dutton.

Kite, M. E., & Deaux, K. (1986) Attitudes toward homosexuality: Assessment and behavioral consequences. *Basic and Applied Social Psychology, 7,* 137–162.

Kolnes, L. J. (1995). Heterosexuality as an organizing principle in women's sport. *International Review for the Sociology of Sport, 30*(1), 61–79.

Kurdek, L. A. (1988). Correlates of negative attitudes toward homosexuals in heterosexual college students. *Sex Roles, 18,* 727–738.

Lancaster, J. B. (1979). Sex and gender in evolutionary perspective. In H. A. Katchadourian (Ed.), *Human sexuality: A comparative and developmental perspective* (pp. 50–80). Berkeley: University of California Press.

Levant, R. F. (1995) Nonrelational sexuality in men. In R. G. Parker & J. H. Gagnon (Eds.), *Conceiving sexuality: Approaches to sex research in a postmodern World* (pp. 9–27). New York: Routledge.

Levant, R. F. (1996) The new psychology of men. *Professional Psychology, Research and Practice, 27*(3), 259–265.

Levant, R. F. (1997). Nonrelational sexuality in men. In R. F. Levant & G. R. Brooks (Eds.), *Men and sex: New psychological perspectives* (pp. 9–27). New York: Wiley.

Levant, R. F., Hirsch, L., Celentano, E., Cozza, T., Hill, S., MacEachern, M., Marty, N., & Schnedeker, J. (1992). The male role: An investigation of norms and stereotypes. *Journal of Mental Health Counseling, 14*(3), 325–337.

MacKinnon, C. A. (1979) *Sexual harassment of working women.* New Haven, CT: Yale University Press.

Mehrtens, C. (1999, June 14). Mystics' Holdsclaw confronts no mystery, just expectations. *Charlotte Observer,* pp. B1, B3.

Messner, M. A. (1996, September). Studying up on sex. *Sociology of Sport Journal, 13*(3), 221–237.

Morgan, G. (1986). *Images of organization*. Beverly Hills, CA: Sage.

Moss Kanter, R. (1977). *Men and women of the corporation*. New York: Basic Books.

National Opinion Research Center. (1996). *General social surveys, 1972–1996: Cumulative codebook*. Chicago: National Opinion Research Center.

Ogburn, W. F. (1964). *On culture and social change*. Chicago: University of Chicago Press.

Penelope, J. (1993) Heterosexual identity: Out of the closets. In. S. Wilkinson & C. Kitzinger (Eds.), *Heterosexuality: A feminism and psychology reader* (pp. 261–265). London: Sage.

Pleck, J. (1981). *The myth of masculinity*. Cambridge, MA: MIT Press.

Pleck, J. (1995). The gender role strain paradigm: An update. In R. F. Levant & W. S. Pollack (Eds.), *A new psychology of men* (pp. 11–32). New York: Basic Books.

Pringle, R. (1997). Male secretaries. In M. B. Zinn, P. Hondagneu-Sotelo, & M. Messner (Eds.), *Through the prism of difference: Readings on sex and gender* (pp. 357–371). Boston: Allyn & Bacon.

Rich, A. (1980). Compulsory heterosexuality and lesbian existence. *Signs, 5*(4), 631–660.

Rosenbluth, S. (1997, December). Is sexual orientation a matter of choice? *Psychology of Women Quarterly, 21*(4), 595–610.

Rosenkrantz, P. (1968). Sex-role stereotypes and self-concepts in college students. *Journal of Consulting and Clinical Psychology, 32*(3), 287–295.

Schwartz, P., & Rutter, V. (1998). *The gender of sexuality*. Thousand Oaks, CA: Pine Forge Press.

Weinberg, M. S., Swensson, R. G., & Hammersmith, S. K. (1983). Sexual autonomy and the status of women: Models of female sexuality in U.S. sex manuals from 1950 to 1980. *Social Problems, 30*(3), 312–324.

Whitley, B. E. (1987). The relationship of sex-role orientation to heterosexual's attitudes toward homosexuals. *Sex Roles, 17,* 103–113.

Williams, J. E., & Bennet, S. M. (1975). The definition of sex stereotypes via the adjective check list. *Sex Roles, 1,* 327–337.

Williams, J. E., & Best, D. L. (1982). *Measuring sex stereotypes: A thirty nation study*. Beverly Hills, CA: Sage.

Wilson, E. O. (1978). *On human nature*. Cambridge, MA: Harvard University Press.

Wilson, E. O. (1980). *Sociobiology: The abridged edition*. Cambridge, MA: The Belknap Press of Harvard University Press.

10

GENDER IDENTITY DISORDER IN THE WORKPLACE

Courtney Prentiss and Richard McAnulty

DEFINITION

Gender Identity Disorder, also known as Transsexualism, is a condition in which the individual experiences persistent discomfort and a sense of inappropriateness with his or her assigned sex. Although individuals with Gender Identity Disorder are sometimes referred to as "cross-dressers" when they adopt the attire of the opposite sex, cross-dressing behaviors may be seen in several situations (Adams & McAnulty, 1993). For example, men with Transvestic Fetishism cross-dress because it is sexually arousing and sometimes serves as a form of stress relief. Some gay men and female impersonators also cross-dress. However, only with Gender Identity Disorder is the cross-dressing associated with identification with the opposite sex; in other words, these individuals wear opposite sex clothing because it fits their gender identity. As defined by the American Psychiatric Association (1994), Gender Identity disorders involve:

1. Strong and persistent cross-gender identification. This is often manifested by repeatedly stating the desire to be the opposite sex, a regular pattern of cross-dressing, preference for opposite sex games and hobbies, or marked preference for opposite sex playmates.

2. Persistent dissatisfaction with one's assigned sex or a sense that one's socially determined gender role is inappropriate.

3. The gender identity confusion causes significant personal distress (often labeled Gender Dysphoria; Blanchard, 1985) or problems in one or more areas of life, such as relationships, school adjustment, or occupation.

Other common features include disgust with one's genitalia and sometimes a preoccupation with getting rid of one's sex characteristics. In males, this may include dissatisfaction with one's penis and testes, body and facial hair, and body shape. In females, the dissatisfaction often extends to genitals, breasts, hairstyle, and physical appearance. Commonly, these individuals describe the experience as feeling trapped in the wrong body or as believing that "nature made a mistake."

Although the exact prevalence of Gender Identity Disorder (GID) is unknown, it is estimated to affect 1 in 100,000 males and 1 in 130,000 females. There are reportedly over 25,000 persons with GID in the United States. This chapter presents a discussion of the problems encountered by individuals with GID in their occupational settings. The condition presents a host of challenges, the majority of which can be directly traced to society's disapproval of nonconformity.

BACKGROUND

Throughout history, the concept of gender role reversal has been a part of every culture and society. For some cultures, cross-dressing had a religious or ritualistic significance. Ancient Greek ceremonies often included rites in which men wore women's clothing. Greek actors dressed as women for theatrical shows because women were prohibited from acting on the stage. However, the Judeo-Christian doctrine prohibited cross-dressing: "The woman shall not wear that which pertaineth unto a man, neither shall a man put on a woman's garment" (Deuteronomy 22:5). The admonition was apparently a reaction to the religious rituals of rival groups including the Syrians and the Greeks (Bullough & Bullough, 1993).

Medieval authorities also disapproved of cross-dressing, especially by men. Because women held a low status, for a man to cross-dress would represent a loss of social status, which was incomprehensible. However, cross-dressing in women was more understandable because it could result in significantly higher social status and privileges. Female impersonation on the stage continued as an accepted practice in the sixteenth and seventeenth centuries. Many Shakespearean productions featured cross-dressed men or boys playing the women's roles.

One source of opposition to cross-dressing by religious authorities was its association with homosexuality. For example, Philippe D'Orleans, the brother of the French king Louis XIV, was a notorious homosexual cross-dresser. He was occasionally seen in the king's palace in full female costume. The image of male cross-dressers as homosexual was bolstered by the formation of cross-dressing clubs in eighteenth-century London. Known as "Molly clubs" (Trumbach, 1977), they are historically recognized as the first gay organizations in England. These developments, along with such visible cross-dressers as the Chevalier D'Eon (Nixon, 1965), brought cross-dressing to a new level; no longer was it only a theatrical performance.

A significant change in women's clothing style occurred in the nineteenth and twentieth centuries. Fashions increasingly emphasized female shapes and sexual attractiveness. Items such as brassieres, stockings, underclothes, and high heels became more prominent in Western cultures. Contemporary writings revealed male fascination with these items, in some cases to the extent of constituting Fetishism. At the same time, fetishistic cross-dressing by heterosexual men was reported by several sources (Bullough & Bullough, 1993).

During this period, pioneering sexologists such as Havelock Ellis and Krafft-Ebing began describing the phenomenon of cross-dressing. Their contemporary, Magnus Hirschfield, actually coined the term "transvestism" in his book titled *The Transvestites: An Investigation of the Erotic Drive to Cross Dress,* published in 1910. During this same time, scientific research shifted from Europe to America where American sexologist Harry Benjamin popularized the term Transsexualism (Pauly, 1990). In 1953, Christine (formerly George) Jorgensen made headlines when she journeyed to Denmark for a "sex-change operation" (Rathus, Nevid & Fichner-Rathus, 1997). This marked the beginning of modern gender identity research and clinical assessment and treatment of GID. Since then, thousands of transsexuals have undergone sex reassignment surgery (SRS).

The observations of the early sexologists remain valid in many respects. There are multiple motives for cross-dressing, the meaning of cross-dressing can vary tremendously according to a person's gender, social role, gender identity, and sexual orientation. Hirschfield's ideas about transvestism are retained in the Transvestic Fetishism label: it applied to heterosexual men for whom cross-dressing is sexually arousing. Transsexual cross-dressing is associated with Gender Identity Disorder; it can occur in either sex, and is not usually associated with erotic desires. In this case, the opposite-sex clothing "fits'" the person's gender identity. Homosexual cross-dressing has been described as a form of entertainment, a political statement, or even a job; "drag queens" or female impersonators are popular entertainers at some gay clubs (Newton, 1972).

In all likelihood, these forms of cross-dressing represent only the most common. There are probably other motives. The persistence of cross-dressing through history and across diverse cultures suggest that it meets important needs for some. The phenomenon is not new, nor is it limited to a few deviant individuals. However, society finds it perplexing that people do not always conform to expected roles and behaviors (Bornstein, 1994).

THEORIES

The causes of Transsexualism remain unknown, although there are many theories. Psychoanalytic theorists have focused on early parent-child relationships. In this view, male transsexuals, may have had extremely close mother-son relationships and fathers who were absent or disinterested. Such family circumstances may have fostered intense identification with the mother, to the point of a reversal of typical gender roles and identity. Girls with weak, helpless mothers and strong, masculine fathers may identify with their fathers, rejecting their own female identities (Rathus et al., 1997).

Some evidence suggests that during childhood male transsexuals tend to have unusually close relationships with their mothers. Similarly, female transsexuals tend to have unusually close relationships with their fathers. Female transsexuals tend to identify more with their fathers and see their mothers as cold and rejecting (Rathus et al., 1997). Yet one problem with the psychoanalytic perspective is that the roles of cause and effect may be reversed. It could be that during childhood, transsexuals gravitate toward the parent of the other gender and reject gender-typed activities encouraged by the parent of the same gender (Rathus et al., 1997). These views also do not account for the many transsexuals whose family dynamics do not conform to these patterns. The majority of children with such family backgrounds do not become transsexuals. In Green's (1987) classic study of 50 extremely feminine boys, virtually all of them eventually accepted their biological sex and developed a homosexual or bisexual orientation. Only one boy displayed conclusive evidence of Gender Identity Disorder as an adult (Green, 1987).

The early onset of transsexual feelings indicates that critical early learning experiences, if they exist, might occur in the preschool years (Rathus et al., 1997). Prenatal hormone imbalances may also influence transsexuals. During fetal development, a random bathing of opposite birth sex hormones may occur, affecting the brain but not the internal or external genitalia (PFLAG, 1998). There is no clear understanding of the cause of Transsexualism, only theories. What is clear is the intensity of their Gender Dysphoria, and the feeling that they can no longer continue living in the gender associated with their physical (birth) sex.

Gender Dysphoria is the overall psychological term used to describe the feelings of distress and anguish that arise from the mismatch between a transsexual's physical sex and gender identity. Some transsexuals discover early on that they are unable to live in the gender of their assigned sex. But the majority struggle to adjust in spite of intense suffering, until their adult years (PFLAG, 1998).

For some transsexuals, living outwardly as the opposite sex does not curb their Gender Dysphoria, and they want to be rid of their own sex organs. In this case, transsexuals seek sex reassignment surgery. Even though this is a long and difficult process, for many it is the only answer (Denvor, 1997).

SEX REASSIGNMENT SURGERY

The Harry Benjamin International Gender Dysphoria Association (HBIGDA) formulated a set of guidelines for transsexuals who are seeking to obtain sex reassignment surgery; these are called "standards of care." Although the standards of care lessen the chance that someone will make a mistake, they have been criticized as a "gatekeeper" system (PFLAG, 1998). Because the surgery is irreversible, professionals conduct careful psychological and medical evaluations of applicants. Transsexuals are usually required to live as a member of the opposite sex for a period of at least one year before undergoing the surgery. This is called the Real Life Test and is crucially important in the decision for sex reassignment surgery. During this period transsexuals must demonstrate their ability to live and work full-time successfully in their preferred gender (PFLAG, 1998). For some the fantasy of living as the opposite gender is enjoyed more in theory than in reality (Pauly, 1990). Whatever the outcome, the Real Life Test aids the transsexual in decision making.

Once the decision is reached, a lifetime of hormone treatments is begun. Male-to-female transsexuals receive estrogen, which promotes the development of female secondary sex characteristics. This softens the skin, inhibits beard growth, and causes fatty deposits to develop in the breast and hips. Androgens are given to female-to-male transsexuals, which fosters male secondary sex characteristics. In this case, the voice deepens, muscles enlarge, fatty deposits in the breasts and hips are lost, and hair becomes distributed according to the male pattern (Rathus et al., 1997). Hormone therapy is highly acclaimed by the transsexual and is a definite step in moving towards his or her cherished goal of complete sex reassignment.

Sex reassignment surgery is largely cosmetic because of medical science's inability to construct internal genital organs or gonads (Rathus et al., 1997). Generally, sex reassignment surgery is the "permanent surgical refashioning of genitalia to resemble that of the appropriate sex" (PFLAG, 1998). For female-to-male transsexuals it also includes breast removal and sometimes a hysterectomy. Male-to-female transsexuals may also undergo cosmetic procedures such as electrolysis to remove facial and body hair, liposuction, breast augmentation, Adams apple reduction, and many types of facial surgeries (PFLAG, 1998). It is quite apparent that transsexuals go to extraordinary lengths to obtain relief from their Gender Dysphoria. In most cases sex reassignment surgery is a very positive aid in helping a transsexual achieve congruency between their body and soul.

LEGAL ISSUES

Once the transsexual has gone through the physical process of living as the other sex, they must go through the legal process. Obtaining legal identification for their new names and gender is often extremely difficult. Legal name changes can be easily obtained in most states but only eight states officially permit preoperative transsexuals to obtain change of sex designation on their driver's licenses (California, Colorado, Connecticut, Massachusetts, Michigan, Minnesota, Illinois, and Wisconsin; PFLAG, 1998). A preoperative transsexual from North Carolina reports, "Once my name change is finished I am hoping to have my sex changed on my driver's license, but that will be left up to the Department of Motor Vehicles." All but two states (Ohio and Florida) allow preoperative change of sex to be noted on a birth certificate (PFLAG, 1998). After the name change is completed, transsexuals have the task of changing school, credit, and employment records. Most often there are no written laws, only written "policies" and even their enforcement is arbitrary. In many circumstances transsexuals are at the mercy of clerks and supervisors (PFLAG, 1998).

WORKPLACE ISSUES

Transsexuals, like members of other minority groups, face discrimination and harassment. Denial of an opportunity to make a living is one of the most damaging and pervasive forms of discrimination. Because changing one's gender is so visible, transsexuals are at a high risk of losing their jobs, are often denied employment, or are underemployed (PFLAG, 1998).

When beginning the transition, employed transsexuals must decide whether to stay at their present job or find a new job. Staying at their present job is the ideal decision because it allows for financial security and the assurance of benefits (Brown & Rounsley, 1996). It is also comforting for transsexuals to remain in familiar surroundings where relationships have already been established with coworkers. At such a stressful time in the transsexual's life, staying with the present employer may be more beneficial than trying to prove themselves to new people in a new workplace (Brown & Rounsley, 1996). Of course, there are negative aspects in both situations.

Transsexuals who choose to transition on the job may find that coworkers may not be able to forget their previous identities. The use of improper pronouns and name slips often occur, which can be discouraging to a transsexual who is trying to fit into the other gender role. Many transsexuals discover that being considered a regular female or male employee may be difficult, if not impossible. He or she may always carry the pejorative label of the "company transsexual" (Brown & Rounsley, 1996).

Some coworkers and employers may be so uncomfortable with the transition that they alienate the transsexual by excluding him or her from events or meetings. Employers may even demote or remove the transsexual from positions where they interact with the public (Brown & Rounsley, 1996). For reasons such as these, many transsexuals start over in a new work environment prior to making the transition.

The advantages of starting over and finding a new job are obvious, but there are three problems that transsexuals face when they take this avenue. The first problem deals with work history. Most transsexuals do not have job references or work experience in their new name and gender. Usually the only way to obtain this information is to come out to the former employer and request a change of documentation (Brown & Rounsley, 1996). Many transsexuals are hesitant in doing this because they want to leave their past behind them, but in most cases they have no other choice. In addition to work records, they also have to change other documents such as school records, diplomas, credentials, licenses, and union cards (Brown & Rounsley, 1996).

The second obstacle pertains to interview. Interviewing can be stressful for anyone, but for transsexuals it may be especially frightening. They must impress the interviewer with their skills and qualifications in a gender role that they may not yet be totally comfortable with (Brown & Rounsley, 1996). This leads into the third problem of ethical dilemmas. In some interviews, questions are asked regarding whether the applicant has ever worked under a different name. Most transsexuals answer truthfully, which often leads to questions about their past. Consequently most transsexuals do not get the job. When new jobs are obtained they are usually of less status and salary than the former job. Some transsexuals can hardly survive and have to file for bankruptcy (Brown & Rounsley, 1996). Financial security is of great concern during the transition because their cost of living increases. Transsexuals now need to pay for a new wardrobe, hormones, therapy and other gender-related expenses. Most transsexuals choose to stay with their current employer simply for financial reasons.

Workplace Transition

Preparation and timing are very important when one decides to transition in the workplace. In rare cases does a person just blurt out that he or she is a transsexual. Some transsexuals start the process by gradually changing their appearance. Male-to-females may pierce their ears, begin to let their hair and fingernails grow and dress more androgynously (Brown & Rounsley, 1996).

A male-to-female maintenance technician used this approach. For the purpose of this chapter, this transsexual will be referred to as Jamie. Jamie began wearing female undergarments and female work pants. She also changed her name on her uniform. When the human resource department at the company questioned her about the change, she explained her intentions about becoming a female. Jamie said, "I found that it is better to do, and let them come to you, and let you get your hand slapped than for you to go to them. I found that I fared better with doing that than going any other way."

Other transsexuals may take a more direct approach by means of a letter or a face-to-face disclosure. A male-to-female attorney worked with a public relations specialist who helped her design a communication plan. She developed six different letters that she sent to current clients, nonactive clients, lawyers, insurance adjusters, and judges. Several thousand letters were sent out and she said this system was "extremely effective." Here is an example of a letter taken from the book *True Selves* (Brown & Rounsley, 1996):[1]

Dear friends and coworkers:

I have known many of you for some time now, and I count you all as friends. What I must tell you is very difficult to me and is taking all the courage I can muster. I am writing this both to inform you of a significant change in my life and to ask for your patience, understanding, and support, which I would treasure.

I have a gender identity problem that I have struggled with my entire life. I have been in therapy for it for nearly four years now and I have been diagnosed as a transsexual. I have felt imprisoned in a body that doesn't match my mind, and this has caused me great despair and loneliness.

I cannot begin to describe the shame and the suffering that I have lived with. Toward that end, I intend to have sex reassignment surgery. The first step I must take is to live and work full-time as a woman. On the first of next month I will become Jane Johnson.

I realize that some of you may have trouble understanding this. In truth, I've had to live with it every day of my life, and even I don't understand it. I have tried hard all my life to please everyone around me, to do the right thing and not rock the boat. As distressing as this is sure to be to my friends and family, I need to do this for myself and for my own peace of mind and to end the agony of my soul. Through it all, I have learned that life is an adventure, and I would like to think that the best is yet to come. I hope we can all enjoy it together.

Jane Johnson

Coworkers' Reactions

Once transsexuals have come out to his or her employer and coworkers, they must deal with reactions. Generally, most coworkers are supportive of the transsexual and react in a positive manner. Many employers acknowledge that the original skills, talents, education and abilities that the transsexual brought to the workplace will not be affected by the change. In most cases the transsexual's job performance improves because they no longer have to struggle with Gender Dysphoria. Of course, there will be adjustments that have to be made, but once everyone gets over the initial surprise, business usually goes on as it has before (Brown & Rounsley, 1996).

Unfortunately, not all transsexuals are met with acceptance. Coworkers and employers may be disturbed and resistant to the transition and act out in a hostile manner. As mentioned before, coworkers may be reluctant to change their perception of the transsexual; name slip-ups, exclusion from meetings, the use of improper pronouns, and even harassment may develop. Some transitioning transsexuals may find that their opinion is no longer valued. Coworkers may even go as far as sabotaging the transsexual's projects (Brown & Rounsley, 1996).

In some instances, employers who previously gave the transsexuals superior job reviews have put them on probation for poor performance after the transition. Because discrimination may materialize in this way it is very important for transsexuals to keep copies of all job reviews, performance reports, commendations, and records of pay raises for the time period before the transition.

More subtle ways of forcing the transsexual out of the workplace have been used by some employers, for example, cutting back their hours, giving them insignificant projects, or extending their hours in an attempt to exhaust them. Transsexuals may also be bypassed for a promotion or pay raise or even demoted (Brown & Rounsley, 1996).

Unfortunately, these are not the only tactics used, in some cases transsexuals are put in unpleasant or even dangerous situations. One case mentioned in the book *True Selves* (Brown & Rounsley, 1996), describes a male-to-female police officer who had been on the force for five years without any problems, but after her transition the problems began. For instance, when she needed assistance in a dangerous situation no one would respond, thus putting her life in danger. Another situation involves a transsexual who worked for the telephone company. After her transition she was given work assignments that she had never done before, such as climbing 60-foot poles without proper training or safety equipment (Brown & Rounsley, 1996).

Other transsexuals have found that their positions have been eliminated entirely. Some may be a corporate executive one day and a dishwasher the next. Transsexuals must be prepared to deal with these difficult situations, even though in some states protection is offered (Brown & Rounsley, 1996). Fortunately, most employers today accept diversity in the workplace and some even value it. Gender discrimination is no longer tolerated and many companies have antidiscrimination policies (Brown & Rounsley, 1996). Many transsexuals have reported that their employers and coworkers have given them lots of encouragement and support.

Bathroom Issues

One issue, however, that has caused some concern and discussion is the use of gender-specific bathrooms or locker rooms. It is both logical and practical that a male dressed in men's clothes does not belong in a female bathroom. This brings up the issue of which bathroom a transsexual should use (Brown & Rounsley, 1996).

Many employees feel uncomfortable being in the same bathroom as a transsexual employee. They may feel that their privacy is being violated or that their transsexual coworker has voyeuristic intentions. Even though it seems absurd that a transsexual would go through much emotional and financial distress just to have the opportunity to be voyeuristic, some people have voiced this concern (Brown & Rounsley, 1996). These are some solutions, taken from the book *True Selves,* that companies have created in order to address the bathroom issue:

- A separate facility is designated for the transsexual that may not be in regular use or is located on another floor or in another part of the building.
- Certain restrooms are made "off limits" for the transsexual, to accommodate the needs of employees who are uncomfortable sharing a bathroom with the transsexual.
- An existing unisex facility is used, or one is designated to be used by both sexes and a lock is installed.
- A specially devised procedure is initiated whereby a "flag" or sign is posted on the door whenever the transsexual is using the facility. This system, which is humiliating to most transsexuals, is designed to allow any of their coworkers who are uncomfortable to wait, if they wish, until the flag or sign is down before entering the bathroom.
- A supportive coworker accompanies the transsexual to the restroom and "stands guard" while he or she is inside.

Jamie, a preoperative male-to-female maintenance technician, found that her company was willing to accommodate her, and they allowed her to use a bathroom that was in another part of the building.

Legally, transsexuals in transition are not restricted from using public restrooms designated for the opposite anatomical sex. However, many have had problems from officials and have been given a letter from their therapist to present in case of a confrontation. Because the workplace is private property, companies have the right to control their facilities. Some companies have instituted some of the less favored policies that have just been discussed (Brown & Rounsley, 1996). Transsexuals who have had sex reassignment surgery legally have the right to use the bathroom that corresponds to their new gender without the interference of the corporation (Brown & Rounsley, 1996).

WAYS TO HELP THE TRANSSEXUAL

In times of change and crisis, everyone looks to their friends for encouragement and support. In dealing with transsexuals in the workplace, one must remember that they are human beings. The transsexual deserves to be treated with respect and to not be looked at as an oddity or freak. They are not sick or perverted, but have a medical condition that is beyond their control. These are some things to remember when dealing with a transsexual. They are taken from the book *True Selves* (Brown & Rounsely, 1996).

- Recognize how important your support and acceptance are to the transsexual.
- Listen and be willing to hear what the transsexual has to say without judgment, anger, argument, or confrontation.
- Learn more about the person's conditions and struggles. Educate yourself.
- Keep the lines of communication open even if at first your communication is about your fears and pain.
- Respect the person as a human being. Offer respect, courtesy and compassion.
- Remember that being transsexual involves perpetual inner conflict and that you are dealing with someone who is constantly struggling and facing challenges. There are few welcome places for transsexuals in this world. Try to create one for them with you.
- Trust that what the transsexual is doing is right for that particular person.
- Admire the courage and determination of the transsexual to do what must be done to survive, and let the person know this.
- Understand that the basic character, temperament, and personality of the transsexual will remain the same as before, with all admirable qualities intact.
- Try to put yourself in the transsexual's shoes. Envision what it would be like to have to go through the lifetime of emotional pain that the transsexual has experienced.
- Anticipate the pleasure of a more positive relationship. If the transsexual in your life seemed troubled and unhappy in the past, with the source of the unhappiness now finally known and addressed, you can look forward to a more satisfying relationship.

CONCLUSION

In spite of all the complex difficulties that transsexuals face, many more are coming out, transitioning or finding new ways to live meaningful lives. The trials and tribulations that transsexuals go through are outlined in this chapter. As one can see, they face many difficulties in their personal and professional life. No one knows better than the transsexual the effects of discrimination, but for many, making the transition is the only way they can live a full and happy life.

NOTE

1. Material from M. Brown & C. S. Rounsley, *True Selves: Understanding Transsexualism for Family, Friends, Coworkers and Helping Professionals* (San Francisco, CA: Jossey-Bass, 1996), Copyright © 1996, Jossey-Bass, reproduced with permission of Jossey-Bass, a subsidiary of John Wiley & Sons.

REFERENCES

Adams, H. E., & McAnulty, R. D. (1993). Sexual disorders: The paraphilias. In P. B. Sutker & H. E. Adams (Eds.), *Comprehensive handbook of psychopathology* (2nd ed., pp. 563–579). New York: Plenum.

Blanchard, R. (1985). Gender dysphoria and gender reorientation. In B. W. Steiner (Ed.), *Gender dysphoria: Development, research, and management* (pp. 365–392). New York: Plenum.

Bornstein, K. (1994). *Gender outlaw: On men, women and the rest of us.* New York: Routledge.

Brown, M., & Rounsley, C. S. (1996). *True selves: Understanding transsexualism for family, friends, coworkers and helping professionals.* San Francisco, CA: Jossey-Bass.

Bullough, V. L., & Bullough, B. (1993). *Cross-dressing, sex, and gender.* Philadelphia: University of Pennsylvania.

Denvor, H. (1997). *Female-to male transsexuals in society.* Indianapolis, IN: Indiana University Press.

Green, R. (1987). *The "sissy boy syndrome" and the development of homosexuality.* New Haven, CT: Yale University.

Newton, E. (1972). *Mother camp: Female impersonators in America.* Englewood Cliffs, NJ: Prentice Hall.

Nixon, E. (1965). *Royal spy: The strange case of the chevalier D'Eon.* New York: Reynal & Co.

PFLAG (1998). *Our trans children: A publication of the Transgender special outreach network of parents, families and friends of lesbians and gays (PFLAG).* Hardy, VA: Author.

Pauly, I. B. (1990). Gender Identity disorders: Evaluation and treatment. *Journal of Sex Education and Therapy, 16*(1), 2–24.

Rathus, S. A., Nevid, J. S., & Fichner-Rathus, L. (1997). *Human sexuality in a world of diversity* (3rd ed.). Boston: Allyn & Bacon.

Trumbach, F. (1977). London sodomites: Homosexual behavior and Western culture in the eighteenth century. *Journal of Social History, 2,* 1–33.

Part V
Societal Issues

11

HIV/AIDS IN THE WORKPLACE

Kristin H. Griffith and Michael W. Ross

The facts about HIV disease and its modes of transmission—primarily sexual, and through blood-borne routes such as injecting drug use and transfusion of contaminated blood or blood products—are well established. It is, however, critical to look at the impact of HIV disease on work, and work on HIV disease, in the wider contexts of the individual, the organization, and the values of the wider society. Because the disease was first identified in the United States in 1981, its origin in central Africa and its subsequent spread to the rest of the world has had major implications not only in health terms but also in terms of work and economics. Because the disease is primarily sexually transmitted, it affects those in the most sexually active years (between approximately 20 and 40), which are also the most productive years for people in the workforce. As a consequence, its impact on the workforce is disproportionate.

In some countries with high HIV prevalence, this impact may lead to significant decreases in the national product and national economy. In Botswana, in the 15- to 44-year-old age group, HIV prevalence is estimated at over 40 percent, which will produce a 44 percent reduction in the labor force (Botswana Ministry of Health, 1997). Companies in Malawi, where HIV prevalence is estimated at between 30 to 50 percent of the sexually active population, have reported increased employee morbidity and mortality. Ntirenda and Zimba (1998) report that for a major company, between 1992 and 1996, death rates of employees increased by 220 percent and retirement rate from illness by 226 percent. They estimate that the cost of HIV/AIDS is about 1.1 percent of total expenditure and 3.4 percent of gross profit. In India, where long-distance truck drivers have high HIV infection rates due to their frequent sexual contact while away from home (Rao, Nag, Mishra, & Dey, 1994), Kanjilal, Forsythe, Ganesh, and Balasubramaniam (1998) estimate that between 1.3 and 2.4 million truck drivers (between 12 and 20 percent of all truck drivers) will be infected in India by 2005. This is likely to create a shortage of skilled drivers and increase costs due to indirect impacts such as loss in output and increase in accidents. In Malawi, Forsythe et al. (1993) calculated that the average HIV-infected Malawian will lose three quarters of his or her productive life to AIDS. The modern employment sector (wage earners in firms with more than nine employees) represents only 6 percent of Malawi's population, but 19 percent of all new AIDS cases and 28 percent of the nation's income. The cost of treating people with AIDS accounts for 20 percent of the national health budget. There are reports in the agricultural sector of villages in east Africa where export crops are not able to be harvested because villages consist largely of orphans and their grandparents, the labor force having succumbed to AIDS. Taken together, these studies indicate the enormous potential economic impact of HIV disease on the workforce in high prevalence areas, but also suggest an opportunity and a strong need for HIV education programs in the workplace.

EMPLOYEE CONCERNS

Psychological Aspects of Work

Almost all research on HIV/AIDS, work, and the workplace has focused on gay men. As Nilsson Schönnesson and Ross (1999) have noted for gay men, HIV disease shatters the self, raising questions about identity and the meaning of life to people whose identity may be closely linked, in their and the public's minds, with the acquisition of HIV infection. Second after one's sexual orientation, for gay men, work and career are important in defining identity. Thus, relinquishing work will often act as an additional assault on the psychological functioning of people with HIV disease. In addition to the psychological distress associated with a loss of career or work identity, the loss of its economic benefits may also create psychological and financial distress. For example, in a study of the impact of life events in gay men, Ross (1990) found that one of the major distresses associated with mood disorder, particularly depression, was loss of job, judged to be equivalent to problems with the police leading to a court case, or a traffic accident that carried serious risk to one's life or health (Rosser & Ross, 1988). Ross (1990) found that the correlations between life events (such as having arguments with one's boss, losing one's job) related to work and mental health were very significantly higher for gay men than those for nonhomosexual samples on the same items, suggesting that at least this stigmatized minority status is likely to exacerbate the impact of negative life events (not just those related to work). As the HIV epidemic in the United States involves other minorities, with disproportionate numbers of African Americans becoming infected, emphasis on this population and the impact of HIV disease on their psychological and social functioning is badly needed. However, it is unclear whether it is possible to also extrapolate to such populations Ross's results with homosexual men, which found that minority status accentuated the relationships between psychological functioning and negative life events. Clearly, more research in this area is needed.

In a major study of the impact of work on psychological functioning in men with HIV disease, Ross (1993) reviewed the evidence demonstrating that employment is a source of self-esteem, provides a secure reality base, and is one of the most positive predictors of mental health. Vaillant and Vaillant (1981) have provided convincing evidence that deprivation of work is a source of grief. They indicated in their over 30-year longitudinal study that unemployment causes—and is not an effect of—significant decreases in mental health. Similar findings are reported by Warr and Jackson (1985), who found that unemployment has a major negative impact on mental health, particularly in the first three months of unemployment, and that mental health will improve when the individual regains work. The type of work bears no significant relation to the distress: Krupinski (1984) found it to be equal for both dependent (within an organizational structure) and independent work, but that the nonfulfillment of people's desires associated with work is the critical variable determining mental health. According to Ross (1993), gay men, who account for a majority of people with HIV disease in the United States, place more importance on work as a source of identification, competence, and self-esteem than do heterosexual men. With regard to HIV/AIDS, there is little work on women and racial and ethnic minorities, and it is probably premature to attempt to generalize.

Unfortunately, a study by Rosevelt (1987) of gay men with AIDS or symptomatic HIV disease found that over a third were victims of work discrimination, and nearly two thirds unemployed. What is most important about her study is that half of her sample reported that after friends and lovers, work associates were their most significant supports. In those who were still employed, three quarters listed work associates as a major source of support. Thus, the impact of work (or loss of work) on ability to cope with HIV disease, life stresses, and provision of some quality of life is likely to be significant and should not be underestimated. Any reasoning that sees work as simply a means of economic survival and as replaceable by unemployment benefits is missing the point: Work may also serve as a critical determinant of mental health, self-esteem, as well as one's identity through its provision of meaning in life.

In Ross's 1993 study, he used a qualitative methodology to interview 16 men who were working with HIV disease. Ross found that there were a number of core categories associated with workplace stress, suggesting that for the worker with HIV disease, staying on the job may also be associated with stress. A number of major categories emerged from his analysis:

- using information (on a person's HIV status) in workplace battles;
- major changes in attitudes of coworkers and management, including alterations in friendships and work relationships;
- inaccurate empathy, both positively and negatively intentioned;
- people with HIV disease seen as being "demanding" in asking for workplace accommodations to their situation; and
- discrimination by being cocategorized (people assuming that because they had HIV disease they were homosexual, a drug user, or promiscuous).

Anticipated discrimination based on previous insensitive jokes about HIV leads a number to hide their disease, making it difficult to explain the need for medical appointments or to take medication in public situations. In addition, when HIV status was revealed to coworkers, the lack of knowledge about HIV disease and its transmission, and the need to educate, was stressful. Equally awkward was the attitude of denial that was sometimes apparent. The need to pretend about treatment, and the difficulty of fitting in treatment, were also core concerns associated with the advent of more complex treatment regimens.

On the other hand, Ross (1993) also found his respondents providing evidence that there were positive changes in work life, including self-induced changes in work habits and work life that enhanced enjoyment of both work and life. Further, many respondents also reported favorable experiences in the workplace, with coworkers and management being more supportive than they had imagined, and attempts by coworkers and management to make the work and work environment more comfortable. In conclusion, Ross notes that HIV tends to exacerbate previous workplace issues, but that people with HIV disease need to feel that they remain valued and accepted members of their workplace community given the fact that work is such an important source of self-esteem and personal gratification. Although psychological costs are difficult to quantify, without doubt they are likely to be as important as financial ones to the person with HIV disease.

Attitudes toward People with HIV Disease

One of the major sources of discrimination against people with HIV disease in the workplace is based on attitudes and beliefs toward HIV/AIDS and fears of AIDS. The components and structure of attitudes toward AIDS have been described by Ross (1988), who administered a questionnaire based on 11 different attitudes toward AIDS reported in previous studies. He found that there were six major dimensions of attitudes toward AIDS. These included homonegative ("homophobic") opinion and attribution of responsibility for contracting HIV, fear of death, unrealistic concerns about HIV transmission, recognition of the risk of nonsexual transmission, fear of the unknown in regard to HIV, and social conservatism. Thus, it appears that negative attitudes toward those seen as being at higher risk for HIV infection, particularly homosexual men and injecting drug users, may play a large part in negative attitudes toward those with HIV disease. This is referred to as "cocategorization"—a belief that because someone has HIV disease, they must be a member of one of these stigmatized groups. Such attitudes, however, refer to the epidemiology of HIV infection in the first decade of the epidemic in the United States and other Western countries. The current epidemiology of HIV infection in the United States is becoming more characteristic of the pattern in Africa and Asia, where the HIV pandemic is heterosexually driven. Further, large numbers of women infected by their husbands who have had sex outside of marriage and the rapid spread of HIV among African American communities suggest that these attitudes are out of touch with the present reality of the HIV epidemic in the beginning of the twenty-first century. Nevertheless, such attitudes are prevalent. Ross and Darke (1992), in a study on attitudes toward injecting drug users, found that drug abuse was viewed as a matter of public concern and personal inadequacy, as a crime, and as a matter of personal distaste leading to avoidance of drug users. Such attitudes, through the process of cocategorization, still exist in some persons and are transfered to people with HIV disease, often unconsciously through association.

Fears of HIV disease are also associated with discrimination, although accurate information about means of transmission of HIV is common. Nevertheless, people usually grossly overestimate the risk of workplace transmission. The Centers for Disease Control (1995a) have estimated, based on thousands of reports of needlestick injuries with HIV-infected sharps (needles, scalpels, and so on), that even when the sharps are infected, the rate of subsequent infection is only about half a percent.

Fears of AIDS were initially measured by Arrindell et al. (1989), and Ross and Hunter (1992), using the Fear of AIDS Schedule, found that in health workers, its structure and subscales were consistent. They found that there were five stable dimensions: fear of loss of control resulting from HIV/AIDS, fear of sex and diseases associated with sex, fear of HIV infection through blood and fear of illness, fear of medical interventions and death, and fear of contact with social "outsiders" (a form of xenophobia). In west Africa, Akande and Ross (1994) replicated the Fear of AIDS Schedule in a large stratified proportional sample of Nigerian people and found the same five dimensions emerging from their data analysis. There appears to be a degree of cross-cultural consistency regarding fears of AIDS, which are associated with the images that AIDS evokes: death, lack of control over one's life, illness, threatening outsider groups, the lack of sexual control, and social conservatism. It is for this reason that education, desensitization, and discussion are such potentially effective interventions in the workplace, and why courts have recently placed such emphasis on the necessity of undertaking workplace interventions regarding HIV/AIDS.

However, the fear of AIDS appears to be related to the fear of threatening outsider groups, sexual issues, and social conservatism. Frieder et al. (1998) reported that concerns about transmission of HIV to health workers differed markedly depending on the group being treated: They reported that fear and apprehension were experienced by 74 percent of health workers providing care to injecting drug users, 62 percent providing care to homosexual or bisexual men, and 32 percent providing care to newborn HIV seropositive infants. These data strongly suggest that it is the stigma associated with the group that triggers fears of HIV transmission, with the HIV transmission issue being the acceptable manifestation or rationalization of the fear.

Return to Work of People with HIV Disease

With the advent of protease inhibitors and other highly active antiretroviral therapies, significant numbers of people with HIV disease, who may have taken medical retirement or disability leave, are able to return to work. This raises additional questions relating to HIV/AIDS in the workplace. Canadian data (Jalbert & Masson, 1998) documented some of the barriers to return to work, which included the fact that although half had disclosed their HIV serostatus to their employer, a fifth of these reported having problems with their employer as a consequence. A third had problems paying for their medication (this in a country with a comprehensive health system) and 11 percent reported not taking medication because they are afraid of being identified in the workplace, afraid of being outed by their insurance company, or afraid of losing their job, among other reasons. Jalbert (1997) notes that 82 percent of people with AIDS have considered returning to work but do not want to return to their former jobs because of concerns about stress, discrimination, or their employer's attitude. Heitman and Ross (1999) also note the difficulty of obtaining new employment without having to explain the long employment gap in one's resume, and maintaining employment while having to hide taking medication and visting the doctor. In Britain, as in other countries, the possibility of returning to work part-time is not a viable option as it would involve loss of benefits (Clarkson, 1998). In the United States, there have been reports of people who would lose their medical benefits if they received income. A recent report (Thomas, Joseph, & Campbell, 1996) suggests that the loss of self esteem and employment experience can be overcome through volunteering, which enhances quality of life. Volunteers are also able to be part-time and do not endanger their medical benefits by making a salary and so continue to qualify for Medicare/Medicaid or other government benefits.

EMPLOYER CONCERNS

AIDS issues are particularly important to employers because HIV primarily strikes people in the prime of their careers, from ages 25 to 45 (CDC, 1995b). In countries other than the United States, this pattern also generally holds. For example, of the almost 120,000 documented AIDS cases up to August 1997 in Brazil, 89.2 percent of the cases were within the 15 to 49 age group, which corresponds to the large majority of the workforce in Brazil (Moreira & Cristina, 1998). In addition, AIDS is quite prevalent in the workplace. A recent survey (Mello, 1995) found that of domestic firms in the United States with over 5,000 employees, 75 percent had had employee cases of AIDS, with an average of six cases. Of firms with over 10,000 employees, 90 percent had at least one case. In many other countries, AIDS is also quite prevalent in the workplace. For instance, a survey of 348 factories in provinces throughout Thailand and districts in Bangkok with more than 100 employees found that 29.6 percent of the factories reported having HIV-infected employees (Atthakha, 1998).

Many employers will experience an AIDS case in their organization, and many employers are very concerned about this situation. In fact, a survey conducted by *Fortune* magazine identified AIDS as one of the top three concerns of American employers (Sprinzen, 1988). Employers in other countries are also very concerned with AIDS in the workplace. For instance, one survey (Fukuzawa, Kamakura,

Sakurai, & Yamagata, 1996) found that of companies who participate in the Japan Association against AIDS (JAA; all large companies with more than 2,000 employees), almost everyone in management indicated a deep concern about confusion in the workplace in the case of an employee infected with HIV (95 percent), had doubts about the protection of privacy (83 percent), and only 38 percent had given any thought to how they would respond to this situation. This shows that even among the most liberal of organizations in Japan (ones belonging to the JAA), these employers are confused and not well educated about AIDS in the workplace.

The majority of employers' fears center around the business costs associated with having an employee with HIV/AIDS. Some of the main business costs associated with an infected employee include reduced productivity of an employee with HIV/AIDS, the loss of clients or customers, conflict in the workplace, increased health insurance costs, and lawsuits brought by a person with HIV/AIDS against the organization.

Productivity of an Employee with HIV/AIDS

There are two main concerns of employers regarding the productivity of an employee with HIV/AIDS. First, employers are concerned that employees with HIV will not be good long-term investments because they will become sick and die very soon after hire. Secondly, employers are concerned that an employee with HIV will become ill while on the job, and their job performance will be impaired. These concerns have some basis in reality, but the situation is not as bleak as most employers believe.

Today, people may live for many years with HIV before showing any signs of illness due to HIV. For example, estimates of normal progression are that 5 to 10 percent of infected people progress to AIDS in 4 years, and about 50 percent in 10 years after initial infection, although the recent advent of highly active antiretroviral therapy has radically changed these figures (Moss & Bachetti, 1989). In addition, antiretroviral therapy has led to significant improvements in the health of many people with HIV/AIDS, since protease inhibitors became available in 1996 (Larade, 1998). As a result, many people with HIV/AIDS are living quite a long time. Consequently, someone without HIV may not necessarily be expected to stay in the company any longer than someone with HIV.

Many employers are also concerned that an employee who is HIV-positive will be unable to perform the job adequately. However, based on the available evidence, the World Health Organization has determined that the presence of HIV itself does not result in impaired occupational performance, and the Presidential Commission on the HIV epidemic has agreed with this finding (Watkins, 1988). Also, it may be many years between the time someone has been infected with HIV and the time they show any symptoms. When someone does develop AIDS, they may exhibit a variety of symptoms, and they will have different life expectancies after diagnosis. Consequently, the ability of those with symptoms to function at their normal level will vary greatly from case to case. However, many people with AIDS have continued to work effectively for several years in their jobs. Some might require frequent or a lengthy sick leave or some minor job accommodations, but while on the job they can function at a normal level. Others may develop AIDS dementia complex (ADC), which may have a severe impact on work performance through impaired behavior and judgment. Signs of cognitive impairments may occur in persons with AIDS (PWAs), especially in the latter stages of the disease. The impairments may include difficulty concentrating, an inability to perform complex mental tasks, deterioration of mental skills and manual dexterity, and behavioral changes such as mild ataxia, anxiety, loss of interest in activities, and some unusual behaviors (Lansing & Loeschen, 1989; Prockop, 1988). AIDS-related illnesses may impair the productivity of an employee at the advanced stages of the disease, but a PWA may be able to perform the job effectively for many years with HIV and/or AIDS before there is any decline in job performance.

Loss of Clients or Customers

Many employers believe that their organization will lose clients or customers if their organization employs someone with HIV/AIDS. Employers fear that an employee with HIV/AIDS could tarnish the company's reputation or could compromise the safety of their clients or customers. Companies fear that if customers or clients find out that an employee at the company has AIDS, that they will refuse to do business with the organization because of fears of contagion or prejudice towards those with AIDS. This fear is not completely unfounded on the part of employers. For example, some organizations suspected of employing AIDS carriers have been boycotted by fearful customers, clients, and patients (AIDS, 1987; Refusal to work, 1986). Also, there have been several cases in which parents would not allow their children to go to a school in which there were either teachers or other children with AIDS, and cases in which clients refuse to go to a doctor or dentist that has HIV. In addition, many restaurant owners have been concerned that if customers find out that they employ waitstaff or cooks who have AIDS, that customers will refuse to dine at their restaurant. Much of the public is still misinformed about how HIV/AIDS is transmitted and do not want to work with or patronize a company if they employ people with AIDS, for fear that they may catch HIV by working with or being served by someone with AIDS. In addition, clients and customers may associate AIDS with homosexuals and injecting drug users and do not want to work with or be served by these types of people.

Employers must also be concerned with the safety of their clients and customers. This has been most at issue where there is extensive interaction between employees and customers, such as the food service, cosmetics, and hairstyling industries, and especially where the transmittal of blood to clients is possible, such as in health care settings. However, there is virtually no risk of transmitting HIV through normal workplace activity. Even in health care settings, where there is a very small chance of transmission (usually from patient to medical worker rather than vice versa), this risk can be drastically reduced if standard procedures and precautions are followed (Shanson & Cockcroft, 1991). Even for health care workers, where the risk of infection is probably the greatest, the Centers for Disease Control (CDC) have found that the risk of hospital employees getting HIV from the workplace is significantly low. In fact, hospital employees who are HIV-positive in most cases have become so from injecting drug use or unprotected sexual contact (CDC, 1985). Also, a summary of studies from the CDC have shown that about 30 percent of accidental incidents were preventable and of those accidental incidents, only very few (maybe 1 in 1,500) are likely to result in the transmission of the HIV virus (Banta, 1988). Also, according to the CDC (1985), the risk of infection from a needle-stick puncture where the needle is contaminated with HIV-infected body fluids is less than 1 percent. There have been rare examples of transmission from health care workers: a Florida dentist (MMWR, 1992) transmitted HIV to five of over 1,100 patients who were evaluated (0.5%): the findings supported dentist-to-patient rather than patient-to-patient transmission as the route. Some questions were raised as to the state of mind of the dentist at the time of the transmission. There have also been rare instances of infected persons who purposely threaten to infect others with HIV, and employers should be aware this could happen and that they are responsible for the safety of their clients and customers.

Employers may be held legally liable for the actions of their employees, so they should be concerned with being taken to court should an employee with ADC or other AIDS-related illnesses inflict harm in the workplace. Harm could arise through negligent or malicious actions, the failure or inability to perform properly, or a lapse of concentration that could lead to an accident (Lansing & Loeschen, 1989; O'Brien, 1995). In jobs where safety concerns are very important, and the potential effects of cognitive and neurological impairments secondary to AIDS/HIV are high, some restrictive actions can and should be taken by employers. If a PWA does develop ADC, it is important that an employer determine whether this employee poses a threat to clients or customers, or other employees, because of impairments in productivity. It should be noted, however, that the instances of dementia associated with HIV infection are extremely rare, less than 5 percent in people with HIV and less than 20 percent in people with AIDS, and then only when extremely ill (Harris, 1990).

Workplace Conflict

Many employers may understand the improbability of transmission of AIDS in the workplace, but fear that coworkers will react negatively to a coworker who is HIV-positive. For example, a survey of 263 Detroit businesspersons (Fremgen & Whitty, 1992) found that 53 percent of respondents said that they think that the presence of an employee with AIDS might lead some of their employees to seek employment elsewhere. Only 11 percent disagreed and 32 percent were uncertain. Managers concerns are not completely unfounded. Some people do not in fact want to work with coworkers who have HIV/AIDS.

In a survey conducted by the Harvard University School of Public Health (Blendon & Donelan, 1988), 25 percent of respondents said they would refuse to work alongside an HIV-infected coworker and 11 percent fully believed that they could be infected by the virus by working alongside someone who was a carrier. In fact, there have even been some cases in which employees have taken collective action to have their coworkers with AIDS dismissed (Leonard, 1985; Rowe, 1986). Also, in certain instances, employees have refused job assignments, threatened violence, and walked off the job when expected to work with people with AIDS (Pave, 1985). As a result of coworkers' negative reactions, many managers who have an employee with AIDS have had confrontations with the patient's coworkers (Bauman & Aberth, 1986). Obviously, the existence of a worker with HIV could create considerable workplace conflict if coworkers and the employer are not educated about the real risks of HIV transmission or if coworkers are very prejudiced toward people with HIV/AIDS. However, most of these extreme reactions occurred in the early years of the HIV epidemic, and increased information and understanding in the second decade of HIV in North America have made reactions like these much less common.

Increased Health Insurance Costs

In countries such as the United States, where industry generally pays for medical insurance and disability benefits expenses, industry often pays for a significant percentage of the costs of AIDS-related disease. According to the *U.S. News & World Report* in 1989, the 44,000 people diagnosed with AIDS in the United States incurred direct medical expenses of about $3.3 billion, and 40 percent was paid for by businesses and private insurers (Pomice, 1990). So, employers can end up paying large sums of money in health benefits for employees with AIDS, and this can have a particularly negative effect on small businesses.

Many employers have tried to exclude HIV-related costs from their health insurance coverage to save money. Although company policies cover procedures and treatments as costly as, or more costly than, the treatment for HIV/AIDS, some insurers have singled out HIV disease for exclusion (The treatment costs, 1990), presumably because of the stigma associated with HIV/AIDS. Although in the United States this practice is illegal, many companies have tried to completely exclude HIV/AIDS from coverage anyway. For example, in late December 1985-early January 1986 a Datsun dealer in Oregon revised its insurance plan to specifically exclude costs associated with AIDS. An employee who had been employed and insured with the company since 1982 brought a complaint against the company with the Oregon Civil Rights Division of the Bureau of Labor and Industries, and the Civil Rights Division found in favor of the employee (*Doe v. Beaverton Nissan,* 1986). Other employers have attempted to put discriminatory limits (caps) on the amount of coverage they will provide for HIV-related treatments. For instance, in Florida, a person with AIDS filed a complaint with the Florida Commission on Human Relations claiming that his employer, Arvida JMB Corporation, changed insurance companies when they found out he had AIDS. The original plan guaranteed $1 million in coverage, but the new plan limited AIDS-related medical expenses to $5,000 with a lifetime cap of $15,000. The employer eventually changed the policy back to a plan that did not contain an AIDS-related cap (Hunter & Rubenstein, 1992). Many companies devise ways out of paying for HIV-related medical insurance costs because of the potential for large expenses associated with AIDS.

Lawsuit Costs Brought by Someone with HIV/AIDS

As a result of employers' concerns, many organizations have chosen to fire employees with AIDS, have attempted to find out who has AIDS by either coercing employees into revealing the information or by requiring mandatory AIDS testing for current employees and/or applicants, and have breached the confidentiality of the employee's medical records. Many of these actions can and have resulted in costly lawsuits for employers. In fact, it is clear from services providing advice and guidance to people with HIV/AIDS in the United States that discrimination, prejudice, and harassment within the workplace, often resulting in the loss of a job either through dismissal or forced resignation, are common (Goss & Adam-Smith, 1995). In addition, every study of AIDS-related discrimination in the United States to date has found that the largest category of complaints concerns employment (Gostin, 1990). This occurs in many other countries as well. For example, there has been an increase in India of the number of infected people being traumatized at the workplace due to peer rejection and hostility from employers, even leading to outright dismissal (Mallikarjuna, 1998). In addition, AIDS has become the most litigated disease in U.S. history (Health-care workers, 1996). It is clear that discrimination based on HIV/AIDS is not uncommon at all.

As a result of harassment or discrimination or both on the job, many people with HIV/AIDS are left unsatisfied at work or may face unemployment. This may result in a loss of income and health benefits that are particularly needed in the case of HIV-related illnesses. Because the incidence of workplace discrimination is fairly common, if a PWA feels wrongfully terminated or harassed on the job, he or she may bring a lawsuit to the company for reinstatement, back pay, and even punitive damages in some cases where such a person is protected under the law. Lawsuits can result in much negative publicity and expense to employers. For instance, in the United States, these expenses have been considerable (Feuer, 1987; Logan, 1987). As a result of most companies' attempts at avoiding these sizable expenses, wrongful dismissal suits involving AIDS patients are almost always settled out of court in the United States (Logan, 1987), and most in favor of the plaintiff.

AIDS AND THE LAW

Given the numerous concerns that employers have about employing someone with HIV and/or AIDS, how should employers decide how to handle AIDS in the workplace? Employers must first consider the applicable laws in their country or locale. Lawsuits can be costly to an organization both monetarily and because of the negative publicity that can result from the lawsuits, so the law should be the starting point for organizations in how to deal effectively with AIDS in their workplace. The specifics of the laws that are applicable to AIDS in employment vary considerably between countries, but there are many common elements to most of the laws. Due to space considerations, this chapter will only examine the applicable employment law in the United States. It must be noted that case law is continually changing and the interpretations of relevant laws by the courts may also be changing. As a result, an expert in employment law should be consulted by an employer before taking actions or developing company policies.

Feldblum (1992) provides a good review of the relevant law in the United States and a summary follows. The major law in the United States that covers employment discrimination and people with AIDS was enacted by Congress in 1990. The Americans with Disabilities Act (ADA) prohibits workplace discrimination based on disability, which includes HIV disease. HIV disease refers to the entire spectrum of HIV-related illness, from asymptomatic HIV infection through AIDS. Congress modeled the ADA on a prior law (the Rehabilitation Act of 1973) that also makes discrimination on the basis of disability illegal. However, the Rehabilitation Act of 1973 only applies to the federal government and to private and state employers that accept federal funds or have federal contracts or subcontracts. The ADA also applies to private businesses with at least 15 employees. The law became effective in full on July 26, 1994. Some of the most common things plaintiffs may receive if they win a lawsuit include reinstatement to the job, back pay, and punitive damages in cases of intentional discrimination or reckless indifference to the rights of others.

Since the passing of the ADA, there has been considerable disagreement among the circuit courts about the interpretation of the law (Circuit courts clash, 1997). The disagreement centers around several issues. First is whether or not asymptomatic HIV infection qualifies as a disability under the ADA. However, the U.S. Supreme Court did recently decide that the ADA covers people who test positive for HIV, even if they have not yet developed AIDS-related symptoms (Rauber, 1998). Also being considered is whether reproduction is considered a major life activity under the ADA. The ADA applies to conditions that affect "major life activities" and thus if HIV affects reproduction and reproduction is considered a major life activity, even in the absence of signs or symptoms, there is no question as to the inclusion of HIV infection as a disability. A third issue is whether a person in the advanced stages of AIDS who has significant enough symptoms to qualify for disability benefits including Social Security or private disability plans is still covered under the ADA. A fourth issue is whether insurance products including those provided through an employee benefit program are covered under the ADA. The specifics of the ADA and the implications it has for a PWA are still being tested in the courts.

Job Qualifications and Productivity of People with HIV/AIDS

Under the ADA, "a qualified person with a disability" cannot be discriminated against in employment. A qualified person under the ADA is defined as a person who, "with or without reasonable accommodation, can perform the essential functions of the employment position that such individual holds or desires" (U.S. Department of Justice, 1990). "Essential functions" are job functions that are not tangential or relatively unimportant to the job in question. Employers, under the ADA, still retain the right to not hire, or to fire someone who cannot perform the essential functions of the job with or without reasonable accommodation. Also, it must be noted that a "qualified person with a disability" is determined at the time of hire and cannot be based on future capabilities. So, employers cannot refuse to hire someone who is HIV-positive but asymptomatic because they believe that it is likely this person will get sick and will be unable to perform the job at some time in the future.

Accommodations for the PWA are modifications or adjustments to the job environment or structure of the job that will enable the PWA to be qualified to perform the job. However, there is a limitation to an employer's obligation to provide "reasonable accommodation" to the disabled employee. If an accommodation would impose an "undue hardship" upon the employer, such as resulting in a "significant difficulty or expense" to the employer, it is not required under the ADA. Judgments of "undue hardship" will take into account such factors as the financial resources of the employer, the size and type of the employer's business, the number of employees, and the nature and cost of the accommodation. Most people with HIV disease do not need accommodations to perform the essential functions of the job. However, when they do need accommodations, the most common ones include flexible work schedules and time off to accommodate treatment schedules or fatigue problems. Other general accommodations could include wheelchair access, accommodations for weight loss, vision problems, fatigue, breathing difficulties, weakness, and concentration or memory problems.

Customer and Coworker Safety

In addition to being "otherwise qualified," the ADA requires that the person with a disability "shall not pose a direct threat to the health or safety of other individuals in the workplace." "Direct threat" is defined under the ADA as "a significant risk to the health or safety of others that cannot be eliminated by reasonable accommodation" (U.S. Department of Justice, 1990). A review of AIDS-related court cases in the 1990s shows that judges tend to side with the argument that disability rights laws must yield to concern about the possible transmission risks (Health-care workers, 1996).

Risk to customers or coworkers could also occur in rare cases in which an infected person threatens to infect others. There have been cases where HIV-positive employees have either acted violently against or threatened to harm customers or coworkers (Passenger sues American Airlines, 1986; "X" Corp. v. "Y" Person, 1993). In the cases where an HIV-infected employee purposefully engages in behaviors that threaten the safety of customers or coworkers, an employer's attempt to take action against the employee with HIV/AIDS will generally be accepted by the courts as an appropriate response (Feldblum, 1992).

Safety threats to coworkers and customers may also occur if the infected employee becomes ill and this affects their job performance to the point where the impairment could put others in danger. If a person with HIV/AIDS shows impaired job performance such that it could threaten the safety of others, this person can and should be relieved of those job duties that cannot be safely performed. For instance, there may be certain cases in which the safety of clients is of utmost concern and ADC is likely, that employers could and should not allow an employee with HIV to continue on the job. For example, an airline pilot can be denied permission to fly because of the potential of cognitive impairments in persons with AIDS and the seriousness of pilot error to the safety of passengers (Two pilots seek reinstatement, 1995). However, in most work environments, employers are not able to take actions based on the speculation that ADC will develop in all HIV-positive people. Generally, employers may only take actions against the employee with HIV/AIDS based on the specific behaviors displayed by the individual that show impaired job performance.

Health Insurance Benefits

The protections for people with AIDS in terms of health insurance in the workplace are not very clear. However, the ADA does say that an employer may not discriminate in the "terms and conditions of employment," and this includes "fringe benefits available by virtue of employment, whether or not administered by the covered entity" (U.S. Department of Justice, 1990). Several principles can be derived from various legislative reports concerned with the ADA (Feldblum, 1992). These include: (1) an employer cannot refuse to hire someone with HIV/AIDS because the individual will cost the company more in terms of insurance premiums, (2) employers may continue to include preexisting condition clauses in their health plans, even though the clauses eliminate benefits for a specified time period, (3) an employer may limit coverage for certain procedures or treatments, but not deny coverage completely to an individual based on a diagnosis, such as HIV/AIDS.

The issues in regards to health insurance may differ considerably between countries depending on whether private companies pick up the bulk of the insurance costs, as in the United States. Organizations in which companies do not offer health benefits or countries where health care is provided by the government or both would not necessarily be concerned with this issue except as it relates to the continued health and treatment of an employee with AIDS.

HIV/AIDS Testing

Some employers want to use the HIV blood test to screen current employees to determine who has AIDS, or to screen job applicants in order to avoid hiring applicants who may eventually be diagnosed with AIDS. For example, in Hollywood, Florida, some city leaders unsuccessfully tried to require mandatory HIV antibody testing for all prospective employers. The purpose of mandatory screening was to limit future claims on the city's health benefits package and to reduce the amount of time and money invested in training employees who might then die of AIDS (Slack, 1991). Only a small percentage of companies in the world use HIV testing as a routine screening mechanism for job applicants or current employees, although it varies considerably between countries. For example, in Mexico, reports of mandatory HIV testing in the workplace are the most frequent human rights violation complaint received at CONASIDA's Human Rights Department in Mexico (Panebianco-Labbe, 1996). On the other hand, in the United States, the CDC found that of businesses with at least 50 employees, only 2 percent screen new employees for HIV before offering health benefits (Jorgensen et al., 1996). Often the costs for HIV testing for everyone is greater than the medical costs associated with those people with AIDS. As a result, most companies opt not to test for HIV. Perhaps, more common than HIV testing, is the practice of requiring or encouraging applicants or employees or both to self-disclose their status. If testing is used, employers need to be aware of the numerous problems associated with HIV antibody testing.

First, many employers are misinformed about the meaning of the HIV antibody test, which does not test for AIDS. A positive HIV test result only means that an individual has been exposed to the virus and has antibodies to HIV virus in his or her blood. Many people who test positive for HIV do not develop AIDS or show any symptoms of the illness for a long time after infection. For example, some research shows that, over a 3-year period, only between 8 percent and 34 percent of those infected with the virus go on to develop AIDS (Goedert et al., 1986). Secondly, the test identifies antibodies to the HIV virus that are undetectable for up to 3 to 6 months after contracting the virus (Goss & Adam-Smith, 1995). So, it is possible for an individual to contract the virus and be tested shortly after the test, and the results would show up negative. In addition, an individual could have a negative test result that is correct, but immediately after the test contract the virus (by engaging in unsafe sex, for example), and now be HIV-positive. Unless individuals are tested on a regular basis, testing will not be effective. Thirdly, employment testing remains highly contentious (Pierret, 1992), and may violate laws. However, initially U.S. courts were supportive of the rights of persons living with AIDS, but currently courts are likely to support mandatory HIV antibody testing of health care employees, criminal defendants, and prison inmates (Health-care workers, 1996). Consequently, HIV testing can be used in certain cases.

In regards to HIV testing in terms of the ADA, an employer must first offer a conditional job offer to an applicant, and then after this offer has been extended may require an applicant to submit to a medical examination or answer medical inquiries. The job offer may be conditional on the results of the medical examination or inquiries. However, this screening must be required of all job applicants of a certain job category, not just particular ones. Also, the information obtained from the medical examinations should be kept confidential. Lastly and most importantly, the conditional job offer can only be withdrawn if the medical results indicate that the applicant is not qualified to perform the essential functions of the job. In terms of testing employees who are already on the job, an employer may require a medical examination of an employee only if the employer can prove that the test is "job-related and consistent with business necessity"; that is, if the employer can demonstrate that the medical examination is needed to measure whether the employee's performance is adequate. So, in general, a person can only not be hired or fired if the results of the medical examination or test show that this person cannot currently perform the essential job functions in question adequately with or without reasonable accommodations.

It is important that consent be given before an employer can screen an employee's blood for HIV. There are cases in which consent was not given, and this is illegal in many places. For example, in a newspaper report (Dodd & Nelson, 1994), over 100 food hall staff were told they would be required to undergo medical tests, including screening for HIV, following an outbreak of food poisoning. However, it is claimed that many workers were very angry about being forced to take an HIV test, but many did not complain because they were afraid they might be fired if they did not submit to the testing. However, one chef took the organization to court and another resigned. There are numerous other cases where blood has been taken where informed consent was not given.

SOLUTIONS

Employees with HIV/AIDS

There are several things that people with HIV/AIDS should be aware of in terms of the workplace. First and foremost, someone with HIV/AIDS should pay attention to his or her mental and physical health. Most individuals with AIDS will require good medical insurance and a steady income in order to maintain a decent standard of living and be able to pay for medical bills that will be incurred because of their AIDS status. As a result, a steady job with good health benefits is very important to most PWAs. In addition, for many PWAs, continuing to work may be very beneficial to maintaining their mental and physical health throughout the course of their illness (Patterson, 1989). However, there may be a point in the more advanced stages of a PWA's illness that continuing to work could actually be harmful to the PWA's health. The job could be too stressful mentally or the physical demands of the tasks required of the job could be too much for the PWA and could result in illness or harm. If the job becomes too physically or mentally demanding, the PWA might try approaching the personnel manager about working reduced hours, obtaining a more flexible work schedule, being assigned different job tasks, being transfered to a less demanding job, or given other accommodations to lessen the stress. If these attempts are unsuccessful, the PWA could consider seeking outside counseling or changing jobs. However, one problem with a PWA changing jobs is that many employers have preexisting illness clauses associated with their health insurance benefits, so PWAs may be without health insurance for some length of time after beginning a new job. Consequently, changing jobs may not be a feasible option for some PWAs.

In order to receive special accommodations on the job, PWAs will likely have to disclose their HIV/AIDS status to their boss or personnel management or both. PWAs should carefully weigh the pros and cons of disclosing their HIV/AIDS status. As workplace discrimination is not uncommon, there is a distinct possibility that PWAs will experience job loss upon disclosure of their HIV/AIDS status to others in the workplace as well as the loss of medical benefits if fired. Also, some coworkers may have unfounded fears about casual transmission of HIV and have negative emotional reactions toward the PWA which may include taunting, jokes, avoidance, social isolation, and even formal physical isolation. Even if a PWA is not fired, he or she might find it very difficult and emotionally taxing to work in an environment filled with negative reactions from coworkers or bosses or both. On the other hand, if coworkers and bosses are accepting and well informed about HIV/AIDS, a PWA may experience considerable emotional support from others in their workplace. Work could be a place of great comfort to the PWA. Before disclosing their HIV/AIDS status, PWAs should be aware of the current company policies in regards to HIV/AIDS and discrimination and what has happened to other employees who have disclosed their HIV/AIDS status, if any have. Finally, PWAs should explore their available options, such as the consequences of job loss and the possibility of obtaining new employment in case they do get fired.

PWAs may have legal recourse for employer's negative reactions. However, if a PWA does bring a lawsuit to the courts, it may take years to resolve (years the PWA does not have). Also, a lawsuit will inevitably make the PWA's HIV/AIDS status completely public, and it may be hard for a PWA to prove that he or she was wrongfully dismissed because of his or her HIV/AIDS status. In addition, many PWAs may not be educated about their rights, the law, or how to find legal counsel, as well as lacking the financial resources necessary to pursue a lawsuit. These are some main reasons many PWAs who have been wrongfully terminated do not choose to file suit against their employer. Of course, it must be noted that in some countries it is *not* illegal to discriminate on the basis of HIV/AIDS status, so a PWA may not have legal recourse in many cases. In the United States at least, most companies choose to settle cases out of court to avoid negative publicity and the even greater costs incurred by paying for court costs and lawyers than what the PWA is usually asking for. So, it seems that a PWA who has been wrongfully terminated and is protected under the law may have a fair chance of prevailing against the employer.

There are other difficult situations that might arise for PWAs in the workplace. Employees with HIV/AIDS do not have to disclose their HIV/AIDS status to their boss or others in their workplace in the United States. However, if the PWA feels that he or she may pose a direct threat to others because he or she has HIV, the PWA may feel under an obligation to disclose to others. For example, physicians who perform direct invasive procedures to patients where the risk of transmission of HIV is possible, may be under an ethical obligation to disclose to others in order to protect the safety of their clients and coworkers. Another situation that might arise in the workplace for a PWA is if an employer violates the confidentiality of a PWA's HIV status or someone is involuntarily tested. Employers should maintain the confidentiality of a person's HIV/AIDS status, but sometimes they do not.

Employers

Some business sectors have dealt with AIDS in the workplace, but many have not. Health care settings have been at the forefront of setting policies and procedures for dealing with AIDS in the workplace, as there is a greater risk of infection in health care than in other settings. Some industrial sectors do not view AIDS as much of an issue as others, depending on the potential risks of transmission in the workplace and the prevalence of employees with AIDS in the particular industry. In addition, efforts to deal with HIV/AIDS in the workplace vary considerably between countries. Many employers that have offices or plants in some developing countries are dealing with some different issues than those located in developed countries. Laws may be very different and the rates of infection may be much higher in developing countries. Also, the population is likely to be much less educated about how AIDS is transmitted than in industrialized countries. Employers in developing countries may need to have more aggressive educational efforts to prevent too many workers from getting infected, resulting in a loss of the relevant workforce.

In 1995, the CDC conducted the first national probability survey of 2,252 U.S. businesses (Jorgensen et al., 1996). Of businesses with at least 50 employees, 95 percent offer health benefits to their employees and 5 percent of these exclude or cap coverage for HIV. Of these businesses, 70 percent report having an antidiscrimination policy for people with disabilities, and of these, 59 percent define AIDS as a disability. About one third of businesses offer workplace education on health issues, and 32 percent of these offer AIDS education, whereas 86 percent of the education offered focuses on occupational risk for HIV. Although 25 percent of businesses reported that employees have potential exposure to blood and body fluids, only 42 percent offer education on occupational risk. Also, 57 percent engage in charitable activities for health-related issues, and 15 percent specifically for AIDS.

Some employers in different countries are very progressive in their response to HIV/AIDS in the workplace despite the relatively low prevalence of HIV/AIDS.

For instance, although Hong Kong has a low prevalence of HIV, a Community Charter on AIDS was launched, and as of the end of 1997, 79 community organizations, public bodies, and companies had joined the charter covering an estimated 270,000 employees. Joining the charter committed these groups to HIV education in their workplace and formulating a nondiscrimination policy in their company/organization (Lee, Chan, & Tan, 1998). A study of factories in Thailand (Bangkok) with more than 100 employees, showed that various AIDS prevention programs were conducted in the workplace. Of these companies, 95.4 percent disseminated educational leaflets, 61.8 percent had training on AIDS prevention, and 46 percent conducted AIDS exhibitions. Also, 77.3 percent of employers thought that HIV would affect the workplace, and 61.5 percent raised the importance of preemployment screening in the workplace to avoid the negative effects of AIDS in the workplace. AIDS prevention programs were found in 20.4 percent of the companies and 25 percent had developed a plan for how to deal with AIDS in the workplace. In addition, several activities were conducted to support those with HIV/AIDS such as assistance and moral support (66.1 percent), confidentiality on blood test results (46 percent), continued employment until having health problems (49.7 percent), and provision of counseling services (38.8 percent). However, a survey of some of the top companies in the Philippines found that only 26 percent of companies responding have an HIV/AIDS program or activity in place (Cucueco, 1998). In the United States, as well as many other countries, there has been considerable progress in adapting to HIV/AIDS in the workplace, but many businesses still may not give equal health benefits to those with AIDS, do not have antidiscrimination policies, or do not educate workers on HIV/AIDS.

Many corporate managers who have confronted the problem of an employee with AIDS recommend planning ahead for AIDS-related problems (Bauman & Aberth, 1986), instead of waiting for an AIDS case to appear, if it hasn't already. Management should obtain information about AIDS, get facts about insurance coverage, review the relevant laws (perhaps consulting a lawyer who specializes in employment law), and examine ethical issues. If a company finds itself in a situation where an employee does have AIDS and the company has not formulated policies to handle the issues, companies could find themselves unprepared, and badly handled episodes could lead to costly lawsuits, negative media attention, angry employees, and conflictual situations. If a company does not have someone on staff that is educated enough on the issues, outside professional consultation such as legal and medical counsel should be sought to help develop sound policies, training efforts, and advice on how to deal with AIDS situations. There are several things that employers can do to deal with either a current situation in which an employee has HIV/AIDS or the future situation in which this may occur. These include, but are not limited to, making accommodations for an employee with AIDS, making organizational policy changes, and implementing educational and training programs about AIDS in the workplace.

Policy Changes

There are several things that companies may want to do when developing an AIDS policy. First, the company should develop a committee of individuals that at least includes senior management, physicians, legal counsel, insurance and benefits staff, human resources staff, and union representatives, if applicable. This group should have the power to formulate an AIDS policy and apply it to the entire organization. Before writing the policy, the committee should examine the current company policies, and interview relevant employees in the company to identify the important issues.

There are several things an AIDS policy might include:

1. "reasonable accommodations" that need to be made for an employee with AIDS,
2. the kind of education that should be provided about AIDS, who will be educated, and for whom the education will be mandatory,
3. a list of referrals to community resources that offer medical and emotional support to people with AIDS,
4. reassurance to employees that their AIDS status is confidential,
5. specific behaviors of coworkers against an employee with HIV/AIDS that will not be tolerated,
6. a policy about HIV testing, if it is used,
7. grievance procedures available to employees with HIV/AIDS or perceived as having HIV/AIDS if they feel they have been harassed or unfairly discriminated against,
8. health insurance and benefits packages,
9. counseling for PWAs and coworkers,
10. hiring and firing practices,
11. a statement of antidiscrimination,
12. procedures to follow when an employee is diagnosed with AIDS,
13. procedures to follow when an employee refuses to work with an employee or client with HIV/AIDS,
14. date the policy takes effect, and
15. exactly whom the policy is intended to cover.

Training and Education

Workplace AIDS training is a recent addition to many companies' agendas. The CDC found that nearly half of American workplaces have implemented HIV/AIDS policies, but only one in six large companies in the United States offer formal HIV/AIDS education programs (CDC, 1996). However, a variety of companies have been recognized for their innovative workplace-based programs including Levi Strauss and Company, IBM, Polaroid, and Gap, Inc. These companies provide a range of programs and services that include employee education, fundraising for local AIDS organizations, public awareness, and family education.

In many countries, the workplace has become a place to educate the community on HIV/AIDS. With a captive audience in the workplace, information can be widely disseminated from the workplace to the family and community (Gallagher & Bonifer-Tiedt, 1998). This is particularly important in places where the workplace may be the only way that many people find out about HIV/AIDS. For example, Red Cross instructors facilitated group discussions about the ways HIV is and is not transmitted to over 1,900 employees. This study showed significant changes in behavioral intentions such as intention to engage in casual contact, use condoms, and discuss HIV information outside the workplace. A study of 213 participants in a number of HIV/AIDS programs showed a positive increase in people's self-assessed AIDS attitude scores after the educational programs (Riley & Greene, 1993). Thus, these training programs do have the potential for positive effects on employee attitudes.

AIDS training could be conducted by an AIDS resource person or by speakers from local AIDS organizations. Some of the educational topics that should be included in the training are

1. the causes, diagnosis, course of illness, and treatment of AIDS,

2. how the HIV virus is and is not transmitted,

3. risk factors for HIV,

4. the difference between HIV and AIDS,

5. the meaning of a positive HIV test,

6. precautions that can be taken to prevent AIDS (occupational and personal),

7. legal and ethical issues,

8. the actual company policies on the issue,

9. the illnesses and impairments that could result from HIV disease and how it might affect a PWA's ability to work,

10. the kind of support people with HIV/AIDS need from others,

11. the grievance procedures available to employees if they feel unfairly discriminated against or harassed, and

12. sharing the same equipment and facilities with people who are HIV-positive.

There are several methods of training that can be used to convey the information about AIDS/HIV. Some common methods include educational videos, educational brochures, small discussion groups, audio materials, training packets of written materials including referrals, question-and-answer periods, having knowledgeable speakers come in (for instance, physicians, employment law specialist, and so on), having an actual AIDS/HIV patient speak about his or her experiences, participatory drama, and an AIDS lending library. Large organizations may wish to create their own AIDS brochures, including issues that are company-specific. However, many organizations choose to use brochures that apply to general issues of AIDS in the workplace. General brochures are often available from the American Red Cross, local community AIDS organizations, and governmental AIDS agencies, as well as national organizations such as the American Foundation for AIDS research (AmFAR) (Seligson & Peterson, 1992). Companies may want to send brochures to employees at home, so they can read them in privacy, but the brochures should also be available through human resources. Participatory drama can be a valuable tool to educate people on HIV/AIDS prevention in workplaces (Mbonde, Tusekelege, & Katende, 1998). Since 1993, the African Medical and Research Foundation has been implementing AIDS intervention programs in workplaces in Tanzania. Drama groups wrote and performed their own AIDS prevention plays for an estimated total of 20,737 people in 13 companies and organizations in the first 6 months of the program. Drama can be an effective way to educate people in workplace settings, and the discussions that emerge following the play's performance can give the actors time to answer questions. This method of drama may work particularly for nonliterate populations and may appeal to a wider range of people.

CONCLUSIONS

AIDS in the workplace can be seen in the context of the individual, the organization, and the wider society. For the individual, meaningful work is one of the major bases of self-esteem, meaning, and identity in life, and thus the withdrawal or removal of work is a significant, and damaging, blow in many cases. For the organization, the costs of developing reasonable adjustments in the work environment are outweighed by the advantages of hiring the most qualified employees, keeping experienced employees and avoiding long, costly and usually unsuccessful lawsuits for wrongful dismissal, and negative publicity. From the point of view of society, issues of marginalization and injustice are associated with badly handled reactions to workers with HIV disease, and the economic costs of the HIV epidemic, particularly in African and Asian countries, are having major negative impacts on national economies and social structures. Workplaces may be useful places to provide education, not only to minimize marginalization of those infected, but also to reduce transmission through provision of information on risk reduction. Despite the advent of effective therapies that make it possible for people with HIV disease to work longer or to return to work, workplace issues and HIV/AIDS are still important and potentially contentious issues with considerable legal, economic, social, and psychological ramifications.

REFERENCES

AIDS: When fear takes charge. (1987, October 12). *U.S. News & World Report, 103,* 62–
70.
Akande, D., & Ross, M. W. (1994). Fears of AIDS in Nigerian students: Dimensions of the
Fear of AIDS Schedule (FAIDSS) in West Africa. *Social Science and Medicine, 38,*
339–342.

Arrindell, W. A., Ross, M. W., Bridges, K. R., van Hout, W., Hofman, A., & Sanderman, R. (1989). Fear of AIDS: Are there replicable, invariant questionnaire dimensions? *Advances in Behaviour Research and Therapy, 11,* 69–115.

Atthakha, P. (1998). AIDS situation, employers' opinion and prevention activities in the workplace in Thailand: Results of a nation-wide workplace survey. *International Conference on AIDS, 12,* 174 (abstract no. 13440).

Banta, W. F. (1988). *AIDS in the workplace: Legal questions and practical answers.* Lexington, MA: D.C. Heath.

Bauman, L .J., & Aberth, J. (1986). Health educators in the workplace: Helping companies respond to the AIDS crisis. *Health Education Quarterly, 13*(4), 395–406.

Blendon, R. J., & Donelan, K. (1988). Discrimination against people with AIDS: The public's perspective. *New England Journal of Medicine, 319,* 1022–1026.

Botswana Ministry of Health. (1997). *Botswana HIV and AIDS second medium term plan 1997-2002.* AIDS/STD Unit.

Centers for Disease Control. (1985, November 15). Summary: Recommendations for preventing transmission of infection with human T-lymphotropic virus type III/lymphadenopathy-associated virus in the workplace. *Morbidity and Mortality Weekly Report, 34,* 681–686, 691–695.

Centers for Disease Control. (1995a). Case-control study of HIV seroconversion in health care workers after percutaneous exposure to HIV-infected blood—France, United Kingdom and United States, January-August 1994. *Mortality and Morbidity Weekly Reports, 44,* 929–933.

Centers for Disease Control. (1995b). *HIV/AIDS surveillance report: U.S. HIV and AIDS cases reported through December 1994* (pp. 1–39). Atlanta, GA: U.S. Department of Health and Human Services.

Centers for Disease Control. (1996). *Business responds to AIDS survey.* BRTA Program, XI International Conference on AIDS, Vancouver.

Circuit courts clash over HIV in the workplace. (1997, September 19). *AIDS Policy and Law, 12*(17), suppl 1–4.

Clarkson, B. (1998). UK coalition back to work project. *International Conference on AIDS, 12,* 496 (abstract no. 24288).

Cucueco, M. T. (1998). HIV/AIDS in the workplace: A Philippine situation. *International Conference on AIDS, 12,* 176 (abstract no. 13450).

Dodd, V., & Nelson, D. (1994). Harrods workers fury over illegal HIV tests. *The Observer, 17,* 4.

Doe v. Beaverton Nissan. (1986). No. ST-EM-HP-870108-1353 (Or. Bur. Labor & Indus.).

Feldblum, C. R. (1992). Workplace issues: HIV and discrimination. In N. D. Hunter & W. B. Rubenstein (Eds.), *AIDS agenda: Emerging issues in civil rights* (pp. 271–300). New York: The New Press.

Feuer, D. (1987). AIDS at work: Fighting the fear. *Training, 24,* 61-71.

Forsythe, S., Namanja, G., Sokal, D., King, T., & Delay, P. (1993). Projecting the socioeconomic impact of HIV/AIDS in Malawi. *International Conference on AIDS, 9*(1), 126 (abstract no. ws-D23-2).

Fremgen, B., & Whitty, M. (1992). Corporate AIDS policy response in one midwestern city. *AIDS and Public Policy Journal, 7,* 234–237.

Frieder, K., Perez, H., Maizliz, M., Beers, S., Cahn, P. (1998). Apprehension to care for HIV infected individuals at a workplace. *International Conference on AIDS, 499,* #24-308.

Fukuzawa, T., Kamakura, M., Sakurai, Y., & Yamagata, S. (1996). Results of the questionnaire about HIV infection and protection of privacy in the workplace. *International Conference on AIDS, 11*(2), 400 (abstract no. Th.D.4956).

Gallagher, A., & Bonifer-Tiedt, P. (1998). Workplace education as a vehicle for community education: an application with results. *International Conference on AIDS, 12,* 177 (abstract no. 13455).

Goedert, J. J., Biggar, R. J., Weiss, S. H., et al. (1986). Three-year incidence of AIDS in five cohorts of HTLV-III-infected risk-group members. *Science, 321,* 992–995.

Goss, D., & Adam-Smith, D. (1995). Organizing AIDS: Workplace and organizational responses to the HIV/AIDS epidemic. Bristol, PA: Taylor & Francis.

Gostin. (1990). The AIDS litigation project: A national review of court and human rights decisions, Part I: The social impact of AIDS. *Journal of the American Medical Association, 263,* 161–170.

Harris, D. (1990). AIDS and employment. In D. Harris & R. Haigh (Eds.), *AIDS: A guide to the law* (pp. 86–110). London: Routledge.

Health-care workers are losing most AIDS lawsuits, study says. (1996, August 9). *AIDS Policy and Law, 11*(14), 1, 9.

Heitman, E., Ross, M. W. (1999). Ethical issues in the use of new treatments for HIV. In D. G. Ostrow, S. C. Kalichman (Eds), *Mental health and behavioral issues in new HIV therapies* (pp. 113–135). New York: Plenum.

Hunter, N. D., & Rubenstein, W. B. (1992). *AIDS agenda: Emerging issues in civil rights.* New York: The New Press.

Jalbert, Y. (1997). Triple-drug therapy and return to work: results of a Quebec survey. *Canadian HIV and AIDS Policy and Law, 4,* 13–16.

Jalbert, Y., & Masson, R. (1998). Returning to work when you are on triple therapy: The reality. *International Conference on AIDS, 12,* 176 (abstract no. 13448).

Jorgensen, C. M., Hammock, A., Iannacchione, V., Lyu, C., Murphy, P., Thompson, C., & Montano, D. (1996). Business responds to AIDS: Results from a national survey in the U.S. *International Conference on AIDS, 11*(2), 246 (abstract no. Th.D.372).

Kanjilal, B., Forsythe, S., Ganesh, V., Balasubramaniam, G. (1998). An assessment of socio-economic impact of HIV/AIDS epidemic among truckers in Indian trucking industry. *International Conference on AIDS, 12,* 976 (abstract no. 44201).

Krupinski, J. (1984). Psychological disturbances and work fulfillment. *Australian and New Zealand Journal of Sociology, 20,* 56–65.

Lansing, P., & Loeschen, J. M. (1989). AIDS dementia complex: A new theory of employer liability. *St. Louis University Law Journal, 33,* 823–858.

Larade, R. (1998). Back to the future: Return to work programming issues for people living with HIV/AIDS. *International Conference on AIDS, 12,* 1096 (abstract no. 60521).

Lee, S. S., Chan, K. C., & Tan, R. (1998). Setting the agenda for promoting a non-discriminatory AIDS policy in the workplace. *International Conference on AIDS, 12,* 173 (abstract no. 13434).

Leonard, A. S. (1985). Employment discrimination against persons with AIDS. *The University of Dayton Law Review, 10,* 681–703.

Logan, W. B. (1987). How to deal with AIDS in the workplace. *Venture, 9*(5), 110.

Mallikarjuna, S. M. (1998). Combating discrimination faced by HIV infected at the workplace. *International Conference on AIDS, 12,* 972 (abstract no. 44178).

Mbonde, J. M., Tusekelege, J. S., & Katende, S. S. (1998). Using participatory drama to communicate STD/HIV/AIDS related messages in workplace settings—The Tanzanian experience. *International Conference on AIDS, 12,* 177 (abstract no. 13456).

Mello, J. A. (1995). *AIDS and the law of workplace discrimination.* Boulder: Westview Press.

MMWR. (1992). Update: Investigations of patients who have been treated by HIV-infected health care workers. *Morbidity and Mortality Weekly Report, 41*(19), 344-346.

Moreira, M. D., & Cristina, P. C. (1998). AIDS prevention in the workplace. *International Conference on AIDS, 12,* 177–178 (abstract no. 13458).

Moss A. R., & Bachetti, P. (1989). Natural history of HIV infection. *AIDS, 3,* S55–S61.

Nilsson Schönnesson, L., & Ross, M. W. (1999). *Coping with HIV infection: Psychological and existential responses in gay men.* New York: Kluwer/Plenum.

Ntirenda, C., & Zimba, D. (1998). The impact of HIV/AIDS on production: The experience with Lonrho companies, Malawi. *International Conference on AIDS, 12,* 496 (abstract no. 24290).

O'Brien, G. V. (1995). Employer defenses to discriminatory actions against persons with HIV/AIDS. *Journal of Job Placement, 12*(1), 7–11.

Panebianco-Labbe, S. (1996). Mandatory HIV testing in Mexico: Successful strategies to reduce its use. *International Conference on AIDS, 11*(2), 349 (abstract no. Th.C.4621).

Passenger sues American Airlines over bite. (1986, September). *AIDS Policy and Law, 1*(17), 2.

Patterson, B. (1989, January/February). Managing with AIDS in the workplace. *Management World, 18*(1), 44–47.

Pave, I. (1985, November 25). Fear and loathing in the workplace: What managers can do about AIDS. *Business Week, 2922,* 126.

Pierret, J. (1992). Coping with AIDS in everyday life. In M. Pollak, G. Paicheler, & J. Pierret (Eds.), *AIDS: A problem for sociological research* (pp. 66–84). London: Sage.

Pomice, E. (1990, April 2). A businesslike approach to AIDS. *U.S. News & World Report,* p. 44.

Prockop, L.D. (1988). AIDS dementia complex. *The Journal of Legal Medicine, 9,* 509–517.

Rao, A., Nag, M., Mishra, K., & Dey, A. (1994). Sexual behaviour pattern of truck drivers and their helpers in relation to female sex workers. *Indian Journal of Social Work, 55,* 603–615.

Rauber, C. (1998). Extending the ADA to HIV: High court rules afflicted workers are covered by act. (1998, July 13). *Modern Healthcare, 28*(28), 26, 28.

Refusal to work because of AIDS. (1986). *Industrial Relations Update, 2*(4), 1–11.

Riley, J. L., & Greene, R. R. (1993). Influence of education on self-perceived attitudes about HIV/AIDS among human services providers. *Social Work, 38*(4), 396–401.

Rosevelt, J. (1987). Support for workers with AIDS. *American Association of Occupational Nurses Journal, 9,* 397–402.

Ross, M. W. (1988). Components and structure of attitudes toward AIDS. *Hospital and Community Psychiatry, 39,*1306–1308.

Ross, M. W. (1990). The relationship between life events and mental health in homosexual men. *Journal of Clinical Psychology, 46,* 402–411.

Ross, M. W. (1993). Mental health issues and the worker with AIDS: The impact of work on psychological functioning in men with HIV disease. In L. Diamant (Ed.), *Homosexual issues in the workplace* (pp. 203–213). Washington, DC: Taylor & Francis.

Ross, M. W., & Darke, S. (1992). Mad, bad and dangerous to know: Dimensions and measurement of attitudes toward injecting drug users. *Drug and Alcohol Dependence, 30,* 71–74.

Ross, M. W., & Hunter, C. E. (1992). Replication of the factor structure of the Fear of AIDS Schedule (FAIDSS) across samples. *Psychology and Health, 6,* 39–44.

Rosser, B. R. S., & Ross, M. W. (1988). Perceived emotional and life change impact of AIDS on homosexual men in two countries. *Psychology and Health; 2,* 301–317.

Rowe, M. P., Russel-Einhorn, M., & Baker, M. A. (1986). The fear of AIDS. *Harvard Business Review, 64,* 28–36.

Seligson, M. R., & Peterson, K. E. (1992). *AIDS Prevention and Treatment: Hope, Humor, and Healing.* New York: Hemisphere Publishing Corporation.

Shanson, D., & Cockcroft, A. (1991). Testing patients for antibodies is useful for infection control purposes. *Reviews in Medical Virology, 1,* 5–9.

Slack, J. D. (1991). *AIDS and the public work force.* Tuscaloosa, AL: The University of Alabama Press.

Sprinzen, M. (1988). *Business responds to AIDS: A national survey of U.S. companies.* New York: Time, Inc.

Supreme Court to rule on application of ADA. (1998, May). *AIDS Alert, 13*(5), 53–54.

The treatment costs of AIDS are not as high as the costs for treatment of some cancers and other diseases. (1990, March 7). *More Workplaces Dealing with AIDS Cases, New Treatments Increase,* Bureau of National Affairs Daily Labor Report.

Thomas, P., Joseph, B., & Campbell, W. (1996). Self esteem and skill building for persons living with HIV through volunteerism. *International Conference on AIDS, 11*(2), 198 (abstract no. 3858).

Two pilots seek reinstatement because they had HIV, not AIDS. (1995, May). *AIDS Policy and Law, 10*(8), 5–6.

U.S. Department of Justice. (1990). Americans with disabilities act, Public law 101-336 of 101st Congress enacted July 16, 1990; http://www.usdoj.gov/crt/ada/pubs/ada.txt.

Vaillant, G. E., Vaillant, C. O. (1981). Natural history of male psychological health, X: Work as a predictor of positive mental health. *American Journal of Psychiatry; 138,* 1433–1440.

Warr, P., Jackson, P. (1985). Factors influencing the psychological impact of prolonged unemployment and of re-employment. *Psychological Medicine, 15,* 795–807.

Watkins, J. D. (1988, June). *Report of the presidential commission on the human immunodeficiency virus epidemic.* Washington DC: U.S. Government Printing Office, 0-214-701:QL3.

"X" Corp. v. "Y" Person. (1993), 2 AD Cases (BNA, 1994), 1201.

12

LEGISLATING BEHAVIOR AND ROLES: INSTITUTIONS AND SEX

Larry M. Lance

INTRODUCTION

According to Wintemute (1995), the freedom to engage in consensual heterosexual and homosexual relations is considered by liberals as a basic human right deserving protection by law. Although the freedom to be involved in heterosexual relations has received greater support than the freedom to be involved in homosexual relations, there has been a gradual, uneven increase in social accommodation of homosexual men and women in the United States (Green, 1997). However, organizations may implement policies that restrict workplace behavior.

Language of the various state statutes is so varied that generalizations are difficult. In some instances, the states are adding criminal overlaps to behavior they already regulate through licensing. For instance, a state court may hear a disciplinary action to revoke a physician's license based on sexual conduct with a patient while also prosecuting the physician criminally for that conduct. In these instances, the criminal law tracks the ethical constraints within the regulated activity. Some states are very specific about who is covered by the statute, naming professions such as teaching or medicine. Some states use catch-all language, such as "position of trust or supervision."

Many criminal laws are not enforced, or are enforced only rarely, as a matter of deliberate law enforcement policy or because of the practical difficulties of enforcement. Both conditions are often encountered in the area of sex crimes. Sexual regulation is an especially clear example of the frequent divergence between the law on the books and the law in action (Posner & Silbaugh, 1996).

In the past substantial institutional trust has been placed in the hands of physicians, clergy, officers and educators. In contemporary society such trust has waned. Newspapers and television frequently document sexual abuses of institutional leaders. Although heterosexual and homosexual relationships exist throughout the institutions of society, these relationships between superiors and subordinates are fraught with problems. In education a sexual relationship existing between a faculty member and a student can cause a student to subject himself or herself to unpleasant or offensive situations to which he or she acquiesces in anticipation of a passing grade. Relationships between physicians and their patients, particularly in psychiatric or psychological problem areas, subject patients to potentially more serious problems. In the military setting, amorous relationships between officers and enlisted staff introduces staff members to situations wherein they must perform in the submissive role not only in their work but also in their personal relationships. When a relationship develops between a minister and a member of his or her congregation, the member of the congregation becomes fearful of going against the minister or leader. In addition, members place extreme confidence in the leader of their religious sect and have minimal defenses to oppose the overtures of this "man of God." In 1997 to 1999, a sexual relationship between the president of the United States and a staff member resulted in impeachment proceedings. While amorous relationships have existed in these institutions over the history of society, the increase in media attention to such relationships has spurred efforts to control sexual behavior within institutional frameworks. This discussion will focus on sexual behaviors in the military, educational, religious, and medical institutions. Within these institutional settings the concern with and consequences from sexual relationships will be explored. Also covered will be the measures taken to control such sexual relationships.

RELIGIOUS INSTITUTIONS

From time to time well-known ministers become involved in intimate relationships that are widely reported to the public. Such was the case in 1987 when Jim Bakker resigned from his powerful television ministry after disclosing that he had been involved in an affair. One of the ministers who started the investigation, Jimmy Swaggart, admitted in 1988 that he had also engaged in sexual misconduct and resigned his ministry. Both of these ministers were widely known and their stories received national attention and notoriety. Although such reports would lead people to think that intimate encounters happen occasionally to ministers, it has been maintained that all clergy and ministers have experienced sexual "come-ons" from parishioners and clients and, to some degree, all clergy and ministers have violated pastoral relationship expectations, if not sexually, then emotionally (Fortune, 1995).

Although actual research on sexual relationships between clergy and parishioners is very limited, one study indicated that about 13 percent of clergy surveyed reported having sexual intercourse with a church member (United Church of Christ, 1986). This percentage is statistically equal across denominations, theological orientation, and gender, but this percentage does not compare favorably with other helping professions. For clinical psychologists, 5.5 percent of males and 0.6 percent of females reported sexual intercourse with clients (Holroyd & Brodsky, 1977), half the frequency that clergy self-reported sexual intercourse with parishioners. Moreover, over 75 percent of clergy in this study indicated they knew of another minister who had been involved in sexual intercourse with a church member (Blackmon, 1984). Sexual relationships between pastors and their parishioners or clients violates the trust necessary in those relationships, changes the nature of the relationship, and invites potential harm. Although the parishioner or client may initially feel flattered by the special attention and perceives himself or herself as "consenting" to the sexual or intimate relationship, often the parishioner or client has asked for pastoral care during a period of crisis and is extremely vulnerable. Over time the parishioner or client feels that he or she is being denied an important pastoral relationship and begins to feel taken advantage of. These people feel betrayed, victimized, confused, embarrassed, and fearful. Later, when anger sets in, they are ready to take action. Spiritually the results are also devastating. The parishioner or client feels not only betrayed by a person representing God, but also betrayed by God and Church. This results in enormous confusion and guilt.

It is considered a violation of professional ethics for anyone in a ministerial role or pastoral counseling to be sexually involved with a parishioner or client within the professional relationship. It is a violation of the pastoral role expectations. The pastor or counselor is expected to make use of resources, knowledge, and expertise to serve the parishioner or client. Sexual involvement is not part of the pastoral, professional role expectations.

Further, sexual contact between pastor or counselor and parishioner or client is exploitative and abusive, involving misuse of authority and power. A pastor or counselor can intentionally or unintentionally use his or her authority to start or pursue a sexual involvement with a parishioner or client. Even if the sexual intimacy is initiated by the parishioner or client, it is the pastor or counselor's responsibility to maintain the boundaries of the relationship and not pursue sexual involvement. Further, even if the pastor or counselor and parishioner or client perceive themselves as "consenting adults," the imbalance of power, and thus inequality between the person in the pastoral role and those whom he or she serves, precludes meaningful consent (Fortune, 1995).

It is important to recognize the influence of sexism on sex in the parish. In a sexist culture males and females do not experience their sexuality in the same way, they do not experience their professional roles in the same way, and they do not experience questions about intimacy in the same way. Ethics of sex in the parish need to reflect these differences. In the same way that the socialization of men leading to the expression of sexual feelings needs to be understood to formulate an adequate framework for intimacy in the parish, so must the socialization of males and females that leads to differences in the experience of power and vulnerability.

What has been done in the past to deal with the sexual involvement of clergy with parishioners or clients? Since 1983 the Center for the Prevention of Sexual and Domestic Violence has been dealing with the issue of professional ethics and sexual abuse by clergy. This center has served as advocate, pastor, or consultant with victims, survivors, offenders, judicatory administrators, and attorneys. In 1986 the first U.S. conference on abuse in helping relationships took place. In 1989 *Is Nothing Sacred? When Sex Invades the Pastoral Relationship* (Fortune, 1989) was published and served as the first critical appraisal of the violation of the pastoral relationship that categorized it as an issue of professional ethics and sexual abuse.

Subsequent to these efforts, the discussion of the problem has expanded. Disclosures by victims have increased and expensive lawsuits against churches have multiplied. In the United States, the Roman Catholic Church expects to spend a billion dollars by the year 2000 in settlement for professional misconduct cases by clergy (Stark, 1989). U.S. case law specifies the Church is responsible for the hiring and supervision of its employees. If the Church credentials its personnel, it is also accountable for their behaviors.

Several denominations at the national and regional levels are striving to develop policy and procedures as they are being confronted with an increasing number of complaints. Some denominational leaders are removing offending pastors to protect the Church and are moving effectively to bring healing to victims and congregations. The Church has the right and responsibility to remove pastors that endanger the well-being of Church members and the Church itself. Failure for not taking action can be costly—morally, spiritually, and legally (Fortune, 1995).

Preventing sexual misconduct between pastors or counselors and parishioners or clients should be given attention by religious institutions. Policies need to provide specific guidelines for professional behavior regarding sexual conduct.

For example, the Presbyterian Church (U.S.A.) has been debating what is referred to as a "fidelity and chastity" amendment to the denomination's Book of Order. Approval of such an amendment requires Church leaders to be faithful to their marriage vows or, if single, to live chaste lives. Such a law also would be employed in Church trials to strip members of Church office. Such an amendment would impose one of the strictest requirements for Church office in any mainstream Church. The amendment states:

Those who are called to office in the church are to lead a life in obedience to Scripture and in conformity to the historic confessional standards of the church. Among those standards is the requirement to live either in fidelity within the covenant of marriage of a man and a woman, or chastity in singleness. Persons refusing to repent of any self-acknowledged practice which the confessions call sin shall not be ordained and/or installed as deacons, elders, or ministers of the Word and Sacrament. (News, 1997, 261).

Those who support the amendment contend that it is overdue. They maintain it clarifies the Presbyterian position on ordaining sexually active heterosexuals and homosexuals. Those who oppose the amendment argue that the amendment's main intention is to ban the ordination of homosexuals.

Another preventive measure would be to provide in-depth training in dealing with personal boundaries, dual relationships, and sexuality. An additional preventative measure would be to have pastors or counselors regularly monitor their attention to self-care both personally and professionally.

If prevention fails then intervention becomes necessary. When confronted with a complaint of professional sexual misconduct by a pastor or counselor, the denomination needs an established procedure through which to adjudicate the complaint and possibly employ disciplinary action. Such an established procedure should be easily available to Church members and be clear, fair, and carefully followed. If the complaint turns out to be invalid, steps need to be taken to restore the minister's credibility. When the complaint is determined to be valid, steps need to be taken to: (1) discipline the offending pastor or counselor; (2) protect, restore, and provide restitution to the victims where appropriate; (3) restore the ministry's integrity; (4) restore the congregation, including notification to the congregation of disciplinary action; (5) where possible restore the offending pastor to professional health; and (6) see that information about the offenses accompanies the movement of clergy to other churches (Fortune, 1995).

EDUCATIONAL INSTITUTIONS

Under what conditions, if any, are intimate relationships between faculty and students at an academic institution morally permissible? "Intimate relationships" refer to both sexual relationships without intimate romantic feelings and romantic relationships without any sexual intimacy. Based upon the right of privacy, adults should normally have the freedom of choosing with whom they have intimate relationships. Thus, if restrictions are placed on faculty-student intimate relationships it is necessary to morally demonstrate why such restrictions are necessary.

Academic institutions can choose from at least five different positions with respect to consensual intimate relationships. They can choose: (1) no statement of policy regarding consensual intimate relationships; (2) a policy indicating concern with such relationships but not providing specific sanctions; (3) a policy prohibiting all consensual intimate relationships between faculty and students, with a specific statement of sanctions; (4) a policy defining and prohibiting "exploitative" consensual intimate relationships and indicating specific sanctions for such relationships; and (5) a policy proscribing the formulation of consensual intimate relationships only within the instructional context where the faculty member has professional responsibility for the student's academic work (Keller, 1990).

In educational institutions where there is no policy concerning consensual intimate relationships, faculty and students may be faced with the whims, pressures, and bias of academic administrators. It must be acknowledged that unwritten rules are very hard to enforce in a fair and impartial manner. To the contrary, fairness would suggest that faculty and students be made aware of the types of consensual intimate relationships the institutions find unacceptable.

As with the institutional approach where there is no policy with respect to consensual intimate relationships between faculty and students, taking the approach of having policy statements that do not expressly forbid consensual intimate relationships but generally caution faculty members against such involvement is also problematic. Such policy statements provide faculty with only a vague idea that such relationships are suspect and associated with unspecified sanctions. Moreover, educational administrators will realize that ambiguous policy statements are hard to enforce. If an educational institution takes action against a faculty member by denying tenure or removing him or her from teaching, administrators open themselves to claims of selective punishment and unfair process.

Taking into account the problems with these approaches, a policy prohibiting all consensual intimate relationships between faculty and students sounds appealing. Such a broad ban would enable faculty and students to have less trouble determining unacceptable behavior. However, proscribing all consensual intimate relationships between faculty and students may produce a chill on other desirable social interactions. Mentoring and close association with faculty, key factors of academic success, may be denied students in an atmosphere of fear where such relationships may be misconstrued (Hoffman, 1986). Further, because a public educational institution's enforcement of administrative policies constitutes state action and is therefore subject to constitutional guarantees, imposing a total ban on consensual intimate relationships may infringe on the constitutionally protected right to privacy.

Between the two extremes—a total ban on consensual intimate relationships and no rule at all—are numerous alternatives that could take into account whether the faculty member is in an evaluative role, differences in age and status of the parties, and who initiated the relationship. Perhaps the most attractive alternative would be a policy proscribing the formation of consensual intimate faculty-student relationships within the instructional context where the faculty member supervises the student's academic work. Such a policy would maintain the integrity of the institution's academic mission while protecting the privacy interests of faculty and student. Intimate relationships between faculty and student in an instructional context raise the question of coercion. Despite good intentions of faculty, the question arises as to whether complete voluntary consent is possible given the power disparity between faculty and their students. Further, faculty-student relationships in an instructional context produce situations where faculty force a conflict of interest that might prevent them from assigning fair grades to the students with whom they have intimate relations.

It is also possible that where faculty-student intimate relationships are initiated by the student, the students may use faculty for their selfish end of getting a higher grade. Moreover, other students in the instructional setting may perceive that such relationships create favoritism or unfair academic advantage.

Faculty-student intimacy cases being investigated under a policy that prohibits amorous relationships only in the instructional setting are far less subjective and intrusive. It is relatively easy to determine if a faculty member had supervisory or evaluative power over a student during the relationship. Under such circumstances it is also possible to find objective evidence of favoritism or unwarranted negative evaluation. Moreover the motivation to report faculty-student intimate relationships is higher when the relationships take place within an instructional context.

It has been maintained that policies must make the crucial distinction between intimate relationships within and outside the professional responsibility context. Academic institutions should impose sanctions on faculty having intimate relationships with students for whom they have professional responsibility. Policies should explicitly state that such faculty-student intimate relationships are immoral, making faculty who are involved in such relationships subject to substantial penalties that institutions impose on unethical behavior. Policies should also explain why intimate faculty-student relationships that cross lines of professional responsibility are wrong (Dixon, 1996). One risk of these intimate faculty-student relationships is the risk of lack of voluntary consent on the student's part. The main risk, however, and the rationale for this prohibition, is the unavoidable conflict of interest that arises for the faculty member with respect to the student. Policies making vital distinctions that are supported by clear and compelling rationales have a much higher probability of being respected and followed by faculty than blanket prohibitions that can be construed as archaic (Davis, 1990). The real task for educational institutions is to provide clear and compelling rationales to discourage faculty-student intimate relationships within the context of professional responsibility or punish faculty when such behavior occurs, not to regulate the whole realm of human behavior (Nelson, 1998).

Rationales need to deal with actual threats to students' ability to provide complete voluntary consent and control conflicts of interest instead of people's perceptions, which may or may not be accurate, of these dangers (Zalk et al., 1991). Providing clearly justified policies prohibiting intimate faculty-student relationships when a conflict of interest exists will lower the possibility of false perceptions of impropriety in intimate faculty-student relationships characterized by no professional responsibility. From such policies members of educational institutions will learn that morally relevant distinctions apply and resist assuming the worst when they see faculty-student couples.

These policies prohibiting faculty-student intimate relationships where professional responsibility exists would protect educational institutions from intimate faculty-student relationships that really are harmful, while providing respect for faculty and students in two ways. One way would be that these policies respect the prima facie right of adults to pursue consensual relationships with whomever they prefer. A second way would be that these policies respect the ability of faculty and students to comprehend and behave in morally relevant different relationships that take place in different conditions (Dixon, 1996).

MILITARY INSTITUTIONS

In recent times, the military has been plagued by a plethora of sexual conduct dilemmas. In a recent case of sexual misconduct by a high-ranking official, a one-star Navy admiral accepted a guilty finding on charges he improperly steered military contracts to his partner in an adulterous affair. Rear Admiral John Surdi effectively pleaded no contest to the charges at a closed administrative hearing, precluding any possibility of a court-martial and prison sentence. The disposition of Surdi's case through administrative means, rather than criminal proceedings, enabled the Navy to bring a quick end to a matter that could have resulted in sustained embarrassment (Admiral punished, 1998).

Intimate and sexual relationships are a part of life. However, in the military intimacy and sexual conduct are at least hypothetically governed by customs and regulations. Becoming a high-ranking officer and leader does not mean that one stops being a human being with respect to the desire for intimacy and sexual involvement. Over time, the professional military has formulated codes to clarify and regulate intimacy and sexual behavior among its members. One such code deals with fraternization, defined as personal relationships within the military services that disrupt good order and discipline. The principal behind this is that good order and discipline might be disrupted when (1) officers date enlistees, (2) senior personnel are excessively friendly toward subordinates, or (3) favoritism or prejudice is revealed.

In keeping with fraternization, it is (1) unwise for officers and enlisted personnel to date; (2) unwise for senior officers to date junior officers, or (3) senior enlisted personnel to date junior enlisted personnel. When the possibility of the abuse of power is present, as when faculty date their students, the practicality of discouraging intimacy is self-evident. However, it is considered acceptable for officers to date enlisted personnel and seniors to date juniors if there is no direct supervisory relationship between them. In other words, it is acceptable for two military members to date if they are not in the same unit and if one does not rate the other.

According to Reed (1990) fraternization is unacceptable because it is disruptive of military order and discipline and mistreats human beings. Take fraternization to the extreme and there is the Tailhook scandal. At a Navy and Marine Corps aviator's convention in 1991 drunken officers fondled and partially stripped several women. Reports indicated that scores of male junior officers lined the corridors of one hotel floor and groped women who passed by. Fourteen female officers and twelve female civilians had their breasts, buttocks, and other bodily parts grabbed by drunken aviators. Further, as appalling as the behavior itself was, the common thread throughout the large majority of interviews with more than 1,500 officers and civilians yielded the reaction, "What's the big deal?" (What's the big deal?, 1992). A month of investigation into the event did not resolve the problem. The secretary of the Navy resigned and the Navy inspector general indicated that there was a sense in the tactical air community that what took place was acceptable social conduct and that the allegations regarding the conduct had been blown out of proportion. However, John Muntha, chair of the House Appropriations Defense Subcommittee, based his decision to eliminate 10,000 Navy headquarters jobs on what he termed the Navy's "obstruction and arrogance" in the Tailhook affair

(Navy harassment, 1992). In May 1993, upon reviewing 120 cases of alleged misconduct, Vice Admiral J. P. Reason disciplined 10 officers for indecent exposure (Officers punished, 1993).

What was the result of the Tailhook investigation that cost an estimated $3 to $5 million (Scarborough, 1993)? The acting Navy secretary acknowledged that the Navy has "a cultural problem which has allowed demeaning behavior and attitudes toward women to exist in the Navy" (Webb, 1992, p. 23). What took place at the Tailhook Convention in 1991 was an example of shameful behavior that resulted in great discredit to the Navy and Marine Corps. The officers that took part deserved to be court-martialed (Toner, 1995).

In addition to the questionable sanctions imposed upon officers involved in sexual misconduct in the Tailhook scandal, other cases also suggest that the military justice system has failed in the handling of inappropriate sexual intimacy in the military institution. The Canadian military has also faced major problems of sex and the military. One example of such a case in the Canadian Forces involved CWO Everett Boyle, who had 37 years of military service and was characterized as a disciplinarian responsible for the morale, conduct, and discipline of the 2,200 noncommissioned personnel at North Bay, Ontario. CWO Boyle was a disciplinarian in charge of conduct and discipline for all personnel except for the officers. In 1990 the North Bay's base commander summed up Boyle's character by stating Boyle will exude military excellence until he leaves the service. Few people could surpass him for leadership or dedication. Six months after receiving the commendation, Boyle's reputation was torn apart by senior officers when he pushed for an investigation into allegations that a high-ranking officer had been sexually harassing one of his married privates. The senior officers intimidated Boyle, tried to fire him, and threatened to court-martial him (O'Hara, 1998).

Based on his extensive experience as a military disciplinarian, Boyle indicated that officers are instructed to stick together from their days in officer training when they memorize the credo: "When a commander goes down, you surround him like a herd of elephants looking outward and you stay in that position until you're dead" (O'Hara, 1988, p. 16).

By retirement in 1991 Boyle had come to believe that the military justice system had dramatically eroded. According to Boyle, every time an officer was in trouble, the military's first instinct was to cover it up. Boyle maintained that if an enlisted man got into trouble, he would be sanctioned and held up as a bad example. However, officers protect officers. If you attempt to get in their way, they abuse their awesome power. Boyle, along with a growing number of past and present members of the Canadian Forces, maintain the military justice system, with its incestuous structure, its closed system of investigations, trials, and punishments, has failed and must be reformed.

Boyle's position has been supported by more recent investigation by the Canadian government. A report in 1997 questioned the fairness and effectiveness of the military justice system. Among the recommendations in this report were that military judges be civilians "totally independent of the military chain of command," that the director of the military police report to the solicitor general rather than the defense minister, and that an independent inspector general be appointed to check systems' problems with military justice and protect whistle-blowers (O'Hara, 1998).

In October 1997, the U. S. Military Personnel Subcommittee conducted a hearing on Army investigations into sexual misconduct and sexual harassment in the U.S. Army and its plans for implementing corrective actions. This hearing was held as a result of allegations of widespread sexual misconduct involving drill sergeants and cadre members of the U.S. Army Ordinance Center and School in Aberdeen, Maryland, Fort Leonard Wood, Missouri and Fort Jackson, South Carolina. Responding to these serious allegations, the speaker of the House, Newt Gingrich, charged House National Security Committee Chairman Floyd Spence, as chair of the committee with principal jurisdiction over the Department of Defense to lead a congressional effort to ensure sexual misconduct was completely investigated and that all appropriate actions to avoid future abuse were taken.

Several steps have been taken to prevent future sexual misconduct. Army Regulation 600-20, Army Command policy, has been revised to include a chapter entirely focusing on the subject of sexual harassment. Two new assessment tools, Ethical Climate Assessment Survey and the Command Climate Survey, have been developed to assist commanders in assessing human relations in their units and identify areas that need attention. In the Army a pamphlet entitled "Leadership and Change in a Values-based Army" has also been distributed to all commanders and command sergeants major in the Army to stress the importance of treating all soldiers with dignity and respect. Values-consistent behavior and the teaching of those values to subordinates are now part of the evaluation and mentoring process (Department of the Army, 1998).

Anti-sexual harassment and fraternization policies have been in force throughout the entire time when the most publicized sexual abuses have taken place. These policies are more than adequate vehicles to prosecute assaults, indecent exposures, and sexual misconduct. Education, training, and administrative actions to resolve the sociological and institutional aspects of discrimination based on sex are being widely implemented. Victims need to be encouraged to report misconduct immediately, and commands must investigate and adequately dispose of charges in a timely way (Chema, 1993).

MEDICAL INSTITUTIONS

Although traditionally not frequently addressed in the medical literature or medical undergraduate curriculum, sexual relationships between physicians and their patients have been condemned since the Hippocratic Oath proclaimed that doctors should "abstain from every voluntary act of mischief and corruption and further from the seduction of females or males" (Karasu, 1981, p. 107). Although seldom discussed, research suggests sexual feelings between doctors and their patients are common. One study of Dutch doctors found that 85 percent of male gynecologists and 17 percent of female gynecologists reported having been sexually attracted to a patient (Wilbers, Veenstra, van der Wiel, & Wijmar Schultz, 1992). A survey in the United States found that 95 percent of male psychologists and 76 percent of female psychologists reported feelings of sexual attraction to a patient (Pope & Bouhoutsos, 1986).

Taking into account prior research on the harm done to patients in sexual contact with therapists, there is a major difference in the findings between studies in the early research and subsequent research. In the early research, McCartney (1966) and Shepherd (1971) reported that sexual contact between doctor and patient could benefit the patient. However, subsequent research (Apfel & Simon, 1985; Feldmann-Summers & Jones, 1984; Gabbard, 1989; Kluft, 1989; Sonne, BufMeyer, Borys, & Marshal, 1985) indicated sexual contact between doctor and patient does not benefit the patient. With few exceptions, patients indicated sexual contact with doctors or other therapists was damaging. Patients involved in sexual contact with a previous-treating psychotherapist reported these contacts as harmful in 85 percent of the cases (CEJA, 1991).

This research is primarily based on reports of patients who have filed formal complaints against previous-treating doctors or of patients involved in subsequent treatment who reported being harmed by previous sexual contact (CEJA, 1991). There were a few patients who reported benefits, and others who have not suffered damage after sexual contact with therapists that may have not been taken into account by the researchers. Less damage appears to be done to the patient when the sexual behavior with the therapist is initiated by the patient (Burgess, 1981; Feldmann-Summers & Jones, 1984; Gabbard, 1989; Kluft, 1989; Pope & Bouhoutsos, 1986; Sonne et al., 1985); when the patient's preexisting psychopathology is not as severe, and when the therapist is not married (Feldmann-Summers & Jones, 1984).

The following two cases illustrate that there is more than one distrust problem in doctor-patient sexual encounters. Dr. Perez, a Missouri gynecologist, started treating Mrs. F. for infertility. When this woman told Perez she was emotionally drained from her inability to conceive, he told her to call him at home when she felt depressed. The two began talking almost daily and about 6 months after her initial appointment, Perez made sexual advances. They soon started having intercourse in Dr. Perez's private office at the hospital and at a hotel.

Then Mrs. F. became pregnant, apparently by her husband. Although she stopped fertility treatments and terminated her affair with Dr. Perez, she continued medical visits to Dr. Perez for other medical problems for 5 years before terminating the physician-patient relationship and filing a complaint. Although Perez maintained that Mrs. F. was a willing participant in their sexual affair, the state board determined he had taken advantage of her vulnerability and abused her trust. Nevertheless, the board, rather than imposing a severe penalty, suspended his license for only 2 months (*Perez v. Board of Registration*, 1991).

In another case, Dr. Gromis, a California doctor, treated Ms. M. for sinus problems. After being treated by him for about a year, she mentioned she was disturbed about marital problems. He invited her out to lunch and she asked him if she should see a doctor about her marital situation. Gromis said no and they had lunch again, which was followed by sexual intercourse at Gromis's house and at a motel.

After the affair had been going on for about a month, Ms. M.'s husband became suspicious. Although Ms. M. and Gromis stopped having sex, they continued to see each other and talk over the phone. In a few weeks Ms. M.'s husband confronted Gromis about the sexual affair and submitted a complaint to the state medical board. Ms. M. then ended the relationship as a result of extreme anxiety and a year later received psychological counseling.

Although the state board found Gromis guilty of unprofessional conduct and suspended his license for 2 months, an appellate court put aside the board's decision. The court maintained that the rule prohibiting any sexual encounters between patient and mental health therapist was justified by the possibility for emotional exploitation. For other physicians, the court maintained that the mere fact of having a sexual contact does not make a doctor unfit to practice medicine. The court maintained there was no evidence that Gromis abused his status to influence Ms. M.'s consent or that he took advantage of information he obtained as her doctor.

Although clear evidence existed that Ms. M. suffered anxiety and her marital relationship suffered from the sexual affair, the court determined that there was no evidence that Gromis's status as her doctor led to this stress. Also, the court did not find that Gromis's sexual interest had compromised his medical judgment. Gromis did not advocate Ms. M. obtaining psychological counseling, but the court maintained that he could be disciplined on this ground only if it was found that he gave this advice to further his personal interest by insuring that her marital problems not be resolved (*Gromis v. Medical Board,* 1992).

These cases indicate three problems in doctor-patient encounters. The physician may abuse his or her power, for instance by threatening to withhold drugs the patient needs. The physician may abuse the patient's trust, for instance by taking advantage of times the patient's body is exposed. A conflict of interest may alter the physician's medical decisions or advice. However, problems of power, trust, or conflict of interest do not always take place (Schulhofer, 1998).

Sexual relationships between doctors and their patients can result in devastating consequences for patients (Bouhoutsos et al., 1983; Feldman-Summers & Jones, 1984; Pope, 1994; Pope & Vetter, 1991) and can harm doctors' ability to make objective medical judgments (CEJA, 1996–97). Patients involved in doctor-patient sexual relations may experience depression, sexual problems, guilt, and lack of trust of both doctors and men in general (CEJA, 1991). Despite the dire consequences resulting from physician-patient sexual relationships, only in the last 30 years has sexual contact between doctors and patients been explicitly condemned by the medical profession.

Without evidence of assault, sexual involvement between patient and therapist remains legal in over two thirds of the states. In spite of widespread concern about the damages of these relationships, the case for punishing the therapist continues to be weak unless it is demonstrated that the patient's consent is defective. If the patient desires sexual involvement and makes her choice freely, laws prohibiting sexual contact would interfere with her autonomy, not support it (Schulhofer, 1998).

Proposals for new statutes dealing with therapist-client relationships are no accident. Professional relationships are the setting for frequent, serious abuses that are largely ignored by existing laws. Further, the ethics rules in most professions are either too vague or too inadequately enforced to provide much protection for patients and clients who are vulnerable to exploitation. However, some of the new solutions go to the opposite extreme, limiting freely chosen relationships and legitimate desires for companionship without effectively dealing with abuses that most strongly require legal regulation (Schulhofer, 1998).

Issues about patient-therapist sex focus on the types of sanctions that should be used as well as basic standards for sexual conduct. Since therapist-patient sex is banned by ethical codes, which are enforced by mental health professional licensing boards, many psychiatrists and psychologists maintain more severe sanctions are unnecessary (Illingworth, 1995). However, professional ethics codes, by themselves, are a completely insufficient way to deal with the problems of sexual abuse.

One difficulty with the enforcement of ethics codes is for the patient to find the board that has jurisdiction over her or his therapist. If the therapist is providing counseling without a license, as most states permit, no disciplinary body is involved and there will be no license to cancel (Bisbing et al., 1995). In reality, fewer than 3 percent of sexual misconduct cases are ever reported to licensing boards or other professional authorities (Parsons & Wincze, 1995).

Even if the proper regulatory board is found and a complaint is filed, the likelihood of an effective sanction is low. Although some licensing boards are conscientious and many therapists have had their licenses revoked for sexual misconduct, licensing boards and ethics committees rarely deal with complaints vigorously (Pope & Bouhoutsos, 1991).

Licensing boards generally operate with limited money and a backlog of cases. Because the staff consists of other professional members, there is often a tendency to hesitate to discipline colleagues whose cases are investigated. Further, although victims are generally female, licensing boards are generally male. Many of the male board members are not inclined to perceive patient-therapist sex as a serious injury (Schulhofer, 1998).

In cases where the licensing board supports a complaint, sanctions are usually a reprimand or suspension. If a therapist's license is revoked, he or she can apply for a license. In most states a therapist can continue to practice after revocation of his or her license if he or she does not describe himself or herself as "licensed" or use protected terms such as "psychologist" or "psychiatrist" (Schulhofer, 1998).

These limits preclude the licensing system from providing adequate assistance to harmed patients, but damage suits for malpractice offer an alternative (Jorgenson et al., 1991). Malpractice liability is evident when the doctor initiates sexual involvement on the pretense that it is acceptable therapy (*Roy v. Hartogs,* 1976). Although a few courts have refused to find malpractice when a doctor does not try to tie sexual contact to treatment (*Atienza v. Taub,* 1987), most courts now maintain that sexual contact almost always involves a mishandling of transference and an unacceptable risk of harm to the patient. On this ground, courts usually impose malpractice liability for sexual contact with a patient currently getting mental health treatment, no matter if the sex happens in or out of the office or if it starts at the therapist's initiative or the patient's (*Simmons v. United States,* 1986). The medical profession still lacks clear standards to determine what types of sexual interaction should be placed off limits and psychotherapy still lacks an effective system of sanctions for misconduct (Schulhofer, 1998).

Sexual conduct that has been condemned fall into two categories: sexual impropriety and sexual violation. Sexual impropriety includes seductive behavior toward patients, inappropriate privacy for disrobing and draping, and questioning sexual function or history when not clinically needed. Sexual violations include doctor-patient sexual intercourse initiated by either party and other behavior with a patient that is sexual or reasonably interpreted as sexual (Sex, 1996).

Based on a review of the health care research of the past several decades, it seems that the injunction prohibiting sexual contacts with patients may have been proposed at an earlier time as mainly intended to protect the doctor and the reputation of the profession. Over time it appears that the main purpose in prohibiting sexual contacts between physicians and patients has moved from a need to protect the prestige and economic and physical safety of doctors to an increasing concern for the welfare of patients. Based on research reporting severe harmful consequences for patients who have experienced sexual contact with physicians, there is demonstrated need for the application of the injunction prohibiting sexual contacts with patients and for its enforcement by ethical and disciplinary organizations responsible for the maintenance of practice standards in all health care institutions (Leggett, 1995).

Physicians who sexually abuse their patients produce considerable harm, which leads to the need to closely monitor the discipline of physicians as an important public health issue. The number of U.S. physicians disciplined per year for sex-related offenses increased from 42 in 1989 to 147 in 1996, whereas the proportion of all disciplinary orders that were sex related increased from 2.1 percent in 1989 to 4.4 percent in 1996 ($p < .001$ for trend). Discipline for sex-related offenses was significantly more severe ($p < .001$) than for non-sex-related offenses, with approximately 71 percent of sex-related orders consisting of revocation, surrender, or suspension of medical license. Taking into account the 761 physicians disciplined, 75 percent of the offenses involved patients, including sexual intercourse, rape, sexual molestation, and sexual favors for drugs. As of 1997, about 50 percent of the physicians disciplined for sex-related offenses between 1981 and 1994 were licensed to practice (Dehlendorf & Wolfe, 1998).

It is far from clear that the patient's consent to sex must be coerced or misinformed. Present law reflects these doubts. AMA's ethical standards, although important, do not constitute "law." These ethical standards take effect only to the extent that courts are willing to put teeth in them. Sexual encounters between patient and psychotherapist are criminal in fifteen states (Schulhofer, 1998) and are considered malpractice everywhere, but the legal system largely declines to enforce the ethical rule against sex between patients and other professionals—and liability for malpractice is limited. Most courts rule that a doctor can be sued for engaging in consensual sex with a patient only when he or she tells the patient the sexual acts are part of treatment (Schulhofer, 1998).

In general, licensing boards give more weight to the norms of professional ethics. A doctor's license can be suspended or revoked for sexual misconduct. Unlike the psychotherapist, the doctor cannot legally practice without a license.

To summarize, discipline against physicians for sex-related offenses is increasing and is relatively severe, although few doctors are disciplined for sexual offenses on a yearly basis. Further, a substantial proportion of physicians disciplined for sexual offenses are allowed to either continue to practice or return to practice.

It has been suggested that the willingness of physicians to take corrective action against offending physicians will be increased by the existence of medical education that covers professional ethics (Dehlendorf & Wolfe, 1998). A study in 1992 reported that 56 percent of physicians indicated they had no education during their training about physician-patient sexual contact and only 3 percent had received continuing education on this topic (Gartnell et al., 1992). Failure to cover this subject in the educational system will leave new physicians with little knowledge of the responsibilities toward patients in their new position. In addition, patients need to be encouraged to protect themselves by knowing their rights in therapeutic treatment and by submitting complaints with state medical boards when confronted with inappropriate sexual contact by physicians.

SUMMARY

In contemporary society realities have changed. Today, on a regular basis, the media covers the alleged wrongdoing of trusted doctors, faculty, clergy, educators, and officers. Documentation of abuses of institutional leaders is virtually an everyday occurrence, and this information compels the general public to expect and demand answers. Often the abuses that demand answers are characterized as sexual exploitation by an institutional official who uses the power of the position for sex.

In 1999, newspapers reported that retired Major General David Hale became the highest ranking Army officer to be court-martialed since 1952 (Cruz, 1999). Hale was accused of having improper sexual relations with women in troubled relationships who were the wives of four of his subordinate officers in Turkey from

1996 to 1998. When Hale retired, members of Congress spoke of a double standard, as others of lower rank had been court-martialed in similar situations.

Although Hale was permitted to retire with honor despite claims of sexual improprieties, the resulting strong outburst led the Pentagon to change its rules to prohibit top officers from retiring while facing allegations. After negotiations, Hale was able to plead guilty to seven counts of conduct unbecoming an officer in exchange for having nine other charges dropped. If he had been convicted on the original charges, Hale could have been confronted with 56 years in prison. As it turned out, Hale did not face any time in prison, being fined only $10,000 and giving up only $1,000 out of $6,312 in monthly pension pay for only one year.

Recent estimates suggest that one third of all money awarded for medical malpractice goes for sexual misconduct damages. Sexual contact with doctors, faculty, officers, educators, and clergy has come to be recognized recently as a major problem. This concern has risen from the large number of reported cases, which probably represents the tip of the iceberg relative to the large number of cases that go unreported. (Friedman & Bounil, 1995).

Indeed, institutional sexual misconduct is clearly a complex and troubling issue, frequently swept under the rug. Without scientific data, scientists are left to speculate how widespread the problem is and how profound the effects are from institutional sexual misconduct. What is striking is the apparent lack of professional interest in this area until recently. Although mental health professionals have been pioneers with respect to institutional sexual misconduct, others have been slow to take action. The legal institutions have been moving cautiously. Although the medical institutions have proscribed sexual misconduct with patients since the time of the Hippocratic Oath, only lately has there been concern with enforcing its own code. Moreover, clergy and teachers have only recently acknowledged the seriousness of the problem within their institutions.

Institutional admission that sexual misconduct exists is one thing; taking action is another. Although institutions have acknowledged the existence of sexual misconduct, only recently has there been a growing effort to investigate the problem, document its prevalence, and devise ways victims may be assisted. Institutions are now making widespread efforts to establish strict ethical policy and encourage legislative control.

However, even now, it is difficult to determine what direction social policy will take. Is sexual misconduct unacceptable, or does it somehow become acceptable under certain conditions? Does a strong sexual attraction, an affair of the heart, excuse irresponsible behavior? It seems that the American culture has come to be characterized as a culture in conflict. On one side of the fence, an increasing number of states are declaring institutional sexual misconduct as criminal. On the other side of the fence, Hollywood is accepting, if not promoting and glamorizing, institutional sexual misconduct (Friedman & Bounil, 1995).

One social scientist has suggested that sex between a man and a woman who have a professional relationship based on power or trust, "specifically when a man is the woman's doctor, psychotherapist, pastor, lawyer, teacher, or workplace mentor," is "sex in the forbidden zone" (Rutter, 1989, pp. 22–23). This statement encompasses the sanctions that are starting to attach to these relationships and the costly professional price sometimes paid by those who step over the line. However, the zone is not completely forbidden, either by law or by social and professional norms. And it is not clear that it should be the case. The weaker party's capacity to withhold her or his consent is clearly at risk in these relationships. However, rules that entirely restrict sexual interactions whenever there is any imbalance of power can endanger autonomy from the opposite side, by endangering voluntary, freely chosen relationships, many of which can result in fulfilling, lifelong commitments.

Military "antifraternization" policies provide an extreme example. American armed forces have always prohibited social contact between officers and enlisted soldiers. The increasing number of females in uniform has raised the importance of the traditional policy, and failure to enforce it vigorously has caused major problems at military bases, as the 1997 trials for the sexual abuse of recruits at the Army's Aberdeen Proving Ground vividly demonstrated. However, on other military bases aggressive enforcement of antifraternization regulations has resulted in abuses of its own, destroying careers and limiting freedom to form mutually desired relationships, in situations where the dangers of coercion and the risks to military discipline are virtually nonexistent (Schulhofer, 1998). Even if parties to a completely consensual officer-enlistee relationship can avoid a court-martial, informal pressure and other sanctions still exist. Military members at times suffer a heavy career price for falling in love.

Problems of this type will increase as more women enter the military and the professions. Standards are needed to identify the types of sexual encounters that should be completely off limits. However, it is also equally important to avoid extreme zealousness. Freely chosen relationships should not be subjected to an extensive regimen of legal regulation and intrusive informal controls. It remains important to respect the freedom of every competent adult to seek intimacy with a genuinely willing partner. The problem is to determine when the potential for abuse of power justifies a ban on sexual involvement even in the absence of a coercive offer or threat. Society should not stop sexual involvements desired by both participants unless decision-making incompetence, the risk of retaliation, or potential harm to third parties indicate a high potential for abuse. The problem of formulating standards for protecting and providing autonomy for one person, without simultaneously destroying it for another, assumes a distinct form in each of the institutions where power differentials influence sexual involvement (Schulhofer, 1998).

Although the various institutions have issued guidelines pertaining to the sexual conduct of members within institutional settings, there is less clarity on the need for sexual conduct guidelines for those professionals whose clients, patients, students, and so on, have left institutional settings. In other words, to what extent are people who leave institutional settings affected by the residual effects of the original relationship with professionals once that institutional relationship has concluded? The solution seems to be to what extent a transference was a part of the relationship and whether it is likely to continue and whether there is a continued imbalance of power.

According to the Code of Ethics of the American Medical Association, it is not acceptable for a doctor to become involved in a relationship with a former patient in which he or she uses or exploits trust, knowledge or influence obtained from a former relationship. Again, there is the issue as to whether a power differential or transference continues after the institutional relationship. In domestic law and medicine, transference and power exist but probably diminish over time.

With respect to the educational institutions, sexual contact between faculty and students after the end of an academic program is not regulated even by those colleges and universities that deem it unethical while the teacher-student relationship exists. In religious institutions, sexual contact between clergy and former parishioners is generally left unregulated unless the clergy provides the services of pastoral counselor.

Almost all mental health and counseling professionals agree that transference and unequal power issues extend beyond the institutional relationship, but there is not agreement as to the direction and severity of the effects (Ulanov, 1979). As a result there continues to be conflict between a concern for people who might be sexually exploited and a desire to permit people to relate voluntarily to each other, without governmental or institutional interference. The trend seems to be toward a "cooling off" period. In all other institutions where issues of transference and power is not at issue, there are few restrictions against those who elect to have an intimate sexual relationship that develops out of the previous institutional relationship.

REFERENCES

Admiral punished in sex, contracts probe. (1998, Dec. 3). *New York Times,* reprinted in *The Charlotte Observer,* p. 9A.

Apfel, R. J., & Simon, B. (1985). Patient-therapist sexual contact. *Psychotherapeutic Psychosomatics, 43,* 57–62.

Atienza v. Taub. (1987). 239 Cal. Rptr. 454 (Cal.App.)

Bisbing. S., et al. (1995). *Sexual abuse by professionals: A legal guide.* Charlottesville, VA: Michie.

Blackmon, R. A. (1984). *The hazards of ministry.* Unpublished Ph.D. dissertation, Fuller Theological Seminary, Fuller, CA.

Bouhoutsos, J., Holroyd, J., Lerman, H., Fuer, B. R., & Greenburg, M. (1983). Sexual intimacy between psychotherapists and patients. *Professional Pscyol Res Proct, 14,* 185–196.

Burgess, A. (1981). Physician sexual misconduct and patient's responses. *American Journal of Psychiatry, 138,* 1335–1342.

Chema, J. R. (1993, Spring). Arresting "Tailbook:" The prosecution of sexual harassment in the military. *Military Law Review, 140,* 1–65.

Council on Ethical and Judicial Affairs (CEJA). (1991). Sexual misconduct and the practice of medicine. *JAMA, 26,* 2741–2745.

Council on Ethical and Judicial Affairs (CEJA). (1996-97). *American Medical Association code of medical ethics: Current opinions with annotations.* Chicago, IL: American Medical Association.

Cruz, Laurence. (1999, March 18) Ex-general pleads guilty to affairs. *The Charlotte Observer,* p. 9A.

Davis, N. (1990). Sexual harassment in the university. In E. M. Cahn (Ed.), *Morality, responsibility, and the university: Studies in academic ethics* (pp. 153–158). Philadelphia: Temple University Press.

Dehlendorf, C. E., & Wolfe, S.M. (1998). Physicians disciplined for sex-related offenses. *Journal of American Medical Association, 279*(23), 1883–1888.

Department of the Army Reports on and Corrective Actions Related to Recent Cases of Sexual Misconduct and Related Matters. (1998). *Hearing before the Military Personnel Subcommittee of the Committee on National Security House of Representatives.* Washington: U.S. Government Printing Office.

Dixon, N. (1996). The morality of intimate faculty-student relationships. *The Monist, 79*(4), 518.

Feldman-Summers, S., & Jones, G. (1984). Psychological impacts of sexual contact between therapists or other health care practitioners and their clients. *Journal of Consulting and Clinical Psychology, 52,* 1054–1061.

Fortune, M. M. (1989). *Is nothing sacred? When sex invades the pastoral relationship.* San Francisco: Harper & Row.

Fortune, M. M. (1995). Is nothing sacred? When sex invades the pastoral relationship. In J. C. Gorsinek, (Ed.) *Breach of trust* (pp. 29–40). Thousand Oaks, CA: Sage.

Friedman, J., & Bounil, M. (1995). *Betrayal of trust: sex and power in professional relationships.* Westport, CT: Praeger.

Gabbard, G. O. (1989). *Sexual exploitation in professional relationships.* Washington, DC: American Psychiatric Press.

Gartnell, N. K., Milliken, N., Goodsen, W. H., Thiemann, S., & Lo, B. (1992). Physician-patient sexual contact. *West. J. Med., 157,* 139–143.

Green, R. (1997). The United States. In D. West & R. Green (Eds.), *Sociological control of homosexuality* (pp. 145–167). New York: Plenum.

Gromis v. Medical Board. (1992). 10 Cal.Rptr. 2d 452, 455, 458–459 (Ct.App.).

Hoffman, F. (1986). Sexual harassment in academia: Feminist theory and institutional practice. *Howard Edmonton Review,* 105–121.

Holroyd, J. C., & Brodsky, A. (1977). Psychologists' attitude and practices regarding erotic and nonerotic physical contact with patients. *American Psychologist, 32,* 843–849.

Illingworth, P. (1995). Patient-therapist sex: Criminalization and its discontents. *J. Contemp. Health L & Policy, 11,* 389.

Jorgenson, L., et al. (1991). The furor over psychotherapist-patient sexual contact. *Wm. & Mary L. Rev., 645,* 684–713.

Karasu, T. (1981). Ethical aspects of psychotherapy. In A. Block & P. Chodoff (Eds.), *Psychiatric ethics* (p. 107). Oxford: Oxford University Press.

Keller, E. A. (1990). Consensual relationships and institutional policy. *Academe,* 29–32.

Kluft, R. P. (1989). Treating the patient who has been sexually exploited by a previous therapist. *Psychiatric Clinics of North America, 12,* 483–500.

Leggett, A. (1995). Origins and development of the injunction prohibiting sexual relationships with patients. *Australian and New Zealand Journal of Psychiatry, 29,* 586–590.

McCartney, J. L. (1966). Overt transference. *Journal of Sex Research, 2,* 227–237.

Navy harassment probe stymied. (1992, May 1). *Washington Post,* p. A1.

Nelson, C. (1998, Sept.–Oct.). Sexual harassment in the academy. *Academe,* 14–23.

Officers punished in Tailhook case. (1993, June 10). *Facts on File,* p. 427.

O'Hara, J. (1998, July 13). Abuse of power. *Maclean's,* pp. 16–20.

Parsons, J., & Wincze, J. (1995). A survey of client-therapist involvement in Rhode Island. *Prof. Psychol., 26,* 171.

Perez v. Board of Registration. (1991), 803 SW 2d 160 (Mo.App.).

Pope, K. S. (1994). *Sexual involvement with therapists.* Washington, DC: American Psychological Association.

Pope, K. S., & Bouhoutsos, J. C. (1986). *Sexual intimacy between therapists and patients.* New York: Praeger.

Pope, K. S., & Bouhoutsos, J. C. (1991). Sexual abuse by psychotherapists. *Am.J.L.& Med. 289,* 293–299.

Pope, K. S., & Vetter, V. A. (1991). Prior therapist-patient sexual involvement among patients seen by psychologists. *Psychotherapy, 18,* 429–438.

Posner, R., & Silbaugh, K. (1996). *A guide to America's sex laws.* Chicago: The University of Chicago Press.

Reed, W., Jr. (1990, Jan. 27–28). In search of moral leadership. *Marine Corps Gazette.*

Roy v. Hartogs. (1976). 381 NYS 2d 487 (App.Div.).

Rutter, P. (1989). *Sex in the forbidden zone.* Los Angeles: Jeremy P. Tarcher.

Scarborough, R. (1993, March 8). Tailhook probe goes first class. *Washington Times,* p. 1.

Schulhofer, S. (1998). Unwanted sex. Cambridge, MA: Howard University Press.

Sex in the consulting room: Ethics of relationships between doctors and patients. (1996). *Student British Medical Journal, 44,* 315.

Shepherd, M. (1971). *The love treatment.* New York: Wyden.

Simmons v. United States. (1986). 805 F.2d 1363 (9th Cir.).

Sonne, J., BufMeyer, C., Borys, D., & Marshal, V. (1985). Clients reactions to sexual intimacy in therapy. *American Journal of Orthopsychiatry, 55,* 183–188.

Stark, K. A. (1989). Child sexual abuse within the Catholic church. In G. Schoener, J. Milgrom, J. Gonsinek, E. Luepker, & R. Conroe (Eds.), *Psychotherapists' sexual involvement with clients* (pp. 793–819). Minneapolis, MN: Walk-In Counseling Center.

Toner, J. H. (1995). *True faith and allegiance.* Lexington, KY: The University Press of Kentucky.

Ulanov, A. B. (1979). Follow-up treatment in cases of patient-therapist sex. *Journal of the American Academy of Psychoanalysis, 7,* 101–110.

United Church of Christ. (1986). *Sexual harassment of clergywomen and laywomen.* Cleveland, OH: Coordinating Center for Women.

Webb, J. (1992, Oct. 6). Witch hunt in the Navy. *New York Times,* p. 23.

What's the big deal? (1992, May 11). *Time,* p. 16.

Wilbers, D., Veenstra, G., van der Wiel, H. B. M., Wijmar Schultz, W. C. M. (1992). Sexual contact in the doctor-patient relationship in the Netherlands. *BMJ, 304,* 1531–1534.

Wintemute, R. (1995). *Sexual orientation and human rights.* Oxford: Clarendon Press.

Zalk, S. R., et.al. (1991). Women students' assessment of consensual relationships with their professors. In M. Paludi & R. Barickman (Eds.), *Academic and workplace sexual harassment: A resource manual* (p. 99–113). Albany, NY: State University of New York Press.

13

ROLE CONFLICTS:
FAMILY LIFE, WORK, AND GENDER

Jo Ann Lee

Work and family are both very important to most American adults. Granted, there is variability in the level of satisfaction with each of these aspects of life. Some employees may view work as a necessity instead of a source of psychological fulfillment, and feel little or no corporate commitment. Similarly, some may not be extremely attached to their families and may change their family situation, as the high divorce rate reflects. However, each of these aspects serves as a major force in most persons' lives, affecting their job satisfaction and life satisfaction. The interest in and importance of understanding the consequences of balancing family and work responsibilities are reflected in the increase in published articles on the topic (Barling, MacEwen, Kelloway, Higginbottom, 1994; Lee, 1997; Neal, Chapman, Ingersoll-Dayton, & Emlen, 1993; Pitt-Catsouphes & Googins, 1999). In addition, the enactment of the Family and Medical Leave Act of 1993 highlights the public demand for assistance (Elison, 1997). Policymakers would not have crafted the legislation without the expressed need of their constituents.

Two major changes in our society have increased the need to balance family responsibilities in general (and elder care specifically) and work: changing demographics and the increase in the number of women in the workforce (U.S. Department of Labor, 1999). With more people living longer, the 85 and older segment is the fastest growing age group of the population. Often those surviving their advanced years experience long periods of illness and disability (Scharlach, Lowe, & Schneider, 1991) and need assistance with various activities of daily living and mobility because of some functional limitation. It is anticipated that the caregiving responsibilities will often fall on the shoulders of relatives or friends or both who work (Anastas, Gibeau, & Larson, 1990). Along with an increasing number of elderly, the concurrent increase in the number of two-career families has resulted in more family members who must balance both elder care and work responsibilities.

This chapter addresses the following questions:

1. Does having both work and family responsibilities lead to role conflict? There are different findings and conclusions regarding the beneficial or deleterious effects of occupying multiple roles. Unlike subscribers to role conflict theory, some researchers argue that occupying multiple roles increases the probability of greater psychological rewards (Sieber, 1974) and less psychological distress (Thoits, 1983).

2. If having both work and family responsibilities does lead to role conflict, are men and women differentially affected by role conflict? Are women more likely to experience role conflict than men are?

3. If so, why are women more likely to experience role conflict than men? What are factors that may increase the probability of conflict? Are there circumstances that are more likely to surround females than males, making the former more likely to experience conflict? Does role identity affect conflict? (Role identity refers to one's expectations and standards of behavior for that role.)

DOES ROLE CONFLICT OCCUR?

Investigating whether fulfilling both work and family responsibilities leads to role conflict is more complicated than it appears. We must first define "role conflict." The definition should consider the following: (a) the identification of conflict, (b) the roles that are involved (that is, the family roles), and (c) the direction of the conflict.

The Identification of Conflict

This chapter is based on conflict theory, which posits that success and satisfaction in one environment results in sacrifices in the other environment (Greenhaus & Beutell, 1985). According to conflict theory, conflicting role pressures between work and family make participation in both roles more difficult (Greenhaus & Beutell, 1985). Furthermore, research indicates that when an individual experiences role conflicts, the psychological response is stress (Baruch & Barnett, 1986; Burke & Bradshaw, 1981; Greenhaus & Beutell, 1985; Greenhaus & Parasuraman, 1986; Jones & Butler, 1980). Others argue that filling multiple roles can have many benefits (Sieber, 1974). Opponents of conflict theory argue that concurrently occurring roles can serve as multiple sources of ego gratification as well as serve as buffers to disappointments in the other roles. When one role demands more time and effort than the individual has, however, then role conflict may occur. This chapter is concerned with situations in which individuals perceive there is insufficient time or money or both. More importantly, this chapter is concerned with whether men and women are unequally affected by role conflict.

My research (Lee, 1997), in which I compared employed caregivers with employees who did not have caregiving responsibilities (noncaregivers), has produced findings that support conflict theory. I found that employees who provided care to an elderly person were absent more days than employees who were non-caregivers. Others have argued that the mere occupation of a caregiving role while being employed may not in and of itself lead to inter-role conflict. It may be important to determine whether boundaries limit the effects of multiple roles (Barling et al., 1994). Barling and his associates (1994) found that employed caregivers who are more involved with caregiving responsibilities experience more inter-role conflict than employed caregivers who are less involved. In other words, the level of caregiving may be critical to the occurrence and degree of conflict and stress experienced. One reason for inconsistent results across studies investigating the impact of balancing family and work may be differences in the participants' levels of caregiving responsibilities.

The Family Roles

Life brings many and various responsibilities. Being a good citizen of the community carries responsibilities, such as voting and paying taxes to maintain public services. The major, and most time-consuming, family responsibility is providing care for a dependent, such as a child, elder, or spouse. The family role that this chapter will focus on is that of caregiver. Not all employed caregivers may experience the same level of conflict. Some dependents require more attention and care than others do. A dependent with a mental or physical disability requires more care. Along the same lines, some caregivers are more doting than others and may feel more obligated to provide more care.

Some roles are easier to identify than others are. The role of parent is defined by the presence of children living with the employee (and usually children of a certain age). Other caregiving roles are more difficult, such as care provider for an older parent or disabled spouse. Caregivers for a spouse or elderly relative are often self-identified. The number of hours spent to provide care is usually used to identify caregivers of the elderly and may be more accurate than money spent (Lee, 1999). But "time spent" relies on memory, which may be distorted, and the period of time used may vary across studies (for instance, the last six months, or the last year). Other studies (Gottlieb, Kelloway, & Fraboni, 1994) may use the types of activities of daily living (ADLs; for instance, bathing, eating, walking) requiring assistance and their frequencies to classify persons as caregivers. Other researchers (Ettner, 1996) have assumed that living with an elderly person equates to caring for that person. In other words, different researchers may use different operational definitions to classify people as caregivers for the elderly.

Direction of Conflict

We must also consider the direction of conflict, whether work responsibilities interfere with family responsibilities, or family interferes with work, or both. Most research has been on work-to-family conflict, then bidirectional conflict, with the fewest studies investigating the interference of family with work (Kossek & Ozeki, 1998). Kossek and Ozeki (1998) conducted a meta-analysis of studies that investigated the relationship between work-family conflict with job and life satisfaction. They found a consistent, negative relationship between all directions of conflict with job and life satisfaction. All directions of conflict were related to lower life and job satisfaction. In this chapter, the phrase "work-family conflict" will refer to both directions, unless otherwise specified.

Summary

The role conflict issue is concerned with whether, on average, employed caregivers experience a degree of conflict and stress as a result of their multiple roles that impairs their ability to execute their responsibilities. When conflict does occur then stress will result. Caregivers may seek a strategy to cope with the stress by withdrawing from the work environment completely (quitting or retiring) or adjusting their work patterns, which may contribute to a labor shortage. Employers of today are very concerned about the attraction and retention of qualified workers. The labor market of the year 2000 was very tight, and employers were competing for qualified skilled workers. Offering fringe benefits, such as dependent care services, may be one way that employers can attract and retain the best employees.

Although other models of the relationships between work life and family commitments have been proposed (Zedeck & Mosier, 1990) this chapter focuses on the model of conflict theory. A growing body of research related to inter-role conflict experienced by individuals who fill an employee role and caregiver role has been accumulating. Barling and associates (1994) found that the level of elder-care involvement predicted conflicts between the roles of employee and elder-care provider. The inter-role conflict, in turn, predicted psychological strain. Scharlach, Sobel, and Roberts (1991) examined a multifactorial model of caregiving strain with a sample of 341 employed care providers of an elderly person. They found that work disruptions related to caregiving responsibilities affected caregiver strain and the perceived probability of job termination. Gottlieb and associates (1994) investigated the aspects of elder care that place caregivers at risk of experiencing adverse personal and job outcomes, including conflict between work and family responsibilities. They found that assistance with activities of daily living, care management activities, and the number of crises related to caregiving increased family-to-work interference and more stress.

The increase in the participation of women, both married and single, in the workforce is probably the most significant societal change that creates a situation ripe for work-family conflict, because more people are taking on both worker and caregiver roles.

On average women are working more outside the home. The number of dual-income families has increased, and the percentage of single mothers working has increased (U.S. Department of Labor, 1999). More married women are working and more men are working longer hours. The percent of married women working full-time year round rose from 23 percent to 46 percent from 1969 to 1998 (U.S. Department of Labor, 1999). The increase in dual-income families is due to two forces: more women seeking psychological fulfillment by working outside the home and an economic need to increase the household income. Being in a dual-income family may differentially affect men and women.

The changing demographics are also likely to increase the need for more assistance to dependents. Individuals are living longer, leading to an increase in the number of elderly, many of whom will need some assistance. Most of the family responsibilities continue to fall on women.

ARE THERE GENDER DIFFERENCES?

Having established that role conflict can and does occur, the question raised in this chapter is whether men and women are differentially affected by work-family conflict. Two issues must be considered: (a) whether women are more likely to have both roles and (b) whether men and women are differentially affected when they each have both roles. Role conflict research is focused on psychological experience, that is, mental health. Another question with respect to men's and women's experiences concerns the organizations' responses to their situations, in terms of career growth opportunities and rewards. An organization's climate regarding a caregiver's situation may influence the degree to which rewards and opportunities for career growth are offered, which, in turn, may affect the employee's stress level.

Are Women More Likely To Have Both Roles?

In examining the state of the current situation, we must remain cognizant that the workforce of today includes three cohorts: pre-baby boomers (those born before 1946), baby boomers (those born between 1946 and 1964), and Generation X members (those born between 1965 and 1980). Each of these cohorts may have different circumstances that affect their and others' perceptions of and responses to work and family demands.

For the pre-baby boomers working today, the societal norms and role expectations extant during their early adult years may be the major force behind any conflict that they have experienced. Most women raised during this era were expected to adopt the roles of wife and mother as their primary roles; working outside the home was quite rare for women. The role conflict issue was not as common and not a major societal concern, because fewer individuals were trying to juggle both work and family. The women who were career oriented may have suffered in their personal relationships, though. Women who succeeded in their careers were more likely to suffer marital instability (for instance, never married or a breakup in their marriage) than professionally successful men (Han & Moen, 1999). Married men with a traditional wife depended on her to take care of domestic responsibilities. The gender differences in career paths could be due to the family responsibilities borne by the women. Han and Moen's (1999) study involved pre-baby boom cohorts, born between 1922 and 1944. Most men in their study had very stable, continuous, and upwardly mobile careers. In contrast, most women had careers characterized as intermittent and part-time. In other words, most pre-baby boom women in their study had to choose between work and family. One explanation of the results is that the stress from filling the two roles—employee and family member—was overwhelming and unbearable. Alternatively, the women could have been victims of gender discrimination by the employing organizations. Their employers may not have retained or promoted married women or women with children, fearing they would follow their spouses. The differences between the career paths of the men and women could have been due to both circumstances. The family issue for pre-baby boom caregivers transitioned from childcare to elder care as they, their children, and their parents aged. Lee, Walker, and Shoup's (in press) study with pre-baby boom caregivers found the women in their study who juggled both work and elder care suffered more depression than did the men.

Today's workforce is constituted primarily of baby boomers. The women's movement of the 1960s and 1970s greatly influenced the participation rates of women in the workforce. More women entered and remained in the workforce and in many male-dominated jobs (Palmer & Lee, 1990). A greater number of baby boom women, compared to their predecessors, are more likely to experience role conflict, because they are more likely to accept both roles of worker and caregiver. For baby boom caregivers, the issue may more likely be elder care or care for multiple dependents (that is, children and elders) than childcare. As the number of dependents needing care increases, it becomes more difficult to balance family and work (Chapman, Ingersoll-Dayton, & Neal, 1994). Thus, work-family conflict has become a more salient societal issue.

More females of the baby boom era may perceive career pursuits as being a source of life satisfaction (Parker & Aldwin, 1994), although they may continue to consider family as their major source of satisfaction. They may try to excel in both roles. However, they may not have succeeded. Goldin (1997), using the National Longitudinal Study of Young Women, found that only 13 to 17 percent of women born between 1944 and 1957 attained both family and career roles by their forties.

However, men's and women's attitudes are changing (Barnett, 1999) and becoming more similar to each other. With the change in attitudes, male and female employees of Generation X may be more likely to share family responsibilities (Barnett, 1999). Barnett's (1999) research reveals that today's young adult men and women are less likely to subscribe to gender roles. Both men and women in her study believed that men and women should share both family and work responsibilities. Also Overman (1998) reports that men are willing to adjust their working arrangements to spend more time with their families. For workers of Generation X, the differential effects on men and women balancing family and work may disappear.

Although attitudes seem to be changing, there continues to be an unequal sharing of domestic responsibilities (Phillips & Imhoff, 1997). Women still carry most of the family responsibilities, whether they work outside the home or not (Leslie,

Anderson, & Branson, 1991; Robinson & Godbey, 1997). According to Robinson and Godbey's research (1997), in 1985 women spent about twice as much time as men on housework. In addition, evidence indicates that women are more likely to be the primary caregiver for the family (MetLife Mature Market Institute, 1999; Soldo & Hill, 1995; U.S. Department of Labor, 1999). There was an increase from 1965 to 1985 in the amount of time spent by employed men on selected family responsibilities (U.S. Department of Labor, 1999). The amount of time employed men spent a week increased from 11 hours to 15 hours; the amount of time spent by employed women changed very little and approximated 26 hours a week. The additional time men spent on family responsibilities does not appear to be devoted to childcare responsibilities, though. When the mother is working, primary childcare responsibilities are twice as likely to be left to a nonrelative or day-care arrangement than with the father of the child (U.S. Bureau of the Census, 1994).

Men may spend more time in pursuing avocations, such as leisure and recreational activities. According to a study by Parker and Aldwin (1994), men who graduated college in 1989 were more likely to identify avocations as sources of life satisfaction than men who graduated in 1969.

Gender Differences in Responses

The other issue is whether employed female caregivers are more greatly affected psychologically or emotionally or both by role conflict than are employed male caregivers. The levels of involvement in family and work experienced by men and women may differ, affecting their respective levels of stress and mental health. Notwithstanding the previously mentioned cohort differences with respect to men's and women's work and family roles, there is evidence that men and women respond to balancing the two roles differently.

Research indicates that it may be that women are more likely to be affected negatively than are men (Baruch, Biener, & Barnett, 1987; Chapman et al., 1994; Lee et al., 2000). Chapman et al. (1994) conducted an extensive study, using participants whose ages ranged from the twenties to the fifties. They found that women caregivers were more likely than men caregivers to interrupt their daily work schedule for caregiving responsibilities. They also found that women and younger workers reported higher levels of stress and absenteeism. Generation X employees may have more difficulty juggling family and work, even though they wish to broaden their nonwork lives. Chapman et al. (1994) also found that women were more likely to have multiple caregiving roles (caring for multiple dependents) and that having multiple caregiving roles led to greater stress.

Using the national data set collected by the Health and Retirement Study (HRS), I found that pre-baby boom females providing care for an elderly parent suffered more depression than did male caregivers. I grouped participants by caregiving status (caregivers vs. noncaregivers) and retirement status (completely retired vs. not retired at all) and gender to compare employed caregivers with employed noncaregivers. Respondents occupying dual roles of caregiver and employee reported more depression symptoms than those occupying either role alone (that is, retired caregivers and employed noncaregivers). Female caregivers reported more depression symptoms than male caregivers and emotional health became poorer as employed caregivers became more involved with their caregiving responsibilities. As the number of caregiving hours increased significantly ($p <$ .05) more depression symptoms ($r = -.21$) and poorer overall emotional health ($r = -.14$) was reported.

Female caregivers may experience more depression symptoms than male caregivers because the former may be more involved with their caregiving responsibilities. The gender difference in terms of caregiver involvement is supported by the significant correlation ($r = -.20$, $p < .05$) found between gender and number of caregiving hours, using only the employed caregivers group. Using all caregivers, the correlation between gender and number of caregiving hours was also significant ($r = -.13$, $n = 254$, $p < .05$). Alternatively, the gender differences found in depression symptoms could have resulted from males' reluctance to report what they considered personal information.

Kramer and Kipnis's (1995) study included only employed caregivers whose average age was 40. They found gender differences in terms of emotional burden. They speculated that the gender differences might be due to women's stronger attachment to the care recipient (Kramer & Kipnis, 1995).

Two interesting studies were conducted with Canadian professional women. Burke and McKeen (1994) found that the successful women in their study were more likely to be single or, if married, without children. Women who were more involved with their families were more likely to have lower level positions with their employing organizations. The average age of their participants was 30 years. The women who were more family oriented, compared to women who were more career oriented, reported lower job satisfaction and less job involvement, but higher life satisfaction and fewer psychosomatic symptoms.

These findings are consistent with those of Roskies and Carrier (1994), who also studied Canadian women, most of whom were 35 to 40 years of age. These researchers found that the professional women in their study who had children worked fewer hours and were less involved with their jobs than were women without children. The women with children, though, reported higher levels of life satisfaction than did single women and women without children.

At first it appears that moderation is the key, and that women may be better off when they juggle both family and work. According to these two studies, high job involvement and career success cannot be equated with life satisfaction. The professional women in these two studies could have had the job flexibility and expendable income to cope with the demands of family responsibilities. Consequently, the results of these two studies may not be generalizable to all women, who vary in terms of economic status. The study of role conflict must consider the various factors that influence the probability of conflict. I will discuss these factors in the next section of this chapter.

One reason women seem to be affected more negatively than men may be that they are more attached to the caregiver role, perhaps expecting a higher standard of performance in that role. The numbers of hours devoted to caregiving provide some evidence of gender differences in terms of attachment to the caregiver role. Stoller (1983) found that working daughters did not provide less time to care for an elderly parent than not-working daughters did. This was not the case for the sons in Stoller's (1983) study. Employed sons devoted fewer hours of caregiving than not-employed sons did. Although more women are participating in the work-force, it is likely that women will continue to be the primary informal caregivers of dependent family members (Soldo & Hill, 1995; U.S. Department of Labor, 1999).

Another indication of the differential effects on men and women who balance work and family responsibilities is the differential impact on the number of hours they work (Ettner, 1995). Ettner (1995) found that caregiving (for an older parent) did lead to a reduction in the number of hours worked for both men and women. However, caregiving did have a larger impact on female work hours. Caring for a parent living outside the home decreased work by 0.15 hours for men per week and 2.14 hours per week for women. The causes of the reduction in work hours could not be identified. Secondary data (the 1987 National Survey of Families and Households) were used and questions about daily activities were not asked. The reduction in work hours is consistent with other findings that indicate that em-ployed female caregivers, in general, do not devote less time to caregiving than not-employed female caregivers. With a finite number of hours in a day, less time is devoted to work.

Corporate prejudices may contribute to the reluctance of men of the baby boom generation to accept family responsibilities that take them away from work. Howard (1995) found that men in dual-career families earned approximately 20 percent less than men in traditional families (Howard, 1995). Marshall and Barnett (1994) found that working fathers are less likely to receive paid parental leave than are working mothers. It is possible that corporate prejudice against in-terference by family matters is a factor in some employees' behavior involving family responsibilities, and especially men's (Lewin, 1994).

FACTORS RELATED TO THE PROBABILITY OF CONFLICT

In my research, I have come across a number of factors that may affect the probability of conflict and stress. Gender differences with respect to these factors are noticeable. Women are more likely to find their circumstances promote the probability of conflict. These factors include job flexibility, company size, earned income, presence of a supportive network, and the nature of work. There is some overlap across these factors, but I will discuss each of them separately.

1. Job flexibility refers to the employees' ability to arrange his or her work activities with respect to time and place. Job flexibility would enable the employee to fit family respon-sibilities in the person's work schedule. Job flexibility is usually positively related to job

level, with higher level jobs characterized by more flexibility. Women, compared to men, are more likely to hold lower level jobs. In 1997, 29 percent of male full-time workers and 26 percent of female full-time workers were able to vary their work hours (U.S. Department of Labor, 1999). Thus, it is more likely that women will be caught in situations where it is difficult for them to arrange their work schedules to accommodate family responsibilities.

2. Company size refers to the number of employees at the employing company. The Family and Medical Leave Act (FMLA) does not apply to companies with fewer than 50 employees, and it requires only unpaid leave. Larger companies are more likely to have more generous leave policies than smaller companies, including paid leave. Paid leave policies have changed and the amount of paid time off has declined. The percent of jobs without paid time off rose from 8 percent in the 1981–1983 period to 14 percent in the 1995–1997 period (U.S. Department of Labor, 1999). Less paid time off means less job flexibility and a reduction in paychecks for employees (primarily women) to care for dependent family members. Women are more likely to work at smaller companies and may not even receive unpaid leave as required by the FMLA.

3. Earned income refers to wages received from employment. There continues to be a gender difference, with women earning less than men. Using the National Longitudinal Survey of Young Women, the National Longitudinal Survey of Young Men, and the National Longitudinal Survey of Youth, Waldfogel (1997) found that in 1991 the female-male pay ratio for cohorts with a mean age of 30 was 84 percent. With higher income comes an increase in the ability to purchase services. As alluded to in the earlier description of two studies involving professional Canadian women, work-family conflict may not exist or may be minimized if family responsibilities can be managed via the purchase of services, for instance, childcare or elder care or both.

4. A supportive network refers to others who assist with family responsibilities or who provide emotional support. Although women are more likely to be the primary caregiver for family dependents, the presence of a supportive network varies. Husbands may provide some to no assistance. Other family members may help. Having the assistance of others will alleviate family responsibilities. The employing organization may also serve as a component in the network by providing dependent care services, for instance, counseling, caregiver workshops, information and referral services, dependent care spending accounts. Having a supportive, understanding supervisor may also help the employee cope with the stress. As mentioned earlier, there may be corporate prejudices against male employees diverting their time to family responsibilities.

5. Nature of the work. Given the technological advances and cost effectiveness, many employees are able or required to complete their jobs from sites away from the office. These employees may be labeled teleworkers. Does the type of work permit work spillover to nonwork hours? Is telecommuting an aid or a bane to balancing work and family? Does current technology (facsimile machines, electronic mail, Internet access, cellular telephones and pagers) create an atmosphere more accepting and encouraging of work spillover into family life? The evidence is mixed (Hill, Miller, Weiner, & Colihan, 1998). Although some may perceive telecommuting as facilitating the ability to balance work and family, others disagree. Hill et al. (1998) compared the perceptions of teleworkers with those of traditional workers. Their results did not support the use of telework as a means to help workers balance work and family. Although some teleworkers

in their study perceived teleworking as helping them balance work and family, other teleworkers commented that the mode of working made it "harder to balance home and work" (Hill et al., 1998, pp. 678–679).

SOLUTIONS

I offer a few solutions to the growing need to balance family life and work—an issue that continues to affect primarily women. These include what employees can do for themselves, what employers can do to assist employees, and what public policymakers can do.

The *caregiving employees* have responsibilities not only to work and family but also to themselves. Employees must realize when they need assistance and must allow others to help. Many caregivers, especially those caring for an older parent, find it difficult to ask for assistance. They must read relevant literature and learn about and use available services, such as those offered by community agencies and their employing organizations. Examples of published literature to help working caregivers cope with their dual responsibilities are Cooper and Lewis's (1998) book, *Balancing Your Career, Family and Life,* and the Visiting Nurse Associations of America (1998) book, *Caregivers' Handbook.*

Employers may take an active role in assisting employees in balancing family and work. Although childcare was considered the benefit of the 1980s, elder care was considered the benefit of the 1990s (Earhart, Middlemist, & Hopkins, 1993) and will continue to be a needed benefit for the twenty-first century. The need to include dependent care assistance as a benefit has been recognized by many corporations as a way to attract and retain their best employees. Ironically, many employees caring for an older parent do not use some of the benefits and services offered by their employing organizations. One possible explanation is that they fear being labeled less conscientious and less committed to their jobs than other employees. If employers are serious about helping employees balance work and family, they must create a culture that accepts diversity. Diversity should include all characteristics, from caregiving status to age, race, and gender. Training supervisors to manage a diverse workforce and to respond to employees' needs is recommended.

Policymakers and researchers must join efforts to address the problem of balancing work and family (see Rayham & Bookman, 1999). The Family and Medical Leave Act (FMLA) of 1993 does not help most of those (primarily women) who desperately need assistance (Marks, 1997). Some argue (Marks, 1997) that the FMLA had little impact. Large companies' policies before 1993 were more generous than, or at least in compliance with, the requirements of the FMLA, and small companies were not covered by the act. Many workers, and most female workers, are unable to take advantage of the unpaid leave required by the FMLA, because they need the income. Policymakers should work to expand the benefits of the FMLA, for instance, to include wage replacement and a longer leave period. Researchers serve as a source of information for policymakers (Lee, DeLeon, Wedding, & Nordal, 1994) and need to provide data that illuminate gaps in current laws.

CONCLUSIONS

The growing "oldest old" population (those aged 85 and over) and the increase in the number of women in the workforce have resulted in an increase in the number of persons who must balance both work and family responsibilities. These persons are likely to be women. Women are likely to serve as caregivers and tend to family responsibilities whether they work or not. There are practical as well as academic reasons for understanding the consequences of balancing work and family responsibilities. Policymakers and corporate decisionmakers need to plan and develop policies for a workforce that will increase in the numbers of caregiving employees. The more academic reason is to understand the psychological advantages and disadvantages of balancing multiple roles.

The emotional impact of providing elder care is not as thoroughly researched as that resulting from balancing childcare and work, and the latter may not be generalizable to caregivers of an older person. Elder care has not yet received the attention and social support that childcare has (Sizemore & Jones, 1990; Wagner & Hunt, 1994), and social support may be critical in ameliorating stress (Scharlach et al., 1991). Caregivers of the elderly may experience crises that caregivers of children do not (Braithwaite, 1992), such as awareness of degeneration, unpredictability, time constraints, the caregiver-receiver relationship (Tully & Sehm, 1994), and lack of choice.

There is evidence that caregivers for the elderly differ from noncaregivers with respect to physical health conditions (Scharlach, Runkle, Midanik, & Soghikian, 1994) and symptoms (Lee, 1997). Other evidence indicates that as the level of involvement with elder care responsibilities increases, psychological strain increases (Barling et al., 1994). The financial costs of providing care for an elderly dependent can be great. A study conducted by the MetLife Mature Market Institute (1999) estimated that caregivers of the elderly may suffer an average loss in total wealth of $659,139 over the lifetime. Furthermore, it appears gender differences may exist in the degree of emotional burden experienced. Women caregivers experience greater emotional burden than do their male counterparts (Kramer & Kipnis, 1995).

Although there is support for both the beneficial (Thoits, 1983) and harmful consequences of occupying multiple roles (Cooke & Rousseau, 1984), more evidence of harmful effects is accumulating. Kossek and Ozeki (1998) found a consistent negative relationship between work-family conflict and job-life satisfaction.

Helping workers to balance work and family will benefit employers. For workers whose partners also work, greater job flexibility is related to greater job satisfaction and reduced work interference with family life. Job flexibility also seems to affect workers' mental health (Marshall & Barnett, 1994). Employers may need to develop interventions that may help caregivers who are highly involved with caregiving responsibilities (Levine, 1993). Although female caregivers may be psychologically affected more by their caregiving responsibilities than male caregivers, employers cannot legally offer different accommodations based on gender. Employers may, however, develop work-family policies based on employees' level of involvement. Caregivers, as a group, may not need treatment or accommodations different from employees who do not have caregiving responsibilities.

Despite the fact that the time needed for elder care will increase, recent actions of the federal government fail to include cargivers of the elderly into their work-family policies. President Clinton sought to expand the scope of the Family and Medical Leave Act by encouraging states to use unemployment insurance funds to pay for leave after the birth or adoption of a child (Clinton lets states, 2000). Such actions are laudable, but they ignore the needs of employees who must take leave to provide care for an older parent. The pro-business orientation of the Bush administration leaves little hope of its expanding family leave benefits.

All stakeholders must work together to help employees balance work and family responsibilities. Employees must take an active role in learning about and utilizing available services and benefits. They must also acknowledge their limitations. Employers and their organizations must promote a corporate culture that accepts and embraces diversity. Academicians and other subject matter experts must research the issues and provide information to policymakers, who must craft and enact relevant legislation.

REFERENCES

Anastas, J. W., Gibeau, J., & Larson, P. J. (1990). Working families and eldercare: A national perspective in an aging America. *Social Work, 35,* 405–411.

Barling, J., MacEwen, K. E., Kelloway, E. K., & Higginbottom, S. F. (1994). Predictors and outcomes of elder-care-based interrole conflict. *Psychology and Aging, 9*(3), 391–397.

Barnett, R. C. (1999). A new work-life model for the twenty-first century. *The Annals of the American Academy of Polictical and Social Science, 562,* 143–158.

Baruch, G. K., Biener, L., & Barnett, R. C. (1987). Women and gender in research on work and family stress. *American Psychologist, 42,* 130–136.

Baruch, G. K., & Barnett, R. C. (1986). Consequences of fathers' participation in family work: Parents' role strain and well-being. *Journal of Personality and Social Psychology, 51*(5), 983–992.

Braithwaite, V. (1992). Caregiving burden: Making the concept scientifically useful and relevant. *Research on Aging, 14,* 3–27.

Burke, R. J., & Bradshaw, P. (1981). Occupational and life stress and the family. *Small Group Behavior, 12*(3), 329–375.

Burke, R. J., & McKeen, C. A. (1994). Work, career, and life experiences associated with different career patterns among managerial and professional women. In G. P. Keita & J. J. Hurrell Jr. (Eds.), *Job stress in a changing workforce: Investigating gender, diversity, and family issues* (pp. 301–310). Washington, DC: American Psychological Association.

Chapman, N. J., Ingersoll-Dayton, B., & Neal, M. (1994). Balancing the multiple roles of work and caregiving for children, adults, and elders. In G. P. Keita & J. J. Hurrell

(Eds.), *Job stress in a changing workforce* (pp. 283–300). Washington, DC: American Psychological Association.

Clinton lets states use jobless fund on sick leave. (2000, June 11). *Charlotte Observer,* p. 11A.

Cooke, R. A., & Rousseau, D. M. (1984). Stress and strain from family roles and work-role expectations. *Journal of Applied Psychology, 69,* 252–260.

Cooper, C. L., & Lewis, S. (1998). *Balancing your career, family and life.* London: Kogan Page.

Earhart, K. M., Middlemist, R. D., & Hopkins, W. E. (1993). Eldercare: An emerging employee assistance issue. *Employee Assistance Quarterly, 8,* 1–10.

Elison, S. K. (1997). Policy innovation in a cold climate: The Family and Medical Leave Act of 1993. *Journal of Family Issues, 18,* 30–54.

Ettner, S. L. (1995). The opportunity costs of elder care. *The Journal of Human Resources, 31,* 189–205.

Goldin, C. (1997). Career and family: College women look to the past. In F. D. Blau & R. G. Ehrenberg (Eds.), *Gender and family issues in the workplace* (pp. 20–60). New York: Russell Sage Foundation.

Gottlieb, B. H., Kelloway, E. K., & Fraboni, M. (1994). Aspects of eldercare that place employees at risk. *The Gerontologist, 34*(6), 815–821.

Greenhaus, J. H., & Beutell, N. J. (1985). Sources of conflict between work and family roles. *Academy of Management Review, 10*(1), 76–88.

Greenhaus, J. H., & Parasuraman, S. (1986). A work-nonwork interactive perspective of stress and its consequences. *Journal of Organizational Behavior Management, 8,* 37–60.

Han, Shin-Kap, & Moen, P. (1999). Work and family over time: A life course approach. *The Annals of the American Academy of Polictical and Social Science, 562,* 98–110.

Hill, E. J., Miller, B. C., Weiner, S. P., & Colihan, J. (1998). Influences of the virtual office on aspects of work and work/life balance. *Personnel Psychology, 51,* 667–683.

Howard, A. (1995). Human resources and their skills. In A. Howard (Ed.), *The changing nature of work* (pp. 211–222). San Francisco: Jossey-Bass.

Jones, A. P., & Butler, M. C. (1980). A role transition approach to the stresses of organizationally induced family role disruption. *Journal of Marriage and the Family, 42,* 367–376.

Kossek, E. E., & Ozeki, C. (1998). Work-family conflict, policies, and the job-life satisfaction relationship: A review and directions for organizational behavior-human resources research. *Journal of Applied Psychology, 83,* 139–149.

Kramer, B. J., & Kipnis, S. (1995). Eldercare and work-role conflict: Toward an understanding of gender differences in caregiver burden. *The Gerontologist, 35,* 340–348.

Lee, J. A. (1997). Balancing elder care responsibilities and work: Two empirical studies. *Journal of Occupational Health Psychology, 2,* 220–228.

Lee, J. A. (1999). Defining elder care. *Psychological Reports, 84,* 625–626.

Lee, J. A., DeLeon, P., Wedding, D., & Nordal, K. (1994). Psychologists' role in influencing congress: The process and the players. *Professional Psychology: Research and Practice, 25,* 9–15.

Lee, J. A., Walker, M., & Shoup, R. (in press). Balancing elder care responsibilities and work: The impact on emotional health. *Journal of Business and Psychology, 16.*

Leslie, L. A., Anderson, E. A., & Branson, M. P. (1991). Responsibility for children: The role of gender and employment. *Journal of Family Issues, 12,* 197–210.

Levine, P. B. (1993). Examining labor force projections for the twenty-first century. In O. S. Mitchell (Ed.), *As the workforce ages* (pp. 38–56). Ithaca, NY: ILR Press.

Lewin, T. (1994, October 12). Men whose wives work earn less, studies show. *New York Times,* pp. A1, A21.

Marks, M. R. (1997). Party politics and family policy: The case of the Family and Medical Leave Act. *Journal of Family Issues, 18,* 55–70.

Marshall, N. L., & Barnett, R. C. (1994). Family-friendly workplaces, work-family interface, and worker health. In G. P. Keita and J. J. Hurrell Jr. (Eds.), *Job stress in a changing workforce* (pp. 253–264). Washington, DC: American Psychological Association.

MetLife Mature Market Institute. (1999). *The MetLife juggling act study: Balancing caregiving with work and the costs involved.* New York: Metropolitan Life Insurance Company.

Neal, M. B., Chapman, N. J., Ingersoll-Dayton, B., & Emlen, A. C. (1993). *Balancing work and caregiving for children, adults, and elders.* Newbury Park, CA: Sage.

Overman, S. (1998, November). Catalyst finds fathers taking steps to balance work, family needs. *HR-News,* p. 13.

Palmer, H. T., & Lee, J. A. (1990). Female workers' acceptance in traditionally male-dominated blue-collar jobs. *Sex Roles, 22,* 607–626.

Parker, R. A., & Aldwin, C. M. (1994). Desiring careers but loving families: Period, cohort, and gender effects in career and family orientations. In G. P. Keita & J. J. Hurrell Jr. (Eds.), *Job stress in a changing workforce* (pp. 23–38). Washington, DC: American Psychological Association.

Phillips, S. D., & Imhoff, A. R. (1997). Women and career development: A decade of research. *Annual Review of Psychology, 48,* 31–51.

Pitt-Catsouphes, M., & Googins, B. K. (1999). The evolving world of work and family: New stakeholders, new voices. *The Annals of the American Academy of Political and Social Science, 562,* 8–15.

Rayham, P. M., & Bookman, A. (1999). Creating a research and public policy agenda for work, family, and community. *The Annals of the American Academy of Polictical and Social Science, 562,* 191–211.

Robinson, J., & Godbey, G. (1997) *Time for Life: The surprising ways Americans use their time.* University Park, PA: Pennsylvania State University Press.

Roskies, E., & Carrier, S. (1994). Marriage and children for professional women: Asset or liability? In G. P. Keita & J. J. Hurrell Jr. (Eds.), *Job stress in a changing workforce: Investigating gender, diversity, and family issues* (pp. 269–282). Washington, DC: American Psychological Association.

Scharlach, A. E., Lowe, B. F., & Schneider, E. L., (1991). *Elder care and the work force.* Lexington, MA: Lexington Books.

Scharlach, A. E., Runkle, M. C., Midanik, L. T., & Soghikian, K. (1994). Health conditions and service utilization of adults with elder care responsibilities. *Journal of Aging and Health, 6,* 336–352.

Scharlach, A. E., Sobel, E. L., & Roberts, R. E. L. (1991). Employment and caregiver strain: An integrative model. *The Gerontologist, 31,* 778–787.

Sieber, S. D. (1974). Toward a theory of role accumulation. *American Sociological Review,* *39,* 567–578.

Sizemore, M. T., & Jones, A. B. (1990). Eldercare and the workplace: Short-term training preferences of employees. *Educational Gerontology, 16,* 97–104.

Soldo, B. J., & Hill, M. S. (1995). Family structure and transfer measures in the Health and Retirement Study: Background and overview. *The Journal of Human Resources, 30*(Supplement), S108–S137.

Stoller, E. P. (1983). Parental caregiving by adult children. *Journal of Marriage and the Family, 45,* 851–858.

Thoits, P. A. (1983). Multiple identities and psychological well-being: A reformulation and test of the social isolation hypothesis. *American Sociological Review, 48,* 174–187.

Tully, C. T., & Sehm, S. D. (1994). Eldercare: The social service system's missing link? *Journal of Gerontological Social Work, 2,* 117–132.

U.S. Bureau of the Census. (1994, Fall, Update). *Who's minding our preschoolers?* (PPL-81). Washington, DC: Author.

U.S. Department of Labor. (1999). *Report on the American Workforce 1999.* Washington, DC: Author.

Visiting Nurse Associations of America. (1998). *Caregivers' handbook.* New York: DK.

Wagner, D. L., & Hunt, G. G. (1994). The use of workplace elder care programs by employed caregivers. *Research on Aging, 16,* 69–84.

Waldfogel, J. (1997). Working mothers then and now: A cross-cohort analysis of the effects of maternity leave on women's pay. In F. D. Blau & R. G. Ehrenberg (Eds.), *Gender and family issues in the workplace* (pp. 92–126). New York: Russell Sage Foundation.

Zedeck, S., & Mosier, K. L. (1990). Work in the family and employing organization. *American Psychologist, 45,* 240–251.

14

GENDER AND CULTURAL
DIVERSITY AND THE WORKPLACE

Ella L. J. Edmondon Bell and Stella M. Nkomo

The now infamous Workforce 2000 (Johnston & Packer, 1987) forecast was viewed as the wake-up call for organizations to attend to the growing gender and cultural diversity of the workforce. It predicted that new entrants into the labor force in the late twentieth century would consist primarily of White women and racial and ethnic minorities. This trend is expected to continue in the twenty-first century. Organizations will be more demographically diverse than in previous decades. This significant workplace change presents both challenges and opportunities to individuals and to the organizations of which they are a part (Triandis, Kurowski, & Gelfand 1994). In this chapter, we review the extant literature to address three questions: (1) What are the effects of gender and cultural diversity in organizations? We examine this question at the individual, group, and organizational levels. (2) How does managing diversity differ from other perspectives on race and gender in the workplace? (3) What practices are organizations using to address this growing workplace diversity? Concomitantly, how successful are these practices in addressing diversity?

GENDER AND RACIAL INEQUALITY IN THE WORKPLACE

Despite the nascent movement to focus on "diversity" in the workplace, it is important to recognize that scholars have been studying the differential status of White women and racial minorities[1] in the workplace for a significant period of time. Prior to 1960, extensive job segregation by race and gender existed in the United States. The level of segregation began to change after the passage of the Civil Rights Act of 1964. However, White women and racial and ethnic minorities still do not enjoy the same status as White men. These groups typically occupy lower status jobs, receive less pay, and experience slower upward mobility

(Bell & Nkomo, 1994; Cox & Nkomo, 1991; Reskin & Padvic, 1994; Sokoloff, 1992; Stroh, Brett, & Reilly, 1992).

The research literature offers two dominant explanations for gender and racial inequality in the workplace. The supply-side human capital theory argues that workers receive returns in the labor market from investments in education, experience, and other human capital attributes (Becker, 1964, 1975). Employers see human capital investments as an indicator of greater productivity and career commitment and tend to reward individuals with greater levels of both (Baldi & McBrier, 1997).

Human capital models suggest the reason women and racial minorities experience inequality is their lower investments in education and work experience. In other words, there is an assumption that a single system of workplace attainment operates regardless of race and gender so that if White women and racial minorities had the same amount of education, experience, and effort as White men, they would enjoy equality in the workplace (Tomaskovic-Devey, 1993).

Empirical studies have found mixed results for human capital theory. In studies of wage differentials, human capital models explain about half the variance, but education itself explains surprisingly little (for instance, see Reskin & Padavic, 1994). Stroh, Brett, and Reilly (1992) examined the career progression of male and female managers employed in 20 Fortune 500 corporations. They found the women lagged behind the men with respect to salary progression and frequency of job transfers. Although the women had done "all the right stuff"—acquiring similar education as the men, maintaining similar levels of family power, working in similar industries, staying in the workforce, and putting their names in for transfer—it was still not enough. Friedman and Krackhardt (1997) also found, in total, human capital models downplay the significance of race and gender dynamics in explaining inequality in the workplace. A number of scholars critique human capital theory for its emphasis on voluntaristic individual behavior and motivations to the exclusion of specific attention to the racialized and genderized nature of work, jobs, and organizations (Acker, 1990; Baldi & McBrier, 1997; Cockburn, 1991; Tomaskovic-Devey, 1993).

Demand-side explanations represent the second dominant social science approach to workplace equality. Demand-side explanations focus on both segmented labor markets and the economic segmentation of firms. Segmented labor market theorists (for instance, Edwards, 1979; Baron & Biebly, 1984, 1986) argue inequality is caused by job segregation in both external and internal labor markets. For example, Black workers tend to be concentrated in a peripheral labor market comprising jobs that offer few of the advantages associated with more attractive jobs in mainstream, bureaucratized companies (Bridges & Villemez, 1994).

Approaches centered on the economic segmentation of firms place emphasis on the resources of the organization in its regional and industrial environment. Firms sharing the same characteristics in terms of size, age, market competition, government regulation, age, and bureaucratic procedures will develop similar reward systems (Bridges & Villemez, 1994). However, to the extent White women and racial minorities are overrepresented in firms operating in environments that possess few of the advantages of bureaucratized procedures, they will have fewer opportunities for job mobility and higher pay (Baldi & McBrier, 1997). Together, labor market segmentation and economic segmentation suggest that the quality of jobs is determined by the power of the jobs within and between organizations. Similar to human capital theory, these demand-side theories assume that if workers of different races and genders were in similar jobs in similar firms operating in similar environments, there would be little difference in workplace outcomes.

Critics of demand-side explanations of workplace inequality fault their exclusion of the specific operation of racism and sexism. Tomaskovic-Devey (1993) argues that demand-side explanations are unable to account for gender and race inequalities because they treat race and gender as variables, not as organizational processes in their own right. Baldi and McBrier (1997) argue that the persistent findings of unequal Black-White outcomes in the workplace may be better explained by race-specific models of workplace attainment in which the determinants of advancement differ for Blacks and Whites.

Indeed, despite the growing emphasis on valuing diversity, White women and racial minorities continue to face "glass ceilings" and discrimination in the workplace (Catalyst, 1996; Glass Ceiling Commission, 1995). They can encounter culturally offensive practices and a hostile work environment if entrenched majority group members feel threatened by greater numbers of women and minorities. Greater gender and racial diversity also creates both overt and subtle psychological and intergroup dynamics. The next section of this review focuses on describing these specific dynamics and their consequences for White women and racial minorities. We discuss the effects for both groups, recognizing there are commonalties and differences in the degree and nature of the barriers.

RACE AND GENDER BARRIERS: THE RESEARCH EVIDENCE

In this section, we describe the barriers to workplace equality for White women and racial and ethnic minorities found in the social science literature. For review purposes, the barriers we identify are grouped into three levels: individual, group, and organizational. These categories allow us to aggregate findings from the psychological, sociological, and organizational literature. The levels are distinguished in order to guide the analysis of the barriers. However, we must add, they are not mutually exclusive and indeed they are highly interrelated. Each barrier can be simultaneously operative.

Individual Level Barriers

The first category of barriers occurs at the individual level. These barriers focus on psychological attitudes, values, and interpersonal styles. The research literature reveals three major individual level barriers: (1) racism, sexism, and prejudice; (2) managing duality and bicultural stress; and (3) tokenism and presumed incompetence. Racism, sexism, and prejudice are the most insidious and tenacious of the barriers and carries strong implications for both the group and organizational level. Although research indicates that the majority of racism and prejudice is subtle, overt acts of racial harassment also occur (for instance, see Feagin & Sikes, 1995; Lester & MacKinnon, 1993).

Racism, Sexism, and Prejudice

Gaertner (1976) and Gaertner and Dovidio (1986) developed a theory of aversive racism to represent a modern, subtle form of bias. The aversive racism perspective that was developed originally to account for Whites' prejudice toward Blacks, has been extended also to other types of social bias directed toward Jews (Gaertner, 1973), women (Dovidio & Gaertner, 1983), and Hispanics (Dovidio, Gaertner, Antastasio, & Sanitioso, 1992). The aversive racism perspective assumes that cognitive and motivational biases and socialization into the historically racist culture of the United States with its contemporary legacy lead most White Americans to develop negative feelings and beliefs about relative superiority to Blacks and other minorities (Gaertner & Dovidio, 1986). Thus, an aversive racist can discriminate against minority group members without challenging his or her egalitarian self-image. Pettigrew and Martin (1987) describe the effects of modern, subtle racism on both Blacks and Whites in the workplace:

Precisely because of their subtlety and indirectness, these modern forms of prejudice and avoidance are hard to eradicate. Often the Black is the only person in a position to draw the conclusion that prejudice is operating in the work situation. Whites have usually observed only a subset of the incidents, any one of which can be explained away by a nonracial account. Consequently, many Whites remain unconvinced of the reality of subtle prejudice and discrimination, and come to think of their Black coworkers as "terribly touchy" and "overly sensitive" to the issue. For such reasons, the modern forms of prejudice remain invisible even to its perpetrators. (p. 50)

Rowe (1990) offers a similar analysis. Rowe suggests that microinequities are small events—often ephemeral, hard to prove, and often unintentional—which are indeed the principal scaffolding for segregation in the workplace. Although these mechanisms of prejudice are usually small in nature, they are not trivial in their effect. Rowe argues they are especially powerful taken together—one prejudiced or racist slight may be insignificant but many such slights cause serious damage. Essed (1991) offers the concept of "everyday racism" to capture subtle workplace racism and prejudice. Everyday racism represents the everyday practices both cognitive and behavioral that activate underlying power relations. She argues that African Americans experience modern racism in their everyday, ongoing, routine encounters with Whites both at work and outside the workplace. Bell and Nkomo (1998) found in their study of Black and White women managers, that the Black women identified "little episodes of racism" as a major barrier.

In the case of women, a subtle form of sexism is what Faye Crosby (1989) calls the paradox of gender—the persistent belief that men and women differ in important qualities in spite of countless studies that have failed to document their existence. Studies of gender in the workplace indicate a subtle bias about whether or not women possess the abilities to be leaders. Ever since the appearance of Schein's (1973) study in which she asked business school students to describe the characteristics and qualities of men, women, and managers, there has been considerable attention to the question of whether men and women exhibit the same behaviors in the workplace. Schein (1973) found the characteristics of managers showed greater similarity to the stereotypes of men than to the stereotypes of women. Subsequent research replicates these results (Heilman, Block, Martell, & Simon, 1989). Eagly, Makhijani, and Klonsky (1992) found that women were more likely to be devalued when perceived as acting in a "masculine" (that is, directive) style. Women were also more likely to receive unfavorable evaluations as a leader in male-dominated settings. This phenomenon has been refereed to as what Nieva and Gutek (1980) identify as sex role congruence.

Research supports Rowe's (1990) assertion that subtle racism and sexism end up having real effects on workplace equality for racial minorities and women. One consequence is marginalization. Marginalization occurs when minorities and women are kept from joining the mainstream of organizational life. They maintain an outsider status, so they never achieve full equality or the same power and prestige as their White male counterparts. The research of Collins (1997) offers an example of how marginalization operates for African Americans in the workplace. She interviewed Black executives who entered corporate America in the 1960s and 1970s. Most of these executives were placed in racialized jobs (for example, affirmative action officer, equal employment opportunity director). However, these racialized jobs underdeveloped Blacks' job skills, and thus, the Black employees themselves. Over time, these Black executives were not able to compete with employees in other mainstream departments such as marketing, sales, finance, or accounting.

Another form of marginalization is "seeing through" an African American or paying no attention to a Native American employee, making them feel invisible. This can also lead to their not receiving promotions or their work being devalued. There is evidence to suggest that Blacks are evaluated more harshly than White men in performance evaluations (Kraiger & Ford, 1985); or that Blacks are subjected to a different set of performance criteria (Cox & Nkomo, 1986). Baldi and McBrier (1997) found that Blacks are half as likely to be promoted as Whites even when education, work experience, firm characteristics, and organizational environment were controlled. Greenhaus, Parasuraman, & Wormley (1990) found that African American managers reported having less job discretion and reported feeling less accepted than did White managers. Schmitt's (1993) study of 2,910 candidates for administrative positions indicated that Black candidates were rated lower than Whites on a majority of the assessment center dimensions.

Another manifestation of subtle racism and sexism is stereotyping. Stereotyping is defined as "a cognitive structure that contains the perceiver's knowledge, beliefs, expectancies about some human group" (Hamilton & Trolier, 1986, p. 133). There is a good deal of research documenting the types of negative stereotypes racial and ethnic minorities experience in the workplace. Although we discuss gender and racial stereotyping together, it is important to understand that stereotyping processes operate differently for race compared to gender. Additionally, racial minorities experience differential stereotyping. For example, in a study in which managers evaluated a Hispanic manager videotaped in four different situations, Ferdman (1989) found that the raters evaluated the Hispanic manager significantly less favorably when he displayed a "Hispanic, nonnormative managerial style" than when he exhibited a "Anglo, normative style." Asian Americans are negatively stereotyped as having the capabilities for technical positions but not those required for people-oriented leadership positions (Cabezas, Tam, Lowe, Wong & Turner, 1989). Consequently, they are not considered for management and leadership roles in organizations. Additionally, they face the assumption of being the "model minority" (Tang, 1997).

In the case of women, sexism and gender role stereotyping are significant individual level barriers (Nieva & Gutek, 1980; Gutek, 1985). Laboratory studies portraying men and women with equivalent characteristics result in different appraisals of performance by both male and female raters (Ragins & Sundstrom, 1989). Women often confront patriarchal ideologies that link womanhood with unpaid work, marriage, and family justifying women being placed in lower status jobs in organizations (Cockburn, 1991). This is the place to point out the importance of acknowledging the effects of the intersection of race with gender. Gender and race interact to create different stereotypes and also different experiences in the workplace for women of color (Bell, Denton, & Nkomo, 1993; Higginbotham & Romero, 1997; Rivera-Ramos, 1992). Contrary to the patriarchal image of White, middle-class women as weak, passive, and dependent, stereotypes of African American women see them as hardworking, strong, dominant, and sexually promiscuous (Essed, 1991). DiTomaso (1989) found differences in how Black women versus White or Hispanic women experienced discrimination, and Yoder and Aniakudo (1997) documented the unique patterns of subordination lived by African American women firefighters.

Subtle racism and microinequities may also have a self-fulfilling prophecy effect (Illgen & Youtz, 1986). That is, the expectation of poor performance, or the lack of expectation of good performance, may do damage because the supervisor treats the minority employee in line with his or her expectations. For example, the supervisor may not give the employee clear instructions or adequate resources. When the employee performs poorly, the supervisor believes he or she was correct in their initial expectations. Or worse yet a supervisor can change the criteria for performance. The Asian American employee who is expected to be docile may later not get promoted because he or she is not assertive enough (Rowe, 1990).

Research suggests that White women and racial minorities engage in behavioral strategies to mitigate these perceptual biases. They become superachievers in order to overcome assumptions of incompetence and to offset stereotypic views and attributions of their abilities. A research study of 461 women executives (primarily White women) by Catalyst (1996) found that women attributed their success to consistently exceeding performance expectations. Studies of African American managers also report similar results (Bell & Nkomo, 1998).

Managing Duality and Bicultural Stress

The next major barrier at the individual level is managing cultural duality (Ferdman & Cortes, 1992; Triandis, 1972) and bicultural stress (Bell, 1990). Here the key issue for a racial and ethnic minority is fitting into a White-dominated organizational culture. For most minorities, their work lives may be embedded in White, male-dominated organizations where the norms, culture, and values are based on Anglo-European tradition and the Protestant work ethic of Western society. Other dimensions of their lives such as family life, personal relationships, leisure activities, and spirituality are usually rooted in their ethnic or racial community.

There is sufficient evidence that racial and ethnic minorities, although having knowledge of dominant culture, still hold on to the norms of their own ethnic group (Triandis, Marin, Lisansky, & Betancourt (1984). Using a laboratory study designed to examine ethnically homogenous and diverse task groups, Cox, Lobel and McLeod (1991) found that Asian, Hispanic, and African Americans had a more collectivist, cooperative orientation to completing the task than did European Americans. Triandis et al. (1984) found that Hispanics are more likely than non-Hispanics to expect high frequencies of positive social behaviors and low frequencies of negative social behaviors. These interpersonal communications are characterized by what Triandis et al. (1984) call the cultural script of *simpatico*— an ability to share others' feelings.

Because they hold onto the norms of their cultures, when they enter White-dominated organizations, racial and ethnic minorities have to manage two cultural contexts: one European American and the other of their ethnic background. Bicultural stress is a psychological barrier that manifests when ethnic minorities feel compelled to suppress and diminish one part of their identity (personal values, political ideology, interpersonal style, self-presentation) in order to exist or advance in one or both of the cultural contexts in which they work and live (Bell, 1990; LaFromboise, Coleman, & Gerton, 1993). In the workplace, racial and ethnic minorities have traditionally been expected to assimilate into the dominant culture suppressing their own cultural identity. Bell (1990) in a study of African American professional women found they felt worn out from attempting to juggle the multiple and conflicting roles in two distinct cultural contexts. Although White women do not experience bicultural stress, all women in the workplace struggle with the duality of managing work and family (Hochschild, 1989). Hochschild found that working women still carry a disproportionate share of the responsibility for housework and childcare in their families compared to men.

Tokenism

The last individual level barrier is tokenism. According to Kanter (1977) tokenism is a phenomenon that occurs when a minority or woman is one of a kind or one of a few in an organization. Skewed numerical representation leads to high visibility and sets into place a variety of negative perceptions of persons resulting in their being viewed as tokens. Most often tokens are assumed to have been employed only because of affirmative action and are not accepted as competent or qualified (Heilman, Block & Lucas, 1992). Tokens are also stereotyped and viewed as the representative of their entire group rather than as individuals (Kanter, 1977; Yoder, 1991). Their behavior and job performance, whether good or bad, is magnified, distorted, and overly scrutinized. When the token employee does not perform well, the assumption is that his or her entire group is incompetent.

Tokens are also subjected to the slippery slope of double standards. To overcome their tokenism, women and minorities feel pressure to outperform in order to influence the perceptions of White males (Biernat & Kobrynowicz, 1997). Yet, high performance may not lead to comparable rewards and the same level of recognition. In a study of corporate managers in a large corporation, Greenhaus and Parasuraman (1993) found that managers judging African American subordinates were more likely to attribute good performance to external and unstable factors (for instance, luck) rather than to the subordinate's ability. Pettigrew, Jemmott, and Johnson (1984) refer to this phenomenon as the ultimate attribution error.

Self-Limiting Behaviors

The individual level barriers White women and racial minorities encounter in the workplace can lead to self-limiting behaviors (Ilgen & Youtz, 1986). According to Illgen and Youtz (1986), self-limiting behaviors are behaviors that have the unintended consequence of restricting and inhibiting career advancement and success. Minorities can gradually develop low self-esteem resulting from the constant negative feedback on performance reviews and other work-related evaluations. Eventually, they may come to believe their work performance is inferior in comparison to their White coworkers (Ilgen & Youtz, 1986). Eden (1992) argues that this can lead to lower effort and hence lower performance in a scenario similar to the "Galatea" effect of the self-fulfilling prophecy construct. Inequity in exchanges may also cause minority employees to exert less effort. Ragins and Sundstrom (1989) examined the longitudinal development of gender differences in power. Women, more than men, typified a "psychological cycle of powerlessness," blaming themselves, losing self-confidence, and limiting their ambitions. However, Ragins and Sundstrom (1989) emphasize that these psychological symptoms are the results of powerlessness, not causes.

GROUP LEVEL BARRIERS

At the group level, researchers have identified two significant barriers to the advancement of minority and women employees: (1) cultural differences and ethnocentrism, and (2) minority group density.

Cultural Differences and Ethnocentrism

Numerous scholars support the idea that because African Americans, Chinese Americans, Mexican Americans, Native Americans and other racial minority groups represent distinct cultural groups, research on the workplace must incorporate cultural differences (Cox, Lobel, & McLeod, 1991; Ferdman & Cortes, 1992). Much of the work examining the effects of cultural differences between minority and majority group employees have focused on African Americans and much less on other racial minorities. Intergroup cultural differences have been shown to have strong effects on the behaviors, attitudes, and interactions between African Americans and Whites in the workplace (Alderfer, Alderfer, Bell, & Jones, 1992; Alderfer, Tucker, Alderfer, & Tucker, 1988; Cox, 1993; Cox, Lobel, & McLeod, 1991; Jackson, Stone, & Alvarez, 1993). For example, there is substantial support of significant differences among racial groups in managing interpersonal conflict, cooperative versus competitive behavior, communication styles, and perceptions of organizational experiences (Alderfer, Alderfer, Tucker & Tucker, 1980; Davidson, 1993; Kochman, 1981. Xin's empirical study (1997) shows that Asian American managers use different impression management tactics than do Anglo managers. Impression management tactics refers to the ways that individuals attempt to control the impressions others have of them. Xin's results suggest important differences in how racial groups attempt to modify the image that relevant audiences have of them.

Davidson (1993) found that African American men reported being more aggressive in the ways they coped with conflict, in comparison to White men, White women, and Black women. He argued that the conflict style of African American managers might clash with the dispassionate behavior expected in a corporate environment. If they are too aggressive in managing conflicts with supervisors, they can be perceived as insubordinate and run the risk of being fired. In fact, statistics indicate that in a laboratory study, Cox (1993) and his colleagues found that groups composed of non-Whites including African Americans held more collectivist-cooperative orientation to a work task than did groups composed entirely of Whites. The Whites in the sample displayed more competitive behavior. Thus, an African American manager oriented toward cooperative behavior in a White-dominated workgroup may be perceived as not possessing what it takes to compete. The display of more cooperative behavior can be attributed to low ability and incompetence (Cox, 1993). Communication style differences between African Americans and Whites have also been reported with Black styles being characterized as more assertive, bold, and emotional compared to Whites (Kochman, 1981). Cox (1993) notes that African American culture, especially among men, is high on verbal bravado and attention-seeking behaviors. Such behavior can be perceived as threatening, demanding, or insubordinate.

Alderfer, Alderfer, Tucker, and Tucker (1980) and Alderfer, Alderfer, Bell and Jones (1992) demonstrated that group membership of Blacks and Whites influence how they perceive their organizational experiences. In an ongoing effort to change race relations in one large corporation, Alderfer and his colleagues examined general perceptions of race relations, racial dynamics, perceptions of the influence of race on hiring, advancement, firing, and the effects of training on race relations. Overall, the research showed the existence of parallel and nonparallel perceptions between the two groups. Whites and African Americans, both males and females, reported that members of the other group socialized more with each other than across groups. And, African American men and women evaluated overall company race relations more negatively than did Whites.

Although cultural differences by themselves have implications for the experience of minority employees in organizations, the major phenomenon making the differences important is ethnocentrism. Ethnocentrism, a form of intergroup bias, is defined as the tendency to view one's own group (ingroup) as the center of the universe, for interpreting other social groups (outgroups). Other groups are judged less positively from the perspective of one's own group in terms of beliefs, behaviors, and values (Tajfel & Turner, 1979). A more common element is the "comfort zone" effect. This effect occurs when one finds greater psychological comfort being with members of one's own racial/ethnic or gender group. Related to comfort zone effect is the concept of homophily (Ibarra, 1995). Homophily is defined as the degree to which pairs of individuals who interact are similar in identity or organizational group affiliations. To the extent that White men dominant organizations and hold the most powerful positions, they enjoy ingroup status relative to women and minorities. Women and minority employees tend to find membership in lower ranking hierarchical groups in organizations. They are relegated to outgroup status. Ingroup status affords grater opportunities and greater access to critical resources. Attaining ingroup status is a major barrier to upward mobility for women and minority employees.

The outgroup status of minority employees results in exclusion from both formal and informal organization groups. There are few studies of the experience of minority and women employees in organizations that do not cite exclusion from the informal networks as one of the key obstacles to equality. The most influential work in this area has been done by Ibarra (1995). In a study of informal networks in a Fortune 500 company, Ibarra found that minority managers had fewer intimate informal relationships compared to White managers.

Minority Group Density

Minority group density refers to the relative percentage of minorities in a workgroup. A number of studies have examined how the varying proportions of minority versus majority group members affect group interactions and attitudes (Blalock, 1967; Hoffman, 1985; Kanter, 1977; Tsui, Egan, & OReilly, 1993). Hoffman (1985) studied the influence of varying relative proportions of Black supervisors on the frequency of different types of group and organizational level communication. Hoffman found decreased interpersonal communication frequency among the supervisory cadre as the minority composition of the workgroup increased.

The effects for gender seem to differ, although there are conflicting results. Sackett, Dubois and Noe (1991) studied over 100 workgroups of varying composition and found that although performance ratings for women increased as their proportional representation increased above 50 percent, this did not occur for racial minorities. Similarly, Riordan, Shore, and McFarlane (1997) studied 98 workgroups in a life insurance company and reported that one's similarity to the race and ethnicity of one's workgroup affected attitudes toward the group. Effects were not found for gender. On the other hand, Ely (1995) found that gender roles were more typical in firms with few women in positions of power compared to firms with balanced representation.

ORGANIZATIONAL LEVEL BARRIERS

At the organizational level, the major barriers include (1) access to mentors and (2) functional segregation into staff-type jobs.

Access to Mentors

Research has long documented the importance of mentoring in actual career advancement (Dreher & Cox, 1996). Mentor-protege relationships provide budding managers with information instrumental to career advancement and also provide psychosocial support (Thomas, 1990). A major element of the classic mentor-protege relationship is a high level of rapport and interpersonal chemistry. In sum, the research literature strongly indicates that lack of access to mentoring creates disadvantages for minorities and women in terms of skill development, promotion opportunities, and career satisfaction. Research indicates that mentors and sponsors are more likely to choose proteges who are similar to them in terms of race and gender (Ensher & Murphy, 1997). To the extent that mentors tend to avoid risk in selecting proteges, stereotypes of White women and racial/ethnic minorities as incompetent pose a substantial barrier to their selection as proteges.

Studies of African American managers' experiences with mentoring and sponsorship do suggest it is more difficult for them to get mentors and to build developmental relationships necessary to long-term careers (Cianni & Romberger, 1995; Cox & Nkomo, 1991; Dreher & Cox, 1996; Thomas, 1990). There is very little research on access to mentoring for other racial minorities. Cianni and Romberger (1995) did find that Asian managers reported the lowest self-efficacy to initiate mentoring relationships compared to Black and White managers in their sample. Dreher and Cox (1996) examined the relationship between mentoring experiences and compensation outcomes for a diverse group of MBA graduates. African American and Hispanic MBAs were less likely than their White counterparts to establish mentoring relationships with White men. Those who were successful in establishing mentoring relationships with White men had higher average annual compensation.

Even when African Americans gain access to mentors, there are a number of racial dynamics that affect the quality and benefits of the relationship. David

Thomas's (1990) study of developmental relationships of African American and White managers in a major public utility company revealed a number of insights about the cross-race and cross-gender dynamics that occur in such relationships. He found that cross-race relationships provided less psychosocial support compared to same-race relationships. However, later research indicated that relationships between African American proteges and White mentors are influenced by the racial awareness of both parties. Complementarity in racial perspectives was identified as a necessary condition for the quality of interaction (Thomas, 1993). Cross-gender mentor relationships are subject to sexual innuendo, and Black women face taboos across both race and sex (Kram, 1985; Thomas, 1986).

The research literature also suggests that to be successful minority managers must develop more complex mentoring and network relationships in organizations. Ibarra (1995) investigated the informal networks of 46 White and 17 minority mid-level managers in four industries. She found that high-potential minorities differed from high-potential Whites and non-high-potential minorities in the range, status, and multiplicity of their network ties. High-potential minorities balanced same- and cross-race contacts compared to less successful minority managers.

Functional Segregation into Staff Positions

The second organizational barrier affecting the advancement of White women and racial minorities is functional segregation into jobs that are not in the pipeline to top management. In private sector organizations, holding line positions or positions that directly impact profit and loss are usually the key to upward mobility. Examination of the career paths of CEOs of large U.S. firms (such as provided in the 1990 annual Business Week 1000 profile) makes it clear that the critical career path for senior management positions has historically been finance, marketing, or operations/engineering, but certainly neither human resources nor community relations. There is a good deal of research indicating that both White women and racial minorities are more likely to hold management positions in the areas of human resources, public relations, community relations, or other staff positions (Catalyst, 1996; Collins, 1989, 1997; Sokoloff, 1992).

Collins (1997) reported that the jobs held by African Americans were racialized. The large number of African Americans who entered corporate America in the 1970s were placed in jobs dealing with community relations, public relations, personnel and labor relations, affirmative action, and equal employment opportunity. Mueller, Tanaka, and Parcel (1989) studied spans of both responsibility and control in a sample of 621 White male and Black male supervisors. They found that Black managers had lower spans of control and less authority over the pay and promotion of subordinates than did White managers. Greenhaus, Parasuraman, and Wormley (1990) discovered that compared to White managers, African American managers perceived themselves as having less discretion in their jobs. Bell and Nkomo (forthcoming) found that a larger percentage of African

American women were concentrated in staff positions compared to the White women in their study of women managers.

Our review of the literature suggests that despite the reported recent gains of White women and racial minorities in the workplace, there are still formidable barriers to equality. A concrete indicator of the recognition of the persistence of these barriers is the sobering fact that White men continue to dominate the higher status jobs in organizations (Catalyst, 1996; Glass Ceiling Commission, 1995). However, organizations are increasingly aware that new entrants into the workplace in the coming decades will be primarily women and racial minorities. In the last section of this chapter, we examine how organizations are investing more resources into ways to better manage the growing diversity in the workplace.

MANAGING DIVERSITY IN THE WORKPLACE
The Challenge and Complexity of Diversity

Before describing the specifics of organizational efforts to address the growing diversity in the workplace, it is important to underscore the underlying debates and tension around the diversity phenomenon. Much of the current literature on diversity acknowledges its complexity. The complexity occurs on two levels. The first level arises from defining diversity. Both scholars and practitioners continue to debate how diversity should be defined (Cox, 1995; Ferdman, 1995; Nkomo, 1995; Nkomo & Cox, 1996). However, there appears to be agreement that the central underlying construct of diversity is identity. It is accepted that individuals have multiple identities, not a single identity.

Intergroup theory suggests individuals in organizations have identities emanating from membership in identity groups (for instance, race and gender) and organizational groups (for instance, position or function). Diversity scholars and practitioners generally identify primary and secondary dimensions of diversity. Primary dimensions of diversity are seen as immutable and include race, ethnicity, age, gender, physical ability, and sexual orientation. Secondary dimensions are mutable and typically include tenure, education, job function, and marital status.

Cox (1993) employs the concept of cultural diversity to mean "the representation, in one social system, of people with distinctly different group affiliations of cultural significance" (p. 6). It is this variation in the patterns of values, beliefs, norms, styles, and behaviors that creates the issue of diversity in organizations. The emphasis on cultural aspects of diversity in organizations leads to efforts to understand the implications of cultural differences for interpersonal and organizational processes and outcomes when members of different cultural groups work together or come in contact. Trying to define who is covered by diversity initiatives can cause tension in organizations.

Sometimes it appears that diversity refers solely to White women, racial minorities, and other historically excluded groups. On the other hand, many corporations are apt to argue that diversity includes everyone, even White males. However, both scholars and practitioners are beginning to recognize that diversity is quite complex. Many are cognizant of Ferdman's (1995) insight that diversity goes beyond between-group differences to also include within-group differences. In other words, there may be individual level variations in group identity. Individuals may view themselves in terms of their membership in many different groups at once, and also may vary in the weight that they perceive each identity having in their self-concept (Ferdman, 1995).

The second level of complexity is rooted in the potential effects of the growing employee diversity in organizations. Diversity has the potential for both positive and negative effects (Chemers, Costanzo, & Oskamp, 1996; Cox, 1993). At the individual level, positive effects are rooted in the idea that more women and minorities should have access to opportunities previously denied them. Organizations stand to benefit by having a broader pool of talents and perspectives to address the challenges of an increasingly competitive marketplace (Thomas & Ely, 1996; Robinson & Dechant, 1997). For example, there is some research to suggest that diversity has positive effects on creativity and problem solving in workgroups.

On the other hand, diversity has the potential to generate negative effects. Traditional organizational practices designed for White males may marginalize and subordinate female and minority employees (Glass Ceiling Commission, 1995). Greater group diversity may lead to greater conflict, less communication, and less integration. Organizations view their challenge as one of maximizing the potential of diversity while minimizing the potential disadvantages. The emphasis on diversity in companies has triggered backlash from some White males who express anxiety and dissatisfaction about being excluded from diversity initiatives and being blamed for workplace inequities (MacDonald, 1993). In an empirical study of 151 organizational groups, Tsui, Egan and O'Reilly (1992) showed that increased work unit diversity was associated with lower levels of psychological attachment among majority group members.

Managing Diversity: Organizational Initiatives

An increasing number of organizations have started initiatives to manage and value the growing diversity of the workforce (Cox & Nkomo, 1991; Kossek & Zonia, 1993). The interest in managing diversity has given rise to new job titles such as, "manager of corporate diversity," and "vice president for work force diversity," positions that did not exist 10 years ago. Prestigious practitioner associations such as the Conference Board and the Society for Human Resource Management (SHRM) have begun sponsoring major conferences on diversity management. A 1995 survey of the top Fortune 500 corporations by A. T. Kearney Executive Search found that 70 percent had formal diversity management programs in place, 8 percent were developing programs, and 8 percent had more scattered programs, whereas only 12 percent had no such programs in place.

Managing Diversity Paradigms

It is important to understand that organizations have employed a variety of approaches and techniques to deal with the increasing heterogeneity of the workplace. In large part, the goals and focus of diversity initiatives depend on the perspective chosen by an organization. Based on a review of organization initiatives and programs, Thomas and Ely (1996) classified organizational approaches to managing diversity into three paradigms: the discrimination-and-fairness paradigm, the access-and-legitimacy paradigm, and the learning-and-effectiveness paradigm. Each of these paradigms has different assumptions and approaches to managing diversity in organizations.

According to Thomas and Ely (1996), organizations that view diversity through a discrimination-and-fairness perspective focus on equal opportunity, fair treatment, recruitment of women and minorities, and compliance with federal equal employment opportunity legislation. Human resource practices in organizations with this perspective establish mentoring and career development programs targeted toward women and racial minorities. For example, a number of organizations have established minority and female network groups. Network groups help women and minorities identify each other, make contacts, and extend the range and depth of their social networks, which in turn, generates greater access to information and support (Friedman, 1996). Friedman, Kane and Cornfield (1998) found that network groups have a positive overall impact on the career optimism of Black managers, and this occurred primarily via enhanced mentoring.

Organizations with this perspective also emphasize recruiting strategies to increase the number of women and racial minorities in the organization. A number of companies use internships to attract underrepresented groups. Concomitantly, efforts are made to create policies to reflect the diversity of employees. These include work-family programs, flexible work schedules, telecommuting, parental leave policies, elder care, and childcare assistance (Lobel, 1999).

Training programs in organizations with a discrimination-and-fairness perspective focus on teaching employees to avoid discriminating against women and minorities. The content may also include modules on stereotyping and prejudice. In a 1994 poll of 2,313 organizations with more than 100 employees, 56 percent reported providing diversity training, compared with 40 percent in 1992 (Silverstein, 1995). Diversity training does not refer, however, to any one activity. It includes workplace interventions, ranging from one-hour briefings to more extensive sessions.

Organizations that take what Thomas and Ely (1996) call the access-and-legitimacy perspective seek to capitalize on the diversity that exists in the workplace. The emphasis is on matching internal employee demographics with diverse customers in the marketplace. The underlying assumption of the access-and-legitimacy paradigm is that an organization needs a diverse workforce to help it compete in a multicultural marketplace. Human resource practices would also center on recruiting employees to match the organization's customers. The goal would not be to assimilate these employees into the organizational culture but to maintain the distinct perspectives they bring. In assigning jobs, efforts are made to match employee diversity to market diversity. For example, Avon Corporation was very successful in hiring African American women in inner city areas to market a new line of cosmetics to its African American customers (Robinson & Dechant, 1997). Training efforts tend to focus on increasing employees' understanding of other cultures. Managing diversity initiatives may also include employee cultural and ethnic days on which employees are encouraged to share their culture with fellow workers through dress or food or both (Gardenswartz & Rowe, 1993).

Thomas and Ely (1996) identified a final approach, which they describe as relatively rare. Organizations adapting a learning-and-effectiveness perspective seek to incorporate the diverse employees into the very fabric of the work and culture of the organization. They emphasize the strategic integration of diversity into all aspects of the organization from products to human resource practices. Organization-wide change initiatives are a hallmark of this particular approach. Managing diversity is not seen as a program or one-time effort but an ongoing change process designed to transform the organization culture from one of exclusion to inclusion of all employees. Much greater emphasis is placed on systemic changes in human resource practices and policies and organizational culture. Typically, this involves (1) creating the awareness of the need to value diversity in the organization; (2) making the business case for developing diversity initiatives in the organization; (3) gaining top management commitment; (4) developing a strategic plan to managing diversity; and (5) identifying the needed structural changes to remove barriers to inclusion of women, minorities, and other nondominant groups in the organizations.

Denny's Restaurant offers a poignant example of the learning-and-effectiveness perspective (Adamson, 1998). Few observers expected Denny's to recover from the devastating revelation in 1993 of systematic racist practices in its locations around the United States. However, by 1998 *Fortune* magazine ranked Denny's as one of "The Fifty Best Companies for Asians, Blacks, and Hispanics." Denny's attributes its turnaround to its diversity initiatives launched shortly after it settled two highly publicized class action suits in 1994. The company made a number of structural changes, which included diversifying its board of directors. Today, women and people of color make up 42 percent of Denny's board. Denny's top management also appointed a chief diversity officer who reported directly to the CEO. Unlike many positions of this type, Denny's gave the position the authority and power to fire anyone who discriminated or who did not act in accordance with the new values. Next, the goal to become a diverse and inclusive company was written into its strategic plan. Every manager in the company is evaluated on how well they value and manage diversity. Human resource systems were audited to ensure they did not inhibit advancement and inclusions of women and minorities. Those policies that created obstacles were revised. Finally, every employee in the entire company attended diversity training programs. The extensive efforts under-taken by Denny's are not widespread among organizations.

CONCLUSION

Although many companies have launched diversity initiatives, survey research suggests only a small percentage believe they are doing a very good job of manag-ing the diversity of their workplace. This raises an important question: How can organizations develop new cultures and climates that are inclusive and supportive of gender and cultural diversity? Organizational scholars appear to be at a critical juncture in making prescriptions. Some scholars believe that the key is building a better business case for valuing diversity (Robinson & Dechant, 1997).

Scholars in this camp argue the reason diversity initiatives have fallen short of their promise is the way management determines and prioritizes a firm's time and resources. Although organizations may recognize the importance of diversity, there are usually more tangible and pressing business priorities that dominate in the short term. In this line of thinking, those responsible for the organization's hu-man resources need to develop a business case for valuing diversity. If the bottom-line impact of diversity can be demonstrated, organizational leaders will then be more likely to prioritize it within the organization. This view is problematic. Evi-dence of diversity's impact on the bottom line has yet to be empirically estab-lished. There are a number of studies that indicate positive effects of diversity on group decision making and creativity, but quantitative measurement of diversity effects is very difficult.

On the other hand, other scholars argue that current diversity initiatives have not been effective because they have not gone far enough in addressing the under-lying issues. For example, a number of psychologists argue that overt racism and sexism has been replaced by new, modern forms (Dovidio et al., 1992). Even though these psychologists make conceptual distinctions when describing these new forms of racism and sexism, they do agree on their common features: (1) Dis-crimination is a thing of the past. Women and minorities are free to compete in the marketplace based on their qualifications just like everyone else; (2) women and minorities are demanding too much and pressing too hard; (3) the demands made by women and minorities are unfair to White men; and (4) recent gains made by women and minorities are undeserved. Proponents of this view argue that diver-sity efforts should also focus on helping dominant-group members understand the complexity and subtlety of their biases. They argue strongly that managing diver-sity initiatives should not be used as a substitute for affirmative action initiatives and antidiscrimination policies. Organizations must continue to rectify discrimi-nation and also work toward creating a workplace that values the contributions of a heterogeneous workforce.

Recent initiatives by the federal government through its Glass Ceiling Commis-sion also seem to emphasize the need for direct interventions to remove barriers to advancement. Research conducted by the commission indicated seven characteristics common to all successful glass ceiling initiatives: (1) CEO support, (2) organization-specific, (3) inclusive (they include all race and gender groups), (4) address preconceptions and stereotypes, (5) emphasize managerial accountability, (6) track ongoing progress, and (7) use a comprehensive approach.

The findings of our literature review point clearly to the key for achieving gender and racial equality in the workplace. The barriers faced by White women and racial minorities exist at the individual, group, and organizational level. As we noted earlier, these levels are not mutually exclusive but mutually reinforcing. Consequently, efforts to remove the barriers must be comprehensive. The focus must not just be on changing attitudes but also on changing organizational structures, human resource practices, and ultimately organizational cultures.

NOTE

1. We explicity use the term "White women and racial minorities" instead of the tendency to use "women and minorities." The latter term simply differentiates between White men and everyone else and obscures other differences and dynamics that should be attended to. The experiences of White women in the workplace are different from those of racial minorities. The term "women and minorities" does not recognize that there are women who are also racial minorities.

REFERENCES

Acker, J. (1990). Hierarchies, jobs, bodies: A theory of gendered organizations. *Gender and Society, 4,* 139–158.

Adamson. J. B. (1998, October 5). The Denny's discrimination story—and ways to avoid it in your operation. *Nation's Restaurant News, 40,* 151.

Alderfer, C. P., Alderfer C. J., Bell, E., & Jones, J. (1992). The race relations competence workshop: Theory and results. *Human Relations, 45,* 1259–1291.

Alderfer, C. P., Alderfer, C. J., Tucker, L., & Tucker, R. (1980). Diagnosing race relations in management. *Journal of Applied Behavioral Science, 16,* 135–166.

Alderfer, C. P., Tucker, R. C., Alderfer, C. J., & Tucker, L. M. (19988). The race relations advisory group: An intergroup intervention. *Research in Organizational Change and Development, 2,* 269–321.

Baldi, S., & McBrier, D. B. (1997). Do the determinants of promotion differ for blacks and whites? *Work and Occupations, 24,* 478–497.

Baron, J. N., & Bielby, W. (1984). The organization of work in a segmented economy. *American Sociological Review, 49,* 454–473.

Baron, J. N., & Bielby, W. (1986). The structure of opportunity: How promotion ladders vary within and among organizations. *Administrative Science Quarterly, 31,* 248–273.

Becker, G. (1964). *Human capital.* New York: Columbia University Press.

Becker, G. (1975). *Human capital: A theoretical and empirical analysis with special reference to education* (2nd ed.). New York: Praeger.

Bell, E. (1990). The power within: Bicultural life experience of career-oriented black women. *Journal of Organization Behavior, 11,* 459–477.

Bell, E. L., & Nkomo, S. M. (forthcoming). *Our separate ways: Black and white women and the struggle for professional identity.* Boston: Harvard Business School Press.

Bell, E., Denton, T., & Nkomo, S. M. (1993). Women of color in management: Towards an inclusive analysis. In E. Fagenson (Ed.), *Women in Management: Trends, issues, and challenges in managerial diversity* (pp. 104–130). Newbury Park, CA: Sage.

Bell, E., & Nkomo, S. M. (1994). *Barriers to work place advancement experienced by African-Americans.* Monograph prepared for the Glass Ceiling Commission, U.S. Department of Labor.

Bell, E., & Nkomo, S. M. (1998). *Our separate ways: Black and white women forging paths to corporate America.* Unpublished manuscript.

Biernat, M., & Kobrynowicz, D. (1997). Gender- and race-based standards of competence: Lower minimum standards but higher ability standards for devalued groups. *Journal of Personality & Social Psychology, 72,* 544–557.

Blalock, H. R. (1967). *Toward a theory of minority-group relations.* New York: Wiley.

Bridges, W. P., & Villemez, W. J. (1994). *The employment relationship: Causes and consequences of modern personnel administration.* New York: Plenum.

Cabezas, A., Tam, T. M., Lowe, B. M., Wong. A., & Turner, K. (1989). Empirical study of barriers to upward mobility for Asian Americans in the San Francisco Bay Area. In G. M. Nomura, R. Endo, S. H. Sumida, & R. C. Leong (Eds.), *Frontiers of Asian American studies: Writing, research and commentary* (pp. 85–97). Pullman, WA: Washington State University Press.

Catalyst (1996). *Women in corporate leadership: Progress and prospects.* New York: Catalyst.

Chemers, M., Oskamp, S., & Costanzo, M. (1995). *Diversity in organizations: New perspectives for a changing workplace.* London: Sage.

Cianni, M., & Romberger, B. (1995). Interactions with senior managers: Perceived differences by race/ethnicity and by gender. *Sex Roles, 32,* 353–373.

Cockburn, C. (1991). *In the way of women: Men's resistance to sex equality in organizations.* Ithaca, NY: ILR Press.

Collins, S. (1989). The marginalization of black executives. *Social Problems, 35*(4), 317–331.

Collins, S. (1997). Black mobility in white corporations: Up the corporate ladder but out on a limb. *Social Problems, 44,* 55–67.

Cox, T. H. (1993). Cultural diversity in organizations: Theory, research, and practice. San Francisco: Berrett-Koehler.

Cox, T. H. (1995). The complexity of diversity: Challenges and directions for future research. In S. E. Jackson & M. N. Ruderman (Eds.), *Diversity in work teams: Research paradigms for a changing workplace* (pp. 235–246). Washington, DC: American Psychological Association.

Cox, T. H., Lobel, S., & Mcleod, P. (1991). Effects of ethnic group cultural difference on cooperative versus competitive behavior in a group task. *Academy of Management Journal, 34,* 827–847.

Cox, T. H., & Nkomo, S. M. (1986). Differential performance appraisal criteria: A field study of black and white managers. *Group and Organization Studies, 11,* 101–119.

Cox, T. H., & Nkomo, S. M. (1991). A race and gender group analysis of the early career experience of MBAs. *Work and Occupations, 18,* 431–446.

Crosby, F. (1989). *Gender and personality: Illusions and reality*. Paper presented at Rutgers University, New Brunswick, NJ.

Davidson, M. (1993). *The effect of racioethnicity on beliefs about coping with interpersonal conflict: a comparison of African-American and European Americans*. (Working Paper #298). Hanover, NH: Amos Tuck School of Business. Dartmouth College.

Davis, G., & Watson, G. (1982). *Black life in corporate America: Swimming in the mainstream*. New York: Doubleday.

DiTomaso, N. (1989). Sexuality in the workplace: Discrimination and harassment. In J. Hearn, D. L. Sheppard, P. Tranced-Sheriff, & G. Burrell (Eds.), *The sexuality of organizations* (pp. 71–90). Newbury Park, CA: Sage.

Dovidio, J. F., & Gaertner, S. L. (1983). The effects of race, sex, status, and ability on helping behavior. *Journal of Applied Social Psychology, 13,* 191–205.

Dovidio, J. F., Gaertner, S. L., Anastasio, P. A., & Sanitoso, R. (1992). Cognitive and motivational bases of bias: Implications of aversive racism for attitudes toward Hispanics. In S. Knouse, P. Rosenfeld, A. L. Culbertson (Eds.), *Hispanics in the Workplace* (pp. 75–106). Thousand Oaks, CA: Sage.

Dreher, G. F., & Cox, T. H. (1996). Race, gender, and opportunity: A study of compensation attainment and the establishment of mentoring relationships. *Journal of Applied Psychology, 81,* 297–308.

Eagly, A. H., Makhijani, M. G., & Klonsky, B. G. (1992). Gender and the effectiveness of leaders: A meta-analysis. *Psychological Bulletin, 117,* 125–145.

Eden, D. (1992). Leadership and expectations: Pygmalion effects and other self-fulfilling prophecies in organizations. *Leadership Quarterly, 3,* 271–305.

Edwards, R. (1979). *Contested terrain: The transformation of the workplace in the 20th century*. New York: Basic Books.

Ely, R. (1995). The power of demography. Women's social constructions of gender identity at work. *Academy of Management Journal, 38,* 589–634.

Ensher, E. A., & Murphy, S. E. (1977). Effects of race, gender, perceived similarity, and contact on mentor relationships. *Journal of Vocational Behavior, 50,* 460–481.

Essed, P. (1991). *Understanding everyday racism*. Newbury Park, CA: Sage.

Feagin, J. R., & Sikes, M. P. (1995). *Living with racism: The black-middle class experience*. Boston: Beacon Press.

Ferdman, B. M. (1989). Affirmative action and the challenge of the color-blind perspective. In F. A. Blanchard & F. J. Crosby (Eds.), *Affirmative action in perspective* (pp. 169–176). New York: Springer-Verlag.

Ferdman, B. M. (1995). Cultural identity and diversity in organizations: Bridging the gap between group differences and individual uniqueness. In M. M. Chemers, S. Oskamp, & M. A. Costanzo (Eds.), *Diversity in organizations* (pp. 37–61). Thousand Oaks, CA: Sage.

Ferdman, B. M., & Cortes, A. C. (1992). Culture and identity among Hispanic managers in an Anglo business. In S. Knouse, P. Rosenfeld, A. L. Culbertson (Eds.), *Hispanics in the workplace* (pp. 246–277). Thousand Oaks, CA: Sage.

Friedman, R. (1996). Defining the scope and logic of minority and female network groups: Does separation enhance integration? In G. Ferris (Ed.), *Research in personnel and human resources management* (pp. 307–349). Greenwich, CT: JAI Press.

Friedman, R., Kane, M., & Cornfield, D. B. (1998). Social support and career optimism: Examining the effectiveness of network groups among black managers. *Human Relations, 51,* 1155–1177.

Friedman, R. A., & Krackhardt, D. (1997). Social capital and career mobility: A structural theory of lower returns to education for Asians employees. *Journal of Applied Behavioral Science, 33,* 316–334.

Gaertner, S. L. (1973, April). *Helping behavior and anti-Semitism among black and white communities.* Paper presented at the Annual Convention of the Eastern Psychological Association, Washington, DC.

Gaertner, S. L. (1976). Nonreactive measures in racial attitude research: a focus on "Liberals." In P. Katz (Ed.), *Toward the elimination of racism* (pp. 183–211). New York: Pergamon.

Gaertner, S. L., & Dovidio, J. F. (1986). The aversive form of racism. In J. F. Dovidio & S. L. Gaertner (Eds.), *Prejudice, discrimination, and racism* (pp. 61–89). Orlando, FL: Academic Press.

Gardenswartz, L., & Rowe, A. (1993). *Managing diversity.* Homewood, Ill: Business One Irwin.

Glass Ceiling Commission. (1995). *Good for business: Making full use of the nation's human capital: A fact finding report of the federal glass ceiling commission.* Washington, DC: Author.

Greenhaus, J. H., & Parasuraman, S. (1993). Job performance attributions and career advancement prospects: An examination of gender and race effects. *Organizational Behavior and Human Decision Processes, 55,* 273–297.

Greenhaus, J., Parasuraman, S., & Wormley, W. (1990). Effects of race on organizational experiences, job performance evaluations, and career outcomes. *Academy of Management Journal, 33,* 64–86.

Gutek, B. (1985). *Sex and the workplace.* San Francisco: Josey-Bass.

Hamilton, D. L., & Trolier, T. V. K. (1986). Stereotypes and stereotyping: An overview of the cognitive approach. In J. F. Dovidio & S. L. Gaertner (Eds.), *Prejudice, discrimination, and racism* (pp. 127–158). Orlando, FL: Academic Press.

Heilman, M. E., Block, C. J., & Lucas, J. A. (1992). Presumed incompetent? Stigmatization and affirmative action efforts. *Journal of Applied Psychology, 77,* 536–544.

Heilman, M. E., Block, C. J., Martell, R. F., & Simon, M. C. (1989). Has anything changed? Current characterizations of men, women and managers. *Journal of Applied Psychology, 74,* 935–942.

Higginbotham, E., & Romero, M. (1997). *Women and work: Exploring race, ethnicity and class.* Thousand Oaks, CA: Sage.

Hochschild, A. (1989). *The second shift: Working parents and the revolution at home.* New York: Viking.

Hoffman, E. (1985). The effect of race-ratio composition on the frequency of organizations communication. *Social Psychology Quarterly, 48,* 17–26.

Ibarra, H. (1995). Race, opportunity, and diversity of social circles in managerial networks. *Academy of Management Journal, 38,* 673–703.

Ilgen, D. R., & Youtz, M. A. (1986). Factors affecting the evaluation and development of minorities in organizations. In K. Rowland & G. Ferris (Eds.), *Research in person-*

nel and human resource management: A research annual (pp. 307–337). Greenwich, CT: JAI Press.

Jackson, S. E., Stone, V. K., & Alvarez, E. B. (1993). Socialization amidst diversity: The impact of demographics on work team old-timers and newcomers. Research in Organizational Behavior, 15, 45–109.

Jackson, P. B., Thoits, P. A., & Taylor, H. F. (1995). Composition of the workplace and psychological well-being: The effects of tokenism on America's Black elite. Social Forces, 74, 543–557.

Johnston, W. B., & Packer, A. E. (1987). Workforce 2000: Work and workers for the 21st century. Indianapolis: Hudson Institute.

Kanter, R. M. (1977). Men and women of the corporation. New York: Basic Books.

Kochman, T. (1981). Black and white styles in conflict. Chicago: University of Chicago Press.

Kossek, E. E., & Zonia, S. C. (1993). Assessing diversity climate: A field study of reactions to employer efforts to promote diversity. Journal of Organizational Behavior, 14, 61–81.

Kraiger, K., & Ford, J. K. (1985). A meta-analysis of rate race effects in performance ratings. Journal of Applied Psychology, 70, 56–65.

Kram, K. E. (1985). Mentoring at work. Glenview, IL: Scott, Foresman.

LaFromboise, T., Coleman, H. L.K., & Gerton, J. (1993). Psychological impact of biculturalism: Evidence and theory. Psychological Bulletin, 114, 395–412.

Lester, T., & MacKinnon, C. A. (1993). Only words. Cambridge, MA: Harvard University Press.

Lobel, S. A. (1999). Impacts of diversity and work-life initiatives in organizations. In Gary N. Powell (Ed.), Handbook of gender and work (pp. 453–476). London: Sage.

MacDonald, J. (July, 1993). The diversity industry. New Republic, pp. 22–25.

Mueller, C. W., Tanaka, K., & Parel, T. L. (1989). Particularism in authority outcomes of black and white supervisors. Social Science Research, 18, 1–20.

Nieva, V., & Gutek, B. (1980). Sex effcts on evaluation. Academy of Management Review, 5, 267–276.

Nkomo, S. M. (1995). Identities and the complexity of diversity. In S. E. Jackson & M. N. Ruderman (Eds.), Diversity in work teams: Research paradigms for a changing workplace (pp. 247–253). Washington, DC: American Psychological Association.

Nkomo, S. M., & Cox, T. H. (1996). Diverse identities in organizations. In S. R. Clegg, C. Hardy, & W. R. Nord (Eds.), Handbook of organization studies (pp. 338–356). Thousand Oaks, CA: Sage.

Pettigrew, T., Jemmott, J. B., & Johnson, J. T. (1984). Race and the questioner effect: Testing the ultimate attribution error. Unpublished manuscript, University of California, Santa Cruz.

Pettigrew, T., & Martin, J. (1987). Shaping the organizational context for black American inclusion. Journal of Social Issues, 43(1), 41–78.

Ragins, B. R., & Sundstrom, E. (1989). Gender and power in organizations: A longitudinal perspective. Psychological Bulletin, 105, 511–588.

Reskin, B., & Padavic, I. (1994). Women and men at work. Thousand Oaks, CA: Pine Forge Press.

Riordan, C., & McFarlane Shore, L. (1984). Demographic diversity and employee attitudes: An empirical examination of relational demography within work units. *Journal of Applied Psychology, 82*(3), 342–358.

Rivera-Ramos, A. N. (1992). The psychological experience of Puerto Rican women at work. In S. Knouse, P. Rosenfeld, A. L. Culbertson (Eds.), *Hispanics in the workplace* (pp. 194–207). Thousand Oaks, CA: Sage.

Robinson, G., & Dechant, K. (1997). Building the business case for diversity. *Academy of Management Executive, 11,* 21–31.

Rowe, M. (1990). Barriers to equality: The power of subtle discrimination to maintain unequal opportunity. *Employee Responsibilities and Rights Journal, 3,* 153–163.

Sackett, P. R., Dubois, C. L., & Noe, A. W. (1991). Tokenism in performance evaluation: The effects of work group representation on male-female and White-Black differences in performance ratings. *Journal of Applied Psychology, 76,* 263–267.

Schein, V. (1973). The relationship between sex role stereotypes and requisite management characteristics. *Journal of Applied Psychology, 57,* 95–100.

Schmitt, N. (1993). Group composition, gender, and race effects on assessment center ratings. In H. Schuler, J. L. Farr, & M. Smith (Eds.), *Personnel selection and assessment: Individual and organizational perspectives* (pp. 315–332). Hillsdale, NJ: Erlbaum.

Silverstein, S. (1995, May 2). Workplace diversity efforts thrive despite backlash. *Los Angeles Times,* pp. 1, 14.

Sokoloff, N. (1992). *Black and white women in the professions.* New York: Routledge.

Stroh, L. K., Brett, J. M., & Reilly, A. (1992). All the right stuff: A comparison of female and male managers' career progress. *Journal of Applied Psychology, 77,* 251–260.

Tajfel, H., & Turner, J.C. (1979). An integrative theory of intergroup conflict. In W.G. Austin and S. Worchel (Eds.), *The social psychology of intergroup relations* (pp. 85–102). Monterey, CA: Brooks/Cole.

Tang, J. (1997). The model minority thesis revisted: (Counter) evidence from the science and engineering fields. *Journal of Applied Behavioral Science, 33,* 291–315.

Thomas, D. A. (1986). Mentoring and irrationality: The role of racial taboos. *Human Resource Management, 28,* 279–290.

Thomas, D. A. (1990). The impact of race on manager's experiences of developmental relationships: An intra organizational study. *Journal of Organizational Behavior, 11,* 479–492.

Thomas, D. A. (1993). Racial dynamics in cross-race developmental relationships. *Administrative Science Quarterly, 38,* 169–194.

Thomas, D. A., & Ely, R. (1996, September–October). Making differences matter: A new paradigm for managing diversity. *Harvard Business Review,* 79–90.

Tomaskovic-Devey, D. (1993). *Gender and racial inequality at work.* Ithaca, NY: ILR Press.

Triandis, H. C. (1972). *The analysis of subjective culture.* New York: Wiley.

Triandis, H. C., Kurowski, L. L., & Gelfand, M. J. (1994). Workplace diversity. In H. C. Triandis, M. D. Dunnette, & L. M. Hough (Eds.), *Handbook of industrial and organizational psychology* (Vol. 4, pp. 769–827). Palo Alto, CA: Consulting Psychologists Press.

Triandis, H. C., Marin, G., Lisansky, J., & Betancourt, H. (1984). Simpatia as cultural script of Hispanics. *Journal of Personality and Social Psychology, 47,* 1363–1375.

Tsui, A. S., Egan, T. D., & O'Reilly, C. A., III. (1992). Being different: Relational demography and organizational attachment. *Administrative Science Quarterly, 37,* 549–579.

Xin, K. R. (1997). Asian American managers: An impression gap? An investigation of impression management and supervisor-subordinate relationships. *Journal of Applied Behavioral Science: Special issue: Asian Americans in organizations, 33,* 335–355.

Yoder, J. D. (1991). Rethinking tokenism: Looking beyond numbers. *Gender and Society, 5,* 178–192.

Yoder, J. D., & Aniakudo, P. (1997). Outsider within the firehouse: Subordination and difference in the social interactions of African-American women firefighters. *Gender and Society, 11,* 324–341.

15

SEX, JOBS, AND THE LAW

Michael H. McGee

INTRODUCTION

As the author of this chapter, I am an attorney who prosecuted discrimination cases for the Equal Employment Opportunity Commission between 1974 and 1991. At present, I represent primarily employers, in the defense of discrimination claims and in setting up internal controls to prevent discrimination from occurring within companies. It is from this diverse legal background that I discuss the issues and solutions regarding sex, jobs, and the law. First to be discussed is the legal status of affirmative action planning in the new millennium. This still very vital antidote for discrimination has been altered in its direction and purposes by the courts. I discuss the changes and trends for the future.

The next subject undertaken is an overview of the basic federal statutory and case law concerning sex discrimination in employment. The primary theories of discrimination are described, along with the current trends in how the courts are interpreting these theories. I evaluate the significance of these trends and offer some predictions for the future.

The final topic is a discussion of some powerful new legal tools that have been developed, and will more frequently be used, in cases where there are allegations of sex discrimination. Although it is outside the scope of this chapter to discuss the different laws of all 50 states, some of these new tools involve using certain state laws that are common to most of the states.

A great many of the observations I make in this chapter also apply with equal force to issues of discrimination against ethnic and racial minorities, persons more than 40 years of age, and persons who are disabled. I discuss the issues here primarily from the point of view of sex and gender discrimination.

It is currently common for well-informed and well-educated people to say that the law and the courts are turning their backs on workplace claims of employment discrimination against women. There is, of course, some truth in this statement.

Recent court decisions have made it much more difficult to prove sex discrimination in employment. Both governmental and private preferential affirmative action has all but disappeared. Sexual and minority preferences and set-asides in contracting and subcontracting are getting harder to find. Big class action lawsuits increasingly take more time and energy to produce fewer benefits. One could go on until pessimism sets in. Then one could conclude that there is no justice abroad in the land.

To draw such a conclusion, though, one must start from unsound premises and ignore a great deal of evidence. For all the losses and negative changes that can be recited, compensating factors can be found. All is not well. All is not rosy. Yet all is not bleak, either.

It is true that it is more difficult to prove in court the presence of sex discrimination in employment. One reason for this increasing difficulty is that there is considerably less "overt" sex discrimination being practiced by employers. Further, when an individual complains of overt sex discrimination, many employers will investigate, and settle the claim promptly if discrimination is found to be present.

Many employers will also settle claims out of court where the situation is not overt but is subject to interpretation. They may do this out of a desire to go the extra mile to be fair. Some may even make a "bottom-line" decision that it is less expensive to settle an uncertain case than to go through the time and attorneys' fees involved in extended legal proceedings.

Another factor that must be taken into account is that many employers, including almost all of the larger companies, now have subdepartments of specialized staff human relations persons. The job of the human relations staff is to analyze the existing composition of the company's workforce on an ongoing basis, and to review and chart the company's hiring, promotion, and termination patterns and practices. Another common activity is to conduct training sessions for supervisors and managers on how to maintain diversity in the workplace, as well as how to comply with the applicable state and federal discrimination laws. These staff analysts and trainers often make sure that intentional discrimination, as well as the discrimination of "looking the other way," doesn't happen—or at least happens with decreasing frequency.

Among other things, this means that a much larger proportion of situations in which intentional or unintentional discrimination might have gone unheeded in the past are now resolved at a very early stage. "Situations" never become "cases." Fewer internal personnel matters remain unresolved long enough to become federal agency charges or lawsuits, which leads to fewer clear-cut cases making it all the way to the appellate stage of litigation, where much new federal case law is made.

Many of the cases today that go all the way through the court system to trial, verdict, and appeal involve the interpretation of subtle legal nuances, factual situations that are open to more than one interpretation, and attempts at razor-thin clarifications of the laws. And these types of cases are more difficult for a claimant to win. Such cases also consume more legal resources for fewer results. There's a well-known legal maxim: "Hard cases make bad law." Much of the new case law reported from the federal trial and appellate courts involves hard cases: the interpretation of highly ambiguous situations.

AFFIRMATIVE ACTION AT THE MILLENNIUM

With regard to the reported imminent demise of affirmative action, it can be said that reports of its death are greatly exaggerated. The perception of grave losses and major setbacks occurs primarily when the ebbs and flows of two distinctly different types of affirmative action are collapsed into a single analysis.

Most of the legal setbacks have occurred in the type of affirmative action activity that requires or encourages an employer to grant an absolute or substantial preference to a qualified female applicant for a job or promotion, until the percentage of females in that job category reaches and maintains parity with the percentage of qualified female candidates available in the relevant labor market. This preference is usually applied regardless of whether there is a similarly or more qualified male candidate in the applicant pool. Mandatory minimum percentages of female-owned subcontractors in construction and service projects also fall into this category of affirmative action.

There is substantive and well-established Constitutional law relating to the equal protection under the law for all citizens. The U.S. Constitution has been consistently interpreted to place meaningful limits on the use of affirmative action as a means of providing for preferential hiring and promotion as well as for mandatory contracting set-asides. The use of such legal remedies is limited to situations where a longstanding intent to exclude females, combined with a statistically significant underrepresentation in spite of qualified female applicants, has been proven.

In addition to the Constitutional law, Title VII of the Civil Rights Act of 1964 and the Equal Pay Act of 1963, as well as most of the other civil rights laws designed to provide equal opportunities for women, have been interpreted consistently by the courts as providing the same protections for men in the workplace that are provided for women.

In the early days of the legal push to eliminate discrimination in employment, it was relatively easy to prove to a judge that (1) women were substantially underrepresented in defined job categories or workforces, *and* (2) the reason for the underrepresentation was an intentional refusal to hire or promote women into the defined job categories or workforces, *and* (3) qualified females had applied, or were available and had been discouraged from applying. Courts or government agencies that ordered affirmative action based on those three pillars *standing together* could easily withstand the closest scrutiny by Constitutional scholars.

In addition, it is clear from the evidence introduced in numerous cases in court that many employers have never used "ability" or "qualifications" as criteria for hiring or promotion. As Scott Adams has pointed out in his *Dilbert* cartoons, it is all too common for a white male to be promoted into a position for reasons other than competence. Once in that position he then proceeds to make life miserable for those who report to him. Even worse, *Dilbert*'s unqualified male managers don't ever get the boot. They go along merrily spreading misery and ill will, getting promoted and being given awards in almost inverse proportion to their productivity and management skills.

At this writing, and *Dilbert* notwithstanding, it is substantially more difficult to establish in court conclusive evidence of each of the three elements of proof necessary in order to impose mandatory preferences. Most employers are now taking the step of basing their decisions on overall qualifications of the pool from which the selection is to be made, regardless of sex. Therefore the decline in mandatory affirmative action quotas is more closely related to a change in our society following the passage of the civil rights laws, than it is to any decrease by the courts in their willingness to take the necessary actions to eliminate discrimination.

There is still a significant place in the employment arena for the second type of affirmative action: the ongoing internal analysis by employers of their own workforce, coupled with active efforts to recruit, develop and promote women, who, in a fair competition, meet the qualifications for hire or promotion that are imposed on similarly situated males.

This second type of affirmative action will likely never go out of style, and it is not controversial at all for most employers. The largely unheralded work is done by corporate staff members who perform their tasks behind closed doors. These highly trained men and women often do an exceptionally good job of taking some of the edge off the blade of discrimination and will continue to do so for the foreseeable future.

FEDERAL STATUTORY LAW

Sex discrimination in employment was not addressed effectively by legal theory and practice until two laws were passed by Congress. The Equal Pay Act of 1963 (1963) for the first time required employers to pay equal wages to men and women performing the same work. Title VII of the Civil Rights Act of 1964 (1964) for the first time prohibited other forms of discrimination against women in the workplace. Title VII was generic and virtually unlimited in covering all types of discrimination against women in situations such as hiring, promotion, training, and overtime opportunities, layoff, and discharge. Both of these laws have been interpreted to prevent discrimination against men as well as women.

The Equal Pay Act of 1963 requires that women be paid the same as men in jobs of equal skill, effort, and responsibility, performed under similar working conditions. A long series of court decisions has made it clear that only jobs that are roughly the same, and located in the same general physical location, will require equal pay. Jobs that are different but involve the same types of skills, efforts, and responsibilities—that is, jobs of comparable worth—do not require equal pay. Similarly, it is unlikely that a woman holding a job in New York can compare herself with a man holding the identical job with the same company in Los Angeles, unless it is unequivocally clear that the hiring for both of the jobs is done in one central location, and selection is from an applicant or promotion pool that encompasses both areas.

Title VII of the Civil Rights Act of 1964, among other things, created the Equal Employment Opportunity Commission as an independent federal agency charged with enforcing Title VII and investigating charges of discrimination filed pursuant to the act. Other duties have been added by Congress to this core responsibility since that time.

The Equal Employment Opportunity Commission is so bogged down with competing constituencies and a reduced workforce that at the millennium it is virtually ineffective at carrying out its statutory mandate to enforce the sex discrimination laws. A woman who believes that she has been discriminated against because of her sex will normally find it necessary to file a charge with the EEOC in a timely manner. This is done, however, primarily to meet a jurisdictional requirement, and without any expectation that the bureaucratic staff of the agency will actually investigate her charge or enforce the law unless evidence of discrimination is handed to them on a silver platter.

Due in part to the inability of the EEOC to carry out its statutory responsibility, a woman must consider all of the different avenues that are available, including retaining a private attorney to prosecute her case in court if the matter is not resolved by other means. Many of these other avenues are discussed in this chapter.

In addition to the EEOC, a majority of the states have passed their own civil rights laws and have their own agencies charged with the responsibility of investigating and resolving claims of discrimination. Some of these state agencies are quite effective and some are not. A person claiming discrimination may in some situations be required to submit the claim to the state agency in their area within a certain time limit in order to preserve all of her rights. It is beyond the scope of this paper to discuss the laws of all 50 states. Statutory state, and even local, agencies, cannot be ignored, though, and a full analysis of the validity of any claim of sex discrimination includes a look at relevant state laws, and compliance with the deadlines and procedures imposed by those laws.

Federal Case Law and Theories of Discrimination

In a situation where there is an allegation of sex discrimination, there are two general schemes of proof that can be utilized. These are referred to as the "disparate treatment" scheme of proof, and the "disparate impact" scheme of proof. A "disparate treatment" case is a claim brought by one or more individuals who are attempting to demonstrate that they were individually discriminated against on account of their sex. The elements of proof in a disparate treatment case will be discussed in detail later in this section.

There is a much more complex set of elements of proof in a "disparate impact" case. This is a claim where a group of persons, or a class of persons, is attempting to demonstrate that certain employment practices of a company result in a negative impact against the entire affected class, usually based on evidence of a statistically significant underrepresentation of the alleged affected group in the workforce, or in certain jobs within the workforce. Normally such cases revolve around a statistical analysis, and the significance of studies of groups of employees, applicants, or persons laid off or terminated. An individual sex discrimination claimant is normally entitled to a finding in her favor only if the court finds that the group of persons that includes the individual claimant was treated differently because of sex. For a good analysis of the correct methodology to use in a disparate impact case, see *Ward's Cove Packing Co. v. Atonio* (1989).

In the classic case of *McDonnell Douglas v. Green* (1973), the United States Supreme Court laid out general principles regarding the elements of proof in a "disparate treatment" employment discrimination case. In order to understand how discrimination in employment is proved or disproved, the method of analysis mandated by the Court in this case must be studied in detail. *McDonnell Douglas* is a case involving refusal to hire because of race. The three-part analysis is, however, equally applicable to a sex discrimination case. It is entirely proper to use the analytical framework in this case to examine the evidence supporting almost any claim of employment discrimination for almost any reason.

I undertook a study (McGee, 1991) of more than 200 individual employment discrimination cases, including claims based on race, sex, religion, age, and disability, and with issues ranging from hiring to failure to promote to discharge. In at least 90 percent of those cases, the *McDonnell Douglas* framework was the sole method by which the evidence in the case could be rigorously analyzed to determine whether, in the end, the evidence in support of a claim was sufficient to merit a decision in favor of the claimant. An analyst should *always* use this framework unless there is a strong reason not to do so.

The *McDonnell Douglas* case, as well as some of the other cases referred to in this analysis, involved situations in which discrimination on a basis other than sex was alleged. Only sex discrimination is referred to in the discussion that follows, in order to avoid confusion and to stay consistent with the subject of the chapter. In each case discussed, the analytical framework is virtually the same for sex discrimination situations as it is for the category of claimant actually involved in the case itself.

In the first element of the *McDonnell Douglas* disparate treatment framework, the "burden of proof" is on the claimant to establish a prima facie case of sex discrimination by producing sufficient admissible evidence to prove certain facts. Only the claimant's evidence is looked at, although the claimant's evidence is usually carefully examined for accuracy by the other side, or tested by cross-examination if the matter is before a court.

If the claimant succeeds in producing sufficient evidence to establish this prima facie case, then she has met her burden of proof. In the absence of contrary evidence introduced by the employer in the second stage or a later stage, the claimant wins, and is entitled to a finding of discrimination. This prima facie case is a very light burden for the claimant to meet. It does not require much evidence.

The evidence that must be produced is, first, that the claimant is a member of a protected class. In sex discrimination cases it is usually obvious that the claimant is female. In other types of cases certain introductory facts may need to be proven that are less obvious: for example, that the claimant is disabled within the definition of the Americans with Disabilities Act (1990), or is over the age of 40 (Age Discrimination in Employment Act, 1967). These threshold facts permit the claimant to invoke the statute and get into court. She is in a category of employees, applicants, or former employees that is protected by a federal or state discrimination statute.

Second, the claimant must establish that she is or was employed by the employer who is being charged, or was a bona fide applicant for such employment, and was qualified for the position held or sought. This analytical piece seems simple and it often is. Many evidentiary battles, though, are fought over issues such as whether the person was an employee or an independent contractor, or whether she was in fact employed by a temporary agency under contract with the named employer, or whether the claimant's application for employment had actually been received by the employer during the time period established for persons to apply for a particular job.

Third, the claimant must demonstrate in a very rudimentary way that she has been actually damaged by the alleged discriminatory actions of the employer. Did the employer continue to accept applications for the job for which the claimant applied, and then select a male to fill the position? Was the position into which an employee sought promotion actually filled by a male after the time that she applied? If the claim is that the claimant was terminated because of her sex, an evidentiary battle may be fought over whether her leaving was a discharge, which would mean that she may have been damaged, or if it was actually a voluntary quit, which may mean that she was not damaged.

It is important to spend a great deal of time analyzing and reviewing these seemingly simple early evidentiary points relating to the initial burden of proof, which is on the claimant. Failure to do so can lead to long and complicated litigation or agency proceedings that could have been stopped at an early stage. Further, in a case where there is significant merit to the claimant's position, a failure to analyze these early points can result in prolonging the agony of a matter that should have been settled favorably to the claimant early on.

In any case, failure to analyze rigorously the early elements of proof can result in unnecessary emotionally painful confrontation for a woman who has already suffered considerable harm, or in an agonizing delay on the part of a company in gaining dismissal of a claim that has no merit. In any case, such a failure can run up each party's attorney's fees or staff time, and consume scarce agency and court resources.

Under *McDonnell Douglas,* once the claimant establishes these minimal elements, then the claimant "wins." She has met her initial burden of proof. That is enough. The claimant can sit and rest at this point.

Although the ultimate "burden of proof," or "burden of persuasion" as it is sometimes called, never shifts from the claimant, at this point the "burden of producing evidence" shifts to the employer. The employer is permitted to "articulate a legitimate nondiscriminatory reason" or reasons, for the actions that the claimant has proven were taken.

Stated another way, the employer must come forward with admissible evidence to show that there are one or more valid and nondiscriminatory reasons for the actions taken. The employer can also put on evidence that the harm alleged by the claimant was not caused by the actions of the employer; or that there is some other reason that the employer should be found not to have violated the law. An example of such an "other reason" is where the employer is able to demonstrate the presence of a "bona fide occupational qualification," as when only males are hired to model men's clothing for a catalog.

For example, a claimant may have alleged that she was terminated by her employer because of her sex. She produced admissible evidence that she was female and that she was regularly employed by the employer on an assembly line, doing the work that she was assigned in an adequate manner. One day her supervisor called her into his office and terminated her without any explanation. The evidence showed that she was the only one in her department who was terminated, and that the next day she was replaced by a male employee.

With the evidence that has been presented, the claimant has established her prima facie case and met her initial burden of proof. With nothing else said, she will be entitled to a verdict in her favor that she was unlawfully discharged from her job because of her sex. The "burden of producing evidence" has shifted to the employer to "articulate a legitimate nondiscriminatory reason" for this claimant's termination.

In this claimant's case, documents and testimony presented by the employer showed that work was slow for the plant where she worked, due to loss of a significant contract. The lost contract, though, had not affected the volume of work on this claimant's particular assembly line. The company's evidence was that the plant's managers, in consultation with their lawyers, had reviewed the whole production workforce and decided, without reference to sex, to terminate the seven employees, plantwide, who were the least effective. This claimant was one of the least effective employees based on attendance, production levels, and rework rates, criteria that had been established over time, and for which records had been kept over time without reference to this particular work slowdown.

The plant manager and others testified that following these evaluation sessions he had permanently reduced the head count in the plant by seven persons, by terminating these seven least effective employees. Once this claimant was terminated, there was a vacancy that needed to be filled on her assembly line. The most junior employee on another assembly line that was directly affected by the contract cancellation was transfered to fill the vacant position on the claimant's assembly line. The fact that the transferee was a man was a coincidence. This decision was made, witnesses say, without reference to the sex of the person who was transfered.

With this information, the employer has articulated more than one legitimate nondiscriminatory reason for the actions that were taken. If nothing further is said, then the employer wins the case. End of story. Everything has shifted. And even if this "articulated" evidence does not rise to the level of formal "proof" it serves to rebut the prima facie case and return the necessity for proof to the claimant.

Part three of the *McDonnell Douglas* pattern of proof is just as important as the other two parts of the formula. Here the claimant has an opportunity to demonstrate that the "legitimate nondiscriminatory reasons advanced by the employer are pretextual in nature." Properly done, this section of the proof is very formal in nature and is handled with precision. This claimant must rebut each of the reasons actually advanced by the employer, then demonstrate that the evidence when taken as a whole makes it more likely than not that unlawful discrimination occurred.

It is often quite difficult for a claimant to prove that the reasons advanced by an employer are pretextual. Here is where cases involving attempts to prove more subtle forms of discrimination often get derailed.

Once the employer has asserted that work was slow due to the loss of a contract, the claimant's attorney may be put in the position of having to examine all of the production and output records of the department, or even of the whole company, in an attempt to demonstrate that there was no change in the amount of work to be done. Another tactic may be to look at the attendance, production, and rework records for all of the employees in the plant in an effort to demonstrate that the claimant was not one of the least effective employees on the payroll.

The claimant's attorney may also need to count and chart the entire workforce of the company over time, to see if there was an actual reduction in the number of employees overall at the time stated by the employer, and look closely at massive volumes of files and records to see if someone was hired to replace the man who was transfered from the other assembly line. There will be many witnesses to interview in an effort to find someone who may have seen or heard that the claimant's supervisor or some other manager really did not believe that women should be on these assembly lines, and for those reasons took action to get this particular claimant removed.

For a claimant's attorney to be able to collect sufficient evidence to prove facts such as these, he or she must often conduct a lengthy "fishing expedition." The term "fishing expedition" is generally used among lawyers in a negative way to describe the gathering of huge volumes of evidence from the opposing party in a lawsuit, in the hopes that after reviewing all of this data, some evidence will appear that will help to rebut the apparently plausible facts offered by the employer, and prove an otherwise unwinnable case.

Collecting and analyzing such a large volume of data, and perhaps interviewing a number of additional witnesses, or even hundreds of additional witnesses, are time consuming and expensive, with no assurances that the additional effort will create a more favorable outcome for the claimant. Further, each attempt to rebut reasons offered by the employer places the claimant's attorney in the uncomfortable position of having to attempt to "prove a negative" fact, which is a most difficult task even with evidence that is not vague.

There is real risk involved in this third-stage activity on behalf of the claimant. The claimant's attorney may spend hundreds of hours of time collecting and analyzing data and interviewing witnesses, and engage numerous very expensive experts to review all of this data. After all of this review and analysis, not only may the claimant's case not be proven, but also it may be clear that what the employer said is correct, or at least not palpably false.

Current Trends in Case Law and Discrimination

Since the 1973 decision in *McDonnell Douglas,* the United States Supreme Court has made it abundantly clear that actions taken by an employer "for a reason other than sex" are not actionable under any law connected with sex discrimination.

In the Supreme Court case of *Texas Department of Community Affairs v. Burdine* (1981), the evidence showed that the claimant was one of a number of qualified applicants who applied for promotion to a supervisory position with the Department of Community Affairs. She was not selected for the position and a male with qualifications similar to hers was selected. The evidence further showed that the Department of Community affairs had never in its history promoted a female to a position at this level of management. The claimant argued that given the past history of the department they should have selected her for the promotion, as her qualifications were equal to those of the male who was selected.

The court enunciated a principle of law that where two or more similarly qualified persons have applied for a position, the employer may in its discretion select either a male or a female from among those candidates without violating the law. The only exceptions are where the claimant is able to prove that the selecting officials deliberately and intentionally refused to select her because of her sex, or where there was in place a court-ordered affirmative action plan that required the promotion of a certain number of females in preference to male candidates. Neither of the exceptions was present in this case, so the trial court was directed to enter a verdict in favor of the employer.

In the case of *St. Mary's Honor Center et al. v. Hicks* (1993), the Supreme Court enunciated yet another principle of law. The Court said that it was merely clarifying the order of proof established in the *McDonnell Douglas* case. Most legal commentators, though, see the *St. Mary's* case as adding an additional and quite difficult step to establishing the proof required of a claimant.

As noted above, the first part of a female claimant's case is to establish a prima facie case of discrimination by proving (1) that she is female, (2) that she was qualified for the position of shift commander, (3) that she was demoted and ultimately discharged, and (4) that the position remained open and was ultimately filled by a male.

The *St. Mary's* case made it clear that when the respondent offers one or more plausible, legitimate, nondiscriminatory reasons for the actions that were taken, this offering completely wipes out the prima facie case that has been established by the claimant.

The new requirement that the Supreme Court added, or, to be entirely correct, reiterated with emphasis, is that at this point the claimant returns to square one, for the prima facie case is never thereafter resurrected. Further, the claimant must, in order to prevail, show *two* things: first, that the legitimate nondiscriminatory reasons offered by the defendant were not the true reasons for the action taken, and second, that the defendant in fact intended to discriminate based on sex when it took the action. The Court said that, "[A] reason cannot be proved to be 'a pretext for *discrimination*' unless it is shown *both* that the reason was false, *and* that discrimination was the real reason."

A claimant, the Court said, in addition to having to prove all of the earlier described elements of her case, retains at all times the burden of proof that she has been the victim of *intentional* discrimination. By focusing strongly on the element of intent, the Court in this case reminded parties that claims of sex discrimination in employment are even more difficult to prove than most people had believed.

Unless there are blatant statements indicating an intent to violate the law, or persuasive circumstantial evidence that the decision makers who carried out the alleged discriminatory act intended to take the negative action against the woman because of her sex, a claimant is required to demonstrate intent "by the totality of the circumstances."

There is an even more difficult burden of proof being placed on claimants by some federal appellate courts. The Fourth Circuit Court of Appeals, which handles appeals from federal district court cases in Maryland, West Virginia, Virginia, North Carolina, and South Carolina, is one such court. The case law in this circuit approves of a principle that has come to be known as "pretext plus."

The United States Supreme Court has not yet addressed the issue, but by refusing to accept for review at least two Fourth Circuit "pretext plus" cases, the Supreme Court has permitted the Fourth Circuit's apparently enhanced standard to remain in effect. Some federal courts in other parts of the country have also been tightening their standards of proof, but the Fourth Circuit has taken some of the boldest steps to date, as can be seen in the following examples.

In the case of *Hughes v. Bedsole* (1995), a female jailer, a shift supervisor, was discharged by a sheriff's department for two security violations at the jail, several weeks after she had complained to the sheriff about sex discrimination. The claimant showed that there were males who had committed worse violations than hers and had not been discharged. The employer agreed that some male employees had not been terminated for similar violations, but showed evidence that some men had been terminated for the same or less. The claimant argued that the proximity in time between the complaints and the discharge demonstrated the requisite intent to discriminate against the claimant and to retaliate against her for her complaints.

The Court found that the claimant had offered no evidence showing that the sheriff himself harbored any personal discriminatory animus toward the claimant. The case was dismissed. In this situation, the ability of a claimant to prove discrimination by demonstrating "the totality of the circumstances" appears to have been weakened considerably.

In the case of *Jiminez v. Mary Washington College* (1995), a professor was denied tenure, and alleged that the denial was discriminatory. After a trial, the district court decided in favor of the professor. On appeal, the Fourth Circuit Court of Appeals reversed the trial court's decision. The primary reason for the reversal was that the claimant had not been able to prove by admissible evidence that the employer's conduct constituted "invidious discrimination."

The Court in its decision did not define how it was using the word "invidious." The dictionary definition of invidious is "calculated to create ill will or resentment or give offense" (Random House, 1987). The word "invidious" is normally used in a context that goes beyond an intention to do the unlawful act that has been alleged.

Significance of Trends and Predictions for the Future

It is unlikely that the Court meant to take things as far as these interpretations seem to indicate, but the language of these decisions appears to leave the door wide open for district court judges to apply their personal opinions and prejudices when making decisions in discrimination cases. When decisions are based more on the personality of the individual judge than on an abstract set of legal principles, abuses can occur that may violate both the spirit and the intent of the discrimination laws and the promise in our Constitution of a rule of law rather than a rule based on the personal whims of individuals.

It is thus easy to see how at the millennium and for the foreseeable future, it is extremely difficult for a claimant to prove in court, by way of a trial on the merits followed by a written opinion by the court, that an employer has violated the federal laws against discrimination. Therefore inventive claimant attorneys have looked at new ways to handle these cases, and new ways to bring lawsuits against companies on behalf of women who believe that they have been discriminated against because of their sex.

THE DEVELOPMENT OF POWERFUL NEW LEGAL TOOLS

Negotiation, Mediation, and Arbitration

Negotiation, mediation, and arbitration have moved to the forefront with blistering speed in the last few years as methods to resolve sex discrimination cases.

These tools are available to both claimants and employers. These methods of resolution are providing results not even dreamed of just a few years ago.

From the passage of the modern civil rights laws until the early 1990s, it was considered absolutely foolish for either an employer or a claimant to negotiate, mediate, or arbitrate a claim. To a large extent this notion was correct at that time.

For a company to negotiate or otherwise seek an undramatic voluntary resolution of a discrimination claim was considered to be a serious sign of weakness. The common belief was that if a company showed a willingness to negotiate with its employees on some issues, it was issuing an engraved invitation to employees to try to bring in or strengthen a labor union. Then the company might be saddled with having to negotiate with their employees on all of the terms of employment, including wages and benefits and working conditions.

Additionally, employers had found from experience that the best results were obtained if they resisted all claims and refused to provide information of any kind to a claimant or to a government agency such as the EEOC. When this practice was followed consistently, up to 80 percent of all discrimination claims initiated against an employer would disappear or be dismissed, due to a lack of resolve or lack of resources on the part of the claimant or the enforcing agencies.

For claimants, the prevailing view was that negotiation rarely produced any significant financial remuneration for claimants, and almost never produced any lasting change in corporate employment practices. It was also believed that most mediators and arbitrators were inherently biased against claimants. In the view of many claimants' attorneys, only a show of massive force resolve, usually by filing a federal lawsuit and insisting on a full trial before a federal district judge, would ever cause an employer to change its employment practices in the fundamental ways that were deemed necessary to eliminate entrenched discrimination.

It has only been since the mid-1990s that these early hardened attitudes have begun to shift into a more cooperative approach. Why did this shift occur?

First, protracted litigation has become more expensive for both sides. The cost of legal representation has increased substantially. There are also collateral costs, such as the sometimes permanent animosities that can attend a hard-boiled litigation approach.

Second, employers who engage in protracted discrimination litigation, or who consistently resist all efforts at compromise, can now find themselves with a great deal of negative publicity. Public opinion has drastically changed since the 1960s. Even in the 1970s a company that "stood its ground" and "refused to give in to the rabble-rousers" was considered to be the embodiment of virtue. At the millennium, a company's stock value can drop several points in a single day if it announces that a discrimination suit against it has been filed.

Most members of the public today find it at least unsettling when a company is branded with the stigma of being involved in discrimination litigation, even if the private views of these same people on the issues have changed very little. Companies are also finding that litigation based on resistance to claims of sex discrimination can generate so much negative publicity that it can seriously undermine the value of the millions they are spending to generate a positive company image through advertising.

Third, with the rise of the Internet, disgruntled employees of all kinds can use such charges and litigation as a hook on which to hang their own resentments, and broadcast their negative views of a company worldwide in a day.

Claimants are finding that meeting privately with employer representatives can and often will result in a solution to the stated problems. By handling the matter privately, the claimant can come across within the company as a team player, and can avoid being seen publicly as a malcontent. Further, the claimant can avoid waiting often for 1 or 2 years for the federal government to act on a charge of discrimination, or waiting for 4 or more years for a lawsuit to make its way through the courts.

Arbitration and mediation have become available as formal methods of resolving sex discrimination cases only recently, as courts and federal agencies have begun to recognize the legitimacy of outcomes achieved using these processes.

In many situations an employer can now invoke a mandatory arbitration procedure, which is usually put into place as a part of the agreement by an employee to be hired or promoted. Also, even without a mandatory arbitration clause, both parties can agree to submit the dispute to binding arbitration.

Arbitration is a process whereby each side presents evidence and arguments, and a neutral arbitrator makes a formal decision on the merits of the case. The arbitrator's opinion is usually binding on all parties and cannot be appealed or otherwise challenged for any but the most compelling reasons.

Mediation is a process whereby a trained neutral meets with the parties, using rules and standards established in advance, and acts as a catalyst to get sometimes contentious parties to talk about what happened and how the claim can be resolved. The mediator will then work with the parties to write up an agreement reciting the terms of the settlement. Once it is formally agreed upon and signed, the agreement is binding on all parties.

The crucial distinction between arbitration and mediation is that a mediator does not usually make findings of fact or decide the issues, and the matter is resolved in mediation only if all parties agree upon a resolution.

Both of these processes are tremendously effective in resolving even extremely thorny disputes. Employers like the processes because they are usually undertaken in private and because the employee has an opportunity to speak her mind without generating any sense that the employer is "giving in" to employee demands— which is that vile precursor to "inviting in a union." Further, the process is inexpensive and can frequently improve the overall morale in the workplace.

Employees like these processes because they are quick and efficient, and do not seem to create as much ill will as a protracted fight within a government agency or before the courts. Further, employees are finding that the historical "biases against employees" of arbitrators and mediators are simply no longer present. The culture has shifted.

The Equal Employment Opportunity Commission historically has used *conciliation* as a means of resolving charges filed with the agency. This process did not have a great deal of success because it was done without much vigor and only because it was a part of the statutorily mandated process. Additionally, the conciliator was an agency employee, who was almost always intensely biased in favor of the claimant and against the employer. The normal procedure would be for the conciliator to make a series of nonnegotiable demands to the employer. Discussion of the facts was, by regulation, not even permitted.

This conciliation process still persists inside EEOC, although this agency as well as many state and local discrimination agencies have in recent years begun to offer mediation as a formal option. The government agency will act as a coordinator to set up the mediation with a neutral mediator if both parties agree on using the process. More and more claims of discrimination will be resolved using these processes, and in many other ways involving the use of private mediators and arbitrators.

Intentional Infliction of Emotional Distress

The tort of intentional infliction of emotional distress is increasingly being used by claimants to leverage upward the dollars that can be recovered in sex discrimination cases. Most state laws permit such "common law tort" claims to be made. They can be added to a federal lawsuit, or be tried in the state courts before a jury. The case law of North Carolina, a state where the courts have tended to be conservative in dealing with employment-related issues, is used as an example in the discussion of state laws that follows. Each state has a different approach, but the general outline given here is followed in principle, if not in the details, by the laws and courts of most states.

The elements that must be proven in order to recover damages under the tort of intentional infliction of emotional distress are (1) extreme and outrageous conduct, (2) which is intended to cause and does cause (3) severe emotional distress (*Stanback v. Stanback,* 1979; *Dickens v. Puryear,* 1981).

Money damages may be collected for emotional distress as well as for any other bodily harm resulting from the actions. The burden of proof is on the claimant to produce admissible evidence of the emotional distress and the resulting harm. Frequently, though, the courts have allowed an inference to be drawn that the claimant suffered emotional distress, where evidence is introduced that the alleged conduct was extreme and outrageous in nature.

In almost every case, though, the courts request that the claimant produce an expert evaluation by a psychologist or a psychiatrist concerning the degree and intensity of the claimant's mental distress. In the absence of such expert testimony, a jury may not be able to justify awarding more than nominal damages. Employers will now usually hire a psychologist or a psychiatrist to testify for the defense, in an effort to demonstrate that the claimant was not emotionally damaged or was only minimally damaged. Punitive damages, those intended to punish the defendant, may be awarded *in any amount* by a jury once the elements of the intentional infliction of emotional distress have been established.

The use of this type of legal action was virtually unheard of in North Carolina in the employment context before about 1985. It was assumed that the worker's compensation laws, which place statutory limitations on the dollar amount of damages due to an employee for injuries that occur in the workplace, were the exclusive remedy under North Carolina law for physical and emotional injuries that were job-related. It was also assumed by claimant's attorneys in the early years of the civil rights laws that bringing claims to federal courts was the only way to achieve justice. State court judges and juries were presumed to be highly prejudiced against claimants. The problem for claimants with this approach was that in most cases the federal courts could award only actual back pay and attorney's fees, and no other forms of compensation for a proven injury.

The North Carolina Supreme Court case of *Hogan v. Forsyth Country Club Co.* (1986), clearly opened the door for a claimant to bring a tort claim in the state courts for the intentional infliction of mental distress, independently from any limitations prescribed by the worker's compensation laws.

The *Hogan* case involved allegations of sexual harassment, and the Court in that case said that sexual harassment is always intentional and always causes great emotional distress, and that money damages in any amount that the jury feels is right may be awarded once the claimant has proven harassment alone, without the necessity of demonstrating the degree or intensity of mental distress suffered by a claimant.

The court noted that money damages in such cases are to be levied only as a personal judgment against the individual who did the harassing, unless the claimant can prove that one or more management employees of the employer had notice of the offending behavior and did not take reasonable actions to stop it. This limitation is significant. Normally individual employees of a company do not have sufficient personal assets to be able to pay large verdicts. Corporations, on the other hand, have "deep pockets" and usually have the means to pay a verdict. The lesson here is that a woman who is being harassed or otherwise discriminated against should make sure that she reports the problem to management and gives them an opportunity to correct the problem, unless one or more of the people who took the actions is a manager, or she is sure that one or more managers already knew what happened and did not take action.

It should be noted in this context that the distinction between a judgment against an individual and a judgment against a corporation is virtually nonexistent in cases tried under the federal laws. Almost all judgments under the federal laws hold the company fully liable for all damages.

The *Hogan* case resulted in a jury verdict of $900,000, which consisted of $150,000 in compensatory damages (for her pain and suffering) and $750,000 in punitive damages (to punish the company). It is easy to see that juries at this time in history can be swayed by emotional arguments in situations involving employment torts, in the same way that "runaway juries" go overboard in other areas of the law. Jurors should in theory always look at the facts and render their verdict impartially based on the facts and the law. Attorneys representing claimants can, though, and frequently do, exploit the personal sentiments of jurors. Here is the jury's opportunity, it is implied, to let all of the bad bosses of the world know just how mad they are at them! They've been waiting most of their lives for just this moment to stick it to a big company! Unfortunately, provoking those sentiments can frequently lead to inflated dollar awards by juries. And such inflated awards usually lead to appeals being pursued by companies, which further delays reasonable payments to claimants, who may be deserving of some amount of damages.

There are numerous other cases in North Carolina in recent years where substantial monetary damages have been obtained for sex discrimination claimants using North Carolina's intentional infliction of mental distress laws. The case of *Moore v. Kroger, Inc. and Hutton* (Guilford County, NC) resulted in a $300,000 settlement before the jury verdict was returned. The jurors were interviewed, and two of the jurors said that they would have returned a verdict of $7,000,000. The case of *Sargent v. Prestonwood and Murray Savings* (Wake County, NC) resulted in a jury verdict of $3,850,000, of which $3,250,000 was designated by the jury as punitive damages. The case of *Brown v. Burlington Industries, Inc.,* (Rockingham County, NC) resulted in a jury verdict of $60,000, which the jury broke down as $10,000 compensatory and $50,000 punitive damages.

By 1992 the North Carolina Supreme Court, in the case of *Waddle v. Sparks* (1992) apparently had seen enough of the big dollar verdicts based on speculation by juries, emotional arguments by claimant's attorneys, or on a jury's anger at the company for what had been done. The court held that in future cases, a precondition for the recovery of significant money damages is clinical evidence that the claimant was actually treated for the symptoms of emotional distress, that such manifestations have been diagnosed, and that the clinician or other experts are satisfied that the cause of the claimant's emotional distress was the defendant's conduct. This development makes the involvement of a psychologist or a psychiatrist almost mandatory for both the claimant and the employer.

There are also times when a claimant has not filed a charge with the EEOC within 6 months, or 240 days in some situations, of the date of the alleged discriminatory act. By missing this deadline she will have lost her right to claim sex discrimination in the federal courts. Such a claimant may in an appropriate situation file a lawsuit in state courts using the tort of intentional infliction of emotional stress or other state laws as a basis for the claim. State statutes of limitations for such claims are typically either 2 or 3 years from the date of the alleged discriminatory act. There are also situations in which the state courts may be used when there is no federal jurisdiction, such as a claim of sex discrimination against an employer who has fewer than 15 employees, or where the claimant is an independent contractor rather than an employee.

Negligent Retention and Negligent Hiring

Under the common law of North Carolina, and of most other states, an employer under certain circumstances may be held liable for monetary damages using the tort of "negligent hiring" or the "negligent retention" of one of its managers, or even one of its nonmanagement employees. This state law liability can attach in some cases even if the manager or the nonmanagement employee was acting outside the scope of his or her employment.

The tort of negligent hiring arises when there is evidence that the employer hired a person when the employer knew or should have known that the person had in the past committed injurious or discriminatory acts against subordinates or coworkers, and the person was hired anyway, and the company did not make sufficient efforts to monitor the known behavior patterns of the individual.

The tort of negligent retention arises when an employer becomes aware of current or past behavior by an employee that is or has been injurious or discriminatory to subordinates or coworkers, and fails or neglects to remove the person from his or her position or adequately monitor the newly discovered behavior patterns. Where the injurious or discriminatory behavior is attributed to a management employee, liability attaches as soon as sufficient behavior occurs for a reasonable person to become aware that there is a problem. For behavior by a nonmanagement employee, liability attaches only if the evidence shows that management became or was made aware of the employee's propensity to do harm, and failed to act within a reasonable time or in a reasonable manner to stop further harm from occurring.

Deliberate or intentional actions of hiring or retaining a problem employee are also included in this tort, and references to "negligence" should also be read to include intentional acts. As an example of an intentional act that is not negligent in any way, a company that is desperate to improve its declining market share may hire a man in order to take advantage of his unique promotional skills or technical talents, even though they know that he has a history of a complete inability to work with female subordinates, or a history of sexually harassing female employees.

Here again, as a common law state tort claim, the injured employee may recover not only the equitable damages of lost wages, but also compensatory damages such as actual out-of-pocket losses, in addition to an unlimited dollar amount of damages for pain and suffering and punitive damages. State court claims using this tort action are more likely than some other types of state law claims to allow the claimant to seek an award of money damages against the company, the one with the "deep pockets."

In the earlier discussed state court case of *Hogan v. Forsyth Country Club Co.* (1986), there was also a claim of negligent retention. The Court found that the employer could be held liable for the negligent retention of a chef who had sexually harassed a waitress, where the waitress alleged that she had repeatedly complained to the employer's general manager, who did nothing to protect her and continued to employ the chef in a position where the harassment could and did continue.

In the North Carolina state court case of *Medlin v. Bass* (1990), a school principal, who had been fired from a previous position for sexually abusing school children, was hired by the defendant school board. While employed in this new job, he sexually abused a student. The Court found that the defendant school board had checked the principal's references and no mention had been made of the man's proclivities. The board had made a reasonable inquiry and had uncovered no reason to suspect this principal of having a tendency to sexually abuse children. Therefore, although the defendant school principal was personally liable for his own acts, the defendant school board was not liable. The trial court's grant of summary judgment dismissing the action as to the school board was upheld as proper.

Thus, the case law thus appears to impose a duty upon employers to make a reasonable inquiry into the background of prospective employees. The burden thus imposed is not a great burden of in-depth investigation, but only a burden of conducting a reasonable inquiry.

The Tort of Wrongful Discharge

The North Carolina state courts in 1985, in the case of *Sides v. Duke University* (1985), for the first time created a very limited right for a claimant to bring an action for money damages against an employer for the tort of wrongful discharge, if the employee is discharged in violation of a clear public policy. In the *Sides* case a nurse-anesthetist gave truthful testimony in a medical malpractice lawsuit, after being ordered to keep silent about what she had observed in surgery. At least in part as a result of the claimant's testimony, a jury returned a medical malpractice verdict against the hospital for $1.75 million.

The claimant was discharged 3 weeks after the verdict. The court said that it knew of no precedent in North Carolina legal history for such an employment-related suit, but felt that it had no choice but to grant this individual a right to sue for substantial damages due to the outrageous nature of what had occurred. No general principles were announced.

It was not until the case of *Coman v. Thomas Manufacturing Co., Inc.* (1989) that the North Carolina Supreme Court relented and, not without controversy, joined a majority of the states in formally creating a clear cause of action for the tort of wrongful discharge based on violation of public policy.

The claimant, Mark Coman, was a long-distance truck driver. He alleged that he had been told by his employer to violate the federal mandatory rest regulations, and to falsify his logs to cover up the violations if he wanted to keep his job. Coman refused to do so and was discharged.

The Court made a general finding that claimants in situations such as that experienced by Mark Coman may bring an action in court using the tort of wrongful discharge and may recover money damages if the facts support the claim and the public policy violation is sufficiently clear.

In the later case of *Amos v. Oakdale Knitting Co.* (1992), the North Carolina Supreme Court made it clear that a state wrongful discharge claim can be brought along with and in addition to any other federal or state statutory or common law claim, including a sex discrimination claim, if the facts support the action.

CONCLUSION

There are two lessons to be learned from what has been covered in this chapter. The first lesson is that companies are for the most part making extraordinary efforts to eliminate the worst aspects of sex discrimination in their organizations. These efforts are in part responsible for the current lack of easy victories in the courts for those who are claiming that they have been discriminated against because of their sex.

The courts and the enforcement agencies, though, have in fact made the proof of cases more difficult for claimants, and have eliminated much mandatory affirmative action. At the turn of the new millennium, it is and will be quite difficult for a claimant to win a sex discrimination lawsuit in court, as has been amply demonstrated in this chapter.

For many years claimants were able to win sex discrimination cases with ease. The evidence of discrimination was often more clear-cut and unambiguous, usually because the employer was actively making efforts to exclude women, or to hire women only into certain jobs.

Many cases are harder to prove now because the evidence often does not show that there was discrimination. If the evidence is there, a competent lawyer should be able to find that evidence. If the evidence is not there, a competent lawyer should at some point concede that there is no evidence. Although it is easy to say that employers are getting better at concealing evidence, it is sometimes more difficult to concede that some employers are getting better in the ways they treat their female employees. Not perfectly, by any means—just "better."

The second lesson is that a woman who believes that she has been discriminated against because of her sex, and her attorney, need to expand their thinking to examine whether there are other routes to victory in addition to "filing a charge" with the EEOC. There are multiple avenues open to a potential claimant, some under federal law and others under state law.

If the woman was in fact discriminated against in her employment, some of these other legal theories can bring a much larger financial recompense for the harm than can be obtained in a classic federal discrimination lawsuit under Title VII and the other federal statutes. In addition, many women are in jobs or seeking jobs that are not covered by the federal statutes, such as independent contractor sales agents, and jobs in companies that have fewer than 15 employees.

Claimants and their attorneys need also to be aware that there are methods of alternative dispute resolution, such as negotiation, mediation, and arbitration that are available for use in appropriate situations, and that employers are much more willing to use these methods now than they were even 5 or 10 years ago.

What is motivating all this compliance activity, when everyone agrees that it is more difficult now than ever before for a claimant to prevail in court? First, the managers of more companies desire to comply with the laws. Second, sometimes huge amounts of money have been awarded by judges and juries when claimant attorneys have persuasively combined several legal theories into a single claim. Third, public opinion has swung so far in favor of equality of treatment between the sexes that a company that is perceived as resistant can find itself under attack in the press and in the communities where their offices are located. They can find that their customer base erodes as those who do not like their resistance to the laws go elsewhere to do business, thus reducing their profits and market share. And that, after all, is the bottom line.

REFERENCES

Age Discrimination in Employment Act of 1967, as amended, 29 USC 621 et seq.

Americans With Disabilities Act, 42 USC 12101 et seq.

Amos v. Oakdale Knitting Co. (1992). 331 NC 348, 416 SE 2d 166.

Coman v. Thomas Manufacturing Co., Inc. (1989). 325 NC 172, 381 SE 2d 445.

Equal Pay Act of 1963. (1963). 29 USC 206(d).

Hogan v. Forsyth Country Club Co. (1986). 79 NC App 483, 340 SE 2d 116; *cert. denied,* 317 NC 334, 346 SE 2d 140 (1986).

Hughes v. Bedsole. (1995). 48 F3d 1376 (4th Cir 1995); *cert. denied,* October 2, 1995, 64 USLW 3239.

Jiminez v. Mary Washington College (1995). 57 F3d 369 (4th Cir 1995); *cert. denied,* October 31, 1995, 64 USLW 3316.

McDonnell Douglas v. Green (1973). 411 US 792, 93 SCt 1817, 36 LEd 2d 668.

McGee, M. H. (1991). Unpublished manuscript.

Medlin v. Bass (1990). 327 NC 587.

Moore v. Krager, Inc. and Hutton. (Guilford County, NC, circa 1990). Unpublished but well-publicized trial court verdict, from author's notes.

Random House. (1987). *The Random House Dictionary of the English Language* (2nd ed., unabridged). New York: Random House.

Sides v. Duke University (1985). 74 NC App 331, 328 SE 2d 818; *cert. denied,* 314 NC 331, 333 SE 2d 490. See also Datesman, S. K., *Sides v. Duke Hospital: A Public Policy Exception to the Employment-at-will rule,* 64 NC Law Rev 840 (1986).

Stanback v. Stanback. (1979). 297 NC 181, 254 SE 2d 611. See also *Dickens v. Puryear,* 302 NC 437, 76 SE 2d 325 (1981).

St. Mary's Honor Center et al. v. Hicks (1993). 509 US 502, 113 SCt 2742, 125 LEd 2d 407.

Texas Department of Community Affairs v. Burdine. (1981). 450 US 248, 101 SCt 1089, 67
    LEd 2d 207.
Title VII of the Civil Rights Act of 1964. (1964). As amended, 42 U.S.C. 2000e *et seq.*
Waddle v. Sparks (1992). 331 NC 73, 414 SE 2d 22.
Ward's Cove Packing Co. v. Atonio (1989). 490 US 642.

16

PERSONAL RELATIONSHIPS AND THE RIGHT TO PRIVACY

Terry Morehead Dworkin

INTRODUCTION

During the 1990s, several incidents involving employer interference with employee associations off the job have gained national attention. The affair of two Wal-Mart employees became national news after they successfully challenged their firing by Wal-Mart because their dating relationship was not consistent with Wal-Mart's "strongly [held] belief [in] and support [of] the 'family unit'" (*New York v. Wal-Mart Stores, Inc.,* 1995, p. 144). The threatened court-martial of Navy pilot Kelly Flinn for adultery likewise captured the headlines (Ricks, 1997). The public interest was not in the relationship itself, but in the fact that employers would interfere in this manner. Even the public disinterest in the impeachment of President Clinton indicated a belief in the right to protect the privacy of certain kinds of activities that do not harm job performance.

Privacy has been an important value in American society since its formation. This value along with freedom of association are recognized and protected in the Constitution. Constitutional recognition of these values, however, only protects the citizen against governmental interference. Protection in the private sector has often lagged behind protection in the public sector. This is especially true in the area of employment (Reibstein, 1988).

Interference with one's associations is considered a special affront to one's identity, dignity, and independence. Such actions interfere with rights that individuals consider important; they often feel especially aggrieved when the actions are taken by an employer. Work life is increasingly intertwined with private life.

Employees spend long hours in the workplace. It is not unusual for an employee's main social contacts to occur in the workplace, and dating between workers is common (Jackson, 1999). Emotional ties develop. The employer, who generally has superior power in the employment relationship, is seen by the employee as especially abusive when it uses that power to interfere with associational privacy (*Rulon-Miller v. IBM*, 1984). This increases the anger and psychological trauma that can accompany interference with personal relationships from any source. Emotions are again heightened when the interference occurs with off-the-job activity, which employees usually consider to be none of the employer's business. Although the employees may feel especially aggrieved, the law does not necessarily protect or compensate for these feelings.

HISTORY

Employer ability to interfere with employee associational rights is largely a result of a legal doctrine called *employment at will,* which applies to most workers (employment at will is discussed in Chapter 15). This judicial invention deprived employees of protection from being fired for any reason—even a bad reason (Mallor, 1986). One result was that employers were free to interfere with employees' private lives. A classic example of this is Henry Ford's control over his workers.

Ford established a "sociological department," which had over 100 investigators to monitor employees' off-the-job activities, often coming into their homes to determine compliance with company norms involving sexual habits, home cleanliness, appropriate leisure time activity, and drinking, among others (Linowes & Spencer, 1990). Being divorced was one of the things that could keep an applicant from getting a job. Because jobs at Ford were highly valued, such interference was tolerated.

Sensitivity to such employer behaviors today is quite different, but employer interference with off-the-job activities continues at a surprisingly high level. For example, employees have recently been fired for smoking off the job, drinking an alcoholic beverage, living with a partner outside of marriage, being gay, having a spouse of whom the employer does not approve, and marrying someone of the "wrong" religion (Dworkin, 1997). In the last example, a man was fired because he refused to divorce his wife. The employer, who disapproved of the wife because she was Catholic, won the lawsuit brought against it by the fired employee (*Frankel v. Warwick Hotel*, 1995), which illustrates the fact that obtaining damages for the emotional and other damages caused by such interference is far from easy.

When employees seek legal recourse for the emotional trauma resulting from interference with their associations, there is not a general theory under which they can sue. Employees are forced to stretch statutory enactments or ask courts to adapt precedent to acknowledge the real damages they have suffered. Even if successful, the recovery of damages for their emotional trauma is often severely limited.

RECOVERY FOR PSYCHOLOGICAL HARM
UNDER STATUTORY THEORIES

Harassment

Employer interference with employee relationships is most easily justified under the harassment laws (sexual harassment is discussed in Chapters 5, 6, and 7). In order to prevent sexual harassment (a form of sex discrimination prohibited under Title VII of the Civil Rights Act of 1964) and to protect themselves from liability for it, employers are usually allowed to prohibit supervisors from dating or having relationships with persons they supervise (Markels, 1995; *Watkins v. UPS*, 1993). Additionally, company rules can prohibit unwanted, repeated attempts to date or have a relationship with a coemployee. However, employer interference with associational relationships often occurs in situations that have nothing to do with sexual harassment. They most commonly involve harassment because the employer does not approve of the employee's moral choices. Even though the rationale for employer interference is absent, employees are struggling to protect their rights to associational privacy in this context.

The case of *Meltebeke v. Bureau of Labor & Industries* is illustrative. The employee in this case was a 20-year-old, learning disabled painter who worked in a one-on-one relationship with Meltebeke, his employer. Meltebeke was an evangelical Christian who tried to dissuade his employee from his "life of sin." Meltebeke repeatedly told the employee he was going to hell because he lived with his girlfriend, and repeated the message to the employee's girlfriend and mother. These, and other attempts to convert him, made the employee feel embarrassed, uncomfortable, humiliated, "bugged," and reluctant to go to work (*Meltebeke*, p. 253). However, the employee felt he could not complain or ask the employer to stop because he feared for his job. Meltebeke fired him after one month, and the employee sued for religious harassment.

The first tribunal to hear the case found that the employer had created an intimidating and offensive working environment and awarded the employee damages; but the Oregon court of appeals and the Oregon Supreme Court denied him recovery. One of the two court of appeals judges who found in the employer's favor thought the employee was not entitled to protection because he was not demonstrably religious, and thus, Meltebeke's comments were about the employee's way of life. A way of life, the judge held, is not entitled to protection when based on secular considerations. The Oregon Supreme Court found that the employer was not liable if he did not know his actions were harassing. If this had been a sexual harassment case, the employee would almost certainly have recovered for his emotional harm (Dworkin, 1993).

If the employee had sued in federal court, he might have been more successful (*Turner v. Barr*, 1993; *E.E.O.C. v. Townley Engineering & Manufacturing Co.*, 1988). The federal courts, including the Supreme Court, as well as the Equal Employment Opportunity Commission (EEOC), have equated protection from discrimination on the basis of race, religion, sex, and national origin. The equality of protection has become a political issue, though, and the strength of protection from harassment often varies with the category, and the court that is hearing the case (Dworkin & Peirce, 1995). The uncertainty of successful recovery is compounded when the venue is a state court. State protection for associational privacy and the ability to recover for the emotional harms caused by interference varies greatly from state to state. California, which protects private employees' privacy rights under its constitution, is one of the most protective; the Southern states are some of the least protective.

If an employee can successfully sue for harassment due to interference with personal relationships, remedies under Title VII are still more limited than under the common law. Before the passage of the Civil Rights Act of 1991, recovery for the emotional harms caused by employer interference was generally unavailable. Relief was typically limited to regaining a lost job, lost wages and benefits, and attorney fees. This meant that for harassing environment cases, such as that in *Meltebeke*, where the injury is almost always psychological, there was no remedy other than an injunction. With the passage of the Civil Rights Act of 1991, damages, including punitive damages, became available in intentional discrimination cases. Plaintiffs who can prove psychological harm resulting from intentional employer harassment through interference with personal relationships can now collect for that harm. However, the remedies are still less than those available under common law theories, for Congress capped damages according to the size of the employer.

In response to the nonavailability of adequate damages, employees started suing under tort theories for their harassment. The most common theories relied on were intentional or negligent infliction of emotional distress, assault, battery, and invasion of privacy (Dworkin, Mallor, & Ginger, 1988). Proof of any of these would allow recovery of damages for emotional injuries, as well as punitive damages in egregious cases. Many courts were open to the use of tort theories in harassment cases in order to allow meaningful recovery and to have an effective disincentive against harassment in the workplace. Today, it is quite common for an employee to sue for harassment under both the common law and Title VII.

In order to counter the awarding of damages for the emotional distress caused by harassment, and to discourage the bringing of claims for such injuries, many employers began to investigate the past psychological history of the suing employees in minute detail ("Eggshell Skull," 1998). A recent decision by the Eighth Circuit Court of Appeals shows the court's desire to curb such tactics as well as its general acceptance of the psychological harm that results from harassment. In *Jenson v. Eleveth Taconite Co.*, a special master was appointed to assess damages in a class action suit for harassment and sex discrimination, including damages for past and future mental anguish. The special master found that mental anguish includes mental suffering caused by painful emotions such as indignation, wounded pride, shame, public humiliation, and despair. The Eighth Circuit found it could also include impairment to living a normal life. It held that the master's award of damages was "inadequate" for the "egregious" harassment and resultant mental suffering that occurred. It also found that much of the discovery about incidents such as domestic abuse, personal relationships, abortions, and childhood experiences were not relevant or were so remote in time that it should not have been allowed. This decision should make it easier for plaintiffs to pursue remedies for the emotional trauma caused by harassment without themselves becoming victims of harassing tactics.

Marital Discrimination Statutes

The great disparity in protection against employer interference with association privacy is illustrated by the various state interpretations of state statutes protecting employees against marital status discrimination. However, it is fair to say that the further an employee's relationship veers from a traditional marriage, the less likely the employee is to win a suit against the employer for the emotional harm caused by the employer's interference. A majority of states have adopted marital discrimination statutes (Humphress, 1992–93), but only a minority of those states interpret the statutes broadly enough to encompass nontraditional relationships.

Some courts limit statutory protection to the literal language of the statute and have upheld the firing of an employee because he is unmarried and living with a person of the opposite sex (*State ex rel. McClure v. Sports & Health Club*, 1985), is homosexual and living with a person of the same sex, is married to a coworker (*McCluskey v. Clarke Oil Refining Co.*, 1986), is married and having an affair (*Slohoda v. United Parcel Service*, 1984), or is unmarried and having an affair with a married person. The case of *Federated Rural Electric Insurance Company v. Kessler* (1986) is illustrative. In *Federated*, the employee was denied protection under the marital discrimination law because it was found not to protect his right to have an affair. The judge stated, "A person who has voluntarily made a decision to become married . . . can be compelled to honor the commitment of that decision while he remains married" (*Federated*, 1986, p. 562). Other states have given a more liberal interpretation to their statutes.

In *Waggoner v. Ace Hardware* (1996), for example, the court found that the purpose of the statute was to protect employees from unnecessary intrusion into their private affairs such as sexual relationships and living arrangements. Other courts have protected employees who were fired or not hired because they were cohabiting with people of the opposite sex to whom they were not married, or refused to marry a girlfriend or have her move out of his trailer. However, even in these cases where the employee was successful, recovery for the emotional harm caused by the interference is limited because the statutes generally limit recovery to lost wages and benefits and similar equitable relief.

Lifestyle Protection Statutes

There is also great variance in state protection for off-the-job privacy under recently passed statutes specifically designed to acknowledge this important right.

The initial impetus for the passage of the statutes was lobbying by the tobacco companies who were trying to avert employer discrimination against smokers (Geyelin, 1989; Woo, 1993). They wanted to counter a growing trend among employers to fire or to refuse to hire people who were smokers because such employees increased health care costs, increased liability exposure for second-hand smoke, were at increased risk for disease due to the synergistic effects of smoking and exposure to products in some workplaces, and increased time missed from work (Garfinkle, 1984; Rothstein, 1987; Sculco, 1991). One company went so far as to ask employees (or visitors) who smelled of smoke to go outside, and the employees faced discipline (Policy keeps smell, 1997). Obviously, such a policy even limits where an employee can go for lunch or who an employee can socialize with off-premises.

Soon after the first statutes were passed in 1989, a majority of states had enacted laws protecting the right to smoke off the job or the right to use legal products off the job without suffering discrimination (Dworkin, 1997). Three states—Colorado, New York, and North Dakota—went further and passed statutes protecting the right to participate in a variety of legal activities during nonwork times. In addition, some municipalities and counties, including San Francisco, passed similar protections. The wide appeal of these statutes reflects the heightened concern about and emotional distress of employees when employers interfere with off-the-job activities. As stated above, such interference is considered a special affront to one's identity, dignity, and independence. Even though smoking was increasingly seen as a socially taboo activity, the employer was seen as not having the right to dictate the proper use of one's free time. As the sponsor of New York's legislation stated,

[S]hould an employer have a right to forbid a person from engaging in a legal activity, such as wearing a button for a particular candidate, simply because the employer does not agree with those political sentiments? . . . We have long since passed the days of company towns, where the company told you when to work, where to live, and what to buy in their stores. This bill will ensure that employers do not tell us how to think and play on our own time (Lack, 1992).

Several courts have interpreted the more expansive statutes of New York, North Dakota, and Colorado to broadly protect privacy including associational privacy. In one of the most important cases, the court found that an employee's right to cohabit with whomever one wishes is protected activity and the employer cannot interfere "simply because the employer does not like the activities an employee engages in after work" (*Pasch v. Katz Media Corp.*, 1995, p. 1578). The New York statute does not specifically protect associational privacy, but does protect "an individual's legal recreational activities outside work hours, off of the employer's premises and without use of the employer's equipment or other property" (*New York Labor Law,* 1994). The court, after examining the legislative history, found that the statute "evidence[d] an intent to include cohabitation as a recreational activity" (*Pasch v. Katz Media Corp.*, 1995, p. 1578).

A different court, interpreting the same statute, found that dating was entirely distinct from and bore little resemblance to recreational activity and denied protection to the dating employees from Wal-Mart mentioned at the beginning of this chapter. The court held that the *raison d'être* of dating was romance, either pursued or realized, and that the statute only protected people engaged in leisure activity if they lacked "amorous interest" (*New York v. Wal-Mart Stores, Inc.*, 1995, p. 152).

Obviously, the lifestyle statutes, like the marital discrimination statutes, can be interpreted broadly or narrowly as these cases illustrate. However, because the lifestyle statutes are targeted specifically to protect off-the-job privacy that does not negatively impact the employer, courts seem more willing to adopt expansive readings. The courts have even interpreted them to accord protection to homosexuals (*Borquez v. Ozer*, 1995; *Langseth v. County of Elbert*, 1996).

Although there is expanded protection under some of the statutes against interference with off-the-job associations, for most employees actual statutory relief will be limited or nonexistent. Two thirds of the statutes, including Colorado's and New York's, establish a statute of limitations of 6 months or 180 days within which a claim must be brought (Dworkin, 1997). This is not much time to recover from the trauma of being fired because one's employer did not approve of his or her relationship, work through to the anger of wanting to pursue a remedy, finding an expert who is sufficiently familiar with the law to know of the statutory remedy, and file suit. Additionally, economic resources are usually limited for people who have been recently fired. Even attorneys who are willing to take cases on a contingency basis will be reluctant to do so on the basis of theories that are stretching the law, and the plaintiff will initially have to pay costs. Assuming that these hurdles are overcome and the lawsuit is won, damages for the emotional distress suffered by the employee are generally unavailable. The legislatures are primarily concerned with the monetary losses associated with a job; the anger, frustration, hurt, humiliation, and other emotional harms suffered by the employee are not provided for in the typical statute. The inability to recover damages for emotional distress or punitive damages also make it less likely that lawyers will take a case on a contingency basis.

Statutory remedies for employer interference with an employee's associations are possible but unlikely without more liberal readings by the courts. In order to attain recovery for the psychological harms that usually result from such interference, legislative changes or enactments may be required.

RECOVERY FOR PSYCHOLOGICAL HARM
UNDER COMMON LAW THEORIES

The inability to recover for psychological harm and the full range of damages under most statutes make common law tort theories attractive. Unfortunately, although tort theories offer adequate compensation, courts have been slow to extend the tort theories to employee associational privacy. The torts most applicable to employer interference with employee associations are intentional or negligent infliction of emotional distress, invasion of privacy, and wrongful firing in violation of public policy.

Infliction of Emotional Distress

In theory, many of the cases where there has been a firing or other job action because the employer does not approve of the employee's associational choices nicely fit the requirements of a cause of action for intentional infliction of emotional distress. This theory requires that the defendant has done an outrageous act that led to severe emotional distress in a person of ordinary sensibilities (Barnes, Dworkin, & Richards, 1995). Most people would consider firing an outrageous act if it were done simply because the employer does not approve of who one socializes with, dates, or lives with when the relationship has no significant impact on the employer's business (Lack, 1992; *Rulon-Miller v. IBM*, 1984). Also, most people who incur such actions suffer significant mental anguish "caused by painful emotions such as indignation, wounded pride, shame, public humiliation, and despair," among others (*Jenson v. Eveleth Taconite Co.*, 1998, p. 1290).

Despite the theoretical convergence, success under this theory has so far been essentially nonexistent. The lack of success may be due to the lack of significant precedent using tort law to protect associational privacy in general, and the unwillingness of judges to classify something as "outrageous" when the behavior (such as employer control over employees' behavior) has traditionally been tolerated. As associational privacy cases become more common and successful, employee infliction of emotional distress cases will grow.

Invasion of Privacy

There is precedent for successful suits by employees utilizing an invasion of privacy theory, but a trend toward successful suits on this basis is slow in developing. The right to privacy is the right to be left alone (Craven, 1976; Gorley, 1992; Warren & Brandeis, 1890). It protects "our thoughts, our emotions, our expressions, our personalities, our freedom of communion and the freedom to associate with the people we choose" (*White v. Davis*, 1975, p. 223). Again, privacy appears to offer a theory that should easily accommodate unwarranted employer interference with associations.

The landmark employee privacy case is *Rulon-Miller v. IBM*. (1984). Rulon-Miller was called into her new supervisor's office and told that her long-term relationship presented a conflict of interest. The supervisor told her she would have a couple of days to decide whether to cut off the relationship or lose her job. The next day the supervisor told her he "had made up her mind for her," and constructively fired her (*Rulon-Miller*, 1984, p. 528). He took this action despite the fact that the company had known about the relationship for a long time and another of Rulon-Miller's supervisors had assured her he had no problem with the relationship when she was promoted to her current job. Rulon-Miller successfully sued IBM for both compensatory and punitive damages. The appellate court sustained the award of punitive damages because it found the company invaded her right to privacy in an outrageous manner.

To be denied a right granted to all other employees for conduct unrelated to her work was to degrade her as a person. [The supervisor's] unilateral action in purporting to remove any free choice on her part contrary to his earlier assurances also would support a conclusion that his conduct was intended to emphasize that she was powerless to do anything to assert her rights as an IBM employee. And such powerlessness is one of the most debilitating kinds of human oppression. (*Rulon-Miller*, 1984, pp. 534-535)

Despite this strong precedent, the plaintiff in the case mentioned at the beginning of this chapter who was fired for not divorcing his Catholic wife was unsuccessful in his invasion of privacy suit. The court in that case stated that the tort of privacy encompasses an intrusion into a person's "private affairs or concerns . . . that would be highly offensive to the reasonable person" (*Frankel v. Warwick Hotel*, 1995, pp. 187–188). However, it found that the intrusion had to be through a physical or sensory penetration of one's zone of privacy and did not include invasion by the employer of one's relationships.

These two cases well illustrate the divergence among courts in recognizing and protecting employee associational privacy rights. The latter case shows that many courts still are not willing to extend protection in this area even in cases involving conventional family values (Ewing, 1977; Linowes & Spencer, 1990).

Wrongful Firing in Violation of Public Policy

A third tort theory that would appear to easily accommodate an employee's association privacy suit is firing in violation of public policy (discussed in Chapter 15). This is the first theory under which employment at will was eroded, and it has been adopted by virtually all states. Despite this, employees relying on this theory in associational privacy cases have been unsuccessful. This is primarily due to two factors. Most employees who are fired for their associations are involved in nontraditional relationships, and the courts, as interpreters of public policy in these cases, have been reluctant to interpret public policy as protecting such relationships (Note, 1991). Secondly, most courts prefer to be able to refer to a clearly expressed public policy as the basis for their opinion and, as noted above, the extension of protection to employees' associations has been for the most part lacking.

Damages

The Eighth Circuit case discussed above, *Jensen v. Eleveth Taconite Co.* (1997), set a very important precedent for tort cases as well as for curbing discovery abuse in regard to claims for emotional harm due to harassment. In this case the court found that the "eggshell skull" rule applies to emotional as well as physical harm.

The "eggshell skull" rule derives from a universal doctrine of tort law, which holds that a tortfeasor, or someone who commits a tort, must take the victim as it finds him or her and is responsible for all damages caused by his or her negligence (Barnes et al., 1997). This doctrine was originally applied to physical injuries, and the typical example was someone with an "eggshell skull"—a person whose skull is so fragile that striking it in a way that would not cause serious injury to the normal person causes grave injury to the person with an eggshell skull. If the injuring blow was caused by a tort of the defendant's, he or she is liable despite the fact that the injury that resulted was not the kind that would usually occur.

The *Taconite* court found that the "eggshell skull" rule would apply to a plaintiff who has a "fragile psyche" as well as those who have special physical conditions. This means that an employee who suffers severe emotional trauma from employer interference with his or her relationship under circumstances to which others might not react so strongly can still recover if the employer's actions can be characterized as an invasion of privacy, intentional infliction of emotional distress, a wrongful firing, or some other tort. Not only should this make it easier for a plaintiff to recover from the emotional harm, it also shows an important court willingness to broaden theories to accommodate recovery for workplace-related emotional harms. In so finding, the court rejected the holding of the special master that there is "no scientifically developed psychiatric model or procedure for determining whether a particular stress caused a particular symptom or mental state." It chided the special master for rejecting the testimony of plaintiffs' psychologists and psychiatrists who were expert witnesses, and for his statement that, "[e]xperts . . . know no more than judges about what causes mental changes—which is to say that they know almost nothing" (*Jenson v. Eveleth Taconite Co.*, 1998, p. 1299).

As privacy rights for employees become more widely acknowledged and protected, there is likely to be an explosion of employee suits in this area. Growth in protection under tort law will make statutory protection or expansion less necessary.

OTHER PROTECTIONS FOR ASSOCIATIONS

The above discussion is not exhaustive in terms of legal protection for associations. For example, the Family and Medical Leave Act is a statement by Congress that certain relationships deserve protection, and employees should not be penalized for spending time caring for family members. It also broadly defines who falls within the definition of "family," and is not limited to the traditional nuclear family. The Americans with Disabilities Act (ADA) also offers some protection for associations. It protects employees from discrimination on the basis of associating with someone who is disabled. The Equal Employment Opportunity Commission has reported that although the number of claims filed for all kinds of discrimination is down, claims alleging discrimination due to psychological or emotional discrimination under the ADA have risen (Work week, 1999).

There are also several common law theories that might accommodate an associational privacy claim. For example, an employee who is fired without the procedural safeguards spelled out in a company manual could sue for breach of an implied contract. Other employees might be able to prove a breach of an implied covenant of good faith or fair dealing, or bad faith breach of contract. Finally, public employees can call upon the federal and state constitutions to help protect their associational rights.

CONCLUSION

The problem of recovering for emotional injuries caused by employer interference with employee associations is not a dearth of statutes or laws; it is convincing judges that employee associational privacy is worthy of protection under the existing laws. A prominent writer has described the lack of workplace rights, including privacy, as "The black hole in American rights" (Ewing, 1977, p. 3). Although this statement was made when employment at will was still in full force, it is not far wrong today regarding off-the-job privacy.

Courts should adjust the way they think about off-the-job privacy vis-à-vis employer autonomy. They should adopt a standard similar to the "business necessity" standard used in Title VII and other discrimination cases. If the employer cannot show that the employee's associational activity has an important negative impact on the employer, the employee should be allowed to recover for the emotional and monetary harm caused by the interference. Colorado, New York, and North Dakota established a precedent for this standard in their statutes, which are specifically targeted at off-the-job privacy. It is time for the courts to follow this lead.

Employer interference with employees' associations, without legitimate business reasons, causes significant emotional injuries. It is time for the law to acknowledge and redress these injuries. Off-the-job associational privacy is a legitimate interest worthy of meaningful protection.

REFERENCES

Barnes, J., Dworkin, T. M., & Richards, E. (1997). *Business law and the regulatory environment.* Homewood, IL: Richard D. Irwin.

Constitutional barriers to civil and criminal restrictions on pre- and extramarital sex. (1991). *Harvard Law Review, 104,* 1660–1680.

Dworkin, T. M. (1993, March–April). Harassment in the 1990s. *Business Horizons, 36,* 52–58.

Dworkin, T. M. (1997). It's my life—Leave me alone: Off-the-job employee associational privacy rights. *American Business Law Journal, 35,* 47–103.

Dworkin, T. M., Mallor, J., & Ginger, L. (1988). Theories of recovery for sexual harassment: Going beyond Title VII. *San Diego Law Review, 25,* 125–159.

Dworkin, T. M., & Peirce E. (1995). Is religious harassment "more equal?"*Seton Hall Law Review, 26,* 44–91.

"Eggshell skull" doctrine applies to victims' emotional psyches. (1998, April). *ABA Journal, 84,* 42.

Ewing, D. (1977). *Freeedom inside the organization.* New York: Dutton.

Garfinkle, L. (1984, Spring). Advocates ban, in Do puffing employees send profits up in smoke? *Business & Society Review, 4.*

Geyelin, M. (1989, April 21). The job is yours—Unless you smoke. *Wall Street Journal,* B1.

Gorley, K. (1992). One hundred years of privacy. *Wisconsin Law Review,* 1335–1441.

Humphress, S. B. (1992–93). Note, state protection against marital status discrimination by employers. *Journal of Family Law,* 31, 919–945.

Jackson, M. (1999, Feb. 14). When office dating abounds, passions spill into the workplace, *Sunday Herald Times,* G3.

Lack, Senator (1992). New York State Assembly, 215th Session, Senate Memo at 9 (1992 Bill #6935-C).

Linowes, D. F., & Spencer, R. C. (1990). Privacy: The workplace issue of the '90s. *John Marshall Law Review,* 23, 591–620.

Mallor, J. (1986). Discriminatory discharge and the emerging common law of wrongful discharge. *Arizona Law Review,* 28, 651–671.

Markels, A. (1995, February 4). Employers' dilemma: Whether to regulate romance. *Wall Street Journal,* B1.

New York Labor Law Sec. 201-d 2.c (McKinney's Supp. 1994).

Policy keeps smell of smoke out of electronics building. (1997, January 25). *Herald Times,* p. A5.

Reibstein, L. (1988, March 29). Firms find it tougher to dismiss employees for off-duty conduct. *Wall Street Journal,* B1.

Ricks, T. E. (1997, May 30). Latest battle for the military is how best to deal with consensual sex. *Wall Street Journal,* A20.

Rothstein, M. (1987). Refusing to employ smokers: Good public health or bad public policy. *Notre Dame Law Review, 62,* 940.

Saunders, K. W. (1991). Privacy and the social contract: A defense of judicial activism in privacy cases. *Arizona Law Review, 33,* 811–857.

Sculco, T. W. (1991). Note, smokers' rights legislation: Should the state "butt out" of the workplace. *Boston College Law Review, 33,* 879–902.

Warren, C., & Brandeis, L. D. (1890). The right to privacy. *Harvard Law Review, 4,* 193–220.

Woo, J. (1993, June 4). Employers fume over new legislation barring discrimination against smokers. *Wall Street Journal,* B1.

Work week. (1999, January 5). *Wall Street Journal,* A1. (citing John Tysse of the Equal Employment Advisory Council.)

Cases

Borquez v. Ozer. (1995). 923 P2d 166 (Colo Ct App).

E.E.O.C. v. Townley Engineering & Mfg. Co. (1989). 859 F2d 610 (9th Cir); *cert. denied,* 489 U.S. 1077 (1989).

Federated Rural Elec. Ins. Co. v. Kessler (1986). 388 NW2d 553 (Wisc).

Frankel v. Warwick Hotel. (1995). 881 FSupp 183 (ED Pa).

Jenson v. Eveleth Taconite Co. (1997). 130 F3d 1287 (8th Cir).

Langseth v. County of Elbert. (1996). 916 P2d 655 (Colo Ct App).

McCluskey v. Clarke Oil Refining Co. (1986). 498 NE2d 559 (Ill App).

Meltebeke v. Bureau of Labor & Industries. (1993). 903 P2d 351 (Or. 1995).

New York v. Wal-Mart Stores, Inc. (1995). 207 AD2d 150 (NY App Div).

Pasch v. Katz Media Corp. (1995). 10 Indiv Empl Rts Cas (BNA) 1574 (SDNY Aug. 7).

Rulon-Miller v. IBM. (1984). 208 Cal Rptr 524.

Slohoda v. United Parcel Service. (1984). 475 A2d 618 (NJ Super Ct).

State ex rel. McClure v. Sports & Health Club. (1985). 370 NW2d 844 (Minn).
Turner v. Barr. (1993). 811 FSupp 1 (DDC).
Waggoner v. Ace Hardware. (1996). 927 P2d 251 (Wash Ct App).
Watkins v. UPS. (1993) 797 FSupp 1349 (SD Miss).
White v. Davis. (1975). 553 P2d 222.

INDEX

ABOUT THE CONTRIBUTORS

Louis Diamant is Professor Emeritus of Psychology at the University of North Carolina at Charlotte, and a clinical psychologist in private practice. His previous, related books include *The Psychology of Sexual Orientation, Behavior and Identity: A Handbook* (1995, coeditor with Richard McAnulty) and *Homosexual Issues in the Workplace* (1993), *Male and Female Homosexuality: Theory and Research* (1987), and *The Psychology of Sports, Exercise, and Fitness: Social and Personal Issues* (1991).

Jo Ann Lee is Associate Professor of Industrial and Organizational Psychology at the University of North Carolina at Charlotte. She worked with the Senate Subcommittee on Aging of the United States Senate Labor and Human Resources Committee from 1990–1991 as an American Psychological Association Congressional Science Fellow. Her research interests include special problems facing older workers, personnel selection, work/family issues, and legal regulations of employment practices.

Ella L. J. Edmondon Bell is Associate Professor of Business Administration at Dartmouth College. Previously, she taught in the Belk College of Business Administration, University of North Carolina at Charlotte, at the Sloan School of Management, Massachusetts Institute of Technology, Yale's School of Organization and Management (1986–1991), and the University of Massachusetts at Amherst (1990–1991). She was Visiting- Scholar-in-Residence at the Bunting Institute, an interdisciplinary research center for women at Radcliffe College and Harvard University. Professor Bell's research has focused on the career and life histories of professional African American and European American women. She is currently inquiring into issues of work–life balance among women.

Rosemary Booth is Associate Professor in the Department of Management at the University of North Carolina at Charlotte. For twenty-five years, she was a writer, editor, and manager in IBM's communication function. Her research focuses on women in business and management communications. Her research has been published in the *Journal of Business Communications,* the *Leadership and Organization Development Journal,* the *Journal of Employment Counseling,* and the *SAM Advanced Management Journal.*

Vern L. Bullough is State University of New York Distinguished Professor Emeritus. Currently he is Visiting Professor at the University of Southern California. He founded the Center for Sex Research at California State University, Northridge. He is a fellow of the Society for the Scientific Study of Sex, and a past president of the organization; he is a fellow of the American Academy of Nursing and a laureate in the Academy of Humanism.

James D. Decker is Associate Professor of Political Science at Macon State College in Macon, Georgia. His areas of interest include American political parties and interest groups, lesbian and gay political issues, and American political institutions.

Terry Morehead Dworkin is the Jack and Linda Gill Professor and Chair of Business Law, and Co-Director of CIBER at Indiana University, Bloomington. She was the resident director for the Program in European Studies at the Center for European Studies, Rijksuniversiteit Limburg in Maastricht, The Netherlands. Her primary research interests focus on employment issues, particularly discrimination, whistleblowing, and privacy.

Ruth E. Fassinger is Associate Professor in the Department of Counseling and Personnel Services, College of Education, University of Maryland, College Park, Maryland. Her primary scholarly work is in the psychology of women and gender, career development, and issues of sexuality and sexual orientation. She is a Fellow of the American Psychological Association Divisions of Counseling Psychology and the Society for the Psychological Study of Lesbian, Gay, and Bisexual Issues, and is a member of the Division of Society for the Psychology of Women. She currently serves on the editorial board of the *Psychology of Women Quarterly.*

Susan R. Furr is Assistant Professor in Counseling, Special Education, and Child Development at the University of North Carolina at Charlotte. She has conducted research in the areas of gifted girls in science, career development of college students, and suicide and depression among college students. Dr. Furr has been employed as a school counselor as well as a psychologist in the university counseling center. She teaches courses in group design, crisis intervention, and grief and loss counseling.

Kristin H. Griffith is a graduate student in the Department of Psychology at Rice University. She has research and industry experience in areas such as Internet applications of organizational effectiveness and human resources, workplace diversity, personnel selection, organizational culture, teams, and training.

M. Karen Hambright is Assistant Professor of Psychology at Coastal Georgia Community College. She conducted her graduate thesis research at the Yerkes Regional Primate Research Center Field Station, where she studied sexual behavior in Macaques. Her research interests include human as well as nonhuman primate sexual behavior.

Larry M. Lance is Associate Professor of Sociology at the University of North Carolina at Charlotte. He has taught and conducted research in human sexuality and the sociology of sport. Some of the areas Dr. Lance has investigated include homophobia, AIDS, mate selection, pornography, and cross-dressing. He has published his research in a variety of journals, including *Public Opinion Quarterly, Human Relations, Journal of Men's Studies,* and the *College Student Journal.*

Richard McAnulty is Associate Professor in the Department of Psychology at the University of North Carolina at Charlotte. His research interests center on issues and problems relating to human sexuality. He coedited *The Psychology of Sexual Orientation, Behavior, and Identity: A Handbook* (with Louis Diamant) and coauthored *Exploring Human Sexuality: Making Health Decisions* (with Michele Burnette). He has served on the editorial board of several journals including the *Journal of Sex Research.*

Michelle J. McCormick is currently Director of Institutional Research for Macon State College but continues to pursue her sociological interest in gender and women's issues. Her most current project is an examination of Ghanaian women's involvement in the informal economy of that country and its significance for the family.

Michael H. McGee is an attorney in Charlotte, North Carolina. He received his undergraduate and J.D. degrees from the University of North Carolina at Chapel Hill. He was admitted to the North Carolina State Bar in 1971 and to the Bar of the Supreme Court of the United States in 1991. He maintains a general law practice with an emphasis on employment and labor law, complex equitable distribution and custody matters, general business law, and litigation in the federal and state courts. He was District Counsel from 1974–1977, and Supervisory Trial Attorney with from 1979 to 1991, for the Equal Employment Opportunity Commission. He has authored or coauthored seven legal and psychology textbooks and several scholarly journal articles, and has been a regular lecturer for Continuing Legal Education programs.

Stella M. Nkomo is the Bateman Professor of Leadership at the University of South Africa's Graduate School of Business Leadership. She is former Chair of the Department of Management in the Belk College of Business Administration at the University of North Carolina at Charlotte, where she taught in both the MBA and management development programs. Dr. Nkomo teaches in the field of human resource management, organization behavior, general management, and change management.

Sue Norton is Professor of Human Resource Management in the School of Business and Technology at the University of Wisconsin, Parkside. Her main research interests are in the area of legal issues related to gender and work.

Courtney Prentiss is a sexual abuse investigator with the Department of Social Services in Denver, Colorado.

Michael W. Ross completed his graduate work in Australia, Sweden, and Finland in psychology and in public health and health education. He taught psychiatry and sexuality at Flinders University Medical School before heading the AIDS Program for South Australia and later serving as Director of the National Center in HIV Social Research at the University of New South Wales. He is a Professor of Public Health and director of the WHO Center for Health Promotion and Prevention Research at the University of Texas, School of Public Health. He has served as a consultant for the Global Program on AIDS of the WHO on several occasions on sexuality and on AIDS burnout in health workers. Dr. Ross is American editor of *AIDS Care* and on the boards of six other journals.

Ronald B. Simono is currently Director of Counseling and Health Services and Professor of Psychology at the University of North Carolina at Charlotte, where he has been since 1967. His practice interests include college mental health as well as the application of psychology to cardiac rehabilitation. His teaching is focused on graduate education in the area of ethics and professional issues.